Festum Voluptatis

Festum Voluptatis
A Study of Renaissance Erotica

David O. Frantz

Ohio State University Press
Columbus, Ohio

LIBRARY OF CONGRESS
Library of Congress Cataloging-in-Publication Data

Frantz, David O., 1942–
    Festum voluptatis : a study of Renaissance erotica / David O. Frantz.
        p.   cm.
    Bibliography: p.
    Includes index.
    ISBN 0–8142–0463–5
    1. Erotica—History—16th century.   2. Erotica—History—17th
century.   3. Erotic literature, Italian—History and criticism.
4. Erotic literature, English—History and criticism.   I. Title.
HQ458.F73   1989
809'.933538—dc19   88–23506
                                                                              CIP

The paper in this book meets the guidelines for permanence and durability of
the Committee on Production Guidelines for Book Longevity of the Council
on Library Resources.

Printed in the U.S.A.

9 8 7 6 5 4 3 2 1

For My Mother
and in
Memory of My Father

Contents

Plates

Preface

Justifications for the study and expressions of gratitude are a risky business when a book deals with erotica. Does one admit to being interested in sex? Do colleagues who have surreptitiously slipped pornographic materials and helpful notes in brown campus mail envelopes really want to be cited? And how does one thank one's wife for help? The justifications for this study will become evident during the course of the book and the expressions of gratitude immediately hereafter, but a statement of several principles is in order at the outset.

John Cleland's *Fanny Hill* has been widely praised as a pornographic book that contains numerous scenes of sexual intercourse without ever using an obscene word. This study cannot be defended on those grounds, for some Renaissance purveyors of erotica insist upon using obscene words, and I have had to use them in this book. I have used them both in translation and paraphrases wherever a sexual or excretory matter is presented in "four-letter word" terms, whether in the verbal or the visual arts. Without recourse to this practice, it is impossible to draw distinctions.

With regard to the texts, I have tried to use sixteenth- and seventeenth-century texts wherever an excellent modern edition is not available, and I have chosen to preserve Renaissance spelling throughout. With the many Italian texts I have incorporated translations for all of the primary materials. I have used translations of others when they are available and not bowdlerized; otherwise, I have provided my own. Wherever I have deemed it unnecessary to provide the original language of a text, I have supplied merely the English translation. There is a good deal of citation in this study; however, since one of my major tasks has been to show the range of erotica in Renaissance, and since so much of that erotica has been ignored for centuries, I felt that extensive quotation of texts was necessary at certain points. I have tried to select both the best and most typical examples for this study.

Over the many years it has taken me to complete this study, I have been fortunate in receiving encouragement and assistance from many teachers, friends, and colleagues. Their generosity shines as one of the great rewards of scholarship, and it is a pleasure to acknowledge my indebtedness here. I bear sole responsibility for whatever in this work is defective or offensive; those named below should be seen only in the spirit of generosity with which they helped or encouraged me in some important way. Three mentors deserve special mention. The late Lawrance Thompson was an inspiration and a model for over twenty-five years, and I would be remiss were I not to begin by acknowledging the debt I shall always owe him. James L. Rosier fostered my interest in English and Italian Renaissance studies and directed my work on Renaissance concupiscence. His friendship and scholarly example have been strong and enduring. Thomas P. Roche, Jr., has been mentor, teacher, and friend for many years. His generous support and active encouragement have helped keep me believing that some day this study could become a book.

For suggestions, information, readings, discussions, and assistance of one kind or another I am indebted to the following: Richard D. Altick, Andy Anderson, the late Hugh Atkinson, John Benton, Morris Beja, Julie Carpenter, Cathy Chopp, Thomas Cooley, Maurice Cope, Edward P. J. Corbett, Robert Jones, Stanley Kahrl, Robbie Kantor, James Kincaid, Lisa Kiser, Charles Klopp, Joseph Krack, Albert J. Kuhn, Gershon Legman, Peter Machamer, Albert Mancini, Richard Martin, John Muste, John Sena, Roger Thompson, and Christian Zacher.

Lorraine Carlat typed the final version, and Linda Wiggins read the entire manuscript, thought about it, and helped me think about it; she also prepared the index and bibliography. Dan Barnes, Julian Markels, and Charles Wheeler all read substantial portions of the penultimate version of the manuscript and provided useful advice at every turn. I am indebted above all to John Gabel, who not only read with consummate attention and skill but also listened, discussed, and cared.

Many libraries were generous in making materials available to me. In particular I would like to express my appreciation to the Ohio State University Library, the Institute for Sex Research at Indiana University, the British Museum, the Biblioteca Apostolica Vaticana, the Bibliotheca Hertziana, the American Academy in Rome, the Istituto Nazionale per la Grafica in Rome, the University of Illinois Library, and the University of Pennsylvania Library. To the Ohio State University, especially the Department of English and the College of Humanities, whose chairs and deans have steadfastly supported my work with the research grants that have made this study possible, I am deeply grateful. I am also indebted to Peter Givler, Charlotte Dihoff, Sally Serafim, and the staff at the Ohio State University Press.

I want to thank all of my students who kept it a joy to be in the classroom while I was working on this study, especially Cynthia Lewis, Nikki Love, Jill Estill Lennon, Chip Nilges, and Bill O'Neil. Finally, my greatest debt is to Joanne, Ted, and Sara, who hold the center.

Acknowledgments and permissions for the photographs reproduced in this book are cited with each plate; here I wish to acknowledge the following publishers: Basil Blackwell Publishers and Barnes and Noble Books, Totowa, New Jersey, for permission to reprint material from *The Works of Thomas Nashe*; Stein and Day for permission to reprint material from *Aretino's Dialogues,* copyright © 1971 by Raymond Rosenthal, translator; Houghton Mifflin for permission to reprint material from *The Riverside Shakespeare,* edited by G. Blakemore Evans, copyright © 1974; Liverpool University Press for permission to reprint material from *The Poems of John Marston,* edited by A. Davenport, 1961; Doubleday and Company for permission to reprint material from *The Complete Poetry of John Donne,* edited by John T. Shawcross; and Guis. Laterza and Figli for permission to reprint material from *Sei Giornate,* edited by Giovanni Aquilecchia.

Introduction

Few scholars in Renaissance studies would accept the claim that the Renaissance was primarily a secular age. While one might say that it was an age in which man rediscovered the importance of functioning in this life rather than preparing for his place in the next, stating this would not deny the formulation that the Renaissance was fundamentally a religious age. Significant attention has been paid to the secular dimensions of the age, however, promulgating a view of the Renaissance as an era notable for the pursuit of earthly delights, not the least of which were reading secular books or looking at secular paintings and prints that depicted earthly delights of a most carnal kind. It is thus the more curious that literary historians have neglected a major body of material dealing with earthly delights of a sexual nature—Renaissance erotica.[1]

Our own age is one that prides itself on its progressivism and liberality of thought, but we have never been quite sure of what to do about erotica. Recent commissions on pornography and obscenity provide ample evidence of this uncertainty. To a scholar concerned with erotica of another era this might be irrelevant except that the attitudes and practices of this century as well as those that intervened between the Renaissance and our own time have greatly influenced our study of the subject. They have had an effect on what of Renaissance erotica has survived, what condition we have it in, how accessible it is, and finally whether it has ever been noticed and subjected to serious study and commentary.

1. All sixteenth-century English erotica is ignored by David Foxon in his excellent study, *Libertine Literature in England 1660–1745* (New Hyde Park, N.Y.: University Books, 1965). Since he is concerned with Italian Renaissance pornography and the "birth" of English pornography, and since his bibliographical knowledge is broad indeed, this oversight is regrettable, for the birth of English pornography falls before 1660. Foxon's work, and especially his comments on definition (pp. 45–51), are among the most sensible in print and have been extremely helpful to me. Steven Marcus, in *The Other Victorians* (1966; rpt. New York: Bantam Books, 1967), p. 285, also mistakenly states that English pornography has its origins in the seventeenth century.

1

The simple fact is that the works which I would group together in the category "Renaissance erotica" have at various times and in various ways been banned, transformed, quarantined, or quietly ignored. And those few works that have been studied as erotica have tended to be treated in isolation, never in a comprehensive context. Obviously, such treatment or lack thereof has hardly been systematic, but all of these factors have combined to keep us from seeing a body of material that existed (and still exists in part), and that was recognized by Renaissance people as a kind of artistic production that existed within a context, within a tradition. It is the purpose of this study to reconstruct that context, that tradition.

Several examples, treated at length in this study, should help to illustrate some of the points made above. The *posizioni* of Giulio Romano, executed in 1524, to which Pietro Aretino appended sixteen sonnets, are well known to us by reputation; we do not, however, have any of the original engravings, for they were destroyed very soon after production. (We know of only one sixteenth-century copy, done in woodcuts, that survives.) Suppression began immediately; so did imitation of both the drawings and the sonnets. Indeed, with regard to the sonnets, we are now faced with an embarrassment of riches, since many collections of verses were produced in the ensuing centuries falsely claiming to be a part of Aretino's appended poems. Tracking down even a photographic copy of the surviving sixteenth-century version of the *posizioni* proved to be no simple task; determining which sonnets made up the original sixteen provided an entirely different set of problems.

Destruction of plates and texts was certainly an extreme method of dealing with erotic materials; quiet quarantining as collections were built up over the centuries was more the rule, making knowledge of and access to such materials the privilege of a select few. The *Enfer* of the Bibliothèque Nationale and the Private Case of the British Library housed erotica apart; even catalogues of such collections, if they existed at all, were traditionally kept under lock and key.[2] Binding practices sometimes put works that would otherwise have been in private cases beyond the pale of such segregation, but it did not make the works any more accessible. For example, I came across a version of Niccolo Franco's notorious *Puttana Errante* in the back of a volume entitled *Elegantiae Latini Sermonis* by one Johannes Meursii the Younger (both title and authorship fabrications for the *Dialogue of Luisa Sigea* or *Satyra Sotadica*

---

2. For a sprightly review of such practices see Richard D. Altick, "Out of the Closet," *London Review of Books,* 20 Aug.–2 Sept. 1981, p. 12.

by Nicolas Chorier).[3] While these are all practices of which scholars are now well aware, we have never admitted that our view of the whole of Renaissance literature and the visual arts has been distorted by a failure to take these materials into account (they have never, for example, passed into any of the academic canons).

Additional factors have prevented us from seeing a whole tradition of erotica. Our picture has been fragmented, for one thing, because writers in the Renaissance tended to think and create in generic terms: that is, they wrote epic, or pastoral, or lyric, or Ovidian poetry. Although subsequent scholarly commentary has also tended to recognize such generic distinctions, even where such scholarship has taken into account the incredible mixing of kinds and intrusions of one genre into another, erotica has rarely been seen as a kind of its own. The disparate categories one might invent to deal with the broad topic of Renaissance erotica—Shakespeare's bawdy, Ovidianism in English Renaissance literature, scatology in English jest books—have admittedly been the subject of occasional isolated studies or commentary; but these have never been put together in any comprehensive fashion to illuminate the entire canvas of Renaissance erotica for scholars. Once one has a sense of that immense painting, filled as it might be with a range of styles and kinds, then one can begin to appreciate the fact that there was a tradition of erotica, a tradition that artists were aware of and that they created in and within which audiences viewed or read. We see this canvas only if we are willing to find what has heretofore been lost or altered, to reveal what once was open but has since been obscured, or to comment upon what has been clearly visible but treated with silence. On this last point, editions of Shakespeare provide a nice case in point. We have had several excellent studies of Shakespeare's bawdy, but one would hardly know this from what editors choose not to comment upon in standard editions of the plays.

The failure of editors to comment in this case ends up as a most subtle form of censorship, since so much else *is* annotated. Dealing with the bawdy sense of Shakespeare's language then becomes the peculiar bent of the professor, in the eyes of student readers, rather than something given authority by the editor. The fact that Shakespeare's audience heard his plays without benefit of editors, and heard them, I hope to show, with some sense of a tradition of erotica, is lost upon modern hearers of the plays.

3. In this instance I was aided by a careful cataloguing job that noted the *Puttana Errante*. For the pseudonymous nature of the *Elegantiae Latini Sermonis* see Gershon Legman, *The Horn Book* (New Hyde Park, N.Y.: University Books, 1964), p. 397, and Foxon, *Libertine Literature,* pp. 38-43.

Before I proceed in my efforts to illuminate the broad canvas, there are some matters of terminology that deserve attention. "Erotica" can be a nebulous term; I am using it in an inclusive fashion to cover a body of writing ranging from the merely titillating to the downright obscene. In doing so, I am following the lead of Roger Thompson in his excellent study of late seventeenth-century erotica, *Unfit for Modest Ears*. Precise definitions of erotica, especially pornography, have proven elusive, as many contemporary attempts to define the term amply demonstrate; but Thompson distinguishes four kinds based on the intention of the author: the pornographic, the obscene, the bawdy, and the erotic.[4] Thompson defines his terms in the following manner:

> (i) *Pornographic,* writing or representation intended to arouse lust, create sexual fantasies or feed auto-erotic desires. The pornographer aims for erection (at least) in the pornophile. (ii) *Obscene,* intended to shock or disgust, or to render the subject of the writing shocking or disgusting. This seems to be the purpose in our period of the use of taboo words or casual descriptions of sexual perversions, and is often a companion of satire. (iii) *Bawdy,* intended to provoke amusement about sex; most dirty jokes, for instance, belong to this category. (iv) *Erotic,* intended to place sex within the context of love, mutuality and affection; orgasm is not the end but the beginning. I occasionally vary these epithets to avoid tedious repetition; thus *ribald* is a synonym for bawdy, and *lewd* for obscene. I use the word *erotica* in its general sense to encompass these four types of writing.[5]

As Thompson himself notes, his terms "are not entirely foolproof. There are grey areas between the groups and isolated passages within a book which are anomalous. It is sometimes difficult to determine what the intention of an anonymous or little-known author was, or to gauge what types of readership he was aiming at."[6] Time and again in this study we shall have to consider questions of plot, character,

---

4. See, for example, Richard Gilman, "There's a Wave of Pornography/Obscenity/Sexual Expression," *The New York Times Magazine,* 8 Sept. 1968, pp. 36–37, 69–82. Also chapter 1 of Morse Peckham's *Art and Pornography* (New York and London: Basic Books, 1969) and the Foxon work cited in note 1 above. Susan Sontag, in her essay on pornography in *Styles of Radical Will* (New York: Farrar, Straus & Giroux, Noonday Press, 1976), p. 35, argues that there are at least three kinds of pornography. "There is a considerable gain in truth if pornography as an item in social history is treated quite separately from pornography as psychological phenomenon (according to the usual view, symptomatic of sexual deficiency or deformity in both producers and consumers), and if one further distinguishes from both of these another pornography: a minor but interesting modality or convention within the arts." Obviously, I believe that her first and third categories should not be separated from one another.

5. Roger Thompson, *Unfit for Modest Ears* (London: MacMillan, 1979), pp. ix–x.

6. Thompson, p. x.

setting, language, and especially audience in order to determine the central aim of a work. Such a procedure assumes, of course, that intention can be discovered, and while this is the most sound practice to follow in such an investigation, we are all aware that under certain circumstances it is the audience that can make a work bawdy or obscene. Who has not been in a social situation where one person has started investing remarks or readings with sexual implications and found that soon virtually every comment, every phrase, however innocent, could be so charged? Any schoolboy knows that you can take a story as innocent as Rip Van Winkle and gets lots of laughs out of the suggestiveness of his fishing "rod as long and heavy as a Tarter's lance" and his willingness to do for the women of the village "such little odd jobs as their less obliging husbands would not do for them." And then there is the matter of shifting sensibilities; what was erotic or pornographic to a proper Victorian, perhaps a glimpse of petticoats, would hardly be suggestive today. A colleague reminds me that a picture of Rita Hayworth in a negligee that appeared during World War II is the finest piece of erotica he has ever seen or would hope to see, and he is a lifelong subscriber to *Playboy*. And there is problematical terminology within Thompson's definitions themselves, especially the tricky term "love." Can one distinguish precisely between "physical love" and lust?[7] Must all pornography be autoerotic?

These are real and important questions; they show how complex the "simple" matters of definition and categorization are. Although Thompson's categories will not withstand all tests, they do at least provide useful distinctions; they give us an effective way of beginning to understand erotica. To catalogue does not explain, but it allows explanation to begin. I am also using Thompson's terms because they have functioned successfully in his hands with late seventeenth-century erotica, and it is my hope that the present work will stand in some kind of continuity with his, although the categories into which he divides his works are perforce different from mine.[8]

Over the many years during which I have been engaged in this study and have struggled with problems of definition, especially the definition of pornography, I have drawn solace from the fact that Renaissance writers themselves struggled to differentiate what they saw as wanton or bawdy from what they termed obscene. Even though most satirists,

7. For an example of a Renaissance author attempting to distinguish between physical desire that is love and physical desire that is lust see Robert Burton, *The Anatomy of Melancholy*, ed. A. R. Shilleto (London: Bell & Sons, 1893) II, 60, and III, 10, 57–60.

8. Thompson's categories are: instructional, anti-puritanical, prostitutional, matrimonial, aristocratical, anti-papistical, "medical," visual, and metaphorical.

moralists, and theologians of that age regarded the whole corpus of erotica as obscene, some few writers drew more careful distinctions. Joseph Hall separated poets who merely "glance" at sexual matters and who "leaue off" at the proper moment from writers like Thomas Nashe, who tell all.[9] John Marston in his *Metamorphosis of Pigmalions Image* begins to tell us what Pigmalion does with his statue when she comes to life and then admonishes his poetry in this manner, "Peace idle Poesie, / Be not obsceane though wanton in thy rhimes" (st. 38).[10] In other words, any fairly explicit description of sexual activity itself was regarded by both Hall and Marston as obscene in their sense of the word. But Renaissance definitions will not do; they did not use the word "pornography," and they were not concerned with making any but the broadest distinctions. And if Marston and Hall seem able to draw those wide distinctions, they were unusual; generally confusion reigned. But if Renaissance writers had difficulty differentiating between different kinds of erotica, they were nonetheless fairly well agreed upon what works made up the corpus of erotica. The writings of Aretino, Poggio, Nashe, and the epigrammatists are always on the list. In addition such catalogues invariably pointed to the fact that English erotica imitated Italian works of a like kind. Since one cannot proceed far in the investigation of English erotica without reference to the Italian tradition, the starting place for this study will be Italian literary erotica of the Renaissance.

I have attempted to deal with all of the well-known (but nowadays little-read) works of Italian erotica in the first three chapters. Much of the primary material discussed there has not been readily available to modern readers; I have thus felt it important to offer substantial quotation. Similarly, I have quoted extensively in chapter 6 in an effort to present a range of English Renaissance erotica; a number of the works, especially the epigrams, have not been reprinted in many years or have long been ignored. The fourth chapter, dealing as it does with the visual arts, takes the literary scholar into foreign territory, but it is an area that I felt could not be ignored, since the visual arts play so central a role in Italian erotica of the Renaissance. Chapter 5 provides the bridge between Italy and England, and chapter 7 extends the study of English erotica through an examination of the works of the self-styled English Aretino, Thomas Nashe. I conclude with a chapter in which I read

9. For a discussion of these attempts at definition and classification, see the beginning of chapter 6.

10. John Marston, "The Authour in prayse of his *precedent Poem,*" in *The Poems of John Marston,* ed., Arnold Davenport (Liverpool: Liverpool Univ. Press, 1961). All references to Marston's poetry are to this edition.

selected works by Marston, Donne, Shakespeare, and Spenser within the context of erotica.

I stated earlier in this introduction that my purpose in this study is to illuminate the broad canvas of Renaissance erotica. I suggested that the canvas is one which has not been seen as an entire painting and that some parts of the canvas have been unexposed to any light, some parts have been covered over like the genitalia in Michelangelo's frescoes in the Sistine Chapel, some parts have been altered, and some parts have been perfectly obvious but never commented upon. I would like to extend my analogy and suggest that Renaissance erotica is only one canvas in a Renaissance palazzo filled with many magnificent canvases. Scholars have been intent upon having us see those other canvases, filled as they are with the ideal, the refined, and the tasteful, and they have apologized for or remained silent about the earthy, the sensual, and what such sensibilities would term the tasteless. As a result, our view of Renaissance artistic production has been obscured, limited, and distorted. We need to recognize that if neoplatonism explains some Renaissance paintings, it need not be made to explain all of them.[11] We need to listen to the dialogues of whores as well as sonnets of chaste and chastened lovers. We need to explain the scatology that is a part of Renaissance literary warfare, not pretend that it does not exist. We need to understand that some elements which we think are only on one canvas in fact also have a place on the canvas called "erotica."

There is a temptation to go beyond the argument made above and try to explain the creation of Renaissance erotica, but no one thesis, it seems to me, will explain why artists in the Renaissance produced erotica. And I must confess at the outset that I am not much interested in questioning the *why* of erotica. Answers to such a question are perhaps better left to other professions; for the literary scholar it is enough to say that we have always had erotica because as human beings we seem to need it. I *am* interested in such questions as these: what forms does Renaissance erotica take and why? can we account in some meaningful way for the differences between the kinds of erotica produced in Italy and England? what are the assumptions artists seem to make as they produce their erotica? can we say anything about audience response to the erotica that was produced?

A final point. We need to recognize that Renaissance erotica in its various forms did not appear *ex nihilo*. There were traditions, well

11. For an excellent discussion of this problem in Italian Renaissance painting see Paul Barolsky, *Infinite Jest: Wit and Humor in Italian Renaissance Art* (Columbia and London: Univ. of Missouri Press, 1978), pp. 17, 165–76, and 209–10.

known in the Renaissance, of bawdy, erotic, pornographic, and obscene writing and painting in the much-imitated authors and artists of classical antiquity. Such traditions were not dormant in the Middle Ages either. These are matters that must also be addressed as we bring light into that Renaissance palazzo and look closely at *all* of the paintings, *including* the one named "erotica."

CHAPTER 1

In Praise of Apples, Figs, and Keys: The Learned Tradition

All' orto nostro is provedesse di buona chiave, essendo di tanta importanza. E da chi si tengon anco le mele, le fiche egli altri frutti degni.

Anton Francesco Doni, La Chiave

If we were to accept the predominant English view of Italy during the Renaissance, we should not have to look far for Italian erotica. Indeed, given one English view of things, any realistic account of everyday life in Renaissance Italy would make racy reading; there would hardly be a need for erotica as a genre of its own. It was in Italy, after all, that Ascham claimed he saw more liberty to sin in nine days than he had seen in nine years in London, and to the Protestant English view the popes were nothing more than the most vicious and venal of vile politicians who, to paraphrase Marlowe, weighed not men, and therefore not men's words; who read Machiavelli to attain Peter's chair; who counted religion but a childish toy and held there was no sin but ignorance. In this portrait the Whore of Babylon was alive and thriving, selling her wares on the banks of the Tiber and in her sister cities throughout Italy. The truth is something quite different, of course. Not that Venice did not have more sumptuous courtesans than any place else in the world, but London was not without its stews and sufficient whores to work them. Erotica in the Italian Renaissance is not to be found in literature that presents "real life"; it is in fact a nonrealistic and quite distinct genre that runs the gamut from a straightforward dirty joke to the most sophisticated of scholarly spoofs. Given this range of erotica, I have divided the Italian Renaissance material into two broad categories—learned and popular. The differences between them may often seem more contrived than real, and to some extent they are, but they do give the literature some semblance of manageability, and they do, in the final analysis, have some validity. The major factors in division between learned and popular erotica are those of purpose, audience, and, to a limited degree, style. The works I have grouped together as being learned erotica are the products of highly educated men, papal secretaries and humanists of the various Italian cities, who produced their works for one another, usually in *cenacoli* or academies, and who sought more to amuse one another with their wit and rhetorical skill than to stimulate one another with stories and poems about sex. Thus we find learned erotica full of metaphors, puns, and elaborate rhetorical and scholarly devices. Vulgar words are not avoided necessarily, but neither are they stressed. The works are, for the most part, what we would term bawdy, and much of the humor stems from the fact that sexual matters are used to make fun of the serious scholarly productions of the same humanists.

The works I have grouped together as popular erotica are rather different. Primarily they are purely commercial endeavors, written with the hope of making money through sale and patronage. Elaborate scholarly and rhetorical devices are avoided; obscene words are insisted upon. On the whole these works clearly are written not to amuse the scholarly intellect but to arouse the sexual appetite; they are predominantly pornographic. As we shall see, however, both the learned and popular traditions also partake of the obscene, and the pornographic frequently partakes of the bawdy.

I

To understand learned erotica accurately we must first understand the circumstances under which the works were produced. Students of the Renaissance are all familiar with the famous Platonic Academy in Florence where scholars, artists, musicians, poets, and princes gathered to discuss matters philosophical and artistic. This academy was part of a long tradition of academies and *cenacoli* that flourished in Italy as important centers for learning and culture from the Middle Ages on.[1] As one might imagine, not all of these clubs and academies confined themselves to contemplating Ideal Beauty; sometimes the members of such groups just got together to exchange their latest jokes, present a ribald farce, or read a bawdy book. It is from such genial gatherings that the first great collection of jokes, the *Facetiae* of Poggio Bracciolini, stems.

Giovanni Francesco Poggio Bracciolini has never drawn the broad scholarly attention equal to his importance. He is often mentioned, usually only in passing, as yet another Florentine humanist, a protégé

1. Michele Maylender, *Storia delle Accademie D'Italia,* 5 vols. (Bologna: Licino Cappelli, 1926–30) remains the starting place for investigating this subject.

of Coluccio Salutati and friend of Niccolo Niccoli and Leonardo Bruni.[2] If nothing else, Poggio can be seen as the representative humanist of the Italian Renaissance. Poggio was born in 1380 in Terranuova and sent to Florence for his education. There he studied Greek with Emmanuel Chrysoloras and Latin with Giovanni Malpaghini and so was in the midst of the most important learning of the Renaissance. With a recommendation from Coluccio Salutati, Poggio went to Rome in 1403 and entered the papal service. While attending the Council of Constance in 1415 Poggio engaged in several of the most successful manuscript hunts of the Renaissance. He discovered the first perfect copy of Quintilian's *Institutiones*, Ascionius' commentary on five speeches of Cicero, works of Valerius Flaccus and Lucretius, and Silius and Statius among others.[3] The importance of these discoveries can hardly be exaggerated. To the functionaries who carried on the work of governments in this period and to many of the rulers whom they served, recovery of knowledge from the past was of vital importance, not a mere pedantic pursuit, if true civilization was to be restored to their world.

Poggio's discoveries in the monastery at St. Gallen made his reputation. Leonardo Bruni wrote to Poggio that in finding the first complete copy of Quintilian's *Institutiones* he had freed Quintilian "from a lengthy and cruel prison sentence among the barbarians."[4] "Quintilian," he said, "who used to be mangled and in pieces, will recover all his parts through you."[5] Francesco Barbaro painted Poggio's accomplishments in even more heroic terms; "You have revived so many illustrious men and such wise men. . . . I should decree a triumph for you, since surely their [great literary figures] learning and their rea-

---

2. The notable exceptions are Poggio's treatment in Nancy S. Struever's *The Language of History in the Renaissance* (Princeton: Princeton Univ. Press, 1970) and in Lauro Martines's *The Social World of the Florentine Humanists, 1390–1460* (Princeton: Princeton Univ. Press, 1963). See also Phyllis Gordon, trans., *Two Renaissance Book Hunters: The Letters of Poggius Bracciolini to Nicolaus de Niccolis* (New York and London: Columbia Univ. Press, 1974).

3. For Poggio as a manuscript collector see John Sandys, *A History of Classical Scholarship* (Cambridge: Cambridge Univ. Press, 1908), II, 25ff; and R. R. Bolgar, *The Classical Heritage* (New York: Harper & Row, 1964), pp. 263–64, 275–76, 279. For Poggio's career generally, see Eugenio Garin, "La Letteratura degli Umanisti," in *Storia della Letteratura Italiana*, ed. Emilio Cecchi and Natalino Sapegno (Milan: Garzanti, 1965–69), III; William Shepherd, *The Life of Poggio Bracciolini* (Liverpool: J. M'Creery, 1837). Some facts are given in the preface to a modern paperback edition of *The Facetiae*, trans. Bernhardt J. Hurwood (New York: Award Books, 1968). Poggio is discussed and given his due as a collector of jokes in Legman's *The Horn Book*.

4. Bruni in *Two Renaissance Book Hunters*, p. 192.

5. Bruni in ibid., p. 192.

soning power could bring the human race more benefit by far than the deeds of a few illustrious generals ever brought."[6]

Of course this praise from friends is hyperbolic; of course they had an interest in seeing one of their kind portrayed as a hero of the first rank, but the fact that they convinced the men with power of their importance in such terms is a fact that should not be lost on us. Nor should we lose sight of the excitement that Poggio's discoveries generated. He was unearthing worlds every bit as important as the ones he would write to Henry the Navigator about. Poggio triumphed in this age by performing two of the most important functions of a humanist—recovering ancient texts and ensuring that good copies were made from those texts.[7]

While at the Council of Constance, Poggio did not confine his visits to the nearby monasteries. He also found time to visit the famous baths of Baden, and his account of that experience is justly famous.[8] The Council of Constance ended in 1418, and Poggio, after some wanderings, eventually took up an offer he had received at the Council to go to England at the invitation of Beaufort, the Bishop of Winchester, son of John of Gaunt and uncle to the reigning monarch, Henry V. The two years that Poggio spent in that cultural backwater were most unpleasant for this cultivated man of learning.[9] Poggio eventually returned to Italy and got himself a place as a papal secretary once again; in all, his papal career spanned some fifty years.[10] At the age of fifty-five, Poggio decided to marry; he put aside his mistress and fourteen children and made a good match with a wealthy, aristocratic, eighteen-year-old Florentine girl.[11] They had six children, and Poggio silenced those skeptical of such a January–May alliance. Upon his marriage and return to Florence, Poggio followed in the footsteps of Salutati and served as chancellor of Florence from 1453 to 1458. He died in 1459.[12] The range of his written works and the experiences of his life make

6. Barbaro in ibid., pp. 197–98.

7. The difficulty of finding a sufficiently intelligent and affordable scribe is mentioned time and again by Poggio and his friends. Poggio himself made a copy of the Quintilian and Flaccus' *Argonautica*. See Sandys, p. 27.

8. See Shepherd, pp. 60–68; and Gordon, pp. 24–31.

9. Poggio's letters to his friend Niccolo Niccoli during this period depict quite graphically the way in which these humanists were at the mercy of their patrons. Always they are angling for financial support and time to pursue their studies.

10. See Gordon, p. 4.

11. Martines, pp. 210–14, covers the marriage superbly. He also details Poggio's economic rise, pp. 123–27. Poggio wrote a treatise entitled "Whether an Old Man Should Take a Wife."

12. Martines, p. 243.

Poggio one of the most fascinating of Renaissance figures, and it is important that we understand something of the life he led, what his pursuits were, if we are to understand the *Facetiae* properly, for the *Facetiae* are every bit as typical of Poggio's work as a humanist as his letters are.[13]

There is a tendency to classify all jokes as a kind of sub-literature, but such a classification is misleading, for "sub" implies "low" in terms of subject, style, and audience. The *Facetiae* were not aimed at an audience of "low" social standing or literary taste, no matter how the collection is billed in modern paperback ("THE RIBALD CLASSIC THAT SHOCKED—AND DELIGHTED—RENAISSANCE ROME").[14] Most of Rome could not read the *Facetiae,* for when they came forth in 1450, they were written in Latin, the learned man's language. The *Facetiae* were in fact the product of a club in Rome that Poggio himself describes as the *Bugiale*—the place for telling tall tales:

> . . . a kind of laboratory for fibs, which the Pope's secretaries formerly instituted for their amusement. Until the reign of Pope Martin we were in the habit of selecting, within the precincts of the court, a secluded room where we collected the news of the day, and conversed on various subjects, mostly with a view to relaxation, but sometimes also with serious intent. There no one was spared, and we freely attacked whomever or whatever met with our disapproval; often the Pope himself was the subject of our criticism, so that many attended our gatherings, lest, in their absence, they be the object of the first chapter.[15]

The *Facetiae* are a product of this group, a group of learned men who enjoyed above all, one supposes, the combination of wit and bawdiness that is found throughout the jests, and their appeal was immediate and wide. Poggio himself attested that copies of his work "flooded all Italy, and overflowed into France, Spain, Germany, England, and every country where Latin was understood."[16]

In his monumental study, *The Rationale of the Dirty Joke,* Gershon Legman salutes Poggio as "the first and most important joke-collector and editor of modern times," and he provides a perspective on the *Facetiae* that reminds us of the long medieval tradition of bawdy tales. *Facetiae* derive from the *novelle* and ultimately the *fabliaux*; "the older

---

13. In addition to collecting jokes and finding manuscripts, Poggio wrote dialogues, letters, polemics, orations, and moral tracts. A few of his major works: *De nobilitate, De infelicitate principium, De varietate fortunae, Historia Fiorentina,* and *De avaritia.*

14. Cover of Hurwood's translation of Poggio, *The Facetiae.*

15. Poggio cited in Hurwood, p. 18; also given in II, 230–32, of the dual-language (Latin and English) edition published in Paris in 1879 by Isidore Liseux.

16. Poggio cited in Hurwood, p. 21.

Arab-Italian *novella,* or lengthy folktale, is seen changing to the brief modern *facezia* or joke—punch-line and all."[17] There is merit to this characterization on several counts. Poggio's *Facetiae* are different from the *novelle* in that they are shorter and often do have punch lines, although this is not the case in all instances, as we shall see. Further, Poggio indeed presents himself as a *collector* of jokes. Many of the jokes are rendered as having been told to Poggio by a friend or heard by him at a gathering of the apostolic secretaries, the *Bugiale.* For a number of jokes the setting of the *Bugiale* is made clear.[18] The setting is given very briefly, however; the story is told, and there is little attempt to link the stories. Occasionally, one story will lead to another, but there is no extended narrative or temporal frame beyond reporting jokes of the same teller, as in CLVIII and the two following, or beyond reporting several jokes from the same meeting (CIII–CVI). There is no "envelope" or "cornice" as we get in collections of *novelle* like Boccaccio's *Decameron* or Chaucer's *Canterbury Tales.*[19] Poggio's unconnected tales are more like what we suppose Milesian tales, antiquity's bawdy stories, were like.[20] Clearly, this was a matter of choice for Poggio. We know that Poggio was familiar with the works of Petronius, Lucian's *Lucius, or the Ass,* and Apuleius' *The Golden Ass,* where ribald tales are

17. G. Legman, *The Rationale of the Dirty Joke* (New York: Grove Press, 1968), p. 35.

18. See for example (in Hurwood): XVII, XXIII, XLVIII, LXIX, LXXVII, LXXXI, LXXXII, LXXVIII, XCII, XCV, XCVIII, XCIX, CIII, CIV, CXII, CLVIII, CLIX, and CLX.

19. For a discussion of the features of the *novelle,* especially the cornice, see Robert J. Clements, "Anatomy of the Novella," in the Norton Critical ed. of Boccaccio's *Decameron,* trans. and ed. Mark Musa and Peter Bondanella (New York: W. W. Norton, 1977), pp. 258–69. See also Janet Smarr's introduction to *Italian Renaissance Tales* (Rochester, Mich.: Solaris Press, 1983).

20. Almost nothing survives of Milesian tales "except a scandalous reputation and a few fragments," notes James Tatum, *Apuleius and The Golden Ass* (Ithaca and London: Cornell Univ. Press, 1979), p. 96. According to P. G. Walsh, *The Roman Novel* (Cambridge: Cambridge Univ. Press, 1970), pp. 10–11, the tales "presumably take their origin from the custom of story-telling as a social accomplishment in Hellenistic society. Theophrastus and Athenaeus reveal how private and club dinners exploited this type of oral entertainment. There may possibly have been edifying stories of true love and chaste wives, and innocent accounts of adventure, but the dominant type of anecdote reflected the seamier sexual proclivities of humankind, reinforced by spooky accounts of sorcery and witchcraft. Aristides of Miletus incorporated the spicier of these into a literary framework probably in the second century B.C., and the Roman historian Sisenna translated the collection into Latin in the first century B.C. The prevalence of eroticism in the book is certainly indicated by Plutarch in his account of the reactions of the Parthians to this bedside reading of Roman officers. Aristides was the most celebrated editor of such collections, but Martial indicates that there were *Sybaritici libelli,* presumably of a similar type." See also pp. 15–17.

contained within a connected narrative, but Poggio chose to present himself as a collector of disparate jokes.[21] Within the *Facetiae* as well, Poggio makes no effort to link his work with that of his forebears from antiquity; rather, he emerges as something of a folklorist doing a collection project. In giving us a context for many of the jokes, Poggio provides us with a sense of a world in which the ability to tell a good story, to remember a witty response, was a social grace.[22] An oral context is provided for enough of the stories so that we can see that we are not always dealing with a shortened form of a literary text (in other instances, Legman's characterization is surely correct). Taken as a whole, both in the context provided for the jest and the details within the jests, the *Facetiae* do give a partial picture of the world of the humanists in early Renaissance Italy. Many jokes have to do with problems of the papacy; several relate directly to the Council of Constance. The uncertain place of a humanist in a world governed by preferment is everywhere reflected.[23] Many of the jests depend on a knowledge of the particular foibles of people from a certain part of Italy or gain our attention because they are the witty response of a famous person. In short, one is tempted to say that there is a kind of realism here, that we have the world of Renaissance Italy at least as reflected by humanist thought in a specialized form. One would not, however, want to press very hard along these lines, for we know that jokes are but another kind of imaginative literature that happens to make use of what seems to be realistic detail.

As has been clear from the foregoing remarks, although a number of the *Facetiae* are not what we would call dirty jokes or bawdy stories, many of them are, and it is to those jokes that I wish to turn my analysis. In *The Rationale of the Dirty Joke* Legman sees aggression, hostility, as the major force behind dirty jokes, claiming that, "under the mask of humor, our society allows infinite aggressions, by everyone and against everyone. In the culminating laugh by the listener or observer—whose position is often really that of victim or butt—the teller

21. See Walsh, pp. 230ff. Poggio made Petronian discoveries in England in 1420 and Cologne in 1423, including the sole manuscript of the *Cena Trimalchionis*. Boccaccio discovered a manuscript of *The Golden Ass* at Monte Cassino in 1355 and transcribed it himself. See also Christopher Robinson, *Lucian and His Influence in Europe* (Chapel Hill: Univ. of North Carolina Press, 1979), p. 95.

22. This is the same context Walsh gives us for the Milesian tales. The ability to tell stories is everywhere evident in the literature of the Italian Renaissance. The ability to tell humorous stories is dealt with extensively in Book II of Castiglione's *Book of The Courtier.*

23. See especially XXVII, XXVIII, XCIV, CXII.

of the joke betrays his hidden hostility and signals his victory by being, theoretically at least, the one person present *who does not laugh.*"[24] This is an even more relentlessly psychological explanation of sexual humor than Legman gave in 1964 in *The Horn Book,* where he wrote that sexual folklore, while it has the "air of being humorous . . . actually . . . concerns some of the most pressing fears and most destructive life problems of the people who tell the jokes and sing the songs." These people, Legman asserts, "are projecting the endemic sexual fears, and problems, and defeats of their culture—in which there are very few victories for anyone—on certain standard comedy figures and situations, such as cuckoldry, seduction, impotence, homosexuality, castration, and disease, which are obviously not humorous at all." He concludes that such people "are almost always expressing their resistance to authority figures, such as parents, priests, and policemen, in stereotyped forms of sexual satire and scatological pranks and vocabulary. It is for these reasons that sexual folklore is generally retailed in a mood of exaggerated horseplay and fun."[25]

Legman's comments are very much to the point, for we do see authority figures as targets in Poggio's *Facetiae,* especially in the form of clerics, and we do find that a great many of the jokes have to do with those deep-seated social/sexual anxieties, especially impotence, cuckoldry, and sexually motivated women clever enough to threaten a male-dominated society. For example, we are told that the tenth jest of the *Facetiae* is one which "illustrates the craftiness of women."

My countryman, Pietro, once told me this ridiculous tale which illustrates the craftiness of women. He had been having an affair with the wife of a peasant who spent most of his nights sleeping in the fields to avoid his creditors. One night when my friend was in the woman, her husband unexpectedly came home. Hastily hiding her lover under the bed, she turned to her husband and upbraided him bitterly for having returned, accusing him of doing his best to make certain that he would spend the rest of his life in prison.

"The governor's soldiers just searched this whole place so they could arrest you and haul you off to jail," she said, "But when I told them that you usually sleep outdoors, they went away threatening to return."

Terrified, the peasant tried to think of a way to escape, but the gates of the town were already closed. So the wife said, "You poor thing, what will you do? If they capture you, you're finished!"

Trembling with fear, he kept asking his wife for advice. She, prepared to deceive, said, "Climb up to the dovecote and spend the night. I'll close the

24. Legman, *Rationale,* p. 9.
25. Legman, *The Horn Book,* pp. 245–46.

trap door and take away the ladder, and no one will suspect that you're there."

He followed his wife's advice, she, meanwhile, locked the trapdoor after him so that he could not get out, and freed her lover from his hiding place. He came out and simulated the return of the governor and his soldiers, kicking up a great rumpus, while the woman defended her husband, who shivered with terror in his concealment. Finally after the tumult was allowed to die down, the lovers went to bed and dedicated the night to Venus, while the husband was left to sulk among the pigeons and their dung.[26]

The first thing we note about this jest is the context that Poggio provides—he is merely repeating a ridiculous tale told to him by a countryman, one that illustrates the craftiness of women. Initially, the tale is repeated as having happened to Pietro, Poggio's countryman. By the final paragraph, however, Pietro has become merely "the lover," as we are distanced from the action and seem to be dealing much more with a literary text from a *novella*. However, the transition from medieval folktale to modern joke "punch line and all" has not been accomplished. The humor, such as it is, is situational, and such humor would probably be improved by the slightly longer and more detailed and dramatic treatment a Boccaccio might give it, since there is no punch line. In terms of the subject matter, we note that the craftiness of the woman is not so much apparent as the stupidity of the husband. He is obviously already a failure in the world of business, and his ridiculous acquiescence to his wife's scheming does not engage our sympathy. He is every bit the figure of scorn the joke makes him out to be; but it is his stupidity rather than her craftiness that holds our attention.

A number of jokes show very clearly the anxiety over sexual potency; jest CXI is a splendid example of male wish fulfillment, for it describes the miraculous cure of a sick woman effected by coitus. In this jest the husband lies with his deathly ill wife because they are newlyweds and he has had little opportunity to enjoy the fruits of his marriage. He wants to make love with her one more time before she expires:

A similar tale was told lightheartedly about the town of Valencia by one of the assistants. Shortly after having married a very young notary, a young bride became so gravely ill that everyone thought that she was at death's door. The doctors gave her up as lost, and after losing her power of speech completely, the young woman began to look like a corpse. Despairing over the loss of a wife with whom he had lain so seldom, and whom he loved so deeply, he decided to lay her once more before she expired. After sending

26. Poggio, *Facetiae,* trans. Hurwood, no. X, pp. 33–34.

everyone present from the room on some secret pretext or other, he climbed upon his wife. At once it was as if new life had been pumped into her body, she began to breathe, she opened her eyes, and after a little while, began to talk, softly calling her husband's name. Joyfully, he asked her what she wanted. She asked for something to drink, after which she ate some food, and finally she regained her health. The outcome of the matter proved the superiority of the marital act. It illustrates also that it is the best remedy for all female disorders.[27]

The final lines of the jest exemplify perfectly the male fantasy of supreme potency and superiority; not only is sexual intercourse the best treatment for this particular ill (whatever it might be), "it is the best remedy for all female disorders." Such a belief is portrayed in jest XXIV, where even madness is cured by coitus:

> A woman from my city who seemed to be mad was taken by her husband and relatives to a soothsayer, who, they hoped, would cure her. In order to cross the Arno River they put her on the shoulders of the strongest man. Suddenly she began wriggling her buttocks simulating the movements of coitus, screaming at the top of her lungs, "I want to be fucked!" Thus she revealed the source of her affliction.
>
> The man carrying her fell into such a fit of laughter that he tumbled into the water. The others burst out laughing also when they learned the cure for this insanity, asserting that incantations would not do the job, but that coition would restore her to health. Then turning to the husband they said, "You will be your wife's best doctor."
>
> So they all went home, and when the husband had fulfilled his marital obligations, the woman's mind returned to its former state. This is the best remedy for the insanity of women.[28]

A reader analyzing this jest might, in thinking about the source of the madwoman's affliction, find the story critical of the husband. Clearly, he has not been fulfilling his marital obligations sufficiently. The jest, however, stays on quite another plane, emphasizing only the fantasy that women always want to be fucked and that it is the best cure for all disorders, including those of the mind.

Jest CX turns on the same fantasy, but it adds several interesting details:

> A woman I know named Giovanna became sick. A stupid and ignorant physician was called in to cure her, and according to custom, asked for a specimen of her urine (the collection of which was left to her young, unmarried daughter). Having forgotten all about this, the girl showed the

27. Ibid,, no. CXI, p. 103.
28. Ibid., no. XXIV, pp. 43–44.

doctor her own urine instead. Immediately he prescribed sexual intercourse for the woman. Hearing this, the husband, after filling his stomach with an ample meal, mounted his wife. Finding the business exceedingly bothersome because of her debilitated state (and being unaware of the doctor's prescription), the woman began shrieking. "What are you doing to me, husband? You're killing me!" "Shut up!" retorted he, "The doctor knows, it's the best thing for you. This is how you're going to be restored to perfect health." Nor was he wrong, for after giving it to her four times he found her fever broke. By the next day it was gone. Thus, by the very means with which the quack had intended to deceive them, she recovered.[29]

We see at once the operation of the fantasy of male potency in the jest (here emphasized by the husband's performance of his marital obligation four times), and we note particularly the way the doctor is ridiculed. While doctors do not come in for as much abuse as clerics in the *Facetiae,* they are nonetheless frequent objects of scorn. We are told that the doctor is "stupid" and a "quack," that he means to deceive his patient by prescribing sexual intercourse. The jest would have us believe that the doctor does not know what he is doing; were it not for the efficacy of coitus, he would be revealed for the charlatan that he is. But the details of the jest as rendered are clearly bungled in order to unmask the doctor. The young, unmarried daughter lamely "forgets" her assignment and substitutes her own urine. This detail is important; we are to understand, I think, that the doctor's analysis is correct, for he has seen the urine of a "young, unmarried daughter" who suffers from what the Elizabethans called the "green sickness." Virginity, as the saying goes, is curable. The myth that young, unmarried women want and need sexual intercourse should be understood as a crucial part of this jest; it is obscured here as the doctor as quack and the efficacious powers of coitus are held up as qualities to be noticed.

The attitudes and fantasies found in the foregoing jest seem to me explained as much by social attitudes as by psychological ones. In fact, we find throughout the *Facetiae* that stupid or uneducated people are targets of humor, and with this recognition, one senses that Legman's explanations, while to the point, do not explain everything. Keith Thomas's comments in "The Place of Laughter in Tudor and Stuart England" have application here. Writing on English jest books (which cull Poggio extensively), Thomas notes:

> Much of the humour in these jest-books is purely verbal, punning and repartee. But, like the comedy of the London stage, the jokes also reveal the social tensions of the time, particularly those arising from the meeting of

29. Ibid., no. CX, pp. 102–3.

divergent customs and unequal knowledge, as town-dweller collided with peasant, noble with plebeian, clerk with layman. Many illuminate the working of contemporary marriage. The stories about ferocious quarrels between husband and wife show that the tradition of Mrs. Noah and the Wife of Bath was still very much alive. Like yesterday's jokes about mothers-in-law, this Tudor humour about shrewish and insatiable wives or lascivious widows was a means of confronting the anomalies of insubordinate female behaviour which constantly threatened the actual working of what was supposed to be a male-dominated marital system.[30]

Even though psychological explanations are certainly relevant and have dominated recent treatment of jokes, social explanations like the ones given by Thomas seem equally important. Thomas himself is acutely aware of the validity of psychological explanations, but he is wary of pushing them too far, and he reminds us that

> . . . laughter did not only reflect contemporary anxieties. It also played a more positive role as a crucial part of the social process. Very often that role was a conservative one, for in its affirmation of shared values laughter could be a powerful source of social cohesion. In the close-knit village communities, mockery and derision were indispensable means of preserving established values and condemning unorthodox behaviour. Not only cuckolds, but scolds, henpecked husbands and unsuitably matched couples were subjected to charivari: burlesque demonstrations outside the victim's house, with shouting, beating pots and pans, blowing horns and parading effigies. Neighbours had many mocking devices to signify their disapproval: they put horns on the door; they stuck rhymes on the wall; and they tolled the church bell in derisive anticipation of their victim's demise. This was a harshly intolerant popular culture, hostile to privacy and eccentricity, and relying on the sanction not of reason but of ridicule. Laughter in the villages was a crude form of moral censorship.[31]

As has been noted, Poggio's jests are wide-ranging in kind and run the gamut from those which clearly reflect anxiety of the kind Legman sees as the basis for bawdy humor to those which have targets of a more socially recognizable kind. The jests do reflect a male-dominated society that senses women as a threat; thus, as we have seen, impotency, cuckoldry, and clever female lechery are frequent targets. But stupidity, especially in uneducated peasants or in professions thought to be filled with fools (i.e., the medical profession), is a commonplace. Above all, however, the venality and lechery of the clergy are prominent. This should not surprise us, for we must remember that these jests are

30. Keith Thomas, "The Place of Laughter in Tudor and Stuart England," *Times Literary Supplement* 3906 (21 Jan. 1977): 77.
31. Ibid., p. 77.

collected and presented as coming from an apostolic secretary, a man who was dependent upon the papacy for his employment but who never took orders himself. The wicked lasciviousness of the clergy, proverbial in the world at large (especially the world of medieval and Renaissance literature) is given fullest play by the church functionaries who remained laymen.

As an example of a jest that shows simple stupidity, we might look at CXXXVI:

> A woman had her hair shaved off because of a skin disease, and had to go out suddenly when called by a neighbor on some urgent business forgetting, however, to cover her head. Seeing her like that, the neighbor upbraided her for publicly displaying such a bald and unsightly pate. So to hide her head, she pulled her skirts up from behind, and in her anxiety to cover her top, she bared her bottom. Everyone laughed at the poor woman, who in her attempt to cover a minor embarrassment, created a great one. This applies to those who try to hide a small offense by committing one more serious.[32]

Sheer stupidity is the target here; even though the humiliation takes the form of the revelation of the poor woman's bottom (always in itself good for a snicker in such works), it is the stupidity of the woman that we laugh at. That we are given a "lesson" at the end of this tale is not totally uncharacteristic of the Italian jest; it is, however, a practice followed much more relentlessly in English jest collections, just as the obsession with bums, farts, and excrement seems much more an English one. Only about nine of Poggio's jests have to do with such matters (see, for example, CXXIX, CLXIV, and CLXV).

A joke that has as its targets both the venality of the clergy and the stupidity of the peasantry is the tale "Of the fool who thought his wife had two vaginas":

> A peasant in our district, an idiotic fool who knew absolutely nothing about sex, got married. Now it happened one night that his wife rolled over in bed so that her bottom fit right into his lap. His spear was standing and accidentally landed right in the target. Delighted by his effortless entrance, he asked his wife if she had two vaginas.
>
> "Of course," she replied.
>
> "Ho, ho!" he answered at once. "I am satisfied with one, the second is indeed superfluous."
>
> With that, the crafty wife, who was having a secret affair with the parish priest, said, "In that case we can give the second one away. Let's donate it to the church, and to our priest, who will be very grateful to have it. You won't be depriving yourself of anything, since one is enough for you."

32. Poggio, *Facetiae,* trans. Hurwood, no. CXXXVI, p. 120.

The peasant agreed at once, believing that this was a good way to rid himself of an unnecessary responsibility. They accordingly invited the priest to dinner and explained the matter to him. After the meal all three climbed into bed, the woman in the middle, facing her husband, and the priest behind her. The gluttonous priest, hungering after this delicate morsel for a long time, finally made the first move. The wife, equally anxious, whispered back softly. At this, the peasant, fearing that his property was being trespassed upon, cried out, "Hold it, friend! Remember our bargain, use your own part and leave mine alone!"

To which the priest replied, "God forbid! I don't envy your property in the slightest as long as I can use the church's portion."

These words reassured the stupid peasant, who then told the priest to go ahead and take advantage of the concession granted to the church.[33]

There is precious little cleverness here. Beyond the verbal play that transforms the clergy's proverbial gluttony into equally proverbial sexual appetite (accurately reflected in the translation here), we see that traditional ability of the wife to maneuver the whole affair to a happy conclusion for herself. She can do so because her husband is so monumentally stupid; no learned man, we suppose, would be so ignorant about the facts of life or so trusting of a priest.

A jest that exposes the particular cynical cleverness of the church is the lengthy tale entitled "How a Minorite's breeches became relics":

A thing very worthy of laughter, and deserving of inclusion in this collection of tales, took place not long ago at Amalia. A married woman, moved, I suppose, by good intentions, confessed her sins to a Minorite friar. While talking to the woman, he was aroused into a state of carnal concupiscence, and little by little, he persuaded her to give in, after which they sought a time and place for their tryst. They agreed that she should feign illness, and that the friar would then be called to confess her. As was customary, everyone would leave them alone so that they might labor in privacy at conversation intended to liberate the spirit. So she feigned illness, withdrew to her bed, and pretending extreme pain, sent for her confessor. As soon as he came, everyone departed. The moment they were alone, the friar partook of her favors repeatedly. They were alone together for so long that someone finally interrupted them, and the friar took his leave, saying that he would return the next day to complete the confession. He did exactly that, and, after laying his breeches on the lady's bed, probed her sins in exactly the same fashion he had on the previous day. The husband, however, suspicious of so lengthy a confession, burst into the room. The friar, startled at this precipitous intrusion, fled, leaving his breeches behind. The husband, seeing the breeches, cried out that the wretch was no friar, but an adulterer, and everyone in the household examined the breeches and clamored for vengeance.

33. Ibid., no. V, pp. 28–29.

The cuckold rushed immediately to the monastery where he complained bitterly to the prior, threatening at the same time to slaughter his betrayer. Being an old man, the prior succeeded in calming the husband down, assuring him that by making an issue of the matter, he would only bring disgrace to his family and himself. The only way to cover the affair up, he insisted, was to employ silence and discretion. The husband pointed out that the discovery of the breeches had already brought things out into the open. But the old man offered to remedy that by asserting the breeches to be those of St. Francis, which the friar had brought to heal the ailing woman. They would be retrieved and taken back to the monastery in a procession of great pomp and ceremony. So the husband agreed, the prior assembled all his monks, and bearing the cross before them, they marched to the house clad in sacred vestments. Reverently they took the breeches like holy relics on a silken cushion, and with uplifted hands, raised them to the lips of the husband, the wife, and everyone along the way. Then with full ceremony and the chanting of hymns they returned to the monastery and lay them in the sanctuary with the other relics. Afterwards, this fraud was discovered, and authorities from the town came to investigate it.[34]

Long as this joke is, the humor is sustained until the final, anticlimactic sentence. Poggio's humor cuts in a number of directions; the traditional lust of the friar is exposed, as well as the foolishness of the cuckold, but it is the venality (and cleverness) of the prior and the abuse of relic worship (in the form of the friar's britches) that are held up most vividly for laughter. Both of the jokes just discussed here are not far removed from the *novelle*. They are fairly lengthy and lack punch lines, although they are punctuated by verbal humor throughout. What is striking about these jests and so many others is the repeated use of certain basic characters and situations, especially the foolish cuckold, the wife who gets her pleasure, and the lecherous and often clever priest. The humor in these jests is humor with a point, and one of the points is that in sexual matters and clever maneuverings and rationalizations, none can surpass the clergy (there are even jokes in which women are taken advantage of by clever priests; see CXCIV and CCXXI).

It would be going too far, I think, to suggest that the *Facetiae* were part of a reform movement out to display the abuses of the church. The clergy had always been the targets of such humor. But even though, as Thomas reminds us, humor is most often conservative, that it makes us laugh at deviations from the norm, he also notes that "there was . . . a current of radical, critical laughter which, instead of reinforcing accepted norms, sought to give the world a nudge in a new direction."[35]

34. Ibid., no. CCXXX, pp. 186–88.
35. Thomas, "Place of Laughter," p. 78.

Perhaps Poggio's jests at least gave a nudge, whether intentionally or not, toward the revelation that corruption in the church was widespread and in need of reformation. In commenting on Poggio's letters, Gordon makes the salient point that it was in Poggio's "interest for the Church to have temporal, military, and financial security and his letters reflect that. Yet they also reflect his concern that the material prosperity of the Church and its hierarchy was contrary to the religious principles upon which it was founded."[36] Perhaps it would be safest to reiterate that the *Facetiae* are symptomatic of much of what the humanists thought and did. In the final analysis we should not lose sight of the fact that above all an audience reading or hearing these jokes did not submit them to the kind of examination to which they have been subjected here. While the political jests and witty sayings of famous men obviously had more meaning in their own era than they do now, one suspects that the *Facetiae* flooded all of Europe because people enjoyed the bawdy jests; for whatever reasons, man has always found man (and woman) in pursuit of sexual fulfillment a comic figure indeed.

II

Poggio lamented when he collected his *Facetiae* that things had changed; "Now that most of those boon companions have departed this life, the *Bugiale* has come to an end; whether men or times are to be held responsible, it is a fact that genial talk and merry conversation have gone out of fashion."[37] Poggio was wrong, however, for the *cenacoli* and the academies were just beginning to come into their golden age in Italy. In an extremely informative article on the origins of the *Accademia Fiorentina,* Richard Samuels has pointed to the connections among the various prominent Italian academies and reminded us of the important function they played in carrying on and developing more fully many aspects of Quattrocento scholarship.[38] In his article, Samuels takes note of the *Accademia Romana* and the later *Accademia dei Vignaiuoli,* or Academy of Vintners, but quite correctly he focuses most of his commentary on the *Accademia degli Intronati* of Siena and the *Accademia degli Infiammati* of Padua, since he is interested in the academies that most directly influence the *Accademia Fiorentina.* Samuels ignores Poggio and his group in his short discussion of the Roman academies, but it seems likely that the meeting of literary figures at the papal court was a fairly

36. Gordon, p. 6.
37. Poggio cited in Hurwood, p. 21.
38. Richard Samuels, "Benedetto Varchi, the *Accademia degli Infiammati,* and the Origins of the Italian Academic Movement," *Renaissance Quarterly* 29 (1976): 599–634.

continuous practice. "The so-called 'Roman Academy,' first founded by Pomponio Leto in the 1460's, resumed its meetings during the pontificate of Julius II, and centered its activities in the sumptuous gardens surrounding the villa of Angelo Colocci," according to Samuels.[39] This academy had as its program the study of classical literature and discussion "of original Latin compositions written in antique forms by its members."[40] However, "there is no evidence that it broadened its literary discussions to include political topics, or that its members were willing to accept the vernacular as a language on a par with classical Latin," important developments that were to come with the later academies.[41] Members of this early *Accademia Romana,* most notably Francesco Bini, later joined with other humanists and poets, the most important of whom was Francesco Berni, to form what became known as the *Accademia dei Vignaiuoli,* the academy that was to be the most productive in terms of learned erotica.

Francesco Berni was born almost fifty years after the death of Poggio, and, like the famed humanist, he received his early education in Florence and then went to Rome. At the age of twenty, Francesco was a secretary to Cardinal Bernardo Davizi da Bibbiena. After passing though the service of several other men, Berni secured a place with Cardinal Ippolito de' Medici in 1532, and he spent his last years in Florence, where he was supposedly poisoned in 1535 for refusing himself to poison one Cardinal Salviati.

Berni's literary output is fairly diverse, though generally he is treated as a great anti-Petrarchan. He gained some literary fame finishing the *Orlando Innamorato* of Boiardo, but the major thrust of Berni's work is to be found in his *Dialogo contra i poeti* (1526) and in his *Rime.* In his *Dialogo,* Berni takes a decidedly anti-Petrarchan stance; consequently critics have been quick to see his own work as earthy and realistic.[42] Berni's work is clearly anti-Petrarchan; its imputed realism is another matter. What Berni so often does is use Petrarchan conventions and explode them, much as Shakespeare and Donne do. The impact of such poetry is felt in seeing the deviation from the norm, which might or might not be realistic. One can say that his two poems to his *innamorata* are earthy; the carnal aspects of his love are clearly spelled out, so clearly

39. Ibid., p. 606.
40. Ibid., p. 606.
41. Ibid., p. 606.
42. See Ettore Bonora, "Il Classicismo dal Bembo al Guarini," in *Storia della Letteratura Italiana,* IV, especially pp. 290–301.

in fact, that modern critics have felt the need to apologize and explain the obscenity in the work of Berni.[43]

Much of Berni's erotica is well masked in bawdy, however, for it is to be found in works of a special literary type, the paradoxical encomium, the favorite literary exercise of Berni's famous *accademia* in Rome. Berni himself has left us letters recalling the gatherings of literary figures in Rome for an evening's dining and entertainment. In a letter to Francesco Bino from Florence in January of 1534, Berni writes fondly:

> A vivere avemo sino alla morte a dispetto di chi non vuole, e'l vantaggio è vivere allegramente, come conforto a far voi, attendendo a frequentar quelli banchetti che si fanno per Roma, e scrivendo sopratutto manco che potete; *quià haec est vitoria, quae vincit mundum.*[44]

> We must live until we die, despite those who don't like it, but the important thing is to live happily, as I invite you to do, by attending those banquets which are taking place in Rome, and by writing as little as you can; because this is the victory which conquers the world.

Then in a letter of April of the same year Berni writes in terms of the *Vignaiuoli* or Vintners. He asks that his regards be given to all

> e sopra gli altri al dabbenissimo signor Molza, a messer Giovanni della Casa, e a tutta quella divina Accademia. Così vi dia Dio grazie di avere un cosone grande per il vostro orto, con una fruscina trabale tra gambe e una falciazza in mano, e che non vi s'accosti mai ne' brinata, ne' nebbia, ne' bruchi, ne' vento pestilente, e abbiate fave e baccelli, e pesche e carote tutto l'anno, sì come desidero di avere io nel mio orticciuolo fallito qua giù, che attendo pure a raffazzonarlo quanto posso; ma trovo finalmente ch' è una gran differenza dagli uomini agli orciuoli. *Pure vo driè fazando al meio che possi, e in termi labor.* Ste. con Dio.[45]

> and above all the others to the very good natured Mr. Molza, to Mr. Giovanni della Casa, and to all the Divine Academy. May God grant you his blessing in giving you for your garden a big "thing", with a pitchfork as long as a beam between your legs and a big scythe in your hand and that neither frost, nor fog, worms or stench wind come close to you, and that you might have beans and pods and peaches and carrots all year round, in the way I desire for my small garden here which I do care to patch up as much as I can; but I finally found out that there's a great difference between

---

43. Francesco Berni, *Rime Facete,* ed. Ettore Bruni (Milan: Rizzoli, 1959), pp. 164–67.

44. Berni, *Opere di Francesco Berni* (Milan: G. Daelli, 1864), II, 112.

45. Berni, *Opere,* II, 124. In the *Opere di Francesco Berni* (Milan: Sonzogno, 1873), "cosone" is rendered "priapone."

men and a small jar. However I will do my best and I'll work by myself. Be with God.

In this letter, Berni refers to the various fruits in the garden he hopes will bloom year round to the delight of the members of this academy. This has direct reference to the name of the academy, the *Vignaiuoli*, and the chief metaphor around which they created many of their works, the various fruits and vegetables of the garden, all of which carried, as we shall see, sexual connotations.

The *Vignaiuoli* were only one group of many that sprang up in Italian cities at this time. A list of some seventeen academies is given by Anton Francesco Doni, a literary hack of considerable interest, in the third edition of his list of books and authors of note, *La Libraria*.[46] Doni himself joined or started literary clubs wherever he went, and a quick glance at his activities is instructive in putting Berni and his friends in proper perspective.

When Doni was in Piacenza, he became a member of the *Academia degli Ortolani*.[47] His name in the group was *il Semenza*, the Seed, and the symbol of the club, as one might expect, was the god of gardens, Priapus.[48] At one point, Doni took over the office of Bartolomeo Gottifredi when the latter was in Hungary,[49] and Doni wrote him an amusing letter sending him the key to the academy. The letter becomes a praise of the key, the humor stemming from the sexual connotation of the word *chiavare*, to turn the key or to lock, which is still a vulgar synonym for sexual intercourse.[50] Doni writes that he thinks the key is the greatest thing in the world, that it seems to him that "all' orto nostro si provedesse di buona chiave, essendo di tanta importanza. E da chi si tengon anco le mele, le fiche egli altri frutti degni"[51] [our

46. For an informative study that includes extensive commentary on Doni, Niccolo Franco, and Ortensio Lando see Paul F. Grendler, *Critics of the Italian World, 1530–1560* (Madison: Univ. of Wisconsin Press, 1969).

47. A detailed account is given in Maylender, IV, 146.

48. Anton Francesco Doni, *La Libraria*, 3rd ed. (Venice, 1558), p. 277.

49. Gottifredi was the author of an interesting text on love, *Specchio d'Amore*, now published in *Trattati d'Amore del Cinquecento*, ed. Giuseppe Zonta (1912; rpt. Bari: Gius. Laterza & Figli, 1967). The work is of particular interest since it deals with a very earthly kind of love, whereas most of the love tracts of this era are definitely neoplatonic.

50. Many of the sexual meanings of Italian words are given in the Italian-English dictionary of John Florio, *A Worlde of Wordes* (London, 1598). For *chiavare* he gives the following definition: "*to locke with a key: but nowe a daies abusiuely vsed for* Fottere" (p. 69). Barolsky notes that Italian Renaissance painters were also fond of punning on *chiave*. See pp. 132–33.

51. Doni, *La Chiave*, in *Scelta di Curiosita Letterarie Inedite o Rare Dal Secolo 13 al 19* (Bologna, 1862) I, 22.

garden must produce a good key, being of so great importance. And also it must have apples, figs and other worthy fruits]. He goes on to say that the world could not exist without a key. He reasons, "non sapete che non è casa al mondo che non si chiavi et in cui non si chiavi? tutte le cose più preziose, non si chiavano?"[52] [don't you know that there's no house in the world which is not locked and in which one doesn't lock? Aren't all the most precious things locked?]. Monks in fact, he assures us, lock everything. Doni proceeds to have a little scholarly fun; he quotes a passage from Petrarch in which Petrarch writes, "Del mio cor, donna, l'una e l'altra chiave / Avete in mano." Doni then explicates the passage:

> Questo so io di certo che molti comentatori s'avilluppano in questo caso. perchè, avendo Laura una cassetta, v'avea due chiavature che vi si adoprava una sola chiave; e facendo agli amori col Petrarca, gli disse in un sonetto, a mostrargli ch' egli aveva ogni sua cosa in mano e mostrar che una buona chiave vale per mille:
>
>> Basta al mio forzerin la vostra chiave.
>> Quantunque di due toppe sia munito:
>
> et in un altro loco:
>
>> Basta a due chiavature una sol chiave:
>
> onde egli imitandola disse:
>
>> . . . l'una e l'altra chiave
>> Avete in mano.[53]

I know this for sure, that many commentators are tangled in this case, because Laura, having a small box with two padlocks for which one key worked, making love with Petrarch, told him in one sonnet to show her that he had all his things in his hands and that a good key was worth more than one thousand:

> Your key is sufficient for my lock.
> Although there are two padlocks:

And in another place:

> One key is sufficient for two padlocks:

then he, imitating her, said:

---

52. Ibid., p. 24.
53. Ibid., p. 27.

... You have both keys in your hands.

Doni then looks at the two possible ways of reading the passage and notes that lo Steracchia takes it in the following manner:

> *O donna del mio core, io avete in mano l'una e l'altra chiave, cioè, la mia e quella del mio avversario;* volendo inferire, *attaccatevi a quella che più v'aggrada.* E questo disse il Petrarca, come colui che sapeva bene di che tempra era il suo chiavone; e venendo a questa prova, il rivale aveva fatto il pane![54]

> *Lady of my heart, you have both keys in your hands,* that is, *mine and that of my opponent;* wishing to imply, *stick to the one which pleases you the most.* And Petrarch said this knowing very well the temper of his big key; coming to this competition the opponent waited!

Doni's letter is a fine example of the way in which these jovial literary groups engaged their talents. He takes a seemingly innocent, insignificant object that happens to have well-known sexual implications, he plays upon these implications, while firing satirically at other targets along the way. He plays critical games, mocking the learned explication of the text that was so favored in the Renaissance, particularly with a poet like Petrarch, whose Laura is here imagined in circumstances that are uplifting only in the physical sense. This tendency to mock scholarly endeavors is an important one, for while the sexual implications were surely amusing to the academy members, the frequency with which they parody pedantic practices seems to indicate that they took almost equal if not more delight in making fun of their own scholarly ways.[55] No form allowed them to do this more easily than the paradoxical encomium, the form most favored by Berni and the members of the *Accademia dei Vignaiuoli* in Rome.

The paradoxical encomium as a rhetorical exercise had a long and distinguished tradition before the Renaissance, but it achieved something of a vogue in the academies, where the praise of an unpraiseworthy object proved a most fitting sport for these scholarly gamesters.[56] It was a sport made all that much better if the trifles they chose to praise had sexual connotations as well, and so we find poems in praise of figs (cunts), melons and apples (buttocks), peaches (assholes),

---

54. Ibid., p. 28.

55. Barolsky finds the tendency to parody one's most serious works in Italian Renaissance painters. See p. 59.

56. See Rosalie Colie, *Paradoxia Epidemica* (Princeton: Princeton Univ. Press, 1966); and H. K. Miller, "The Paradoxical Encomium with Special Reference to Its Vogue in England 1600–1800," *Modern Philology* 53 (1956): 145–78.

and string beans (cocks).[57] Other favorite topics were those that were
known to be unpleasant or unmentionable, related as they were to
sexual or excretory functions; thus we find poems in praise of urinals
and syphilis (the French disease to the Italians and English, the Nea-
politan disease to the French).

Berni's most noteworthy work in this mode is his poem in praise of
peaches, a fruit which was understood to suggest the ass or more
particularly asshole—especially of a boy; in fact his poem was so taken
as an expression of his true preference sexually that he was charged by
his enemies with being a sodomite. Berni's poem makes the sexual
references fairly explicit. He writes:

> O frutto sopra gli altri benedetto,
> buono inanzi, nel mezzo e dietro pasto;
> ma inanzi buono e di dietro perfetto![58]

> O fruit blessed above all others
> good before, in the middle and after the
> meal, but good before and perfect behind!

He tells us that peaches are a fruit that particularly delights the clergy;

> Le pèsche eran già cibo da prelati;
> ma, perché ad ogniun piace i buon bocconi,
> voglion oggi le pèsche insino a i fratti,
>   che fanno l'astinenzie e l'orazioni:
> così è intravenuto ancor de' cardi,
> che chi ne dice mal Dio gliel perdoni.[59]

Peaches were for a long time food for prelates, but since everyone likes a
good meal, even friars, who fast and pray, crave for peaches today. The same
thing happened to thistles; may God forgive whoever talks against them.

Berni takes a traditional gibe at the clergy here while reminding his
readers about his poem on thistles (cocks). Certainly the clergy were
not the only ones reputed to be obsessed with young boys—Boccaccio,
in his reworking of the episode in Apuleius' *Golden Ass* where an ass
steps on the fingers of a lover being hidden by an adulterous wife, adds
as an element to his story the husband's preference for young boys—
but this special predilection among the clergy was a proverbial belief

---

57. Florio, in *A Worlde of Wordes*, adds to his definitions of *fica* and *fava* as fig and bean
the following: of *fica*, "*Also a womans conie or quaint*" (p. 130): of *fava*, "*Also vsed for the
prepuse or top of a mans yard*" (p. 177).

58. Berni, *Rime*, p. 32.

59. Ibid., p. 33.

of long-standing and widespread currency.[60] We shall see it in the works of the writers of popular erotica as well. The point of any paradoxical encomium is to take the argument as far as possible, to be outrageous; Berni's is certainly that to the heterosexual; if, of course, one is decidedly not heterosexual (and some charged that Berni was not) then this poem loses some of its force as paradoxical encomium.

Berni's poem on urinals is more typical of the paradoxical encomium of antiquity; it turns not on double entendres but on his rhetorical skill and wit in praising such an insignificant item. In this poem Berni is at his zestful best, first comparing the urinal in its shape to the world in its roundness; he reminds us of its "profundity"; he speaks of the various colors we might find in it. He then lists the various uses the urinal might have, among them a purse, a lantern, a drinking glass, and of course, how old the folklore, a carrier of the French disease.

Other members of the *Accademia dei Vignaiuoli* contributed poems in the same vein. One of the most famous is Francesco Bini's poem on the French disease. Bini presents his praise in nicely turned terza rima, and one of his points is to show us how this great disease keeps us from the seven deadly sins:

> Voi sapete, che aspro, e gran difetto
>   È la Superbia, ei la fà star humile
>   Assai più d'un agnello, o d'un capretto.
>
>   . . . .
> E la lussuria come brace spenta
>   Riman, l'ira piaceuole, a la gola
>   D'ogni picciola cosa si contenta.[61]
>
> You know that pride is a harsh and serious fault,
>   but it keeps it more humble than a lamb or kid
>
>   . . . .
> And luxury remains like extinguished charcoal,
>   The anger pleasing, every little thing
>   contents the throat.

Not only does the disease prevent us from sinning, it also aids us in various virtues—prudence, sobriety, and modesty. Further it is an inspiration and aid to all kinds of arts and sciences. Of poetry:

---

60. In *The Decameron*, Fifth Day, Tenth Story; in Apuleius' *Golden Ass*, IX, 14–32. On sodomy in the Middle Ages see Ernst Robert Curtius, *European Literature and the Latin Middle Ages*, trans. Willard Trask (New York: Harper & Row, 1963), pp. 113–117.
61. Francesco Bini, "Capitolo in lode del mal Franzese," in *Opere Burlesche del Berni, Casa, Varchi, Mauro* (Venice, 1603), p. 122r.

Facci far uersi, che non fe mai Musa,
    Nè Vergilio in Latin, nè in Greco Homero,
    Nè l'Petrarca in Arquato, od in Valclusa.[62]

It makes us write verses, that neither the Muses,
    Nor Virgil in Latin, nor Homer in Greek,
    Nor Petrarch in Arqua or in Vaucluse ever wrote.

Bini assures us that it helps in figures, grammar, rhetoric; even sculptors and painters are aided:

Quanti Scultori, e Dipintor pregiati
    Fur mai, costui gli faria star a drieto.
Non uedete uoi i uisi delicati,
    Ch' ei fà? come che i membri rozi ingrossa:
    Empie gli smilzi, e doma gli sforzati?
Come imbianca la carne troppo rossa,
    Come fà comparir, ch'e'l fondamento
    De l'arte, le gionture, i nerui, e l'ossa.
Come il capo, le ciglia, e gli occhi, e'l mento
    Sì gentilmente pela, netta, e sbuccia,
    Ch' un par di cinquant' anni, ed hane cēto.[63]

How many sculptors and famous painters.
    It leads through the right path,
Don't you see the delicate faces
    Which it makes? It makes the rough members big,
    Fills the thin ones, and tames those which are strained.
It makes the red skin white, it makes one important because
    it is the foundation of art; it gently shaves, cleans
        and feels
The joints, nerves, bones, head, eyelashes, eyes
    And the chin; so that he doesn't look
    Like a fifty-year-old and is a hundred.

Syphilis as sculptor! It is this kind of extravagant logic that typifies so many of the paradoxical encomia. Such logic, and the particulars of the argument, using the seven deadly sins and the academic and artistic disciplines in a poem on what was to the Renaissance one of the most horrifying of all diseases, must have been both outrageous and amusing to the learned poets and scholars of the *Accademia*.[64]

There are many other poems in praise of sexually related subjects; Dolce's poem on the nose should certainly be of interest to Shandean

---

62. Ibid., p. 122ᵛ.
63. Ibid., p. 123ʳ.
64. For a fuller discussion of the horrible as comic, see chapter 5, pp. 152–55.

readers of Renaissance materials; Varchi's poem on Priapus strikes a note on a subject that will be of significance in a later chapter. There are also paradoxes that were written on various topics or propositions rather than on objects. The greatest collection of these was written by Ortensio Lando, one of the most curious and fascinating of Renaissance writers, who deserves far more attention than I can give him here.[65] A good many of the thirty paradoxes in a 1544 Venice edition of the *Paradossi* do not deal with sexual matters. We find them on such topics as "That Aristotle was not only ignorant but also the most wicked man of his age" and "That Cicero was ignorant of not only philosophy, but also rhetoric." There are several, however, that deal with sexual matters in which Lando shows himself a master of this kind of writing. He pens one on the proposition that it is better to have a sterile wife than a fecund one, and another on the proposition that it is not a detestable or odious thing to have an adulterous wife.[66]

Something of a high point was reached in the mock encomium tradition with the work of Francesco Molza and Annibale Caro. Molza's poem in praise of figs (female pudenda, metaphorically) was included in a collection published with works by Berni and the other *Vignaiuoli*. Molza had the name *Il Fico* in the *Accademia*, and in this poem he sings of the honor the ancients did to the fig tree; only from this wood would they carve a Priapus, for example.[67] Molza tells us this fruit is preferable to peaches and apples; men, in fact, cannot live without the precious fig.

The inevitable, given the kinds of rhetorical games these men enjoyed playing, occurred. Annibale Caro, member of a different academy in Rome, the *Accademia della Virtù*, came out with an elaborate mock

65. Lando is a quixotic figure indeed. His works are as strange, various, and humorous as his own accounts of himself within them. For example, in a work entitled *Sette Libri de Cathaloghi A Varie Cose, Appartenenti, Non Solo Antiche, Ma Anche Moderne: Opera Vtile Molto Alla Historia, et Da Cui Prender. Si Po Materia di Favellare D'Ogni Proposito Che ci Occorra* (Venice, 1552–53), we find Lando listing himself under a catalogue of ugly men; he is also in a catalogue of irascible, choleric, and disdainful men and in a catalogue of those who hate literature; he is among the unhappy, and he lists himself along with Doni among those who have written on base subjects. Another work of interest is Lando's *Varii Componimenti* (Venice, 1552). In this collection of varied works there is a long section devoted to amorous questions and answers. Lando is discussed by Grendler, pp. 21–38.

66. See paradoxes VII and XI in Lando, *Paradossi* (Venice, 1544). Lando's *Paradossi* were translated into English from a French version in 1593 by Anthony Munday under the title of *The Defense of Contraries*.

67. Francesco Molza, "Capitolo in lode de' Fichi" in *Opere Burlesche del Berni, Casa, Varchi, Mauro*, p. 145ᵛ. The quotations from the poem cited hereafter will be from Caro's *Commento* (see note 70).

commentary on the poem in praise of figs.[68] In the *Commento,* published by one Barbagrigia in 1538 or 1539, Molza is given the name Padre Siceo (literally Father Cunt) and Caro takes the name Ser Agresto (Mr. Bitter Grape). The work begins with an address by the publisher, Barbagrigia, to Molza and Caro.[69] He refers to the works as having "sciocchi concetti,"[70] and then, very interestingly, Barbagrigia answers the objection that he should not publish the work because it is licentious. He says:

> As far as the lasciviousness, although I know well that I don't understand other language except slang, Mr. Ludovico Fabbro da Fano, who is to me a Dragonman of these languages and my counselor for the works which I print, tells me that they have the same kindness, modesty as those of this kind among the Greeks, Latins, and the Vulgar who are mostly naked and without pants, whereas the former are completely dressed and with underwear.[71]

Barbagrigia explains at the end of his comments that he has published the work because he believes he can make some money; if he can create some controversy, so much the better for sales:

> . . . because I printed them for your honor and for the affection which I have for them, and to tell you the truth, because I earn some money. And if anyone among you is offended, it is too bad; and if you want to take revenge, write against them, and I will print it underhand. Repress this anger for now and be well.[72]

The commentary proper begins with Caro's Preface, in which we see that he will parody scholarly commentary of all kinds: points of grammar are examined in excruciating detail, methods of allegorical interpretation are strung out in both theoretical fashion and practical application; the pedantic obsession with etymology and dialect, including the question of whether Tuscan dialect and rules should hold sway,

---

68. See Samuels, p. 607.

69. The publishing history is interesting in that this same Barbagrigia was the publisher of Aretino's dialogues. He has been identified as a Roman publisher, Antonio Blado. See Pietro Aretino, *Sei Giornate,* ed. Giovanni Aquilecchia (Bari: Gius. Laterza & Figli, 1969), p. 400n. When Aretino's dialogues were published in England in 1584 by John Wolfe (see pp. 300 and 328 n. 7) a later Barbagrigia, in this case probably Petruccio Ubaldini, wrote a preface in which he refers to his "grandfather," the original publisher. It was a pseudonym both men seem to have found convenient and humorous to adopt.

70. Annibale Caro, *Commento di Ser Agresto da Ficarvolo, sopra la prima Ficata del Padre Siceo,* in *La Prima Parte de Ragionamenti di M. Pietro Aretino* (Bengodi [London], 1584), p. 6.

71. See ibid., p. 7.

72. See ibid., p. 8.

is pursued throughout; extended citation of divergent opinion on a point is lovingly considered beyond the bounds that any reader wishes to journey; mythology, philosophy, philology, folklore, proverb-lore all receive their due. For anyone who has labored in serious Renaissance commentary on any classical author, Caro's work is a remarkably successful, highly comic work. And through it all, Caro spices his commentary with sexual double entendres, reminding us that he is, after all, commenting upon a poem in praise of figs that plays upon the metaphor of figs as cunts.

Several examples should serve to illustrate Caro's parody. He makes fun of the obsession with points of grammar, allegorical interpretation, and dialect in a passage in which he takes up the problem of gender for the Italian word for fig:

> It soggetto sono i FICHI, o le FICHE: Che nell' vn modo, & nell' altro son chiamate dall' Autore: con tutto che i Toscani se ne scandelezzino: perche vorrebbon i Fichi sempre nel genere del maschio. Laqual cosa (in questo loco massimamente) non mi da briga, ne ancho presto lor gran fede: sappiendo che s'intendono piu tosto dell' altre frutte, che di questa. Oltre, che io potrei mostrar loro, che si truouano Fichi maschi, e Fiche femine, & allegarei da vn canto le Fiche lesse, le Fiche pazze: Dall' altro i Fichi Atteroni, i Fichi delle Tribadi, il Fico de Modena, di che altra vilta habbiamo disputato nella Diceria de S. Nafissa—& addurrei mille altre ragioni, che muouono l'Autore à così chiamarle: le quali mi passerò, per non intricarmi fuor di proposito nella questione del Valla; che per dichiarare i generi, & le variationi de Fichi, fece anch' egli vna ficata, & vno scompiglio di grammatica, che non lo' ntenderebbe, Va qua tu. Bastiui per hora di sapere, che'l Poeta, non senza misterio li battezza hermafroditi; & che per tutta l'opera trouerete, che hanno confusamente due sessi, & due sensi, & di questi vno è secondo la lettera, l'altro secondo il misterio, come di sotto vedrete. [73]

> The FIGS or the FIGESSES are the subject, because they are called by the Author in one way or the other: although the Tuscans are scandalized, because they want the word Figs always masculine. But (especially in this place) I don't care and I don't have any faith in them, knowing that they are rather familiar with other kinds of fruits than these. Besides, I can show them that there are masculine figs and feminine figs, and I could place on one side the boiled Figess, the crazy Figess: on the other side the ripe Figs, the Figs from Tribadi, the Fig from Modena and other meanness which we have discussed in the Tale of S. Nafissa, and I would add one thousand other reasons which have moved the Author to call them in this way: I will skip them, in order not to get involved out of place in the question of Valla; that in order to declare the gender and the variations of the figs, he himself made

---

73. Ibid., pp. 9–10.

a ficata and he made so great a mess of the grammar that nobody can understand it. It is enough to know that the Poet, not without mystery, calls them hermaphrodites; and through all his work you will find that they have confused two sexes, and two senses, and of these one is according to the letter and the other according to the mystery, as you will see below.

The question of whether Tuscan dialect and rules should hold sway lies at the heart of this part of the commentary, and this question of Tuscan hegemony over the Italian language was an extremely serious one. A writer like Castiglione felt the need to justify at great length his unwillingness to be bound by the Tuscan dialect in the preface to his *Book of the Courtier.*[74] Here the Tuscan sensibilities (those of Berni and his friends?) are dismissed in a rather less genteel fashion as Caro accuses them of preferring the masculine gender and fruits other than figs.

Concerned as he is with the careful explication of words, Caro proceeds to explain the significance of Padre Siceo's name. He is called father "come so ognuno li fosse figliuolo: Et come Alberto fu detto Magno, per havere scoperti i segreti delle donne; esso è cognominato Diuino, & perfetto, per hauer riuelati i segreti de Fichi . . ."[75] [as if everyone were his son: and as Albertus is called the Great, for having discovered the secrets of women; he is given the family name Divine and Perfect, for having revealed the secrets of Figs. . .]. The absurd logic, the outrageous comparison, carried off in the most learned manner—these are the stock in trade of the commentator, and they are in constant evidence as he goes through the poem tercet by tercet explaining the possible meanings.

A splendid parody of the practice of citing conflicting learned commentary is attached to the tercet, "Io sarò teco & t'aprirò la via, / Per la qual venghi à si lodata impresa, / Senza pur mescolarui vna bugia" [I will be with you, and I will open the way for you, in order that you may come to this worthy deed without mingling in it any lie]. Caro writes:

Dove gli altri, dice Apollo, hanno per iscorta le Berte & lodano le cose, come Sophisti; io che sono lo Dio della Verità, sarò tua scorta à dir le vere lodi del Fico, senza fare argomenti a rouescio, Il Forca li dà vn senso piu recondito: & dice così: Perche tu non hai si penetratiuo ingegno, come si conuerrebbe a vna si profonda materia, io che fò le mie cose con fondamento, ti farò la via innanzi, & mostrerò ti tutti i colpi maestri, senza vscir mai del suo dritto: & vuole, che in questo loco le BUGIE siano, come dire, punte

74. Baldesar Castiglione, *The Book of the Courtier,* trans. Charles S. Singleton (Garden City, N.Y.: Doubleday, 1959), pp. 4–6.
75. Caro, pp. 10–11.

false. Ma il Giuccari leggendo questa gran liberalità d'Apollo, cominciò a ridere, & disse: in verità, che il faceua vn gran seruigio à volerli aprir la via del Fico; come se non fosse pur troppo larga. Io li replicai, che, aprir la via, era Metafora. O metter fuora, o metter dentro, disse egli, non bisognava, che pigliasse questo disagio, perche il Poeta era tanto pratico, che sapeua andar da se. Io soggiunsi: intendi sanamente Giuccari: Aprir la via vuol, come dir, far lume. O tu sei vn balordo, rispose. Non sai tu, che vi s'entra à chius' occhi? Hora intendetela come voi volette, che io non vò combatter col Giuccari.[76]

Where others, says Apollo, have for a guide Berte and praise things, like the Sophists, I being the god of truth, will be your guide in order to tell the true praises of the Fig without treating the subject wrongly; Forca gives to it a more hidden meaning, and he says: Since you don't have a sharp intellect, which such a deep subject would require, and because I treat my things very deeply, I will make the way for you and will show to you all the master strokes, without going out of the right path; and he wants in this place lies that are, as they say, false points. But Giuccari in reading this great liberality of Apollo began to laugh and said: In truth, he would do a great service by opening to him the way of the Fig; as if it would not have been already wide enough. I answered him that to open the way was a metaphor. He said that sticking it out or sticking it in didn't matter, and therefore he didn't have to go into so great trouble, because the Poet was very practical, and he knew how to go ahead alone. I answered; Giuccari you are talking wisely; to open the way means to make light. You must be silly, he answered. Don't you know that you can enter it with your eyes closed? Now you can take it in the way you like, I don't intend to contradict Giuccari.

Stock scholarly phrases—"deep subjects" that require "sharp intellects," "opening the way" and "entering in"—prove ready material in the hands of one working to invest them with bawdy connotations; the fun of arguing over different meanings is punctuated by the quibbling over "metafora" ("metaphor") and "metta fuora" ("stick it out"). The "metta fuora" of the commentary is followed by "metter dentro" ("stick it in"); the bawdy connotations of the passage are not left to chance. And of course the reader must also remember (he can hardly forget) that this is a commentary on a poem that itself depends upon an understanding of a bawdy double entendre.

Caro passes through the poem offering extended commentary now on the quality of the wood of the fig tree, now on the name of any place or thing in Italy related to the fig. The pedantic obsession with etymology, questions of dialect, and folklore is paraded forth; allegorical readings that are both philosophical and mythological are proffered;

76. Ibid., pp. 16–17.

and always explanations of particular metaphors and special features of style are treated.[77] In discussing the question of allegory, Caro employs the traditional language of the Renaissance literary scholar; the narrative is a mere "veil" (*velame*) for the mystery or true meaning of the work:

> Questo è quel gran punto, che comprehende tutta la Filosofia. Et questo è quello, che l' altissimo nostro Poeta ha voluto dire sotto il velame di questo antico misterio, cioè, che i Priapi s' intagliassero nel legname del Fico: Percioche fatta vna cosa della Natura & del Naturale, si componeua la Materia prima.[78]

> This is the main point which comprehends all philosophy. And this is what our very great poet wanted expressed under the veil of a mystery, that is, that Priapuses were carved in the wood of a Fig; therefore making a thing from Nature and from the Natural which contains the First Matter.

A sweeping, crass, comic generalization, blandly asserted under the quintessential scholarly method of reading texts. That our commentator uses allegory to find a bawdy meaning is in fact a wonderfully ironic reversal of the Renaissance tendency to use allegory in order to find "serious" meanings in works that were bawdy, or erotic, or even obscene. Such is the commentary of a scholar who would convince us that he deals with "legitimate" fruit while the pedants prefer apples and peaches.[79]

Caro's work is in many ways the ultimate in learned erotica, for it takes the one step beyond a comic sexual poem that itself displays and mocks learned traditions; Caro provides us with a line-by-line excursus of the poem in which he is able to mock not only sexual matters but every scholarly procedure practiced by Renaissance literary commentary as well.

There remains one other famous work to be discussed in the context of learned erotica, *La Cazzaria* of Antonio Vignale, the Arsiccio Intronato of the *Accademia degli Intronati* of Siena. The *Accademia degli Intronati* in Siena is generally considered the oldest academy in Italy. At the forefront of the earliest gatherings was Aeneas Silvius Piccolomini, later Pope Pius II; by the first half of the fifteenth century the Academy had become more of an organized body and was called the *Accademia*

---

77. See ibid., p. 21. At one point Caro humorously notes that the Sicelide (Muses of Sicily) really should be muses of figs and that Virgil should have invoked them in the *Priapeia* rather than in the *Eclogues*. My thanks to Mr. Anthony Foddai, who pointed out the allusion to Virgil's fourth eclogue in this passage. For etymology as a category of thought, see Curtius, pp. 495ff.

78. Caro, p. 50.

79. Ibid., p. 46.

Grande. By 1525 it is assumed that the *Accademia Grande* became the *Accademia degli Intronati,* although Maylender points out that this has never been proven conclusively.[80] The *Intronati* (or "Dunderheads," as the name has been most commonly translated) "were devoted to 'reading, disputing, composing, interpreting and writing' in what they regarded as the three most important languages: Tuscan, Latin, and Greek."[81] In terms of their own literary productions the *Intronati* are most famous for their numerous dramas, but the *Cazzaria, or Book of Cocks,* by the "Burnt Dunderhead" achieved a certain notoriety as well. The *Cazzaria* consists of a dialogue between Arsiccio and Sodo, or "Thick Dunderhead." In the Dialogue Sodo is presented, as one might expect, as a dense and somewhat prim character, while Arsiccio might be described as a naturalist.[82]

Arsiccio starts off the dialogue by explaining to Sodo why he should study about cocks, cunts, and fucking. It is shame for a scholar not to know about such things, he says, "quanto che tu fai professione, oltra a la disciplina legale, di lettere humane, volgari e latine, e mescolatamente di Philosophia, la quale non è altro che cognitione de le cose naturali: onde essendo il cazzo cosa naturale, e la potta et il fottere cose naturalissime e necessarie a l'esser nostro, mi pare grandissimo vituperio che tu te ne faccia ignorante . . ."[83] [since you make a profession, other than the legal discipline, of humanistic letters, vulgar and Latin, and of mixed philosophy, which is nothing other than the awareness of natural things: therefore, the cock being a natural thing, and the cunt and fucking most natural things and necessary to our existence, it seems to me the greatest shame that you remain ignorant about them . . .]. Arsiccio gives a number of specific reasons beyond the general principle as to why scholars must know about such things, and he explains why women want to be fucked above all by a knowledgeable scholar:

Et io ti dico il vero, che s'io fossi una Donna, vorrei inanzi essere fottuta

80. Maylender, III, 350–54. See III, 355–56 for a description of their activities and an explanation of their emblem.

81. Samuels, p. 608. For the translation of the name and a description of the work see Legman, *The Horn Book,* p. 476; and Victor Robinson, ed., *Encyclopedia Sexualis* (New York: Dingwall-Rock, 1936), pp. 491–92. According to Patrick J. Kearney, *The Private Case* (London: Jay Landesman Ltd., 1981), two modern versions of the work have appeared in recent years as *The Love Academy* (Brandon House of North Hollywood, trans. Rudolphe Schleifer, 1968) and *Dialogue on Diddling: La Cazzaria* by Sir Hotspur Dunderpate (Collectors Publications, 1968).

82. Legman has noted a good deal of comic homosexual play in the work. *The Horn Book,* p. 80.

83. Antonio Vignale, *La Cazzaria* (Paris: Isidore Liseux, 1882), p. 10.

cento volte da uno scolare, che una sola da questi ignoranti; imperoche essi
che studiano sanno mille colpi buoni e mille tratti dolci sopra quel fatto, li
quali trovano scritti ne i libri, e come quei che sanno come la potta sta
dentro, sanno ritrovare tutte le vie piacevoli e segreti.[84]

And I tell you the truth, that if I were a woman I would prefer being fucked
one hundred times by a scholar to only once by these ignorant ones; because,
since they study, they know one thousand good strokes and a thousand sweet
pulls concerning that fact, which are written in books and since they know
how the cunt is made inside, they can find all the pleasant and secret ways.

The glories of being able to read! Arcane knowledge only the learned
can have makes such men better lovers. Here is an argument for a
learned audience indeed. Further, he points out, scholars know how to
defame and praise in print, which can do much for a woman's reputation, and they know such practical things as how to prevent or abort
pregnancies.[85] Such is the nature of Arsiccio's opening remarks, where
we are struck by the juxtaposition of the "scholarly inquiry" and the
use of vulgar terms. Arsiccio overcomes Sodo's objections that such
matters are not important in Sodo's philosophy, which deals with things
"pui perfette, e di piu gloria, e di maggiore honore che non sono coteste
. . ."[86] [more perfect, and of more glory and of greater honor than
these . . .].

Arsiccio then launches into his discourse proper. He explains why
man has the smallest cock of all animals, why women have big cunts,
and why cocks have nodes. He attacks friars and monks for their sexual
abuses, and always he has an eye out for sexual connotations as he
writes. For example, as he moves from considering cocks to cunts, he
writes, "Ma lasciamo stare il cazzo, et entriamo ne la potta . . ."[87]
[But let us leave the cock and let us enter into the cunt . . .]. But not
all of Arsiccio's topics are sexual. He goes off on tangents, among them
a timely discourse on the Tuscan dialect.

A great part of the work is devoted to a long, pseudo-mythological
account of a golden age long ago when the cocks were the most honored
organs of the body. The story tells how the big cocks became proud
and, in conjunction with the beautiful cunts, assumed total power,
deposing the little cocks and ugly cunts. In time, the rulers so abused
their power that the little cocks, ugly cunts, assholes, and balls joined
together to lead a rebellion. At the last minute, however, the balls turned

84. Ibid., p. 13.
85. Ibid., p. 14.
86. Ibid., p. 16.
87. Ibid., p. 19.

informers. The rebellion was crushed; one of the punishments was that ugly cunts were made to smell like herrings, and no longer were they known as *potte* but as *fiche* and "conni, et altre cose piu sozze e puzzolenti"[88] [cunts and other things more filthy and smelly]. In time, however, a successful rebellion was mounted, and the resulting punishment, meted out to the cocks, cunts, and especially the traitorous balls, accounts for the present body structure. For punishment the balls were to be enclosed by pairs in a sack and placed between the cock and the asshole, there to remain a constant witness of all things but a participant in nothing.

The myth then becomes a fantastic way of explaining all sexual bodily functions. But there is a good deal more than this pseudo-explanation of sexual organs.[89] Vignale invests the myth with long discourses after the successful rebellion on proper government and justice. The three major forms of government are discussed, and the wisdom of the old cunt of Modena is what carries the day. She is a wise and fair-minded individual who, speaking on victory after the rebellion, notes, "la prima parte de la vera vittoria è il deporre la superbia e la prosontione di se stessi, e disporsi non a guidicarsi, ma a volere essere giudicato"[90] [the first part of a true victory is to give up pride and presumption of oneself and be willing not to judge oneself but to be judged by others]. It might possibly be argued that the discussion on government and rebellion is the real focus of this work, but I think such an argument would not stand up given the context in which the material is presented. Vignale seems more intent upon having fun with learned dialogues, mythology, discourses on government, all matters of great moment to Renaissance humanists, and he keeps us aware of this fun when we remember (and we can hardly forget) that he is talking about cocks, cunts, assholes, and balls. Here is an instance in which the juxtaposition of obscene words and learned discourse is central in having the work function. *La Cazzaria* is a typical albeit brilliant example of learned erotica. The main business is bawdy above all, but as a product of an academy, it parodies all kinds of important endeavors that these men undertook in their more serious work. There is another dimension to Vignale's work, however, that I think finds its fullest expression in various forms of Renaissance art; this is the desire to return to the golden age, to see a world in which human bodies were

88. Ibid., p. 71.
89. There is a poem that tells the same story entitled *Il Libro del Perche*. This verse imitation was published in the eighteenth century, according to V. Robinson, *Encyclopedia Sexualis*, p. 491.
90. Vignale, Liseux ed., pp. 86–87.

not fettered by the Fall. Arsiccio the naturalist looks back with admiration in his mythological account to a world of beautiful cocks and cunts. The wonderful state could not last, he realizes, but the myth itself shows a certain longing quite common in the turning of the Renaissance to classical antiquity.[91]

The literature produced in the academies in Italy, like much of the literature produced in the universities and inns of law in England, has long been neglected. One of the reasons for that neglect, in Italy especially, has undoubtedly been the subject matter of much that was written, but there are other reasons as well. Essentially, materials like the ones dealt with in this chapter are comic productions of humanists whose major efforts were given to other, more "serious" work. If a humanist spent a large part of his life producing a learned edition of a classical text or composing a history of a major Italian city, we are hardly likely to give more than a passing notice to bawdy rhymes he composed and contributed to a collection of similar rhymes written by his friends and fellow humanists. But produce such works these humanists did, often, it seems, as part of a joint project for a club, and when we see them gathered and published together, when *we* gather these productions together, we see that there was a corpus, a body of literature, that a humanist in England in the 1590s could look at and see as a kind, to be imitated, translated, and explicated. There was, in short, a tradition of learned erotica. The literature in this tradition demands a great deal of its audience. The humor of this literature, even when couched in the most forthright of language, depends upon the reader's knowledge of the world of scholarship. It is a literature produced by a very specialized segment of society of its own members. Such a context and such intentions are considerably different from those that inform the production of the commercial erotica of the Renaissance, as we shall see in the next chapter.

91. I do not wish to argue that the Renaissance was pagan or that this aspect of the Renaissance marks a Counter-Renaissance. (Poggio's jokes, for example, surely show a desire to expose the vices of the church, but they are not anti-Christian.) I do think that Vignale's work expresses a longing for sexual freedom and glorification. See p. 122 for more on the Renaissance concept of the Golden Age.

CHAPTER 2

The Scourge of Princes as Pornographer: Pietro Aretino and the Popular Tradition

Io te lo ho voluto dire, ed emmisi scordato: parla alla libera,
e dì "cu', ca', po', e fo' . . ."
    Pietro Aretino, Ragionamento Della Nanna e
    Della Antonia

Pietro Aretino was the first great commercial writer of the Renaissance. Indeed, it is now something of a commonplace to call Aretino the first public relations man, the first gossip columnist, the first journalist, and the first realist to reject classical traditions. In his own time he was called the Teller of Truth and the Scourge of Princes (surely a result of his own successful self-promotion). These are the nice things he was called. His enemies called him everything from a pimp to a cocksucking sodomite. One thing that can be agreed upon is that Pietro Aretino is the first modern pornographer.

The danger in writing about Aretino is that one is tempted to concentrate more on his life and times than on his works. It might be argued that Aretino's life-style itself—that hedonistic reveling in the splendors of this world—is the essence of the man. From the resplendent Villa Farnesina in Rome to his opulent abode in the Ca' Bolani in Venice, Aretino, Scourge of Princes, friend and agent of Titian, companion and champion of the most famous courtesans of the time, sensualist and libertine, artist and blackmailer, moved in the highest and lowest circles. Aretino not only lived, he also wrote; he wrote widely and successfully, and it can be fairly said that Aretino was the first man to "make it" as a literary man in the modern world; he was the first to write professionally for a public press and make a considerable livelihood that way.[1] He was not concerned with reaching the scholarly

---

1. This is an overstatement, of course. Aretino did curry favor with any nobleman or woman from whom he thought he could get either money or presents, and he tried to blackmail those whom he could not flatter. Nonetheless, he was no court writer

audience of his world. He wrote in the vernacular, aiming at a wider audience (albeit one limited still to those who could read). This helps explain why Aretino wrote religious tracts as well as pornography; he would write anything he thought would sell, and knowing what would sell was a questionable proposition in the first great age of printing.[2] Aretino saw clearly the potential of the printed word, and he explored every possible avenue of that potential from the safety that Venice afforded him.[3]

Certain biographical matters must be dealt with, however, if we are to understand the nature of Aretino's pornography, and one of the problems in dealing with Aretino's life is that many of the "facts" that we find in biographies of Aretino are drawn from literary sources— especially from the attacks of his literary enemies.[4] Such sources must always be dealt with cautiously. Equally troublesome is Aretino's fondness for shaping the truth of his life to meet the needs of any moment and his consistent coloring of events by his heroic view of himself.

Aretino began his literary career in Rome, where he got a place in the service of Agostino Chigi, richest man in Rome and not coincidentally banker to the papacy. Pietro, born to a shoemaker father in

---

dependent upon any one prince at any one time once he arrived in Venice. Arnold Hauser, in *The Social History of Art* (New York: Vintage Books, n.d.), II, 80–81, sees Aretino as a member of the new, "theoretically, free literary profession. . . . The freedom to which he owes his existence first became possible in an age in which the writer was no longer absolutely dependent on a single patron or a strictly limited circle of patrons, but had so many potential customers for his products that he no longer needed to be on good terms with all of them. But, after all, it was only a comparatively small educated class on whom the humanists could rely for their public, and, compared with the modern man of letters, they still led a parasitical life, unless they had private means and were, therefore, independent from the very start." A good summary of the life and works of Aretino can be found in *A Concise Encyclopaedia of the Italian Renaissance,* ed. J. R. Hale (New York and Toronto: Oxford Univ. Press, 1981), pp. 33–34.

2. Among Aretino's works one finds several plays, the most notable being *La Cortegiana* ; an epic poem, *La Marfisa* ; his famous letters; the pornographic *Ragionamenti* and *sonetti lussuriosi* and a number of religious tracts, including *Parafrasi sopra i sette salmi, Dell'umanita del Figliol di Dio,* and *Vita di Maria Vergine.*

3. At a time when various *Indexes* were first taking hold, culminating in 1559 with the first Papal *Index Auctorum et Librorum Prohibitorum* of Paul IV, Venice remained remarkably free from enforcement of the *Index.* See George Haven Putnam, *The Censorship of the Church of Rome* (1906; rpt. New York: Benjamin Blom, 1967), I, 29–37. Even before Aretino's time, Venice had become the place for the business of printing. See Martin Lowry, *The World of Aldus Manutius* (n.p.: Cornell Univ. Press, 1979).

4. There are a number of very readable biographies of Aretino: Thomas Caldecot Chubb, *Aretino Scourge of Princes* (New York: Reynal & Hitchcock, 1940); James Cleugh, *The Divine Aretino* (New York: Stein & Day, 1966); and Ralph Roeder, *The Man of the Renaissance* (1933; rpt. Cleveland: World, 1958).

Arezzo, came to Rome to make his way in the world. He came, after having spent several years in Perugia, without the letters of recommendation that accompanied a Poggio or a Berni, and he came without their education as well. In all probability, Aretino could read neither Latin nor Greek.[5] In acquiring a position, however humble, in the household of Agostino Chigi, Aretino moved into the most sumptuous service in Europe. The Villa Farnesina is still there on the Via della Lungara; the frescoes of Raphael can still be seen, and the gardens, a small part of what they once were, still offer a cooling shade from the burning Roman sun.[6] Even what are surely apocryphal stories give some sense of the glory of the villa. This was the palace so splendid that the Spanish ambassador, caught in a coughing spell, spit in the face of his servant, for, he allowed later, it was the only thing of no value he could find in the place.[7] Here Chigi lived with his mistress, Impera, one of the most famous of Roman courtesans, widely known for her refinement and learning. And here Agostino Chigi entertained as one might have expected one of the richest men in the world to entertain. The story is told of how at one dinner party given for the Pope, the gold dishes were tossed into the Tiber after each course. Chigi was no spendthrift, however; he had nets in the water to catch them.

This was the household in which Aretino worked, and the Rome in which this household thrived was the Rome of Julius II and Leo X. Again, popularizers have tended to distort the historical picture. They conjure up the Rome of Alexander VI and the corruption of the Borgia papacy—masked balls that approached orgies and the randy voyeurism of a pope who enjoyed nothing so much as watching with his daughter Lucrezia as horses copulated. Rome was much more complex than this, as all serious historians have shown, but popular biographers of men like Aretino have tended to overlook complexity in favor of showing us the "pagan," "liberated," "sensual" aspects of the Renaissance. Aretino is one figure who has been treated within the context of erotica; ironically the "pagan and sensual world" pictured by the popularizers as the one in which Aretino worked is as distorted a view as that which pretends that the earthy, the bawdy, and the pornographic do not exist.

5. Grendler, p. 39.

6. The Gabinetto Nazionale delle Stampe is now housed in the Villa, which allows scholars one of the most delightful of places to work.

7. See Chubb, *Aretino,* p. 44. For an excellent scholarly account of Chigi's household and patronage see Ingrid D. Rowland, "Render unto Caesar the Things Which Are Caesar's: Humanism and the Arts in the Patronage of Agostino Chigi," *Renaissance Quarterly* 39 (1986): 673–730.

The religious, philosophical, ascetic, and humanistic aspects obviously cannot be ignored if one is to have a sense of Renaissance Italy in all of its complexity.

Aretino managed to get the attention of his employer—and the Pope—by a literary effort, a kind of *jeu d'esprit* that was first published anonymously. It seems that Leo had a pet elephant of which he was extremely fond, and the elephant died. There appeared a "Last Will and Testament of the Elephant." In this testament, the elephant wills the parts of his body to the various cardinals; each cardinal is fitted for his vice (Cardinal Grassi got the elephant's genitalia). Once Aretino discovered that the Pope was amused by this, he was quick to make known his authorship. Thus Aretino began his literary career mocking the clergy—something he was to do throughout his life.

When Leo died in 1521, Aretino, supporting Giulio de' Medici's candidacy, attacked various rivals for the papacy in print. Adrian of Utrecht was elected to succeed Leo, and Aretino continued his offensive attacks upon the election of this northern outsider to the throne of Peter. Aretino attacked under the guise of Pasquino, the name given the defaced trunk of a statue still found off the Piazza Navona where pamphleteers traditionally appended their works. Pasquino Aretino's works soon had Rome buzzing with the viciousness of his attacks upon Adrian. Though the verses Aretino turned out at this time were not obscene, they were nonetheless good practice in the art of invective, which was to serve him well in later years.

Aretino had been wise enough to leave Rome, and in removing himself to Mantua, he went into the service of Federico Gonzaga. It was here that his friendship with Giovanni de' Medici delle Bande Nere, the condottiere descendant of Cosimo's younger brother, began.

In 1524, after Giulio de' Medici had become Pope Clement VII (his election took place in November 1523), Aretino, having returned to Rome, became part producer of what is certainly the most famous piece of erotica created in the Renaissance, the so-called Aretino-Romano *posizioni.* Various accounts of the creation of the *posizioni* are conflicting, and as with so many of Aretino's works, the efforts of imitators have been added, so that it has become difficult to know exactly what Aretino did contribute in the way of sonnets to the famous drawings of Giulio Romano as engraved by Marcantonio Raimondi.

As nearly as fact can be separated from fiction, Giulio Romano for some reason drew a series of sixteen positions of men and women copulating.[8] Marcantonio Raimondi, one of the leading engravers in

8. An account of the story exists in Legman's *Horn Book,* pp. 23, 79, 80. I am

Rome, made copies of these cartoons and printed an edition of them that included sonnets by Aretino.[9] The Pope reportedly saw the book and ordered all copies destroyed. Raimondi was put in jail; Giulio Romano had already left Rome, and Aretino departed before he could be attached.[10] Later, according to Aretino, his own intervention brought about Raimondi's release. This book of *posizioni* is extremely important for any study of the visual aspects of Renaissance erotica, for it inspired in its pictorial aspect a whole series of works dealing with *posizioni,* usually involving the loves of the gods, a topic that will be dealt with in a later chapter. The Aretino-Romano book is of central importance for written erotica as well, since the *sonetti lussuriosi* are the first in a series of sonnets on erotic subjects. Aretino's "positions," as they came to be known in the English Renaissance, gained wide notoriety from the outset, perhaps because Aretino became so adept at promoting himself and his works. But though the *sonetti lussuriosi* and the *posizioni* became almost immediately a byword for erotica in the Renaissance, they were also censored from the outset, and there are no extant copies of the original copper engravings. As I mentioned in the introduction, the ironic fact is that suppression of the original version of the work has not led to a paucity, but rather a plethora, of materials as far as Aretino's sonnets are concerned. Writers following in Aretino's footsteps wrote erotic sonnets that got attached, in later editions, to Aretino's originals. Thus in several later editions of the sonnets there are

---

drawing on Legman; Frederick Hartt, *Giulio Romano* (New Haven: Yale Univ. Press, 1958), 2 vols.; Foxon; Mark W. Roskill, *Dolce's "Aretino" and Venetian Art Theory of the Cinquecento* (n.p.: New York Univ. Press, 1968), pp. 304–06; and information gathered at the Institute for Sex Research in Bloomington, Indiana. There has been considerable debate about the manner in which the book was composed; there is a question as to whether Aretino's sonnets were printed with the *posizioni* originally or only added some three years later in 1527. Roskill argues for Aretino's adding the sonnets in 1527 and sending out copies of the prints and sonnets in that year. The subsequent history of the prints is recounted in Roskill. One copy of the book, done in woodcuts, survives from the sixteenth century; it was owned by Mr. Walter Toscanini in New York; it sold at auction in New York for $32,000 in 1978. A photographic copy of the book can be found in the Fine Arts Library of Harvard University.

Whether Aretino wrote the sonnets in 1524 or 1527, the fact is that he did write them and place them at some time with the Romano prints; his association with the *posizioni* became so strong that in England in the Renaissance the combined production was often referred to as Aretino's positions.

9. For a discussion of the *posizioni,* see chapter 4, pp. 119–23.

10. Aretino joined up with Giovanni delle Bande Nere; he then returned to Rome where the papal datary, Giovanmatteo Giberti, tried to have him assassinated; Aretino was wounded but escaped. He again joined Giovanni and was with him when Giovanni died, later writing a famous account of the condottiere's death. After a stay in Mantua, he arrived in Venice in 1527.

as many as twenty-six poems. Even in an abundance of materials, then, there are problems for the literary historian. Exactly which sonnets are Aretino's? With one notable exception, the lone sixteenth-century copy of the poems resolves this question. The fact that this text, with the Romano *posizioni* executed in woodcuts, has been held in private hands has made accessibility a major problem. Simple questions have been difficult to answer, and the sonnets then, like the *posizioni* themselves, have been the subject of much speculation, folklore, and romanticizing. Put in the context of Renaissance erotica, as they have been for this study, they become prototypical, for in these sonnets Aretino sets the tone and defines the method for much of popular erotica in the Renaissance.

Aretino launches forth in the opening sonnet (the only one discussed here that does not appear in the unique extant sixteenth-century copy of the poems) with an insistence that he is doing something quite different.[11] This sonnet, which does appear in later editions of the *sonetti lussuriosi,* may or may not be one of the two missing sonnets from the sixteenth-century copy of the text; that matter is certainly open to debate. However, the sonnet bears citation because it says so much that lies at the heart of Renaissance erotica.[12]

> Questo è un libro d' altro che sonetti,
> Di capitoli, d' egloghe o canzone,
> Qui il Sannazaro o il Bembo non compone
> Nè liquidi cristalli, nè fioretti.
>
> Qui il Marignan non v' ha madrigaletti,
> Ma vi son cazzi senza discrizione
> E v' è la potta e'l cul, che li ripone
> Appunto come in scatole confetti.
>
> Vi sono genti fottenti e fottute
> E di potte e di cazzi notomie
> E ne' culi molt'anime perdute.
>
> Qui vi si fotte in più leggiarde vie,
> Ch'in alcun loco si sien mai vedute
> Infra le puttanesche gerarchie;

11. There are fourteen woodcuts and sonnets in the sixteenth-century edition; two are missing. Mr. Toscanini felt he was able to select the missing sonnets from the total of twenty-six that appear in later editions.

12. This poem may have been Aretino's, and it may well have come before any of the plates (sigs. Ai^r and Ai^v are missing in the sixteenth-century edition). The case cannot be made conclusively, however, from the evidence at hand.

In fin son pazzie
A farsi schifo di si buon bocconi
E chi non fotte in cul, Dio gliel perdoni.[13]

This is not a book of sonnets, chapters, eclogues or cantos; here neither Sannazaro nor Bembo compose liquid crystals or sweet flowers.

Here Marignan does not have madrigals, but there are cocks without description and there are cunts and ass-holes that are kept like candies in a box.

There are people who fuck and people who are fucked, and some cunts and famous cocks, and many who lost their souls in the ass-hole.

Here one can fuck in many charming ways which are not found in any other place, even among the hierarchy of whores;

One is real crazy if he is disgusted by such good bits, and he who does not fuck in the ass-hole, may God forgive him!

Our attention is immediately drawn to the assertion that this is not the typical literature of the day. This poetry is different; it does not partake of the normal traditions or forms. It is a *sonetto caudato,* or "tailed" sonnet, one with three additional lines appended to the first fourteen, rhyming *a b b a a b b a c d c d c d d e e.* One usually does not think of Aretino's worrying about such niceties as wedding form to function, but I think the tailing of the sonnet does precisely this, as it indicates a metaphoric as well as a formal departure from the traditional sonnet. Aretino tells us that he is not writing the sonnets of a Bembo or rendering the pastoral glories of a Sannazaro; he is not penning madrigals; he is writing about cocks, cunts, assholes, and fucking. Aretino insists on using vulgar words. He will not let us avoid them. In so doing, Aretino establishes a major line of difference between his erotica and that of Berni and his school, between the popular and learned traditions. All of Aretino's followers employ vulgar words; they insist on them as Aretino himself seems to in his dialogues, where, as we shall see, he has his two speakers discuss this issue.

I take the tone of the first sonnet cited to be typically Aretine. The outrageous ending, asking God to pardon those who do not practice sodomy, is typical of Aretino in its extremity. It is like Aretino to push things to the limit, to stand forth and assert himself without qualification. At the end of the first sonnet in the sixteenth-century edition Aretino tells us not to look for satire in these sonnets, only for sexual intercourse. The sonnets partake of both the bawdy and the pornographic, I think, although Aretino himself defended them on philo-

13. Pietro Aretino, *Dubbi amorosi, Altri Dubbi e Sonetti Lussuriosi di Pietro Aretino* (copy at the Institute for Sex Research; "Fottropoli," n.d., from 1759 edition), p. 39.

sophical grounds. One of the fascinating aspects of Aretino's character and literary talents seems to have been his total unscrupulousness. When it was expedient, he could defend any point of view in any tone. Thus in a letter to Messer Battista Zatti of Brescia, Aretino tells the story of the *sonetti lussuriosi* and defends the prints and sonnets on philosophical grounds. As a document of a great Renaissance libertine, the letter is worth citing in full:

> No sooner had I persuaded Pope Clement to set free Messer Marcantonio of Bologna who had been imprisoned for having engraved on copper the sixteen methods, etc., than I had a sudden desire to see those pictures which had caused tattle-tale Giberti to insist that the worthy artist ought to be hung and drawn.
>
> When I saw them I had the same kind of impulse which made Giulio Romano do the original paintings, and inasmuch as the poets and sculptors, both ancient and modern, have often written or carved—for their own amusement only—such trifles as the marble satyr in the Chigi Palace who is trying to assault a boy, I scribbled off the sonnets which you find underneath each one. The sensual thoughts which they call to mind I dedicate to you, saying a fig for hypocrites. I am all out of patience with their scurvy strictures and their dirty-minded laws which forbid the eyes to see the very things which delight them most.
>
> What wrong is there in beholding a man possess a woman? It would seem to me that the thing which is given to us by nature to preserve the race, should be worn around the neck as a pendant, or pinned onto the cap like a broach, for it is the spring which feeds all the rivers of the people, and the ambrosia in which the world delights in its happiest days.
>
> It is what made you, who are one of the greatest living physicians. It is what has produced all the Bembos, Molzas, Fortunios, Varchis, Ugolin Martellis, Lorenzos Lenzis, Dolces, Fra Sebastianos, Titians, Michelangelos, and after them all the popes and emperors and kings. It has begotten the loveliest of children, the most beautiful of women, and the holiest of saints.
>
> Hence one should order holidays and vigils and feasts in its honor, and not shut it up in a bit of serge or silk. The hands indeed might be hidden since they gamble away money, sign false testimony, make lewd gestures, snatch, tug, rain down fisticuffs, wound and slay. As for the mouth, it spits in the face, gluttonizes, makes you drunk and vomits.
>
> To sum up, lawyers would do themselves honor if they added a clause about it in their fat volumes with something too about my verses and his attitudes.
>
> When you write to Frosinone, greet him in my name.[14]

14. Thomas C. Chubb, trans., *The Letters of Pietro Aretino* (Hamden, CT: Shoe String Press, Archon Books, 1967), pp. 123–25. The Italian text can be found in Pietro Aretino, *Tutte Le Opere di Pietro Aretino. Lettere. Il Primo e il Secondo Libro,* ed. Francesco Flora, notes by Alessandro del Vita (Verona: Arnoldo Mondadori, 1960), pp. 399–400. Chubb weakens Aretino with his phrase, "What wrong is there in beholding a man *possess* a woman" (italics mine). The Italian *montare* is clear enough.

When forced to defend his erotic works on serious, philosophical grounds as he is here, Aretino shifts his arguments rather cleverly from his stance in the sonnet, where intercourse as intercourse is defended, to a defense of the activity involved as making love toward a regenerative end. Aretino does not sing the praises of the human body as the most beautiful form on earth and argue, as he might have, that in the act of love the human body finds its fullest expression. Such an argument, I suppose, would be the ultimate in the Renaissance return to paganism, but Aretino does not argue this; he argues on the grounds of use and on the concept that in sexual intercourse we are all—the most talented and the most elevated of us—created by this very basic act; therefore it ought to be glorified. Aretino is easily able to overlook the kind of statement he makes at the end of the first sonnet, as he disregards the fact that sodomy never produced any offspring. But then the letter is a defense after the fact.

Nowhere in the sonnets, in fact, is any mention made of sexual intercourse for the purpose of producing offspring. James Cleugh, in his biography of Aretino, feels that "these sonnets have no literary touches, unlike the author's later pornography. The wit is coarse and blunt, meant to shock like a blow in the face, an almost exact analogue of talk among the more ferocious and facetious inmates of a modern boarding-school dormitory or barrack-room."[15] In terms of our definitions, he would see the sonnets as obscene. But if Cleugh has caught the tone of the sonnets correctly, if not the precise way in which the sonnets depart from "literary touches," he has missed some of the humor and, again in our terms, the frankly pornographic nature of the poems.

The sonnets are dramatic poems in which one or both of the figures in the print speak about how they are enjoying sexual intercourse. The focus in the sonnets is primarily on describing the positions being employed. Whether stated or not, this is surely one of the conventions of pornography of all eras—how many ways are there to copulate and how can one describe them. Indeed, in his full verbal descriptions of the prints, Aretino sets another pattern for most of the popular pornographic erotica of the Renaissance, for subsequent pornography shows an abiding concern for including detailed descriptions of positions. Both Romano and Aretino understood that pornography is about sexual activity; whatever else it does, it must describe sexual activity.

The second sonnet in the sixteenth-century edition runs:

> Mettimi un dito in cul, caro vecchione,
> E spingi il cazzo dentro a poco a poco;

---

15. Cleugh, p. 70.

Alza ben questa gamba e fa buon gioco,
Poi mena senza far ripetizione.

Che per mia fe' quest' è il miglior boccone
Che mangiar il pan unto presso il foco;
E s'in potta ti spiace, muta loco,
Ch' uom non v'è che non sia buggerone.

In potta tel faro questa fiata
Ed in quest' algra e'n potta e 'n cul il cazzo
Mi farà lieto e tu lieta e beata

E chi vuol esser gran maestro è pazzo
Ed è proprio un uccel perde giornata
Chi d'altro che di fotter ha sollazzo.

E crepi in un palazzo
Ser Cortigian e aspetti ch'i tal muoja,
Ch'io bramo per me sol trarme la foja.[16]

Put a finger in my ass-hole, dear old man, and push the cock in little by little, lift up this leg, and make a good game, then wield it without repeating. For by my faith this is as great a feast as eating greased bread by a fire. And if you don't like it in the cunt, change places; what man is there who is not a buggerer.

In that cunt I'll do it this time, and in the ass-hole (with) the cock another; it makes me happy and you happy and blessed. And who wants to be a great master is crazy and is just a gull to lose the day, who from other than fucking takes solace.

And burst into a palace, Mr. Courtier, and wait, that it so moves that I think the sun drags the itching desire through me.

In this sonnet the woman urges the man to seize the day and to fuck her in a number of ways. He responds joyously. The poem is not without consistency in its imagery, but the focus is clearly on positions at the outset (see figure 1). From there our attention is centered on the desire of the woman to achieve pleasure, and she is insistent upon teaching her lover exactly how she wants that pleasure given. He in turn reminds us of another world, the world of courtiers and advancement. The world of sexuality is set in contrast to this; it is its own world.

In another sonnet for which a plate survives (figure 2), we once more are given the ardor of the woman:

Oh saria ben una coglioneria
Sendo in potestà mia fotterti adesso,

16. Aretino, *Dubbi amorosi*, p. 43.

Avendo il cazzo nella potta messo,
Del culo mi facessi carestia.

Finisca in me la mia genealogia,
Ch'io vo' fottervi dietro spesso spesso.
Piochè è più differente il cul dal fesso
Che l'acquarola dalla malvasia.

Fottimi e fa di me ciò che tu vuoi
O in potta o in cul, ch' io me ne curo poco
Dove che tu ci facci i fatti tuoi.

Chè non ho meno in cul ch' in potta il foco,
E quanti cazzi han muli, asini e buoi
Non scemerian di tanto ardore un poco.

E saresti un dappoco
A farmelo in al potta, usanza antica,
Chè s'io foss' uomo non vorrei mai fica.[17]

O you are playing a rotten trick, being in my power, fuck now, having put your cock in my cunt, don't make a famine in my ass-hole.

Finish my genealogy in me, because I want you to fuck me from behind again and again, because the ass-hole is somewhat different from the crack as water from wine.

Fuck me, and make me however you want, either in the cunt or the ass-hole, I care little where you do your deeds.

For I have no less fire in my ass-hole than in my cunt, and don't lessen your ardor by however many cocks mules, asses, and bulls have.

And be ready in a little while to make me in the cunt in the antique way; if I were a man I would never want cunt.

Again Aretino has the woman demanding her pleasure; here he invents a personality that has no necessary relation to the picture at hand, since the woman in this case seems to want her lover's penis in her anus. It is the ardent sexual drive of the woman, her insistence that she cannot get enough fucking, that makes Aretino's sonnet pornographic, for it feeds one of the major fantasies of pornography—that women want it all the time in every way. In having this woman think of cocks on mules, donkeys, and bulls, Aretino reveals her obsession with long cocks. She is Poggio's young bride who thought her husband had too small a penis brought to life.[18]

Part of what makes Aretino so significant as a pornographer is his

17. Ibid., p. 60.
18. See Poggio, *Facetiae*, trans. Hurwood, no. XLII, pp. 55–56; in this tale a young bride accuses her husband of having too small a penis; it turns out that she has been comparing his member to that of a donkey.

pioneering use of what were to become the staples of pornography. How conscious he was of this is difficult to gauge; so much of what he does is aimed at flying in the face of the conventional. Be that as it may, his use of vulgar words, his insistence on variety of positions, seen here and in the sonnet previously noted, and his presentation of limitless sexual energy show that Aretino had mastered the essentials of pornographic writing. George Steiner, who has stimulated thoughtful discussion on the matter, has argued that the obsession in pornography with positions is part of what makes it so boring that "the actual sum of possible gestures, consummations, and imaginings is drastically limited." He goes on to note that there "are probably more foods, more undiscovered eventualities of gastronomic enjoyment or revulsion than there have been sexual inventions since the Empress Theodora resolved 'to satisfy all amorous orifices of the human body to the full and at the same time.' There just aren't that many orifices."[19]

Renaissance writers, shaping as they did many of the conventions of modern pornography, do not seem to have found these conventions either limiting or boring, and although one might not want to go as far as Morse Peckham does in praising the "audacity and . . . endless invention" that strike one in examining a great body of pornography from the late fourteenth century to the present, Steiner's judgment seems excessively harsh and limited, if not completely wrong-headed.[20] Steiner in fact mixes two elements indiscriminately here, the number of orifices available for sexual activity and the sensations that humans can have while engaged in that activity, and even as he mixes these two elements, he ignores completely the essence of pornography—that it is *writing* about sex.[21] Pornography, as we have noted, aims to stimulate the reader, and it has many rhetorical ways of doing this, by appealing to the imagination through words that suggest sounds, sights, tastes, smells, and tactile impressions, and by describing at any chosen length the sensory experiences of characters. Even single words can be sexually exciting, as Faulkner's Joanna Burden knew so well.

19. George Steiner, "Night Words: High Pornography and Human Privacy," in *Perspectives on Pornography,* ed. Douglas A. Hughes (New York: Macmillan, St. Martin's Press, 1970), pp. 97–98. Steiner continues his argument by saying, "What emerges when one reads some of the classics of erotica is the fact that they too are intensely conventionalized, that their repertoire of fantasy is limited, and that it merges, almost imperceptibly, into the dream-trash of straight, mass-produced pornography" (p. 99).

20. Peckham, p. 298.

21. For a provocative discussion of the relationship between sex and artistic endeavor see John Richardson, "The Catch in the Late Picasso," *The New York Review of Books,* 19 July 1984, pp. 21–28.

Steiner's analogy with gastronomic enjoyment or revulsion is surely self-defeating. At the level of orifice, there is only one for eating. On the level of sensory perception, it is certainly true that all the sensory perceptions may come into play with food, but one need only think of the standard vocabulary of the oenologist ("presumptuous," "fruity," "nut-like flavor," "robust," "finishes well") to see how limited the "eventualities" are. Writing about sex, on the other hand, is not so limited—nor, what is truly to the point here, is it as limited as sexual activity itself. Even if the end of pornographic writing is arousal and ultimately orgasm, it need not always and at every point aim at orgasm, so that it can continue with more variety and for a longer duration than any real sexual activity. It is a *fiction,* not a reality. And good pornography, like all good writing, can and does use a variety of rhetorical and stylistic tools. Purveyors of erotica from antiquity on have presented the variety of sexual activity, and while there may be "no transcendental series," there has been more than enough for pornography to be anything but boring in the hands of an artist. Just how many ways are there? Have we tried them all? What other stimuli are important in the pursuit of this activity? Does music help? Does the uttering of sounds and words make it more exciting? Do certain foods stimulate the activity? (Perhaps we can have our cake and eat it too.) These are questions both "normal" people and pornographers ask, and the pornographer deals with these issues, if he is an artist, without boring us. Aretino, in his sonnets, focuses on the positions, for they are a given for him, composing his sonnets as he did for existing pictures that emphasized modes of sexual intercourse. He also focuses on positions because they are among the most interesting aspects of sexuality. Further, he adds the energy and dramatic qualities that give his poems their distinctive character. What he does is add to the fictive world first created by Giulio Romano, and he does so, I think, primarily by subverting not the real world but another fictive world, the world of sonneteers, Petrarchanism. We need to remember that by Aretino's time Italy had seen not only the apotheosis of Petrarch's sonnets but also two centuries of slavish imitation as well. Several centuries of slavish imitation inevitably led to reaction. The Petrarchan mode was one that lent itself readily to satire and parody; writers like Berni, we recall, were noted for their anti-Petrarchanism. But parody is not Aretino's mode of subversion; his attack is far more radical. If we generalize crassly and say that the qualities that characterize Petrarchan poetry are an intense focus on the emotional and spiritual state of the poet-lover (the self, in short), an ingenious use of metaphor and paradox, an elevation of the unattainable loved one, especially an admiration of her spiritual qualities, then we understand at once how different the general qualities of Aretino's poems are. The "world" of Petrarchan poetry is a world where love is never meant to be consummated physically; the "world" of Aretine poetry is one where there is nothing but consummation. Pleasure comes without paradoxes in the Aretine world; there is no freezing in summer or burning in winter, there is no lack of peace without being at war; in the Aretine world there is only heat and, as he insists on saying, cocks, cunts, assholes, and fucking. No metaphors here. The poems are not self-reflexive but dramatic and intensely involved with the physical pleasures achieved through sexual activity. The point is to find gratification, not to explore frustration or transformation of feelings.

Far from being concerned about "literary touches," Aretino is insistent about being nonliterary in these sonnets. The names used do not conjure up goddesses or other sonneteers' ladies; they are the names of common courtesans. What characterization we get is given to us through direct discourse, not through physical descriptions filled with tired or even inventive metaphors (something Aretino is able to manage superbly in his dialogues).

We see these qualities displayed in a final example, in which Aretino extends the dramatic mode of the sonnet by having both parties speak in an attempt to render something of the immediacy of the situation:

> Dammi la lingua, punta i piedi al muro
> Stringi le cosce e tiemmi stretto stretto,
> Lascia che vada a traversar il letto,
> Chè d'altro che di fotter non mi curo,
>
> Ah traditore! hai il cazzo molto duro,
> Oh come in su la potta mi confetto,
> Un dì di torlo in culo ti prometto
> E di farlo uscir netto t'assicuro.
>
> Io vi ringrazio, cara Lorenzina,
> M' ingegnerò servirvi; or via spingete
> Appunto come fa la Ciabattina.
>
> Io faccio adesso, e voi quando farete?
> Adesso, dammi tutta la linguina.
> Ohimè ch'io muoio e voi cagion ne siete!
>
> Dunque voi compirete?
> Sì sì, già faccio, ohimè spingi, ben mio.
> Ohimè già ho fatto, ahi che son morta, o Dio![22]

22. Aretino, *Dubbi amorosi,* p. 58.

Give me your tongue, point your feet to the wall, squeeze your thighs and hold me as tight as you can. Let it go across the bed, for I don't care about anything but fucking.

O traitor, you have such a hard cock, O how you ram it in my cunt; one day I'll give you a twirl in my ass-hole and make it exit cleanly, I assure you.

I want to thank you my dear Lorenzina; I exert myself to serve you, now, push away, just as Ciabattina does.

I am doing it now, and when will you come? Now, give me all of your tongue. O that I die and you be the cause.

Now then you understand? Yes, yes, I am coming, o, push well my love. O, I have come, o I am dead, o God!

Aretino creates a world through the conversation he imagines in this poem. It is a world in which the lovers will have their pleasure now one way (described in detail), another time another way; so that not only is the position of this sexual act detailed, but the possibility of another position for another time is set forth. Fucking, cocks, cunts and assholes are explicitly insisted upon in Aretino's attempt to give something of the psychological nature of the physical act, at least its immediacy, in the increasingly rapid shifts of speaker through the final lines of the poem.

In these sonnets Aretino does show a flair for the dramatic; the picture is most often merely a starting point for him as he develops the sexual encounters. In the sonnet just cited, the woodcut is not explicit at all; the couple are half-reeling, almost falling onto the bed, and their bodies are so intertwined that one cannot see genitalia. There is no necessary relationship to the picture at hand; the world becomes even more relentlessly pornographic in Aretino's poems.

Aretino manages to suggest through his sonnets in a radical fashion some of the ways in which certain crucial aspects of Petrarchanism came to be transformed. We praise Shakespeare for his anti-Petrarchan poetry, and especially Donne for his introduction of dramatic situations where physical love does occur, for his use of colloquial language, and for his wit. While one certainly could argue about whether Aretino's sonnets show much wit, those other qualities—dramatic situations and colloquial language—are present in good measure in Aretino's relentless pursuit to be different, daring, outrageous, and pornographic.

Aretino's beginnings as an upstart satirist and pornographer in Rome were an indication of greater things to come; from the safe port of Venice he was able to pursue his literary career as a promoter of Titian, the Scourge of Princes in his letters, a blackmailer, poet, playwright, pornographer, theological writer, and literary combatant.[23] Again, it is difficult to avoid writing about Aretino's life in Venice—his splendid palazzo in which he kept open house, the beautiful courtesans, the ambitious young men hoping to emulate the great Aretino, the sensual Titian with whom Aretino had so much in common. But if we restrict ourselves to the literature, we can learn even more, I think, about this Renaissance man and the nature of his times than any "facts" about his life are likely to reveal. First, the very range of Aretino's literary endeavors is instructive. As the first man of letters trying to succeed as a professional writer, not attached to a court but dependent upon sales (and gifts, it is certainly true, and bribes given so that Aretino would not write nasty things about certain people), Aretino was willing to write anything that might make him money. Admittedly, he tried some of the traditional literary paths to security. For some time he peddled an epic poem, first to one noble family and then to another, promising to make the family immortal through his efforts, but mostly he made his way through his published materials.[24] Aretino might denigrate writing for public sale ("he who every evening visits the bookstore to pick up the money earned by the day's sales, . . . [is] like a pimp who empties the purse of his woman before he retires to bed") and wish for the patronage of princes ("I hope God will grant that the courtesy of princes rewards me for the labor of writing, and not the small change of book buyers; for I would rather endure every hardship than to prostitute my genius by making it a day laborer of the liberal arts"), but that was his line when writing to a printer.[25] He was dependent upon the press. His letters were his great stock-in-trade. He churned out volume after volume in his lifetime, hoping for reward for letters praiseworthy to people or for blackmail fees for letters of a more derogatory nature that might be stricken from the next edition or dropped even before they hit the press. But the letters were also successful because they sold.

Aretino prided himself in being something of an antihumanist to the extent that he paraded his poor Latin and nonexistent Greek (his way of saying it was to cite a remark by Gian Giordane, "I don't know how to dance or sing, but I can fornicate like a jack donkey").[26] Yet

23. In terms of freedom from papal interference, Venice was a stronghold in the Renaissance. See Putnam, *Censorship,* II, 281, 293ff; Grendler, pp. 3–19.

24. Aretino first offered the poem to the Marquis of Mantua, Federigo Gonzaga; then when Aretino quarreled with Federigo, he offered it to Alessandro de' Medici. The poem was finally dedicated to the Marquis of Vasto.

25. Chubb, *Letters,* p. 66.

26. Ibid. p. 98.

when he turned to writing pornography again, he used a form, the dialogue, characteristic of the humanists' return to the classics. One of the reasons he did so, I think, was not so much from any desire to imitate Lucian's *Dialogue of the Courtesans* but rather to write in such a way as to enable the courtesans to speak in a language Aretino himself knew so well. What classical influence there is in Aretino's dialogues probably comes from Ovid and is found in the second part of the *Dialogo,* where Pippa learns how to be a whore, and even this is tangential.[27] The authenticity and vitality of his language are something for which Aretino is continually praised, and nowhere is he in better command of his language than in his dialogues.

By our standards, informed by all of the pornography we have been exposed to in recent years, Aretino's dialogues hardly fall into any "hard core" category. After the first dialogue, comparatively little space is given to the description of sexual intercourse.[28] Aretino the satirist

27. The dialogues of Lucian were certainly available at this time, but I find no evidence that Aretino knew them at first hand. See C. Robinson, p. 95; and Bolgar, pp. 518–19. Aretino does borrow material from *The Aeneid* in *The Betrayals of Men,* and then draws jesting attention to this borrowing; see Aretino, *Aretino's Dialogues,* trans. Raymond Rosenthal (New York: Stein & Day, 1971), p. 253.

28. A careful reading of Putnam, *Censorship,* shows that only rarely were books placed on the *Index* for reasons of salaciousness or obscenity, although the categories were spelled out much more clearly in the *Index* of the Council of Trent in 1564 (the first *Index* to have the authority of a general council behind it). Rule VII of this *Index* reads:

> Books professedly treating of lascivious or obscene subjects, or narrating or teaching these, are utterly prohibited, since not only faith but morals, which are rapidly corrupted by the perusal of them, are to be considered; and those who possess them shall be severely punished by the bishop. But the works of antiquity, written by the heathen, are permitted to be read, because of the eloquence and propriety of the language; though on no account shall they be suffered to be read by young persons. (I.184)

The basis for the *Index* of 1564 was an *Index* issued by Pope Paul IV in Rome in 1559, and this is the first *Index* in which works of Aretino are mentioned. In the introductory remarks we read that there are three categories of books banned:

> In primis nomina, uel cognomina disponuntur eorum, qui prae caeteris, et tanquam ex professo errasse depraehensi sunt, ac ideo uniuersae ipsorum conscriptiones, cuiuscunque argumenti sint, omninò prohibentur.
>
> His succedunt nomina, siue cognomina certorum quorundam auctorum, quorum libri aliqui, ea ratione reijciuntur, quòd uel ad haersim, uel ad aliquod praestigiosae impietatis genus, uel omnio ad intollerabiles errores subindè allicere, satis expertum est. Postremo loco redactae sunt inscriptiones librorum, qui ut plurimùm ab incerti nominis haerecticis conficti pestilentissimis doctrinis respersi sunt. (*Index* [Rome, 1559], sig. Aii^v)

Under Category II we find "Petri Aretini opera omnia" (sig. Giv^r)

and parodist is never far removed from Aretino the pornographer, as I shall show in the ensuing discussion. Having said this, one must nonetheless acknowledge that Aretino breaks new ground here just as he did with his *sonetti lussuriosi*. His dialogues are much more explicit than anything the Italian Renaissance had seen in the vernacular with the exception of his *sonetti*. We are in a world quite different from that of the *novelle* or even the *facetiae*, especially in the first dialogue, for often the emphasis is not on the trickery that allows sexual activity but on the sexual activity itself explicitly described.

Originally, the dialogues were published in two parts, *Ragionamento Della Nanna e Della Antonia* in 1534 and *Dialogo Quale La Nanna Insegna La Pippa* in 1536.[29] In the first part, comprising the first three days, Nanna, in a dialogue with Antonia, tries to determine what life her daughter Pippa should lead. On successive days they consider the life of nuns, the life of married women, and the life of courtesans. Having decided upon the life of a courtesan for her daughter, Nanna instructs Pippa in the second part, again on successive days. The fourth dialogue deals with the whore's trade, the fifth with the wiles of men, and on the sixth and final day, a nurse and midwife discuss the bawd's trade.

The introductory elements of the first part of the dialogues give us a good idea of Aretino's intentions. The book begins with an address by Aretino to his pet monkey, the female ape whom Aretino compares to great personages. Aretino takes up the convention of dedications and the problem of obscenity at the outset:

> Ma per tornare a te, Baggattino, dico che se tu non fussi sanza gusto come sono i gran maestri, farei un poco di scusa del licenzioso parlare della opera che mando fuora alla ombra tua (che li gioverà come giovano quelle dei gran maestri a quelle che tuttodì si gli intitolano indegnamente), con allegare la *Priapea* di Virgilio e ciò che in materia lasciva scrisse Ovidio, Giovinale e Marziale.[30]

> But to return to you, Bagattino, I say that if you were without taste, as princes are, I would try to excuse the licentious speech in this work which I publish under your protection (which you will enjoy as much as those great personages enjoy the works which every day are unworthily dedicated to

29. Both parts have recently been edited by Giovanni Aquilecchia under the title of *Sei Giornate* (Bari: Gius. Laterza & Figli, 1969). This is an excellent edition with fine notes. My citations will be from this edition, but I have carefully checked against the 1584 "Bengodi" edition, since this was the edition most readily available in Renaissance England.
30. Aretino, *Sei Giornate*, ed. Aquilecchia, p. 4. All subsequent references to Aretino's dialogues are to this edition.

them by mentioning in its behalf Virgil's *Prispea* [*sic*] and all those salacious works which were written by Ovid, Juvenal, and Martial.[31] (P. 12)

While Aretino calls attention to the licentious nature of his work, he does so with a parody of dedications. We see from the outset Aretino's tendency toward satire, and so first to be pilloried are those tasteless aristocrats to whom works are dedicated; next to be indicted are authors who resort to mentioning the pornographic writings of Ovid, Juvenal, Martial, and Virgil as a defense for what they themselves have done. Aretino does not need to put himself in this tradition. Of course, in implying that he has no need for the tradition, Aretino clearly reminds his audience of it. He goes on to note:

> tu, che vorresti forse, per il dire che farà la Nanna delle moniche, che io fussi tenuto della buccia della tua malignità. La Nanna è una cicale, e dice ciò che le viene alla bocca; e alle suore sta bene ogni male, da che si fanno vedere dal vulgo peggio che le femine del popolo; e avendo già empito ogni cosa di Antecristi, con la puzza della lor corruzione non lasciano spirare i fiori della verginatà delle spose e ancille di Dio che ci sono. (Pp. 4–5)

> Perhaps you would have liked, when it comes to what Nanna says of the nuns, that I hadn't been as malicious as she is. Nanna is a chatterbox, and she says anything that comes to her lips, and it is right to say as much evil as possible about the nuns, since they exhibit themselves to the vulgar in a way that is worse than streetwalkers. And having by the stench of their corruption already filled the world with Anti-Christs, they prevent us from knowing the true brides of virginity and hand-maidens of God, who do exist. (P. 13)

There are several matters of interest here. First, from an artistic point of view we are struck by Aretino's assertion that Nanna must talk as she does if she is to be true to her character. That Aretino thought of the speakers of his dialogues in such a way accounts for the liveliness of the discussion. Doubtless his experience as a dramatist served him well here. Second, and more importantly, we see Aretino taking a moral stance. He can describe the awful sexual adventures of nuns because nuns are truly corrupt and deserve to be exposed. Aretino states his position as moralist more directly when he writes:

> . . .così non arei avuto ardire di pensare, non che di scrivere, quello che

31. For the English translation I am using the Rosenthal translation cited in note 27 above. All page references are to this edition. In spite of the unclosed parenthesis and botched rendering of the *Priapeia* in this particular passage, Rosenthal's work is lively and gives us a language much closer to our own (and Aretino's) than we find in the Isidore Liseux Paris edition of 1889.

delle moniche ho posto in carta, se non credessi che la fiamma della mia penna di fuoco dovesse purgare le macchie disoneste che la lascivia loro ha fatte nella vita d'esse: che dovendo essere nel monistero come i gigli negli orti, si sono lordate di modo nel fango del mondo, che se ne schifa lo abisso, non che il Cielo. Onde spero che il mio dire sia quel ferro crudelmente pietoso col quale il buon medico taglia il membro infermo perché gli altri rimanghino sani. (P. 5)

. . . so I should never have dared to think, much less write, what I set on paper about the nuns if I did not believe that the flame of my fiery pen would clean away the shameful stains which their lewd behavior has left on their lives. Those who should live in their monasteries as lilies do in their gardens have covered themselves with the muck of the world, so that not only heaven but the very abyss is revolted by them. Therefore I hope that my book will be like a scalpel, at once cruel and merciful, with which the good doctor cuts off the sick limb so that the others will remain healthy. (P. 13)

Now the assertion of a moral position need not be taken seriously, nor need it preclude reading the dialogues as pornography. Indeed, I think it is safe to say that the moral stance is one adopted only when convenient by Aretino (as it clearly is in this preface); it provides him with a defense should his work come under attack for being licentious. After all, what one could get away with in publication, even in Venice, was an unknown. A moral stance would allow Aretino to claim that such a position should be taken seriously, were he forced to it.

Placed as this statement is, however, in a dedication to a monkey, we must recognize the strong element of parody. Aretino gets in all of the traditional language of the biting satirist: his pen is a flame that will cleanse with fire; what should bloom like lilies is covered with muck; his book is like a surgeon, wielding a scalpel that will excise the diseased limb.[32] Comedy is the aim here, as it is through much of the work.

I would argue that a satirist is at work through much of the dialogues, but Aretino is a very special kind of satirist. He complicates the issue by parodying the very stance he purports to maintain, but throughout the work we see him taking on some of the traditional targets of the satirist. Literary conventions and peculiarities come in for ridicule; the abuses of society and the clergy in particular are presented as such. Part of the literary *persona* Aretino was developing was the Veritiero, the Teller of Truth, il Flagello de' Principi, the Scourge of Princes—in other words, the satirist who exposes the vices of the

32. For a discussion of the traditional language of the satirist, especially the medical language, see Alvin Kernan, *The Cankered Muse: Satire of the English Renaissance* (New Haven: Yale Univ. Press, 1959), pp. 26 and 93.

world in order to rid the world of them. Aretino's aims as satirist in his dialogues are complex, however, since they do not stem from a traditional moral stance. Literary excesses and abuses are held up for ridicule in a fashion that poses few problems once we recognize that Aretino's stance is always against the tradition of the learned humanist. The abuses of society in general and the clergy in particular are held up in a rather more problematic fashion, however, since the stance of the author flies in the face of traditional morality. Aretino's assumption in the dialogues is that people in this world are driven primarily by one thing—sex. One should face this fact and be honest about it as one pursues the pleasures of this driving force. Traditional morality might admit Aretino's premise, given the fallen nature of man, but it would certainly not endorse his conclusion. Aretino keeps us off balance throughout this work, and it is hard to take too much seriously; that is how Aretino would have it.

All of this posing as satirist and parodist argues for seeing the work as something other than pornographic, and that fact is that the stances of the author and the constant movement toward comedy work against the involvement of the reader in a world of total sexuality. Beyond the first day of the dialogues, there is little striving for what Steven Marcus has termed "pornotopia."[33] But the fact remains that in the first dialogue there are scenes that exist merely to arouse lust, that is, that are pornographic. Aretino is not consistent with any stance. Part of his genius, I would argue, is his ability to be pornographic and satiric or even pornographic and realistic in the same work—often, paradoxically, in the same passage. A final crucial point: even though the world Aretino immerses us in is not always pornographic, it is always sexual in some fundamental way.

The dialogue of the first day, the life of nuns, is the most pornograhic of the six dialogues. Aretino seems to have taken a special delight in looking at the supposed sexual practices of the clergy. He feeds on what was a commonplace fantasy, as the jests have shown us. Nanna tells Antonia of her experiences as a nun so that Antonia may advise her as to what life Pippa should follow. Nanna starts by describing her induction into a nunnery, beginning with her first meal with the members of the clergy. Here we get one of our first indications within the dialogues proper that even where he is most intent on being pornographic, Aretino cannot resist writing satire. He goes into a long description of the gluttony and drunkenness of the refectory. Only after several pages of this does he lead into salacious elements, beginning with a descrip-

33. Marcus, p. 245.

tion of how the nuns seized upon some glass dildos that were brought to the table. Aretino's efforts at satire rather than pornography are carried forward in Nanna's description of the paintings on the walls of one of the main rooms of the nunnery. One wall shows the life of Saint Nafissa—a young nun who was a whore. Her life cycle, complete with depictions of the "succour" she provided to all pilgrims, is described in some detail. A second wall shows the story of Masetto from Day Three, story i of Boccaccio's *Decameron*. The story of Masetto is obviously appropriate for these walls, since it shows us how Masetto, pretending to be deaf and dumb, was able to service all the sisters in a small nunnery. On the third wall, Nanna tells us, "ci erano (se ben mi ricordo) ritratte tutte le suore che fur mai di quello ordine, con i loro amanti appresso e i figliuoli nati di esse, con i nomi di ciascuno e di ciascuna" (p. 16) ["if my memory serves, were portrayed all the nuns who had ever belonged to the order, with their lovers beside them and their children too, and the names of each man and woman" (p. 24)]. With his description of the fourth wall Aretino brings the reader closer to sexual activity itself, for here "Nell' ultimo quadro ci erano dipinti tutti i modi e tutte le vie che si può chiavare e farsi chiavare" (p. 16) ["The last picture depicted all the various modes and avenues by which one can fuck and be fucked" (p. 24)]. Aretino goes into some detail on this favorite of Renaissance erotic topics. Nanna tells Antonia that there is an instructress who teaches the positions painted on the walls:

> Nanna. C'è la maestra che mostra a chi non sa comme si deve stare, caso che la lussuria stimoli l'uomo sì che sopra una cassa, su per una scala, in una sede, in una tavola, o nello spazzo voglia cavalcarle; e quella medesima pacienza che ci ha chi ammaestra un cane, un pappagallo, uno stornello e una gazzuola, ha colei che insegna le attitudini alle buone moniche: e il giocar di mano con le bagattelle è meno difficile a imparare che non è lo accarezzare lo uccello sì che ancora che non voglia si rizzi in piedi. (P. 17)

> Nanna. . . . there's a mistress. She shows the ignorant how to set themselves when lust so excites a man that he wants to mount them on a chest, a ladder, a chair, over a table, or on the bare floor. And in order to teach the proper postures to the good nuns, she must be as patient as the man who trains a dog, parrot, starling, or magpie. Indeed, juggling with little balls is much less difficult to master than learning how to stroke a prick so that, even if the desire is not there, it stands up straight and stiff. (Pp. 24–25)

The art of copulation is the issue here, and it is described as a difficult one. The lust and sexual imagination of men make it necessary for women to adapt to so many circumstances; a woman must know positions. A woman must also know how to arouse the man, make his "bird" stand, if she must.[34]

From here to the end of the first dialogue, there is a good deal of sexual intercourse, some involving Nanna, most of it seen by her through cracks in walls, windows, and keyholes. It is the closest Aretino comes to creating a pornotopia, and in these scenes we see Aretino's grasp of what devices will work well in pornography. Since all readers of pornography are in large measure voyeurs, pornographers have always (since Aretino at least) made much of voyeurism within pornography. The writer of voyeuristic scenes plays on both the sexual action as well as the sexual arousal of the person viewing the action, and he can do this to a variety of ends. The whole notion of seeing sex performed, of seeing nude women or large cocks is one that Aretino uses throughout the dialogues. The fact that Nanna's initiation into the world of sexuality should begin with her seeing paintings of it turns out to be most appropriate.

Nanna has been taken to a cell with numerous cracks in the wall; the sexual activity begins with her telling us what she sees through one of those cracks:

> Vidi in una cella quattro suore, il generale e tre fratini di latte e di sangue, i quali spoliaro il reverendo padre della tonica rivestendolo d'un saio di raso, ricoprendogli la chierica d'uno scuffion d'oro sopra del quale posero una berretta di velluto tutta piena di puntali di cristallo, ornata d'un pennoncello bianco; e cintagli la spada al lato, il beato generale, parlando per "ti" e per "mi", si diede a passeggiare in sul passo grave di Bortolameo Coglioni. Intanto le moniche cavatosi le gonne e i fratini le toniche, esse si misero gli abiti dei fratini, cioè tre di loro, ed essi quelli delle moniche: l'altra, postasi intorno la toga del generale, sedendo pontificalmente contrafacea il padre dando le leggi ai conventi. (P. 19)

> In the cell I saw four sisters, the General, and three milky-white and ruby-red young friars, who were taking off the reverend father's cassock and garbing him in a big velvet coat. They hid his tonsure under a small golden skullcap, over which they placed a velvet cap ornamented with crystal droplets and surmounted by a white plume. Then, having buckled his sword at his side, the blissful General, to speak frankly, started strutting back and forth with the big-balled stride of a Bartolomeo Colleoni. In the meantime the sisters removed their habits and the friars took off their tunics. The latter put on the sisters' robes and the sisters—that is, three of them—put on the friars'. The fourth nun rolled herself up in the General's cassock, seated

---

34. Barolsky, pp. 107–11, discusses the use of "bird" as phallus in Renaissance literature and painting.

herself pontifically, and began to imitate a superior laying down the law for the convent. (P. 27)

This is a scene at once wonderfully comic and pornographic, beginning with the comparison of the "General" to Bortolameo Coglioni, for Coglioni's name (commonly spelled Colleone) literally means "balls." It is part of Aretino's genius that he is able to serve both his satiric and pornographic ends here. He does this in the following fashion. We begin with the transvestism. This act, the nuns donning the robes of the friars and the friars those of the nuns, is a parody of Nanna's investiture as a nun, an event that had occurred earlier in this same day, a sacred ceremony that Aretino had described at some length. In that scene, we had been told how Nanna had put on her spiritual garb and been sprinkled with holy water. Ecclesiastical clothing ought to be a reminder of one's office in the service of God; we see that meaning debased in this act of transvestism. If transvestism calls the masculinity of the friars and femininity of the nuns into question, it is meant to, for acts are to be performed by both sexes with both sexes here. The General is described as being aroused by both sexes; Aretino is not going to miss an opportunity to describe the cleric's proverbial desire for young men, nor is he going to miss an opportunity to display, comically, woman's proverbial desire to rule. Initially, the General is not sufficiently aroused, and it takes the actions of a young friar and then a young nun, approached as one expects here, from the rear, to excite this jaded cleric:

Perché la reverenda Paternità chiamò i tre fratini e, appoggiato su la spalla a uno cresciuto inanzi ai dì tenero e lungo, dagli altri si fece cavar del nido il passerotto che stava chioccio chioccio; onde il più scaltrito e il più attrattivo lo tolse in su la palma, e lisciandogli la schiena come si liscia la coda alla gatta che ronfiando comincia a soffiare di sorte che non si puote più tenere al segno, il passerotto levò la cresta di maniera che il valente generale, poste le unghie a dosso alla monica più graziosa a più fanciulla, recatole i panni in capo, le fece appoggiare la fronte nella cassa del letto: e aprendole con le mani soavemente le carte del messale culabriense, tutto astratto contemplava il sesso, il cui volto non era per magrezza fitto nell' ossa, né per grassezza sospinto in fuore, ma con la via del mezzo tremolante e ritondetto, lucea come faria un avorio che avesso lo spirito. (Pp. 19–20)

Because the reverend father summoned the three friars and leaning on the shoulder of one of them, a tall, soft-skinned rascal who had shot up prematurely, he ordered the others to take his little sparrow, which was resting quietly, out of its nest. Then the most adept and attractive young fellow of the bunch cradled the General's songster in the palm of his hand and began stroking its back, as one strokes the tail of a cat which first purrs, then pants, and soon cannot keep still. The sparrow lifted its crest, and then the doughty General grabbed hold of the youngest, prettiest nun, threw her tunic over her head, and made her rest her forehead against the back of the bed. Then, deliberately prying open with his fingers the leaves of her ass-hole Missal and wholly rapt in his thoughts, he contemplated her crotch, whose form was neither close to the bone with leanness nor puffed out with fat, but something in between—rounded, quivering, glistening like a piece of ivory that seems instinct with life. (Pp. 27–28)

Antonia, to whom all of this is being recounted, asks whether the General then spent the whole day in contemplation of this sight, and Nanna replies:

Nol consumò miga: che posto il suo pennello nello scudellino del colore, umiliatolo prima con lo sputa, lo facea torcere nella guisa che si torceno le donne per le doglie del parto o per il mal della madre. E perché il chiodo stesse più fermo nel forame, accennò dietrovia al suo erba-da-buoi, che rovesciatoli le brache fino alle calcagna, mise il cristeo alla sua Riverenza *visibilium;* la quale tenea fissi gli occhi agli altri dui giovanastri che, acconce due suore a buon modo e con agio nel letto, gli pestavano la salsa nel mortaio, facendo disperare la loro sorellina: che per esser alquanto loschetta e di carnagion nera, refutata da tutti, avendo empito il vetriolo bernardo di acqua scaldata per lavar le mani al messere, recatasi sopra un coscino in terra, appuntando le piante dei piedi al muro della camera, pontando contra lo smisurato pastorale, se lo avea riposto nel corpo come si ripongono le spade nelle guaine. Io all'odore del piacer loro struggendomi più che non si distruggono i pegni per le usure, fregava la monina con la mano nel modo che di gennaio fregano il culo per i tetti i gatti. (Pp. 20–21)

No, I wouldn't say he consumed it, because placing his paintbrush, which he first moistened with spit, in her tiny color cup, he made her twist and turn as women do in the birth throes or the mother's malady. And to be doubly sure that his nail would be driven more tightly into her slit, he motioned to his back and his favorite punk pulled his breeches down to his heels and applied his clyster to the reverend's *visiblium,* while all the time the General himself kept his eyes fixed on the two other young louts, who, having settled the sisters neatly and comfortably on the bed, were now pounding the sauce in the mortar to the great despair of the last little sister. Poor thing, she was so squint-eyed and swarthy that she had been spurned by all. So she filled the glass tool with water heated to wash the messer's hands, sat on a pillow on the floor, pushed the soles of her feet against the cell wall, and then came straight down on that great crozier, burying it in her body as a sword is thrust into a scabbard. Overcome by the scent of their pleasure, I was more worn out than pawns are frayed by usury, and began rubbing my dear little monkey with my hand like cats in January rub their backsides on a roof. (Pp. 28–29)[35]

35. The Rosenthal translation misprints *visibilium* as "visiblium."

Aretino gives us action here, action that is meant to arouse, I think, but he also wants to entertain us with inventive and outrageous metaphors. The penis is a sparrow again, nothing unusual about that metaphor, but others are more startling. While we are never in doubt about the nature of the action, the metaphors are not far removed in that sense, we are struck by Aretino's inventiveness. The General contemplates an exquisite profanation of a religious text, the "leaves of her asshole Missal," and he puts his "paintbrush" in her "color cup." The favorite young monk applies his "clyster" (that with which one gives an enema should be understood) to the essence of the General, his *visibilium*. The other young monks are "pounding the sauce in the mortar," and the one lone nun is left to impale herself on a "crozier." We admire Aretino's cleverness here, and we may also be offended by that very cleverness which constantly uses terms that remind us of what should be the religious nature of events in this household.

The players of the scene try enough combinations to satisfy the particular fetish of any reader, and the scene culminates in the following action:

> Menatosi e dimenatosi mezza ora, disse il generale: «Facciamo tutti ad un'otta; e tu, pinchellon mio, basciami; così tu, colomba mia»; e tenendo una mano nella scatola dell'angeletta, e con l'altra facendo festa alle mele dell'angelone, basciando ora lui e lei, facea quel viso arcigno che a Belvedere fa quella figura di marmo ai serpi che l'assassinano in mezzo dei suoi figli. Alla fine le suore del letto, e i giovincelli, e il generale, e colei alla quale egli era sopra, colui il quale gli era dietro, con quella dalla pestinaca muranese, s'accordaro di fare ad una voce come s'accordano i cantori o vero i fabbri martellando: e così, attento ognuno al compire, si udiva un "ahi, ahi", un "abbracciami", un "voltamiti", "la lingua dolce", "dàmmela", "totela", "spinge forte", "aspetta ch'io faccio", "oimè fà", "stringemi", "aitami"; e chi con sommessa voce e chi con alta smiagolando, pareano quelli dalla *sol, fa, mi, re*ne; e faceano uno stralunare d' occhi, un alitare, un menare, un dibattere, che le banche, le casse, la lettiera, gli scanni e le scodelle se ne risentivano come le case per i terremoti. (P. 21)

> When they had pushed and squirmed and twisted for half an hour, the General suddenly cried: "Now all at the same time, and you, my dear boys, kiss me, and you too, my dove!" and holding one hand on the lovely angel's box and with the other fondling the cherub's behind, now kissing him, now kissing her, he wore that frowning look the marble statue at the Vatican Museum gives the snakes that are strangling him between his sons. In the finale the nuns on the bed with the two young men, the General and the sister he was mounted on, together with the fellow at his behind, and, last of all, the nun with her Murano prodder, all agreed to do it together as choristers sing in unison, or more to the point, as blacksmiths hammer in

time, and so, each attentive to his task, all that one heard was: "Oh my
God, oh my Christ!" "Hug me!" "Ream me!" "Push out that sweet
tongue!" "Give it to me!" "Take it!" "Push harder!" "Wait, I'm coming!"
"Oh Christ, drive it into me!" "Holy God!" "Hold me!" and "Help!" Some
were whispering, others were moaning loudly—and listening to them you
would have thought they were running the scales, *sol, fa, me, re, do*—their
eyes popping out of their heads, their gasps and groans, their twistings and
turnings making the chests, wooden beds, chairs, and chamber pots shake
and rattle as if the house had been hit by an earthquake. (P. 29)

Aretino continues his attempts to be both titillating and amusing. The
musical allusions might be said to provide a rhythm, but we are never
totally caught up in it as the bounding and rattling of furniture and
pots are surely intended to make us laugh. Nanna, however, watching
this sexual activity, is aroused, and she tells us that she was "non
potendo più sofferire la voluntà della carne che mi pungea la natura
bestialmente, non avendo acqua calda come la suora che mi avvertì di
quello che io avea a fare de' frutti cristallini, sendo fatta accorta dalla
necessità, pisciai nel manico della vanga" (p. 22) ["No longer being
able to withstand the desires of the flesh, which were goading my
nature like a wild beast, and not having the hot water the sister had
told me to use if I wished to employ the glass fruit, my wits sharpened
by necessity, I pissed right into the handle of the spade" (p. 30)]. As
readers, we are voyeurs to the voyeur, and Aretino allows us a reaction
that is primarily comic, while Nanna's remains one of sexual arousal,
which she satisfies by employing her glass dildo. Nanna describes the
action as painful, pleasurable, and scary. She tells Antonia that she
wanted to cry out. We see some attempt by Aretino at realism here in
having Nanna assure us that all has not been pleasurable for her at the
outset of her actions, but above all we are to be convinced that she has
been highly aroused sexually. Antonia certainly "reads" Nanna this
way, and she asks Nanna why she felt compelled to cry out. Nanna's
answer again moves toward realism; she tells us she was scared and in
pain, "Perché, ah? Mi credetti esser ferita a morte: io mi metto la mano
alla becchina, e immollandola la tiro a me; e vendendola con un guanto
da vescovo parato, mi reco a piangere: e con le mani in quei corti
capegli che, tagliandomi lo avanzo, colui che mi vestì in chiesa mi avea
lasciati, cominciai il lamento di Rodi" (p. 22) ["Why, you ask? I
thought I had mortally wounded myself. I put my hand on my pretty
little mouth, brought it away wet, and when I saw that it too was
scarlet, like a Bishop's gloves on a high holy day, I began to cry and
tear out the few hairs that butcher who cut them off had left me when
he dressed me in church. So then I began the lamentations of Rhodes"

(p. 30).] Aretino, of course, could never be content with realism; he must go beyond that. His comparison of Nanna's hand to that of a bishop's gloved for a holy ceremony is outrageous. Its effect, aside from whatever shock value this might have (and Aretino glories in shocking), is to remind us once again of the disparity between appearance and reality in this holy house. Corruption, Aretino makes clear, especially sexual corruption, is everywhere in this world, but especially in ecclesiastical houses. Again, whatever the truth of this, it is certainly a favorite myth of the Italian Renaissance, one bound to appeal to sexual fantasies. It is Aretino the pornographer who plays upon this, but Aretino the satirist carries a note too. This myth is one Aretino manages to keep in front of the reader not just by the many overt scenes of sexual intercourse engaged in by the clergy but also by the language he uses throughout day one. His similes and metaphors, like the one used here, work in just this fashion.

The fact that Nanna is led to masturbate by what she sees has the effect of reminding the reader that this is the "normal" reaction to visualizing sexual intercourse, barring the immediate availability of a sexual partner. Time and again in the dialogues we are reminded of the power of sight to arouse, and in the world of erotica sexual creatures always find a way to satisfy their sexual urgings. Later in the day Nanna once again looks through a chink in the wall, and once again she is treated to a scene of group sex. Aretino begins by using battle terms to describe what becomes a daisy-chain:

> Eccoti i giostranti in ordine; e avendo fatto inguintana del sedere di quella lusca negretta che dianzi mangiò vetro a tutto pasto, fu tratto la sorte, e toccò il primo aringo al trombetta: che facendo sonare il compagno mentre si movea, spronando se stesso con le dita, incartò la lancia sua fino al calce nel targone dell' amica; e perché il colpo valea per tre, fu molto lodato. . . .
>
> Mosse dopo lui il generale tratto per poliza; e con la lancia in resta correndo, empì l'anello di colui che l'avea empito alla suora; e così stando, fissi come i termini fra dui campi, toccò il terzo aringo a una monica: e non avendo lancia di abeto, ne tolse una di vetro, e di primo scontro la cacciò dietro al generale, appianttandosi per buon rispetto le ventose nel pettignone. . . .
>
> Ora vien via il fratoncello secondo, pur tóccogli per sorte, e ficcò la freccia nel berzaglio all bella prima; e l'altra monica, contrafacendo la sozia con la lancia da le due pallotte, investì nello *utriusque* del giovanetto, che sguizzò come una anguilla nel ricevere il colpo. Venne l'ultima e l'ultimo: e ci fu molto da ridere, perché sepellì il berlingozzo che era tocco la mattina a pranzo ne l'anello della compagna; ed egli, rimaso dietro a tutti, piantò dietro a lei il lanciotto: di odo che pareano una spedonata di anime dannate,

le quali volesse porre al fuoco Satanasso per il carnasciale di Lucifero.
(Pp. 23–24)

Now the jousters are lined up for the fray. They made a quintain out of the
backside of that swarthy, squint-eyed nun who had been stuffing herself
greedily with the glass cock, and then drew lots. The first tilt fell to the
trumpeter. He told his companion to continue to blow as he started to run,
spurring himself on with his fingers in his asshole, and then drove his lance
into his darling's shield right up to the hilt. Since that one stroke was as
good as three, he was roundly applauded. . . .

After him came by lot the General, who ran, lance at rest, and filled the
bung-hole of the novice as he had just filled the sister's. So there they were,
firm and tightly fixed, like the boundaries between two fields. The third tilt
fell to one of the nuns, who, not having a pine lance, picked up a glass one,
and at the first crack buried it deep in the General's buttocks, while planting,
for good measure, the bells in her own love-patch. . . .

Then the second friar, whose turn had come, rushed forth and at the very
first thrust drove his arrow straight into bull's-eye. The other nun, copying
her sister, plunged her two-balled lance in the backside of the young man,
who, when he felt the impact, squirmed like an eel. Then came the last
woman and the last man, and there was plenty to laugh at here because she
buried her glass patty-cake, on which she had dined that morning, in her
sister's oven. And then the monk, who was behind them all, planted his
javelin in her behind, so that they all looked like a spit of damned souls that
Satanas was roasting at the fire for Lucifer's carnival. (P. 32)

While the jousting language dominates this passage, we note that eating
and cooking comparisons are used as well, and the whole scene culminates in an image that is both culinary and religious—the linked
sexual warriors described as morsels on a spit roasting in an infernal
cookout. Nanna finds that in watching this she has "tolto il luogo alla
predica" (p. 24) ["lost me my seat at the sermon" (p. 33)].

Cut off from the group sex scene, Nanna looks into another cell,
noting that she thinks the sisters enjoyed watching each other. She next
sees two nuns masturbating with dildos. She hears them lament the
inadequacy of such measures and plan to leave the nunnery for real
men. Nanna turns to another chink, and she sees the Abbess in difficulty with her confessor:

Egli, in sul più bel dello spasso, le avea cavato lo stoppino della botte e lo
volea porre nel vaso del zibetto; e la poveretta, tutta in sapore, tutta in
lussuria, tutta in sugo, inginocchiata ai suoi piedi, lo scongiurava per le
stimmate, per i dolori, per le sette allegrezze, per il *pater noster* di san Giuliano, per i salmi penitenziali, per i tre magi, per la stella e per *santa santorum*:
né poté mai ottenere che il nerone, il caino, il guida le ripiantasse il porro
nell' orticello; anzi, con un viso di Marforio, tutto velenoso, la sforzò con i

fatti e con le bravarie a voltarsi in là, e fattole porre la testa in una stufetta, soffiando come un aspido sordo, con la schiuma alla bocca come l'orco, le ficcò il piantone nel fosso ristorativo. . . .

E si pigliava un piacere da mille forche nel cavare e mettere, ridendo a quel non so che che udiva allo entrare e allo uscire dei piuolo, simigliante a quel *lof tof* e *taf* che fanno i piedi dei peregrini quando trovano la via di creta viscosa che spesso gli ruba le scarpe. . . .

La sconsolata, col capo nella stufa, parea lo spirto d'un sodomito in bocca del demonio. Alla fine il padre, spirato dalle sue orazioni, le fece trarre il capo fuora; e sanza schiavare, il fratacchione la portò su la verga fino a un trespido; al quale appoggiata la martorella, cominciò a dimenarsi con tanta galantaria, che quello che tocca i tasti al gravicembalo non ne sa tanto; e come ella fosse disnodata, tutta si volgea indietro volendosi bere i labbri e mangiare la lingua del confessore, tenendo fuora tuttavia la sua che non era punto differente da quella d'una vacca; e presagli la mano con gli orli della valigia, lo facea torcere come gliene avesse presa con le tanaglie. (P. 26)

Just when they were at the peak of their pleasure, he pulled the bung-peg out of the bung-hole and wanted to put it in the shitspout, and the poor woman, all lathered up, dying of lust, her love-mouth streaming, got down on her knees and begged him by the stigmas, by the sorrows, by the seven joys, by St. Julian's Our Father, by the three Magi, by the star, and by the *santa santorum*—but she could not convince that Nero, that Cain, that Judas to plant his leek in her little garden. Just the opposite. With the glower of Marforio's statue in Rome, malicious as a snake, he whacked and bullied her until she turned her back; then he made her stick her head in a small stove, and hissing like a deaf asp, his mouth frothing like an ogre's, he plunged his enormous plant deep in her refreshing ditch. . . .

And he took a delight that merited a thousand trips to the gallows in pulling it out and shoving it in, laughing all the while at something he heard as he drove his pole back and forth; in fact it sounded like the slurping pilgrims' feet make when they walk on a road of sticky clay, which often robs them of their shoes. . . .

The inconsolable woman, with her head poked in that stove, looked like the soul of a sodomite in the mouth of the devil. At last the father, moved by her prayers, permitted her to pull her head out; without removing his key, the dirty monk bore her on his rod all the way to a stool, where he placed the poor martyr and began to twist and jiggle so boldly that the man who plays the organ in church could not have touched the stops more deftly. And then as if her body had become boneless, she bent all the way back, trying to drink her confessor's lips and eat his tongue, sticking her own so far out that it looked like a cow's, and at the same time gripped his hand between the edges of her valise, making him writhe as if she had seized it between a pair of pliers. (Pp. 34–35.)

Aretino employs traditional Renaissance sexual fantasies in the most extraordinary fashion in this scene. One of those major fantasies—

women can never get enough sexual intercourse—clashes with the
other—priests always want anal intercourse. Aretino plays these two
fantasies off against one another in a scene that is meant to be both
erotic and comic. The sexual activity, after all, is described in great
detail and meant to arouse the reader. The attitudes of Nanna in describing the action and Antonia in hearing it described (Antonia inter-
jects into the narrative two exclamations, she calls the confessor a
"poltronaccio" ["scoundrel"] and says, "Che sia squartato" ["He
should have been drawn and quartered"]) support the notion that
women want sexual intercourse, and they want it in their "natures" as
the Abbess later says, not their anuses. Nanna and Antonia sympathize
with the Abbess; they condemn the confessor, but only for the way in
which he wants his satisfaction. He is a "Nero," a "Cain," a "Judas,"
a "dirty monk." While they feel sorry for the Abbess and condemn
her confessor, we are amused by the lengths to which Aretino goes in
perverting the world of religion. The Abbess begs by all the holy things
she can think of, the sound of the confessor's actions is like "the slurping [of] pilgrims' feet," she looks like one of the condemned in a
painting of the Last Judgment, she is a "martyr" being played "like an
organ in church." Aretino could hardly go further in putting the world
of the church into the service of the world of pornography.

Another of the fantasies upon which pornography is built is that the
sexual appetite is never sated for long. Nanna's narrative continues
apace, for soon after the confessor finally "intertenendo la piena che
volea dare il passo all macina" (p. 27) ["loosed the flood that turns the
mill wheel" (p. 35)] the Abbess nibbles his "reliquary" (surely the most
appropriate of all of Aretino's metaphors in this scene) in an effort to
arouse him. Finally the confessor's novice enters the room, and the
threesome are at it forthwith. The scene is described at length, and
Antonia asks Nanna how she could control her "desire for a man after
seeing all that fucking," and Nanna confesses that she was indeed made
"horny" by the scene and used her dildo again (p. 36). If the effect on
the reader has not been one of arousal, it has been that for Nanna, as
Aretino once again reminds us of the "natural" reaction of a voyeur.

More adventures follow quickly; the two nuns seeking to leave the
nunnery are caught, but they invite the muleteer of the convent to their
room. He takes a wrong turn, however, and ends up in a room where
two other nuns, awaiting a vicar, battle over him. It is a scene done
with broad comic strokes that ends when Nanna discovers that the
young clergyman sent to care for her is suddenly in her cell. He begs
for mercy in parodic religious terms, calling her "il mio altare, il mio
vespro, la mia compieta e la mia messa" (p. 32) ["my altar, my Vespers,

my Compline, my Mass" (p. 41)]. Nanna confesses that she "e lascia-
tami vincere dal suo proemio fratino, nel quale dicea maggior bugie
che non dicono gli oriuoli stemperati, egli me entrò a dosso con un
laudamus te che parea che egli avesse a benedir le palme" (p. 33) ["Won
over by his monkish preamble, in which he told me greater lies than a
laggard clock, I let him get on me and shove it inside me with a
Laudamus Te, as if he were blessing the palms on Palm Sunday" (p. 41)].

Aretino is not content to play a few simple variations on the device
of using religious terminology in the service of sexual activity. It is
typical of him to push such usage to the limits, to be as extravagant
as possible in the practice. The reader is to be shocked, amused, and
aroused. On the face of it, such extensive use of religious terminology
in erotic scenes would seem to heighten the satiric purpose of the work
at the expense of the erotic. As I have said before, it does have the effect
of reminding us of the disparity between appearance and reality in
what was supposed to be a holy house. But it also has the effect of
heightening the erotic effect, since part of the prevailing mythology of
Renaissance Italy (its own mythology, that is) was that members of
ecclesiastical orders were the most highly sexed of any group in society.
Although I would argue that *any* language can be invested with sexual
meaning given the proper context, it might be worthwhile noting that
language we think of as belonging to the world of sex and the language
we think of as belonging to the world of religion share many affinities.
It is part of Aretino's genius that he is able to have it both ways—be
satirist and pornographer at the same time.

Aretino takes no chances on a reader's missing his many inventive
metaphors drawn from all walks of life, for soon after the foregoing
scene, Antonia interrupts Nanna and castigates her for what she considers to be an excessive use of metaphors in describing sexual intercourse. Such an objection is in character for the matter-of-fact Antonia,
who had stated at the outset of the dialogue in response to Nanna's
assertion that nuns, married women, and whores live differently nowadays from the way they used to, "Ah! ah! ah! La vita visse sempre a
una foggia: sempre le persone mangiaro, sempre bevvero, sempre dor-
miro, sempre vegghiaro, sempre andaro, sempre stettero, e sempre
pisciaro le donne per il fesso" (p. 9) ["Ha! Life has always been lived
in the same way: people have always eaten, have always drunk, have
always slept, have always looked, have always lain awake, have always
gone and always stayed, and women have always pissed through the
crack" (p. 17)]. Antonia objects:

Io te lo ho voluto dire, ed emmisi scordato: parla alla libera, e dì "cu', ca', po' e fo' ", che non sarai intesa se non dalla Sapienza Capranica con cotesto tuo "cordone nello anello", "guglia nel coliseo", "porro nello orto", "chiavistello ne l'uscio", "chiave nella serratura", "pestello nel mortaio", "rossignuolo nel nido", "piantone nel fosso", "sgonfiatoio nella animella", "stocco nella guaina"; e così "il piuolo", "il pastorale", "la pastinaca", "la monina", "la cotale", "il cotale", "le mele", "le carte del messale", "quel fatto", "il verbigrazia", "quella cosa", "quella faccenda", "quella novella", "il manico", "la freccia", "la carota", "la radice" e la merda che ti sia non vo' dire in gola, poi che vuoi andare su le punte dei zoccoli; ora dì sì al sì e no al no: se non, tientelo. (P. 35)

Oh, I meant to tell you and then I forgot: Speak plainly and say "fuck," "prick," "cunt," and "ass" if you want anyone except for the scholars at the university in Rome to understand you. You with your "rope in the ring," your "obelisk in the Colosseum," your "leek in the garden," your "key in the lock," your "bolt in the door," your "pestel in the mortar," your "nightingale in the nest," your "tree in the ditch," your "syringe in the flap-valve," your "sword in the scabbard," not to mention your "stake," your "crozier," your "parsnip," your "little monkey," your "this," your "that," your "him" and your "her," your "apples," "leaves of the missal," "fact," *verbigratia,* "job," "affair," "big news," "handle," "arrow," "carrot," "root," and all shit there is—why don't you say it straight out and stop going about on tiptoes? Why don't you say yes when you mean yes and no when you mean no—or else keep it to yourself? (Pp. 43–44)

This insistence upon the use of vulgar words is a keynote, as I have already suggested, in the popular erotica of the Renaissance. Elsewhere Aretino and his imitators respond to Antonia's request, but in Nanna's description of a copulating couple immediately following Antonia's advice we see that Aretino cannot resist the obviously delightful task of finding more and more metaphors for sexual intercourse. As a consequence the sexual activity is described as the "knife cutting the kid," the "stiff wild poppy-stem in the bed of creeping thyme," and the "seal in the wax."[36] Perhaps Aretino was aware of the limited power of suggestion in words equivalent to "fuck," "cunt," "cock," and so forth (even granting them a power, as taboo words, of sexual arousal). Throughout his dialogues, Aretino continually delights in finding metaphors for sexual organs and sexual intercourse; his love of his own inventive use of language that draws attention to itself always seems

---

36. Aretino raises the issue again in the final dialogue of the work, where the nurse and midwife discuss the use of "vulgar" terms. The discussion concludes with the midwife giving the same argument that Aretino used in the letter to Zatti, that is, that cunts and cocks deserve to be talked about and shown since they have made us all, whether we are kings, popes, poets, muses, or midwives (pp. 298–99 in Italian text; pp. 325–26 in translation).

stronger than his desire to create "hard-core" pornography. Ironically, then, while he insists in his sonnets on using vulgar words and makes the argument for using them in his dialogue, Aretino himself constantly tries to find new metaphors that display his wit and extend the world of sexuality.

This last point is an important one. One might argue that metaphors that are radically different from the ones conventionally used to describe sexual intercourse would seem to lessen rather than heighten the erotic effect of a passage, for one is apt to think about that differentness. Such is often the case with Aretino's dialogues, where he wants us, above all, to be amazed by his ability to be inventive. Yet if Aretino diminishes the erotic effect of a given passage by using so many inventive metaphors, he also manages to get us to start thinking that all things can be turned to the service of sex. The context is crucial, I think. For much of the first day the context in which Aretino uses these inventive metaphors is one of such heightened sexuality that we can hardly forget that we are reading about sex in some form or other, even though the metaphors may seem farfetched indeed. We are forced to the conclusion that while some metaphors may be more powerful, effective, and sexually suggestive than others, better for arousing the reader, the context in which we encounter those metaphors is also a crucial factor in determining the overall effectiveness of such comparisons.

There is a further point: Marcus, in defining pornotopia, would cast pornography out of the realm of "literature" on a number of counts, chief among them its singleness of purpose. For Marcus much of the limitation found in singleness of purpose can be located in the language, since "language for pornography is a prison from which it is continually trying to escape. At best, language is a bothersome necessity, for its function in pornography is to set going a series of non-verbal images, of fantasies, and if it could achieve this without the mediation of words it would."[37] For Marcus even the metaphors of pornography "*de-elaborate* the verbal structure."[38] I take issue with this notion of singleness of purpose. Granted that the chief intention of pornography is arousal of the reader. Granted that this is the chief reason people read pornography; intelligent readers (and there are intelligent readers of pornography) want more—they want to be amused and entertained too. I would argue that *part* of what distinguishes good pornography from

---

37. Marcus, p. 282.

38. Marcus, p. 283. Marcus might not argue with this point here on Aretino, but he would no doubt dismiss it by saying that Aretino's work does not qualify as pornography. I would still make the same argument about "hard-core" pornographic works.

the mediocre or bad are those elements which carry it beyond its chief end. The most important of these elements is inventive language— language that reminds us that we are in a fictive world and amuses us even as it arouses us.

Nanna concludes her narrative by relating several more adventures, including an incident where her special cleric friend catches her in bed with another man, beating her so that she finally leaves the convent. She tells Antonia that she has "been a fool to promise to tell you the life of nuns in a single day, for what they manage to do in an hour would take me a year to relate" (p. 53). This is certainly the fantasy upon which the most pornographic of the dialogues is built.

The whole of the second dialogue, the *Life of Wives,* is comprised of numerous cuckoldry tales of a Boccaccian type. The emphasis is on the turning of the plot so typical in the *fabliaux* and *novelle,* not on detailed description of sexual activity. They are primarily bawdy tales with wives switching beds, favoring lecherous priests, finding willing men with big tools; all are built on the premise stated at the end of the book: "per una che le piace il marito, son mille che se ne fanno schife: ed è chiaro che per due persone che faccino il pane in casa, son sette-cento che vogliono quello del fornaio perché è più bianco" (p. 89) ["For each woman pleased with her husband there are thousands disgusted with theirs; what's more, it is obvious that for every two people who make their bread at home, there are seven hundred who want the baker's because it is whiter" (p. 102)]. Given this premise, it is not surprising that our overwhelming sense of this dialogue is of Aretino's reworking the tale-types of the *novelle.* There are several points of interest in the *Life of Wives* beyond watching Aretino play his variations on a form. Nanna's account of her wedding night is well-turned comic drama.

Coupled by her mother to a rich old man, Nanna conspires with her mother to convince the fellow that he is taking a virgin to his nuptial bed. Taking the blood from a capon and filling an eggshell with it, Nanna's mother smears the mouth of her pudendum with it. Nanna has also received careful instructions on how to act like a virgin, and so the wedding night proceeds, with Nanna performing her part expertly. She laments; she starts; she stops. Finally, even though the old man provides no more than "greased bread," Nanna can no longer control herself:

Io non mi potendo tenere, gustando il pane unto, di non mi abandonare come una porchetta grattata, non gridai se non quando la menchia mi uscì di casa. Allora sì che i gridi fecero correre su le finestre i vincini e mia madre di nuovo in camera: che, visto il sangue del pollo che avea tinti i lenzuoli e la camiscia allo sposo, fece tanto che quella notte egli si contentò che io andassi a dormir seco; e la mattina tutto il vicinato era in conclave per la mia onestà, né si parlava d'altro per la contrada. (P. 51)

When I tasted that piece of larded bread, I couldn't hold myself back and let go like a scratched pig and didn't make a single cry until his mighty mite slipped out of my house. Then I really began to shriek, so loud that all the neighbors ran to their windows. My mother rushed into the room again, and seeing the capon's blood, which had stained the sheets and my husband's nightshirt, kicked up such a fuss that for that night he was happy to let me go and sleep with her. In the morning the whole neighborhood was gathered in conclave, discussing my respectability, and that's all they talked about throughout the district. (P. 61)

Nanna's husband, in a society that demands ocular proof that women are virgins on their wedding night, is held to be very foolish indeed. If Nanna's loss of control over the "larded bread" at first strikes us as out of character, we must remember that Aretino has not abandoned his pornographic intentions entirely. Thus even in the midst of this comic scene, he would have us believe, when all is said and done, that women really enjoy sexual intercourse; they cannot do without it. Aretino is careful to feed this fantasy, so essential if his dialogues are to work as pornography.

Aretino also continues to exploit the notion that seeing sexual intercourse is always stimulating. In two episodes in the *Life of Wives* Nanna is witness to sexual encounters. In both instances she is not hidden away, peeking through chinks in a wall; rather, she is the confidante and witness of unhappy wives with lovers. In the first instance, a woman has a husband who "looks good on the piazza" but is nothing at home. The wife shows Nanna a fellow whom she had hidden in her closet, "e fu pure il vero che ella in sul mio viso si gli coricò sopra, e ponendo la casa in sul camino gli fece fare duo chiodi a un caldo e due schiacciate in un fiato, dicendo: ‹‹Io voglio piuttosto che si sappia che io sia trista e consolata che buona e disperata›› " (p. 52) ["And I swear that right there and then, before my very eyes, she pulled him on top of her and, fitting her house over his chimney, made him forge two nails in the heat of her furnace, two flat cakes dripping in oil, hip, hop, saying meanwhile: 'I would prefer that people know me as a horny woman who is content than a good woman who is desperate' " (p. 62)]. Seeing this act has the predictable effect on Nanna; she rushes home to seek out her manservant. She finds, however, that her mother is engaged with him, and so she is reduced to working off this "whim" as best she can with her husband.

In the second such episode, Nanna is with a wife who has a yen for a disgusting, unkempt but sexually well endowed pedant (she decides he must be well endowed by the size of his nose).[39] One evening when her husband is away, the pedant overhears the wife and Nanna discussing the prospect of entertaining him sexually, and he boldly enters the room. The wife exclaims: "«Maestro, tenete in su la briglia la bocca e le mani, e serviteci per istanotte del vostro battisteo»" (p. 61) ["Maestro, put a rein on your mouth and hands and tonight use only your baptismal sprinkler" (p. 72)]. Nanna is, naturally, aroused by what she witnesses; "Io in quel mentre simigliava una mona che mastica il boccone inanzi che lo abbia in bocca: e se non che mi stuzzicai con un pestello di metallo che ivi trovai sopra una cassa (il quale, secondo che me ne venne lo odore, avea pestato canella), certo certo mi moriva per la invidia del piacere altrui" (p. 62) ["Meanwhile I felt like a slut who masticates a mouthful before she has it in her mouth, and if I hadn't macerated myself a bit with a metal pestel that I found on a chest, which, judging from the odor it gave off, must have pounded cinnamon, I would surely have died of envy at the others' pleasure" (pp. 72–73)]. By painting explicitly both the sexual activity itself as well as the reactions of someone watching sexual intercourse, Aretino manages to heighten the pornographic nature of the scene. The arousing effect the sexual activity has on Nanna is, of course, the same one that pornography tries to achieve on the reader. Such scenes of explicit sexual activity are the exception in the second dialogue, however. More often than not what is emphasized is the sorry state of wives; they are married to sexually inadequate men and must use their wits to find those who can satisfy their sexual desires. The object of their designs is usually someone known to have a large penis (in one instance, it is a priest, seen pissing, who arouses a deprived wife). Variations of all kinds are played, including a wife who substitutes herself for a woman sought after by her husband.

In Aretino's version of this well-known plot, the husband is described as a ne'er-do-well who plans to have his pleasure with a friend of his wife's, and he proposes to share his bounty with his friends in a "thirty-one" or gang-bang.[40] In this instance the wife, who overhears

39. Chaucer's Miller with his distinctive nose comes to mind here. It was a commonplace to read the face as emblematic of the sexual nature of a person. See Walter Clyde Curry, *Chaucer and the Mediaeval Sciences*, rev. ed. (New York: Barnes & Noble, 1960), pp. 85–90.

40. Florio, *A Worlde*, p. 431, defines a trentuno as:

. . . one and thirtie. Also a game at cards called one and thirtie, or else the game on

the plan, substitutes herself, not because she wishes to keep her husband faithful but because she says, "«Io ho inteso dire che chi gode una volta non istenta sempre»" (p. 73) [" 'I've heard it said that a woman who enjoys herself fully once will never feel hard up again' " (p. 84)]. The husband begins the parade, which is described in great detail, but before the full thirty-one has been completed, the identity of the woman is revealed, and the husband must acknowledge his many horns. Antonia's reaction to the story bespeaks the fantasy underlying all of these stories, "Beate quelle che si sanno cavare delle voglie" (p. 75) ["Blessed are the women who can satisfy their desires!" (p. 86)]. The pornographer must insist on this notion—that women are driven by sexual appetite and will do anything to satisfy it. Nanna concurs with Antonia's statement, but she goes on to aver that "ma a chi se le cava per via di questi trentuni non ho veruna invidia; e ne ho provati anche io, per grazia di chi me gli diede, qualcuni; e non ci trovo le beatitudini che la gente si crede, però che durano troppo. Ti confesso bene che, se durasseno la metà, sarebbeno una cosa sfoggiata, e farebbero un buon pro' " (p. 75) ["But I don't envy anyone who satisfies them by these thirty-ones; I have tried them once or twice myself, thanks to those who gave them to me, and I didn't find in them the delight people claim for them, because they go on too long! I'll tell you the truth: if it lasted only half as long it would be a splendid thing and quite worthwhile" (pp. 86–87)]. Momentarily, it would seem that Aretino breaks through the fantasy, but he has Nanna recover with her wish for half a thirty-one. Elsewhere in the dialogues, however, thirty-ones are presented for what they truly are, crimes of violence. Aretino does not appear to present them in this way to appeal to sadistic readers; rather, in one instance the scene is given to show the most vicious way that men betray women in a dialogue (the *Betrayals of Men*) where Aretino more than once allows a kind of realism to enter his works for the purposes of furthering his pose as the biting satirist and moralist.[41]

As the passages cited above from the *Life of Wives* make clear, Aretino continues to delight in inventive metaphors. It is an issue he never drops for very long, and, near the end of this second dialogue, Antonia complains about a woman with genteel airs who has been teaching her

the head. Also a punishment inflicted by ruffianly fellowes vppon raskalie whores in Italy, who (as we pump them in England) so they cause them to be occupied one and thirtie times by one and thirtie seuerall base raskalie companions. Also an occupying of one and thirtie times to such a colmon hedge whore or ouer-ridden iade, as we say in England a pumping of a common whore.

41. See pp. 266–67 in Rosenthal for a depiction of a violent thirty-one.

daughter to speak in a manner that can only be described as highly euphemistic. In response to Antonia's complaint, which concludes, "E intendo che quei dalla scuola vogliono che il K si metta dietro al libro, e non dinanzi: che sarà una signoria" ["And so far as I can see, the followers of this school want us to put the prick in the back of the book, not the front—which would be a gentlemanly way to do it"], Nanna says, "Per chi lo vuole: io, per me, lo vo' porre dove mi fu insegnato dalla potta che mi cacò . . ." (p. 82) ["For those who like it. As for me, I want to put it where I was taught by the cunt that shit me out" (p. 94)]. It would seem that Nanna has been converted to Antonia's unembroidered style of speech, but we notice that she concludes the story she has been in the midst of by saying, "Egli lo fece due volte alla biasima-tutte sanza levare il becco da molle" (p. 82) ["He did it twice to Madame Blame-All, without even taking his beak out of the pool" (p. 94)]. Language, its richness, its suppleness, in its metaphoric and direct modes, is one aspect of the dialogues always consciously on display.

In the *Life of Whores* on the third day, sexual activity is described but not nearly in so graphic a fashion as it has been heretofore, and this part of the dialogues reads a good deal like Greene's cony-catching pamphlets where the art of cross-biting (the con games worked by whores and their pimps) is set forth. Occasionally, Nanna confesses, "e se qualche volta toccano una grossa chiave, il fanno per un certo appitito di donna pregna, che mangia uno aglietto e una susina acerba" (p. 116) ["And if every now and then a whore does get a fleeting desire for a big prick, she gets it in much the way that a pregnant woman eats a clove of garlic or a green plum; it is but a passing whim" (p. 131)]. Such desires, of course, are bad for business, and above all the life of whores is presented as a business. Time and again Nanna reminds us that she has made men pay. Money, as she tells her daughter in the next dialogue, when Pippa's instruction in the life of a whore begins, can make the stench of men with bad breath and fartitious assholes bearable (p. 175). For this same reason, money, men with it are always preferable to great lords and courtiers. She says, "La maggior parte dei cortigiani simigliano lumache che si portano la casa a dosso; e non hanno fiato" (p. 104) ["The majority of courtiers are like snails; they carry their houses on their backs and have nothing else to their names" (p. 117)]. Because Aretino is consistent in presenting the life of whores as a business, there is little that can be described as pornographic in the third dialogue; rather, the appeal is to society's fascination for finding out how the seamier side really works. By the end of the third dialogue, Antonia has come to the conclusion that Nanna should have Pippa become a whore, since they are the most honest of women.[42]

The second part of the work, or the *Dialoghi* in the Italian title, deals with the instruction of Pippa in her trade. Here Aretino seems to be doing little more than updating Ovid, however much he might want to deny his classical fathers; there is little that might be termed pornographic. Only when Nanna is instructing Pippa specifically on how to arouse a man and prolong his arousal do we get anything resembling an extended scene of sexual activity. Nanna delivers chapter and verse on how to drive men wild with lust, providing details so that Pippa will be financially successful at her trade. Aretino has her drag out this scene at great length:

> Mentre egli ti gualca, piagni, diventa ritrosa, non ti movere, ammutisci; e se ti domanda ciò che tu hai, rugnisci pure; e ciò facendo, è forza che si fermi e dicati: «Cor mio, fovvi io male? avete voi dispiacer del piacer che io mi piglio?»; e tu a lui: «Vecchietto caro, io vorrei . . . » (e qui finisci); ed egli dirà: «Che?»; e tu pur mugola; a la fine, tra parole e cenni, chiariscilo che vuoi correre una lancia a la giannetta. . . .
>
> Se tu sei con la fantasia a far quel che io vorrei che tu facessi, acconciati bene adagio; e acconcia che sei, fasciagli il collo con le braccia e bascialo dieci volte in un tratto; e preso che gli arai il pistello con mano, stringegnelo tanto che si finisca di imbizzarrire: e infocato ch'egli è, ficcatelo nel mozzo e spigneti inver lui tutta tutta; e qui ti ferma e bascialo; stata un nonnulla, sospira a la infoiata e dì: «Se io faccio, farete?» lo stallone risponderà con voce incazzita: «Sì, speranza»; e tu, non altrimenti che il suo spuntone fosse il fuso e la tua sermollina la ruota dove ella si rivolge, comincia a girarti; e s'egli accenna di fare, ritienti dicendo: «Non anco, vita mia»: e datogli una stoccatina in bocca con la lingua, non ischiodando punto de la chiave che è ne la serratura, rispigni, rimena e rificca; e piano e forte, e dando di punta e di taglio, tocca i tasti da paladina. E per istroncarla, io vorrei che facendo quella faccenda tu facessi di quelli azzichetti che fanno coloro che giuocano al calcio mentre hanno il pallone in mano: i quali schermiscano con artificio e, mostrando di voler correre or qua or là, furano tanto di tempo che, senza esser impacciati da chi gli è contra, danno il colpo come gli piace. (Pp. 157–58)
>
> . . . while he's pumping away, start to cry, hold back, stop moving, and fall silent. If he asks you what's wrong, you can even let out a groan, and then he will have to stop and say: "My dear heart, am I hurting you? Are you displeased at the pleasure I am taking?" And you say to him: "My dear old chap I should like . . ." But stop right there, and he'll ask you: "What?"

42. See pp. 139–40 in the Italian edition, p. 158 in Rosenthal.

and you just moan. Finally, by words and hints, make it clear to him that
you want to break a lance with him in the Giannetta style, man on bottom,
woman on top. . . .

If you in your fantasy are doing what I want you to do, squat down over
him; and when you are nicely settled twine your arms around his neck and
kiss him quickly, ten times in a row. Then, after grabbing his pestle in your
hand, clutch it so tightly that it begins to go wild; and when it is blazing
hot, shove it straight into your socket and push against it so hard that the
spoke goes in all the way, and then, suddenly, come to a dead stop and kiss
him. After having lain there quietly for a while, sigh as though you were
dying with delight and whisper to him: "If I come, will you come too?"
The stud will answer in a voice blurred with passion: "Yes, my hope!" Then
you must act as if his halberd was a spindle and your patch of wild thyme
the wheel on which it revolves, and start pushing down on it with a rolling
twist. And if you see that he is about to come, stop again and say; "Not
yet, my life," and ramming your tongue deep into his mouth, while making
sure not to let his key slip out of your keyhole, push, wriggle, and bear
down mightily, driving it in firmly and sweetly, thrusting with the point
and cutting with the edge, touching all the keys like a true paladin and, to
cut the story short, I would wish that you did this business with all the
clever feints and moves and twists and turns soccer players adopt when they
have the ball in their hands—they fake so adeptly, pretending to run this
way or that, that they slip by the man who tries to block them and kick the
ball just where they please. (Pp. 174–75)

Nanna as narrator draws out her *description* of sexual action just as she
wishes Pippa to draw out the actions themselves. The premise upon
which these scenes (upon which much pornography for that matter) is
based is that man is "incazzito." To translate the phrase "con voce
incazzita" as "in a voice blurred with passion" is, literally, to reduce
Aretino's conception of men obsessed, driven wild, with wanting their
cocks satisfied, to men by driven by some abstract force ("passion").
The point of the passage, after all, is to prolong the erection. We are
to see men as little more than extensions of their cocks. To master
their cocks is to master them—this is Nanna's message to Pippa. Aretino knows it is also the key to writing successful pornography, but
again we see that even in a scene like this, he will not be mere pornographer. On one level, we laugh at men who are so easily manipu-
lated; as readers we distance ourselves from such fools. We are helped
in this by Nanna's presentation of the "incazziti" as victims at the
mercy of the art of whores. But the scene is calculated to involve us
and arouse us too; who, after all, has not been subject to such "passion"
at one time or another? Only at the end of the scene does Aretino make
it truly comic in his comparison of the artful whore to a clever open
field runner in the Renaissance version of *calcio*.

In this dialogue Aretino paints few scenes like the one just analyzed for the "incazziti," but he does have a good deal to say about writing in general, scholars, poets, and society as a whole, that is important for any overall evaluation of his work. For example, Aretino begins the second part of the dialogues by describing his creative process in the dedication to Bernardo Valdaura:

> E per dirvi, Omero nel formare Ulisse non lo imbellettò con la varietà de le scienze, ma lo fece conoscitore dei costumi de le genti. E perciò io mi sforzo di ritrarre le nature altrui con la vivacità che il mirabile Tiziano ritrae questo e quel volto; e perché i buoni pittori apprezzano molto un bel groppo di figure abozzate, lascio stampare le mie cose così fatte, né mi curo punto di miniar parole: perché la fatica sta nel disegno, e se bene i colori son belli da per sé, non fanno che i cartocci loro non sieno cartocci; e tutto è ciancia, eccetto il far presto e del suo. (P. 146)

> Homer, for example, when forming his Ulysses, did not deck him out with the variety of sciences, but made him the wise knower of the customs of the peoples. So I try to describe other kinds of characters with the same vividness that the admirable Titian portrays this or that face. And just as good painters greatly appreciate a beautiful group of sketched figures, so I allow my works to be issued in the same way, without at all caring to embellish my words, because the real work lies in the design, and if this is well done the colors are so lovely in themselves and do not prevent cartoons from being what they are—cartoons. The whole thing is a game, yet you must do it quickly and by your own hand. (P. 162)

Aretino seems to be concerned with the work primarily as a demonstration of his dexterity, imagination, and facility of creation. He goes on to assert, "Eccovi là i *Salmi,* eccovi la *Istoria di Cristo,* eccovi le *Comedie,* eccovi il *Dialogo,* eccovi i volumi divoti e allegri, secondo i subietti; e ho partorito ogni opera quasi in un dì" (p. 146)[43] ["Over there are my *Psalms,* further along is my *History of Christ,* beyond that are my plays, and here are my *Dialogues*: devout or entertaining works, according to the subject. And I have given birth to each work in almost a single day" (pp. 162–63)]. This is an exaggeration, no doubt, made so that we may admire Aretino's breadth, quickness, and inventiveness, qualities we may still admire while rejecting the exaggeration of a "single day." The effect, of course, is to draw our attention to Aretino as a writer, and Aretino does want us to pay attention to writers and writing in the second part of the dialogues. Nanna tells Pippa that

---

43. Aretino sounds like a Renaissance Robert Frost. Unfortunately, scholars have not been able to prove or disprove this statement as Lawrance Thompson has done so brilliantly with Frost. It is generally conceded that Aretino at least rewrote some of his plays.

when she is at a courtly gathering, "e se ci è alcun vertuoso, accostategli con faccia allegra, mostrando di apprezzar più loro che (mi farai dire) il signor ch' è ivi" (pp. 163–64) ["If there is a scholar present, approach him with a happy countenance, showing him that you hold him highly, even more highly than the lord of the manor" (p. 181)]. Writers are to be feared and honored, since they can do so much for one's reputation.

Aretino has Nanna follow this advice by defending herself against those who criticized the idiom of speech she employed in the first part of the dialogues. It is a defense in which Aretino deflates literary high-style; in such defenses he is always on the side of plain-speaking.[44] His writing itself is not. Aretino is never content to confine himself to direct and vulgar expressions. But it is important for his pose as *Il Veritiero,* the teller of truth, that he assert freedom of speech and attack euphemism. In practice he rarely employs euphemisms, it is true, but he is not about to abandon inventive metaphor for plain speech any more than he is to confine himself to describing sexual intercourse in the missionary position.

Aretino has Nanna ever wary of poets and reading and writing in general. Several examples in the dialogue entitled the *Betrayals of Men* show women falling prey to the flowery phrases of poets or duped by their own ability to read.[45] Nanna is consistent in her advice to Pippa; she must be kind to poets. Pippa complains that Nanna has in fact urged her to give herself to them. Nanna retorts, "Cotesto non ti ho detto io; io voglio che gli accarezzi senza dargnele mai fetta: e questo si fa perché non ti dileggino con la baia de la lor laude, e acciò che, beffeggiandoti con la poltroneria del biasimo, non paia che dichino a te" (p. 273) ["I never said anything like that. I want you to caress them but without ever giving them even a slice of it. And you should do this so they won't tear you apart with their sarcastic praises; or if they do mock at you with their vicious cracks, it won't seem that they're really talking about you" (p. 299)]. Aretino could never resist striking a blow in favor of the power of the pen. He keeps this power in front of us in other subtle ways that shall concern us at the end of the chapter.

There are two other striking and interconnected topics brought forward in the last dialogues that demand passing attention—a defense of whores and a praise of the lower classes.[46] Nanna presents the fullest

44. See p. 165 in the Italian version, p. 182 in the English version.
45. See pp. 270–71 in the Italian version, pp. 296–97 in the English version.
46. Also noteworthy is Aretino's praise of Venice. As Nanna instructs Pippa on how to deal with different kinds of men, she describes the important characteristics of each kind of national type and each Italian type by cities, all of whom, except for the Venetians, come in for faint praise. Of the Venetians Nanna says, "perchè son iddii e padroni del

defense of whores in the fifth dialogue, the *Betrayals of Men*. Here Aretino allows Nanna her say as a working woman and human being. She bursts forth against men who preach that it is quite all right to trick whores out of payment for their services in the manner we have come to expect from the pen of Aretino, *Il Veritiero*. Prostitution, after all, is a business; he has insisted upon this throughout the dialogues, but he has said it in passages imbedded in instruction on sexual techniques; in this section he is at pains to remind us that whores too must eat.[47]

Aretino's praise of the lower classes is, on the face of it, a curious one. Nanna explains to Pippa why she prefers men of a lower social order:

> Perché i fattori, gli staffieri, i ragazzoni, gli ortolani, i facchini e i cuochi almen ti sono schiavi, e andrebbono a porre il capo nel fuoco e fra il ceppo e la mannaia per compiacerti; e se gli tritassi a minuzzoli, non gli cavaresti il segreto di bocca; e poi non si crederia, quando ben si dicesse «Lo spenditor di messer tale gli soprescia la moglie». Oltra questo, simili gentarelle non sono svogliati, e pigliano il panno pel verso, e secondo che son recati si acconciano, né pigliano mai la lucerna in mano acciò che il suo lume gli faccia veder quanti borselli ha la tua fica, strupicciandole gli orli; né ti fanno alzare il culo in alto, sculacciandolo can la palma e graffiandolo con l'unghia; né ti fanno spogliare ignuda nel bel mezzodì, voltandoti ora di drieto e ora dinanzi; né si curano, mentre ti sforicchiano il cioncio, di alcuno azzichetto, né che tu dica parole disoneste per crescergliene la volontà, né ti stanno quattro ore in il corpo; né ti scommettano l'ossa col disnodarti tutta, ne le forge di alcuni "alza le gambe in suso e incavicchiale insieme", le quali essi trovano, hanno trovato e trovaranno per iscialacquarci le persone: ed è un zuccaro quei pascipecora e quelle altre poltronerie che ti dissi ieri, pare a me. (P. 259)

> Because stewards, lackeys, grooms, gardeners, porters, and cooks are at least your slaves and would even put their heads in the flames or between the block and the axe to please you; and even if they chopped them up, they couldn't pull a secret out of their mouths; and besides, nobody would believe it even if it were said: "The Messer So-and-So's factor ploughs his wife." What's more, these ordinary folk are not listless and go with the nap of the

---

tutto e i più bei giovani e i più begli uomini e i più bei vecchi del mondo" (p. 181) ["for they are gods and the lords of all—the most handsome youths, grown men, and old men in this world" (p. 199)].

While Aretino claimed to be a revealer of truth, he was a flatterer of monumental proportions when it served his needs. Venice was probably the only city in Italy where Aretino could write as he did and get away with it, and he was acutely aware of this fact. Thus he paid homage to Venice whenever possible. His flattery of Michelangelo is also well documented; it continued as long as Aretino felt there was some chance that Michelangelo would send him an autographed scrap of his work.

47. See pp. 237–38 in the Italian edition, pp. 260–61 in the English version.

cloth; and no matter how they are set in the saddle, they adapt themselves to the prevailing conditions. Nor do they grab a lantern so that they can see how many wrinkles you have in your cunt, stroking it and pushing back its lips. Nor do they make you lift your ass up high, slapping it with the flat of their hands or scratching it with their nails. They don't force you to take off all your clothes and go stark naked in the middle of the day, compelling you to take it first in the back and then in the front. Nor do they care, while driving their staff into your trill-hole, whether you give a little twist or a wriggle or shout dirty words to magnify their potency. Nor do they lay for four long hours on top of your body. Nor do they dislocate your bones by making you twist into those positions where you lift up your legs high in the air and let yourself be screwed at the same time—all those positions which men invent, have invented and will continue to invent in order to distort the pelvic regions of poor working whores. And all those positions I told you yesterday—the grazing sheep and those other filthy postures— are sweet as sugar compared to these. (Pp. 283–84)

Perhaps as a teller of truth, and as one from humble origins himself, it is not out of character for Aretino to give such praise for the lower social classes, but it is strange for a work of erotica in that what is condemned here is the variety of sexual experience. Were Aretino interested in writing only pornography in his dialogues, this would be seen as a serious lapse indeed. From a whore's point of view, however, the variety of sexual intercourse is simply more work; the gentleman is more demanding and less grateful than the humble man.

Of course, by attacking the sexual oddities of "gentlemen," Aretino does get to list them. He give us some mild titillation even as he attacks.[48] Just as Aretino brings a double perspective of humor and arousal in the first day of the dialogues, so in Nanna's praise of the lower classes he brings a double perspective of what he would have us believe is realism and arousal.

In Nanna's instructions to Pippa, Aretino returns in a direct way to the power of seeing as a sexual stimulant. Elsewhere we have seen that he demonstrated this power in scenes employing voyeurism; here he has Nanna discuss this power directly with Pippa. Men, she insists, are always stimulated by what they see:

E che risa gli escano di gola nel vedercelo entrare e nel vedercelo uscire; e dando alcune spinte a schincio e certe punte false, par tramortischino per la dolcezza del farci male. Talotta tolgano uno specchio grande grande, e ispogliatici ignude, fanno starci nei più sconci modi che si sappino fantasticare: e vagheggiandoci i visi, i petti, le pocce, le spalle, i corpi, le fregne e le

48. For Nanna's catalogue for Pippa, see p. 177 in the Italian edition, pp. 195–96 in Rosenthal.

natiche, non potrei dirti come se ne sfamano il piacere che ne hanno. E quante volte stimi tu che faccino stare i lor mariti, i lor giovani ai fessi perché vegghino cio? (P. 260)

And what a roar of laughter comes from their throats as they watch their prongs slide in and out of our backsides. And when they push it hard on an angle or jab it in some soft spot, you'd think they were going to faint away with the pleasure they get from hurting us. Sometimes they get a huge mirror, undress us and make us go about completely naked, and then they force us to hold the most obscene postures and positions that the human fantasy can concoct. They gaze longingly at our faces, breasts, nipples, shoulders, loins, cunts, and thighs, nor could I possibly tell you how that satiates their lust and the pleasure they get from looking. And how many times do you think that these punks set their husbands and young boys at the peephole so that they can see it all too? (Pp. 284–85)

That such a belief in the power of sight should be expressed should not surprise us in an age where the sense of sight as the primary respondent to beauty was a commonplace. The difference is, of course, that Aretino gives us no neoplatonic ladder; we do not move from what the eye sees to some imagined ideal beauty; we stay on the most fleshy of levels. But of course, we are not really seeing; we are imagining as a result of Aretino's powerful words. The power of words, finally, to stimulate the sexual imagination is what every writer of erotica counts on. Aretino makes that power concrete within the world of his dialogues in a number of different ways, but most notably by having a listener within the dialogues react to a graphic description with some sort of sexual activity, usually masturbation. We have noted this pattern from the very first of the dialogues; it is one that Aretino continues through the final dialogue.[49]

For the Midwife in the final dialogue language is part of her stock in trade as a bawd. She no longer has the looks to work as a whore herself, so she uses language to entice men to those who can satisfy the itching she has created. Sometimes she is so successful, the man cannot wait. In one scene she describes to a customer how she washed the intended mistress:

«E per dirlo a la Signoria vostra, io la lavai con queste mani, con l'acqua rosa, e non con l'acqua schietta; e mentre le spurava le pocce, il petto, le reni, il collo, stupiva de la sua morbidezza e de la sua bianchezza. Il bagnuolo era tepido e il fuoco acceso, e io sono stata la colpa d'ogni male: perché nel lavarle le cosce, e le meluzze, e la cotalina, mi venne meno per la dolcitudine del piacere. Oh che carni delicate, oh che membra candide, o che spesa non

49. See p. 321 in the Italian version, pp. 349–50 in the English translation.

più fatta da veruno: io l'ho palpata, l'ho basciata e maneggiata per una volta, sempre parlando di voi». A che fine sprolungarla? Io il messi in volontà: e rizzandosigli il-piei-del-trespolo, mi si lascia cadere a dosso, e diemmene una che se gli poteva dir "arcivoi", non pur "voi". (Pp. 307–08)

"And to tell your lordship the truth, I washed her with these very hands, using rosewater, not ordinary water, and while I was cleaning her nipples, tits, loins, and neck, I was amazed by their softness and whiteness. The bathwater was tepid and the fire lit, and so I was to blame for all the trouble, for as I washed her thighs, her melons, and her cute little slit, I almost fainted from the unbearable sweetness of my pleasure. Oh what delicate flesh! Oh what white limbs! What a beautiful body! Nobody can afford such flesh. I palped it, kissed it, and fondled it just once, all the time talking about you." But why drag it out? I got him so worked up that he lifted his third leg and, letting himself fall on top of me, gave me the kind of screw that one could call a super-screw, not just a run-of-the-mill one. (P. 335)

Such is the power of language to excite the sexual imagination. Aretino is entirely conscious of this, as scenes like the foregoing demonstrate. It is also a fact that he has the Midwife assert directly, for he has the Midwife tell the Wetnurse that the bawd's profession depends upon fantasy. "Perché il punto nostro sta nel cacciar carote, in far creder quello che non è e non pò essere" (p. 315) ["Because our main task is making people believe in that which is not and cannot be" (p. 343)]. The translation here omits the idiom that literally translated means to hunt the carrot (Florio translates it as "To make one swallowe a gudgeon, to make one beleeue the moone is made of greene cheese").[50] *Cacciar carote* is a nice image for the man who is "*incazzito*." And just as the bawd's profession depends on the building upon fantasy, so too does the pornographer's.

This is the way in which Aretino's genius as eroticist is, in the final analysis, truly felt. His richness of expression, the wide range of his topics, all within the context of an erotic work, serve to make his writing an extension of his sexuality. On one level, it would appear that I have argued against this very case, for I have been at pains to show that while there is much that is salacious, especially in the *Life of Nuns,* there is a good deal more than that. Aretino has so many other irons in the fire; the satirist, the parodist, or even the realist is never far removed from the pornographer, and so he must discourse on the abuses of the clergy, flowery language, the nobility, misogynistic literature, the power of the pen. In addition, he seems too enamored with his own talent with characters and words to envelop us in a

50. Florio, *A Worlde,* p. 52.

pornotopia, and we are constantly amazed at least as much by the way in which he says things as by what he says. But on further reflection, we must grant that more often than not when Aretino deals with what appear to be nonsexual topics, he does so in a context that relates to man's sexuality. Must we speak without euphemisms? To do so is to recognize the sexuality of human beings. Should poets be courted? To do so is to protect one's good name as a reputable whore. Are courtiers worthless drones in society? They are bad for the business of prostitution. And his verbal pyrotechnics, especially his inventive metaphors, have the effect, given their context, of heightening sexuality in an imaginative way. They become a kind of sexual embellishment, a joining together of the world of sexuality with all other worlds; this is intercourse in every sense of the word. Such is the power of Aretino's seeing, saying, writing. All the things we can think of become grist for his sexual mill; his pen becomes a true extension of his penis.[51]

51. In his article on Picasso, Richardson makes an analogous argument about Picasso (although he is talking about art as compensation, the point about the artist's tools as surrogates for sexual parts is relevant here). He says (p. 22):

But let me go back for a moment to Picasso's statement about the way bullfight drawings compensated him for missed pleasures, because this has an obvious relevance to the artist's sex life, or lack of one. In the circumstances, the raunchy subjects of the last decade (cf., the earlier bullfight scenes) must be seen as a form of compensation for an inability to have sex. But does this entitle us to claim, as some critics have done, that Picasso's baleful nudes flaunting their sexual parts are allegories of impotence? I don't think so, for this negative view leaves out of the account some very positive aspects of Picasso's final works.

For while Picasso's sexual powers may have waned, his artistic ones had if anything done the reverse. Whatever he may have felt about the onset of impotence, the compensatory pattern that the artist himself described enabled him to see sex and art as metaphors for each other. The tools of the artist's trade—his brushes—became surrogates for sexual parts to be used on a canvas that was a surrogate for the model.

CHAPTER 3

The Aretines: Imitation and Vilification

Aretino . . . Tu sai mangiare vn cazzo e crude e cotto.
Niccolo Franco, La Priapea

Aretino's success as a literary figure attracted a number of aspiring young men to his household. Niccolo Franco, Ambrogio degli Eusebui, Lorenzo Veniero, Lodovico Dolce, Anton Francesco Doni came to make their fortune or fame by whatever means they could. On the whole, Franco, Eusebui, and Doni proved to be a considerable problem for Aretino both personally and professionally. Originally, Franco and Eusebui were taken on as secretaries to prepare the first edition of Aretino's letters. Aretino had difficulty with the physical act of writing, reputedly having lost two fingers to a jealous husband in Rome, and these two young men wrote out the copy for the press.[1] As was the case with most young men hoping to follow Aretino, they soon turned out works of their own in the mode of Aretino, often attempting to out-Aretino the master himself. For the most part, Aretino's followers seem to have thought that if they could include more scenes of sexual intercourse described in more basic terms, they could surpass Aretino. The Aretines were much more intent on producing pornography, as the term is used in this study.[2] Further, some of the followers of Aretino eventually became his enemies, and out of the rift in their relationships grew quarrels carried on in print in which obscenity was the order of the day. The obscene literary quarrel, for which there was already a strong tradition, became a standard feature of the Renaissance literary scene, and by no one was it performed in a more scabrous fashion than by Aretino's followers.

Even though none would claim that the works of the Aretines are superb artistic productions, some are illuminating in what they attempt

1. See Chubb, *Aretino,* p. 281.
2. The term "Aretines" has been used variously to describe the courtesans living in Aretino's household and his literary imitators. Since those imitators themselves used the term, I apply it to them here.

artistically; and for the present study they are all important for revealing more fully the canvas of erotica in Renaissance Italy. Since most of these works are pornographic or obscene in nature, and since they were produced by men of far less repute than the humanists examined in chapter 1, one understands why they have either been totally ignored or remained the private preserve of specialists in esoteric erotica. For many of these works one looks in vain for accurate bibliographic information, modern critical editions, translations, or genuine scholarly commentary.

These works were not unread in their own day, however; clearly there were printers with an eye toward the marketplace willing to produce them. One of these works, Niccolo Franco's prose *La Puttana Errante,* gained a good deal of notoriety. Aretino, in order to encourage the success of a book by one of his followers, went so far as to allow his own name to be put on the title page,[3] and *La Puttana Errante,* always attributed to Aretino, became the most famous of all Italian pornographic works in Renaissance England.[4] No doubt it is precisely because the book was associated with Aretino that it has survived, gained such notoriety, and been more widely published than some of the other works considered in this chapter.

In *La Puttana Errante* there is much that is characteristic of Renaissance pornography: an overriding concern for sexual positions, a strongly anticlerical bent, a "how to" section on pleasing men, and an insistence on vulgar words. It is one of the few examples of Renaissance pornography that deals almost exclusively with sexual intercourse; it is nearly the pure world of pornographic fulfillment Steven Marcus calls pornotopia. There is some attempt at plot line in the work, but it is barest kind of business concocted merely to allow more copulation scenes. What is remarkable about the work, beyond its very real historical importance as a touchstone for the pornographic, is Franco's attempt at what might be termed realism, both in terms of description of place and in terms of the psychology of his heroine.

La Puttana Errante derives its title from the actions of its protagonist, Maddalena, who describes her initiation into the world of sexuality and

---

3. See Legman, *The Horn Book,* p. 91; and Foxon, p. 28n.

4. John Marston, Everard Guilpin and John Donne make this attribution, for example. Ben Jonson in *Volpone* mentions Aretino in the context of the *posizioni.* References to Aretino and the "errant," "arrant," or "wandering" whore became the touchstone for obscene literature in Renaissance England. For an article dealing with Aretino's reputation in England see David C. McPherson, "Aretino and the Harvey-Nashe Quarrel," *Publications of the Modern Language Association,* 84 (1969): 1551–58.

whoredom in a dialogue with Giulia.[5] The dialogue begins with Giulia and Maddalena admiring the rich dress of a certain Tortora, one of the leading courtesans of Rome. Maddalena explains that Tortora had the good fortune, after having been abandoned in Rome, to attract a chief secretary who became a cardinal "e quindi alquanto arricchito, cominciò a comprarle vesti e mille altre cose"[6] [and then as he became rich, he began to buy her clothes and a thousand other things]. Afterward she was loved by an old man who was an apostolic secretary, and then by other priests and cardinals; thus she rose to the top of her profession. Giulia is amazed and wonders what the secret of attracting men is, and Maddalena gives her some persuasive instruction. Giulia asks how many ways men and women may have sexual intercourse. Maddalena replies that to answer she will have to use naughty words; Giulia assures her, "Non restare per questo, ma fammi tanta grazia, dimmeli e non abbi meco rispetto. Già so bene io che cosa sia cazzo, potta e culo; parla pure liberamente; tu sai pure che d'allora in quà ch'io ti conobbi, io ti ho sempre amata come sorella"[7] [Don't stop for this, but make me very thankful, tell me and don't have any respect for me. I already know very well what a cock, cunt, and ass are; speak freely, you know that ever since I have known you, I have always loved you like a sister]. The way is thus cleared for Maddalena's uncensored narrative. Franco is very much a part of the popular tradition, and he is much less interested in the possibilities of inventing metaphors than Aretino. Vulgar words and obscene slang terms are used throughout.

As Maddalena begins her life's story, the work virtually ceases to function as a dialogue; at one stretch there are twelve pages of uninterrupted narrative and soon after that thirty-six more. Such extended first-person narrative is surely one of the factors that tempts a literary scholar to treat the work like an eighteenth- or nineteenth-century piece of prose fiction. Franco covers a variety of sexual activities through having Maddalena recount her initiation into sexual life. She tells how at age eleven she saw her fifteen-year-old cousin, Federico, masturbating. In great wonder, she tells her sixteen-year-old sister about what she has seen; her sister, in response, uses her finger to show her what men do to women. Later, Maddalena sees Federico engaging in anal

5. I am using an 1862 edition of the work attributed to Aretino that is owned by the Institute for Sex Research in Bloomington, Indiana. The University of Pennsylvania also has an edition of the work bound in the back of a volume, Meursii, Johannes the Younger, *Elegantiae Latini sermonis*.

6. Franco, *Puttana Errante,* p. 70.

7. Ibid., p. 76.

intercourse with his friend Roberto, and not long after this her sister marries and moves away, forcing Maddalena to share a bed with her aunt as the sleeping arrangements in the household are changed. Her aunt shows her ways in which a woman can please another woman. And then one day, now sixteen or seventeen, Maddalena sees her cousin Federico and his wife making love. For a literary scholar the passage is surely the most interesting in the book, since Franco makes an attempt at psychological realism in presenting the scene through the eyes of Maddalena as a virgin. Maddalena relates that

> . . . vidi la Caterina che s'aveva tolta la camicia di dosso ed era nuda e cercava se vi era dentro alcun pulce; dall'altra parte Federico nudo era sopra il letto con le reni verso quello, e sopra il ventre aveva la sua faccenda ritta, ed era così grossa e lunga che pareva un coniglio; mentre la riguardavo, maravigliandomi che in quattro anni fosse tanto cresciuta, diceva tra me; ohimè! costei è si piccola, com'ella può ricevere in sè tanto lavoro? come è possibile che colei non la squarci? e poi pensava fra me: egli la deve solamente fregare come faceva a me la zia: In questo, odo che Federico dice: Caterina vien quà; ed ella rivolta e vistolo a quel modo, disse sorridendo: Che volete? a cui egli disse: Vien quà se tu vuoi; ed ella si mise la camicia e vi andò, e posta la mano sopra quella colonna, disse: Non avete vergogna a stare in questo modo? egli disse: Baciami pure; ella lo baciò e collocossi vicino a lui, che così le toccava le poppe e il conno, e le dava colle mani in su le natiche, e la baciava; ed ella così lui, e la mordeva, e poneva la sua gamba sopra la sua. Or ecco nel baciare egli la volta con le reni in giù con il volto verso il cielo, poi le montò sopra il corpo, e con le mani aprendole un poco le labbra del conno, vi pose dentro il suo palo ritto; allora fra me stupefatta, aspettava che costei gridasse e dubitava che non morisse; quando la veggo legare ambe le gambe alle spalle di Federico, e colle mani gli aveva preso le natiche, e tirando cosi a sè, alzava il culo premendo le calcagna, quasi temendo che egli nol cavasse: dopo, menando l'uno e l'altro, ed anelando ella continuamente, diceva: Anima mia dolce, spingete pure che anch' io faccio, ed egli non poteva tanto spingere che più non paresse desiderare; alla fine ambidue menando con grandissima fretta, e con gemiti e con sospiri, distese le gambe e le braccia, rimasero pallidi e quasi fuor di loro. Allora, a dirti il vero, tenevo per certo che la Caterina fosse morta; ed ecco Federico che spiccato, ed ella come se fosse svegliata dal sonno, pigliava la sua camicia e gli rasciugava l'istrumento, il quale era diventato piccolo e rugoso, e non pareva più quello: poi baciava Federico nel viso, nelgi occhi, nelle spalle e per tutto, si chi io compresi ch'ella aveva avuto in ciò grandissimo piacere; onde mi nacque tanto desiderio di provare anch'io simil diletto, che quasi era venuta in rabbia, e tenevami le dita nel conno e fregava, e nella mente sempre rivolgeva come poteva fare ancor io trovarmi un giovane in braccio, e questa cosa tutta notte pensando, pervenni senza sonno fino alla mattina, nella quale la fortuna assai benevola a' miei desiri, apparecchiò qualche compenso.[8]

8. Ibid., pp. 87–90.

I saw Caterina, who had taken off her shirt and was nude and was looking to see if there were any fleas inside; on the other side, nude, Federico was on top of the bed on his back, and beyond his belly he had his erect thing, and it was so fat and long that it looked like a rabbit; while I was looking at it wondering to myself how much it had grown in four years, I said to myself: Oh my, she is so small, how can she receive so much work into herself? How can he possibly not tear her apart? and then thinking to myself, he will surely have to rub her as my aunt did me. Then I heard Federico say: Caterina come here: and she turned and seeing him in that state, said smiling: what do you want? to which he said: Come here if you like; and she put down the shirt and went there, and putting her hand on that column, said: aren't you ashamed to sit around like this? He said, come on kiss me; she kissed him, and bit him, and put her leg over his. All the while he was kissing her he turned her on her back with her face toward the sky, then mounted on top of her, and opening the lips of her cunt a little with his hands, stuck his erect pole in; meanwhile I was stupefied and waiting for her to scream and expecting her to die, when I saw her lift both her legs to Federico's shoulders, and she had taken his buttocks in her hands, and pulling herself so to him, lifted her ass by pressing her heels, as if fearing he would fall out of her: then, pressing both of them and panting continuously she said, My sweet soul, you push too as I am doing, and he could not have pushed as much as it seemed he wanted to; at the end both were panting very fast, and with sighs and moans, stretched out their arms and legs, both pale and almost outside themselves. Now, to tell you the truth, I was afraid that Caterina was dead for sure; and Federico was exposed, and as if she had just awakened from sleep, she took her shirt and wiped off his instrument which had become small and wrinkled, and no longer seemed what it had been before: then she kissed Federico on the face, on the eyes, on the shoulders, and everywhere, so that I realized that she had enjoyed doing it very much; thus such a great desire to try similar delights sprang up in me that I almost went mad, and putting my fingers in my cunt and rubbing, and all the while thinking how I could do more with a young man in my arms, and thinking about this all night, spent the entire night without sleep until morning, at which time fortune, a little more kind to my desires, prepared some compensation.

Aretino's extensive use of voyeurism was not lost on Franco, and the difference between the pupil's usage and that of the master in *Life of Nuns* is notable. While Aretino had Nanna describe the sexual activity in considerable detail, we noted that a comic element entered into the one early description with the musical terminology and the shaking furniture, all calculated to make us laugh. There was, then, a difference in our reactions as readers from the reaction of Nanna, who was viewing the action and who was led to masturbate as a result of the scene in front of her. Franco's description has some similarities with Aretino's; Maddalena is driven to masturbation by the scene that she sees. The sexual activity is presented with a directness and immediacy whose purpose is the arousal of the reader by involving him in seeing first the copulation and then Maddalena's reaction. We see the scene as Maddalena sees it, and she renders the scene for Giulia as she experienced it at the time. Franco seems to be striving for psychological realism in this scene. At the time of the events, Maddalena knows about the sexual relations of men and women only through what she has been told and shown by her sister and aunt; thus her shudder of fear at seeing an erect penis about to enter what she thinks is a small, tight vagina. Maddalena herself could have presented this scene comically, making much of her sexual naiveté, but Franco chooses to have Maddalena present the scene straight; she tells all to Giulia just as she experienced it then, and so she is reassured within the scene only when she sees that all has been pleasurable for Caterina. Any comedy that exists in the scene derives from the superior knowledge of the reader; it is not provided by the narrator. Franco's attempt at such psychological realism is unusual in Italian Renaissance literature, pornographic or otherwise.

That such an attempt should come in a pornographic work should not be surprising, however, since the pose of the pornographic writer is that he is presenting the real world, the way it really is, the way sex really operates in it. This is the fiction, the fantasy if you will, on which pornography is built; sex enters into and finally overwhelms the whole world, the world as we know it. That is what pornophiles want to believe. We know that the world of pornography is no more real than the world of any other literary construct, say the pastoral, but the pornographer would have us believe otherwise. This is not then, I think, psychological realism for its own sake or for the sake of effective characterization; it is psychological realism in the service of pornography, and it is a keynote of Franco's use of "realism" throughout the work. It is surely for this reason that Franco provides so much detail early in his narrative about specific family relations and particularized places. He would have us believe that all of this is happening here and now, in places we know with people we know, people who do such mundane things as check their shirts for fleas.

Soon after her voyeuristic and masturbatory episodes, Maddalena begins her own heterosexual life with Roberto, Federico's old friend. We are treated to descriptions of Maddalena and Roberto copulating in a number of positions, most of them of the standing or sitting variety, since they find a bedroom difficult to come by. Again it would seem that Franco has invested his story with realistic particulars. We are told that the family went to the country for the month of August and that sleeping quarters are crowded. The exact layout of the house and its adjacent shelter are given to us in great detail.[9] One is sorely tempted to argue for the existence of literary realism long before its reputed rise in the eighteenth century.[10] But again this is realistic detail in the service of pornography; the physical arrangements are specified merely so that we understand why the lovers are forced to positions that are exclusively of the standing or sitting variety (Maddalena eventually has a large chair stored in the unfurnished shelter where she and Roberto meet). No one, presumably, even in the world of pornography would *always* choose such positions. The "realistic" setting is a device for exploring the Renaissance obsession with positions. All is given to impress upon us the ardor of the lovers, the supremacy of the world of sexuality, a world where human beings will do anything in any place to satisfy their sexual appetites.[11] It may be that a psychological or social historian could make more of such details.[12] The constraints of space, the living together of extended families in single households, surely did present barriers to gratification in the world of Renaissance Italy; Franco's work provides a fantastic surmounting of those barriers. It is ever thus in the world of pornography. On any given day or night, in any given place, one can have sex.

Maddalena's early heterosexual life is most completely fulfilled when Caterina leaves home for a time, and Maddalena and Federico consummate an affair. The description of their intercourse fills page after page; always the positions are detailed elaborately in vulgar terms. Though Franco does employ some metaphors in his descriptions, sometimes referring to Federico's "key" that brings an "amorous delight," he still insists upon using the Italian equivalents of "fuck" and "cunt" as he elaborates on the positions, ever the staple of Renaissance pornography. Indeed one of Franco's shortcomings as a pornographer is the rapidity with which he moves the reader from one position to another without painting any one scene at length, so that his descriptions lose their pornographic impact. Too often he lapses into merely listing, ignoring the sensations involved. Franco's plan is clearly to provide descriptions of as many different positions as he can think of; thus the rapidity of his scenes, and the detailing of events leading quickly to orgasm. For

9. Ibid., pp. 86–87.

10. Ian Watt, *The Rise of the Novel* (1957; rpt. Berkeley and Los Angeles: Univ. of California Press, 1959), p. 18.

11. Marcus, defining pornotopia, describes the qualities of time and space; see especially pp. 271–77.

12. See Gaston Bachelard, *The Poetics of Space,* trans. Maria Jolas from 1958 French ed. (New York: Orion Press, 1964).

example, we discover that even Maddalena's menstrual period does not dampen the lovers' ardor for sexual activity, for they find new ways to please one another during that time, and Franco finds many positions to describe. Federico, desperate in not having had Maddalena for several days, visits her

> e così ragionando, baciandomi e toccandomi, l'avea duro come un legno, me lo fece toccare, e talora me lo poneva fra le coscie, e talvolta presso le poppe, talchè io vedendo la grandissima voglia che aveva, ebbi di lui compassione e mi contentai che me lo tenesse fra le mammelle, ed egli premendo or l'una or l'altra con le mani, tenendole strette presso le sua faccenda, e menandola per quelle ora in su ed ora in giù, mi sentii bagnato tutto il collo, il quale asciugato, ebbi piacere di aver mitigato in quel modo alquanto il suo ardore, e dopo molti baci e regionamenti ci addormentammo. Ed a caso tenendogli volte le reni, non essendo lo ardente desiderio diminuito, levando il panno di lino che per nettezza in quel luogo teniamo, me lo pose fra le natiche, non già nel conno comme le oltre volte fece, ma nell' altro buco ivi appresso, il quale per esser molle per la umidità del vicino, facilmente lo ricevè, il che sentendo io, non dissi nulla, ma lo lasciai fare, perciocchè non solamente non mi fece male, ma oltre al mio pensiero qualche diletto mi recò; per il che un'altra volta, avanti che si levasse, volle farmelo nel medesimo luogo, ed io di ogni cosa gli compiacqui. e tre notti che mi durò quel male, volle che sempre dormissimo insieme, onde non solamente fra le mammelle, ma fra le coscie, fra le gambe e sotto le braccia mel fece.[13]

and so talking, kissing, and touching me, his prick hard as wood, he made me touch it, and sometimes he placed it between my thighs, and sometimes against my breasts, so that seeing the extreme desire he had, I had compassion for him and contented myself with his putting it between my breasts, and he squeezed first one and then the other with his hands, and holding them close against his prick and rubbing against it up and down, I felt all my neck wet; and having dried it, I was happy to have allayed in that manner some of his ardor, and after many kisses and talking we went to sleep. And by chance turning my back to him, his ardent desire not being diminished, lifting the cloth that we wear in that place for cleanliness, he put it between my buttocks, not in the cunt as he had the other times, but in the other hole near there, which being wet on account of the humidity of its neighbor, easily received it, and feeling it, I said nothing, but let him do it, because not only did it not hurt, but instead it brought some delight to my thoughts; for this reason another time, before he got up, he wanted to do it to me in the same place, and I was happy to do what he wanted, and for the three nights which that malady lasted, he always wanted to sleep with me, and so not just between the breasts, but between the thighs, between the legs, and under the arms he did it to me.

13. Franco, *Puttana Errante,* pp. 118–19.

Once more it might seem that we are in a world of realistic detail, for it is surely rare, even in works of pornography, to intrude matters like menstrual periods into the world of sexuality. But again, all is done so that Franco can describe more positions, more ways of satisfying the sexual drive. This is what is relentlessly pursued here; there is always a road to satisfaction; one can always find some position that will lead to orgasm, and obviously Franco did not feel himself limited to orifices in exploring those roads. His emphasis is on the variety of positions, the different ways one can achieve orgasm rather than on the intensity of any one orgasm.

Franco finally moves the plot to the point where Maddalena must make her way in the world, and she does so as a courtesan. In recounting her adventures here, Franco stabs at the clergy through Maddalena's account of her experiences with a canon. Maddalena occasionally favored a young man who was handsome but poor, and as the canon had his eye on the same young man, he arranged and paid for an evening for the three of them. Needless to say, this *ménage à trois* brings even more elaborate descriptions of positions. Maddalena scornfully states, however, "nè mai quel traditore di canonico me lo volse porre nel conno"[14] [never did that traitor of a canon want to put it in my cunt].

The dialogue comes to a close with a recapping and naming by Giulia of the thirty-five positions for sexual intercourse that Maddalena has described in the course of her narrative and some final advice by Maddalena to Giulia on how to please a man.[15] The listing of positions serves to underline once again Franco's preoccupation with this aspect of sexual activity. It is certainly the most limiting factor in his pornography. All in all, Franco's work is remarkable for the Italian Renaissance in the single-mindedness of its sexuality; it is obviously written to arouse and please the salacious reader, and that purpose remains at the forefront at all times, even if Franco is often less than successful in achieving his purpose. The work seems carefully calculated to play on all the typical aspects and interests of Renaissance erotica, especially in its concern for positions; and in its exclusion of virtually all subjects and interests other than sexual ones, it is unique. It is unadulterated pornography; it is, as I have stated, as close as we come to Marcus's pornotopia, and a steady diet of such texts would undoubtedly lead one to formulate a thesis about the ways in which pornography is not lit-

14. Ibid., p. 132.
15. Ibid., p. 138, for example: "Il *decimonono* è quando l'uomo giace col corpo in su e la donna gli sta sopra, e questo si chiama *alla giannetta*" [The nineteenth occurs when the man lies with his body up and the woman sits on top of him, and this is called the *giannetta* (literally, in the mode of the Spanish mare)].

erature.[16] Of the characteristics Marcus lists for pornotopia two, the single intention of the author (arousal of the reader) and the extensive use of taboo words, seem especially applicable to Franco's work. But when we consider that Franco wrote early in the sixteenth century, that single intention of the author (seen especially in the use of realistic detail in setting and psychology for pornographic purposes) and that insistence on taboo words can be seen as innovative and radical.

Confusion about *La Puttana Errante* has existed for some time because there is a poem by the same title, composed by another of Aretino's secretaries, Lorenzo Veniero.[17] Veniero was no vagabond, hoping to make a living by his pen; he was from an aristocratic Venetian family, and he seems to have followed the literary life for a while for the pure enjoyment of it all.[18]

Besides his poetic *Puttana Errante,* Veniero wrote a poem entitled *La Zaffetta.* This is a work more interesting for its historical and folk aspects than for its literary and pornographic aspects. There was an historical Angela Zaffetta: she was a noted courtesan in Venice, especially highly esteemed by Aretino, who once wrote her a remarkable letter of praise.[19] Aretino, "the Teller of Truth," lauds her in his letter as the best of courtesans, one who uses none of the wiles that Aretino the pornographer had Nanna teach Pippa; more than anyone else, he tells her, "you know how to put the mask of decency upon the face of lust, gaining by your wisdom and discretion both riches and praise."[20] In his notes to Flora's edition of Aretino's letters, Alessandro del Vita characterizes this letter as being in the style of the *Ragionamenti* (a work which he sees as being unique in Renaissance literature). This seems to me an acute observation. While the letter is characterized by the exaggeration typical of Aretino in his praise of someone, the elaboration in the letter is all on what Angela is *not*. "You do not," he says, "use your wiles—which are the essence of a harlot's trade—to betray men,

16. Marcus, pp. 280–89; chapters 2 and 3 of this study call for a modification of Marcus's developmental theory, I believe.

17. Scholars favorable to Aretino have long looked upon the prose work as a dubious part of the canon, but attribution to Franco is still disputed. See Foxon, pp. 27–30; and Legman, *The Horn Book,* p. 91. Also see Alessandro Luzio, *Pietro Aretino Nei Primi Suoi Anni A Venezia* (Turin: Ermanno Loescher, 1888), p. 45 and pp. 15ff. See also Aretino, *Lettere,* p. 1066. I have not been able to locate a noncensored version of the poem.

18. Chubb, *Aretino,* pp. 272–75.

19. Angela del Moro was called *La Zafetta* because she was the daughter of a sergeant of the law, *un birro,* or in Venetian dialect, *un zaffo.*

20. Chubb, *Letters,* pp. 120–21. The Italian text can be found in Aretino, *Lettere,* pp. 366–68.

but rather with such skill that he who spends his money on you, swears he is the gainer." You are not suspicious, he continues, and you do not "rowel the flanks of gullible suitors with the spurs of your serving maids whom you have taught to swear that you do not eat, drink, sleep or find any peace on their account." You are not ready with tears at any moment, he says; and lying, envy, and slander "do not keep your mind and your tongue in a constant turmoil."[21] The detailing of all the practices that Angela does not engage in of course reminds us of all the wiles Nanna had instructed Pippa to use. In this letter we see Aretino's ability to create a world, to detail it, to give it life by describing human actions. So successful is Aretino in separating Angela from vices that he can assure us that she caresses virtue and adores the virtuous![22]

Veniero's poem shows us a different kind of courtesan from Aretino's letter, one who two-timed a customer who in turn took his revenge on her in the form of a *trent-uno,* a thirty-one or gang-bang, of the kind we saw in Aretino's dialogues. The main business of the poem has little to recommend it. Veniero says that he is writing *La Zaffetta* in order, among other things, to show that Aretino did not write the verses of the *Puttana Errante.*[23] The poem is thus of bibliographical importance, for it helps in establishing the authorship of the poetic *Puttana Errante.* Veniero also makes a jocular reference to Aretino that places Aretino squarely at the head of these writers of pornography and shows that his secretaries considered themselves Aretines.[24]

There is one final work of note in this pornographic tradition by Aretino's followers. Entitled *La Tariffa delle Puttane di Venegia,* probably written by Antonio Cavallino, it is a poem listing the cost and qualities of the various whores of Venice.[25] The catalogue is rather straightforward; there are stories thrown in to keep up the interest of the foreigner to whom this information is being given by a gentleman of Venice, but the stories are not much more compelling than the list of whores. Several points should be made about the work, however.

There is an introductory sonnet that is a close adaptation of the introductory sonnet of Aretino's *sonetti lussuriosi.* The adaptation makes direct reference to Aretino and his dialogues and sets the purpose of the work:

21. Chubb, *Letters,* pp. 121–22.
22. According to del Vita, even after the thirty-one, Angela was able to count among her protectors Cardinal Ippolito de' Medici; Aretino, *Lettere,* p. 1083.
23. Lorenzo Veniero, *La Zaffetta* (Paris, 1861 from the 1531 edition), p. 6.
24. Ibid., p. 2.
25. Aretino, *Lettere,* p. 1040.

Questo è un libro d'altro che Sonetti,
Di Capitoli d'Egloghe, e Canzone,
Qui il Sannazaro e'l Bembo non compone
Nè liquidi christalli, nè fioretti;

Qui il Marignan non fa madrigaletti,
Nè inni il Rosso, che sì ben gli espone;
Nè v'ha di cavaliero o di pedone
L'Ariosto a cantar con versi eletti;

Qui l'Aretin non pon sopra le stelle
Il suo gran Re, o in queste rime mie
Si ragiona di Monache e Donzelle;

Ma de le puttanesche hierarchie,
Di Ruffe, e per qual prezzo e queste e quelle
Vi prestino al chiavar tutte le vie.

    In fin le son pazzie
A farsi schifi de i dolci bocconi:
E chi legger non vuol, Dio gliel perdoni![26]

This is not a book of sonnets, chapters, eclogues and songs: here Sannazaro and Bembo don't write either liquid crystals or sweet flowers. Here Marignan does not compose madrigals, nor does Rosso create, who knows well how to set things forth; Ariosto has neither horsemen or footmen to sing about with his well chosen verses; here Aretino does not place his great king above the stars, and in my rhymes one does not discourse on nuns and ladies, but of the hierarchy of whores, of bought women, and for what price these and those will charge to fuck in all ways. Finally, they are crazy who scoff at such good pieces, and he who does not wish to read, may God forgive him.

Just as Aretino had declared the difference of his erotic sonnets from traditional Renaissance literary fare, so does Cavallino in his opening imitation of Aretino's sonnet. He goes on to point out the difference of his work from that of his master's, for the social class of his subject will ostensibly be lower.

In the address of the author to his lady, Cavallino tackles the problem of vulgar words:

Ma se alcun altro vi dirà che qui si passa di grossi i termini dell'honestà, col spesso nominare d'un K, d'un P e d'un Q, voi, che da voi stessa lo sapete, dite loro, che essendo queste le proprie arme e le instrumenti delle Puttane, fu egli di necessità a scriverli, anzi sarebbe state vitio a tacergli.[27]

26. Antonio Cavallino, *La Tariffa delle Puttane Di Venegia* (Paris: Isidore Liseux, 1883), p. 2.
27. Ibid., p. 6. K, P, and Q are abbreviations for cazzo, potta, and culo.

But if someone should tell you that here we go beyond the boundaries of honesty, with the naming of a K, of a P and of a Q, you, who know this thing well, tell them that these being the proper arms and instruments of the whores, he was forced to write about them, and it would have been a fault not to talk about them.

The popular insistence on vulgar language is neatly handled here under the name of authenticity, and Cavallino employs it throughout.

In the poem proper, the foreigner states his case directly at the outset:

> Ecco una enigma: Io vorrei San Fotino,
> Far sacrificio, e s'io nol faccio adesso,
> Io mi mangio i coglioni, e mi ruino.[28]

Here is an enigma: I would like to make a sacrifice to Saint Fucking, and if I don't do it now, I shall eat my balls and ruin myself.

There is very little subtlety to this statement, and the foreigner objects when the gentleman tries to warn him of the wiles and evils of the whores:

> Deh! lasciate le prediche in buon punto
> Ai Frati, che pur c'habbiano a gridarci,
> Di cio che fanno hanno levato il punto.
>
> . . . .
>
> Nè qui s'ha à disputar di theologia,
> Ma di fotter al dritto et al riverso
> E de la puttanesca monarchia.[29]

Bah! Leave the sermons to the friars at a good point, because even if they yell at us about what they've done, they have raised the point. . . . We don't have to discuss theology here, but fucking in front and behind and the monarchy of whores.

So the gentleman begins, invoking the aid of Veniero's style. Cavallino will occasionally try to characterize a whore through his description, as he does with Bianzifiore Negro:

> Se Bianzifiore Negro chiaverete
> Premer paravvi una vesica vuota,
> E nuotando in gran mar morir di sete.[30]

If you will fuck black Bianzifiore, it will seem you strain on an empty bladder, and die of thirst while swimming in a great sea.

28. Ibid., p. 12.
29. Ibid., p. 16.
30. Ibid., p. 34.

But more often than not he does little more than list:

> Lucina Ferro volentier s'imbrocca
> Per mezzo scudo, o vogli drieto o avanti,
> Vada pur cazzo come stral da cocca.
>   Marina Stella, inferno degli amanti,
> Per un scudo suol dar quanto ha di buono,
> E fa col cul maravigliosi incanti.[31]

Lucina Ferro will willingly embrace for half a scudo, and from either the front or the back will take a cock like an arrow from a bow. Marina Stella, hell for lovers, for one scudo will give away her best and do marvelous things with her ass.

It is rather dreary business, failing as pornography or anything else one might try to make of it. The poem ends on a rather anticlimactic and atypical note; the foreigner stops the account because he says he has decided to hate all whores!

In summary, the imitative works of Aretino's followers, works dealing primarily with the lives and ways of whores (in other words, doing exactly what the word "pornography" means literally) are similar not only in their subject matter but, with the exception of the extended prose in Franco's *Puttana Errante,* in their manner as well. All of the works show an interest in positions, all of them insist upon vulgar words; rarely do any of them deal with any subjects other than sexual ones. They are the works of not very inspired imitators, but they show us that such men thought creations in the pornographic mode would help them make their way in the literary world; pornography was a way to notoriety at least.

While a major part of the popular erotica in the Italian Renaissance consists of works like the ones discussed above for which Aretino's dialogues stand as the inspiration, there was another form of erotica for which Aretino would also seem to have provided the model—the lascivious sonnet.

Niccolo Franco published a collection of sonnets in 1541, with subsequent editions in 1546 and 1548.[32] Ironically, these were primarily poems written against Aretino (we would classify them as obscene). Added to them was a work Franco called his *Priapea,* a quasi-imitation

---

31. Ibid., p. 46.

32. The publishing history of Franco's works is well covered in Carlo Simiani's *Nicolo Franco, La Vita e Le Opere* (Turin and Rome: L. Roux, 1894), pp. 35ff; and in Grendler, pp. 38–49, 215–21.

of the classical body of poems entitled *Priapeia,* poems of disputed
authorship (probably primarily by Ovid and his imitators) about the
god of gardens, fertility, and constant erection—Priapus.[33] The classical
Priapeia enjoyed a great popularity in the Renaissance; there were
twenty-two editions of the work before 1517, when the circle of the
publisher Aldus Manutius brought out its critical edition. Edgar Wind
notes that "according to the statutes of the Aldine Academy, editorial
labors were to be combined with convivial amusement, and no subject
was more suited for this dual exercise than a study" of the *Priapeia*.[34]
Clearly the circumstances surrounding such an editorial labor would
place this work within the "learned" tradition of erotica as it has been
defined in this study. But the poems within the collection itself are
another matter, and the service to which the imitative work by Franco
was put places it more appropriately in the popular tradition. In the
classical collection we find some poems addressed to Priapus, but more
often than not Priapus speaks, threatening those who would steal from
his garden with sodomy, irrumation, and straight heterosexual intercourse. The tersest example:

> Paedicare puer, moneo: futuere puella:
> Barbatum fuerm tertia poena manet.

I warn thee, my lad, thou wilt be sodomised; thee, my girl, I shall futter;
for the thief who is bearded, a third punishment remains.[35]

Even though the writers of Renaissance erotica like to stress their originality, as Aretino did in his address to his monkey, they also allied
themselves with the great poets of antiquity who wrote bawdy verses.
There was, after all, a tradition, and Renaissance writers of erotica
wanted to have it both ways. On the one hand they felt the need to
stress their originality (and thus their difference from Renaissance humanists who imitated the classics slavishly); on the other they desired
the protection and prestige of being associated with great writers who
had written erotica. Franco's *Priapea,* rather than being an updating of
the classical collection, was primarily a means of attacking Aretino.
Leaving Aretino aside for the moment, however, since I wish to place

33. See Edgar Wind, *Bellini's Feast of the Gods: A Study of Venetian Humanism* (Cambridge, Mass.: Harvard Univ. Press, 1948), pp. 32–33; and Richmond Thomason, *The
Priapea and Ovid: A Study of the Language of the Poems* (Nashville, Tenn.: George Peabody
College for Teachers, 1931).
34. Wind, *Bellini's Feast,* p. 33.
35. The citations and translations are from the edition of the *Priapeia* (with notes)
printed by the Erotika Biblion Society in 1888, pp. 16–17.

Franco's attack on him within the context of literary quarrels, we find that Franco singles out a number of other targets for his obscene jibes in these poems. In the *Priapea* Franco asserts early in the collection through Priapus (as in the classical collection, Priapus speaks in some poems, in others he is addressed) that he will use vulgar language; no flowery euphemisms of Boccaccio or metaphors for him:

> Non vorrei, perch'i sia si liberazzo,
>   Alcun di voi mi pensi lapidare,
>   Perche ne gli orti miei si puo ben fare
>   Doue non e crianza da palazzo.
> La Potta io chiamo Potta, il Cazzo Cazzo,
>   E' il Culo Culo, & questo e il vero andare
>   Perche da furbo non si dee parlare
>   Se con furbi non siamo, e per solazzo.
> Anzi vi dico, che se mai mi tocca
>   Doue fra donne vassi ragionando,
>   Lascio al Boccaccio la sua filostocca.
> Et senza cerimonie parlando,
>   A punto come viemmi in su la bocca,
>   A voi donne da fottere dimando.[36]

I wouldn't like it, because I am so free, if one of you thought to stone me, because in my gardens one can do everything he wants, for the manners of the palace are not here. The cunt I call cunt, the cock, cock, and the ass, ass, and this is the correct way to speak because one cannot speak slyly if he is among the sly, and for sport. And I tell you, if it would happen to me to reason with women, I would leave it to Boccaccio with his long string of words; and speaking without ceremony, in the way it comes to my mouth, I will ask you ladies to fuck.

As one might expect in a work that purports to be imitative, there are a good many more classical and mythological allusions in Franco's collection than one finds in Aretino's work, and in spite of the state-ment in the sonnet just cited, Franco does take advantage of his garden setting to play upon the sexual implications of the various fruits and vegetables, just as Berni and his friends had done. We find sonnets on peaches, beans, and figs, for example. A few of the poems do imitate works in the classical collection, but more often than not Franco does not imitate the general situation of the classical *Priapeia* with Priapus as the god of gardens.[37] Many of Franco's poems merely involve invi-

---

36. Franco, *Delle Rime di M. Nicolo Franco Contro Pietro Aretino, et de la Priapea del medesimo* (London, 1887, from the 1548 edition), p. lxx[v].

37. In Latin *Priapeia*, pp. 10–11; in Franco, *Delle Rime*, p. lxxi[r].

tations to women to enjoy his cock. There are several poems that do show Franco capable of real bawdy, however, capable of adapting other forms to the sonnet within the context of erotica. The best of these is a variation of a riddle in praise of cocks:

> Gran cosa e il cazzo se'l vogliam guardare.
>   Che non ha piedi, & entra, & esce fuore.
>   Ch' e disarmato, & ha cosi gran core.
>   Che non ha taglio, & basti a'nsanguinare.
> Gran cosa e poi, e gran miracol pare,
>   Ch'e senza orecchi, e sente ogni rumore.
>   Che non ha naso, e piacegli l'odore.
>   Che non haue occhi, e vede doue andare.
> Gran cosa, & ben da croniche, e da annali,
>   Che non ha mani, e cerca di ferire.
>   Che non ha gambe, e vuole gli stiuali.
> Ma cosa piu mirabile a sentire,
>   Ch'entrando in corpo a furie infernali
>   Et sano & saluo se ne sappia vscire.[38]

A cock is a great thing if we want to look at it. It doesn't have feet but goes in and out. It is disarmed, and it has great courage. It doesn't have an edge, but is sufficient to cause blood. It is a great thing, then, and it seems a great miracle because without ears it hears every noise, because it has no nose and yet likes the smell. It has no eyes, but sees where to go. It is a great thing, something worthy of chronicles and annals, because it has no hands but tries to wound; because it doesn't have legs and yet longs for boots. But the most remarkable thing is that entering in the body with infernal fury, it knows how to get out safe and sound.

If one comes at this sonnet having read even marginally in structural analyses of riddles, one can appreciate Franco's artistry more fully. Robert Georges and Alan Dundes define a riddle as "a traditional verbal expression which contains one or more descriptive elements, a pair of which may be in opposition; the referent of the elements is to be guessed."[39] In one sense, of course, Franco has ruined the poem as riddle since he specifies the referent at the outset—a cock.[40] The first

38. Franco, *Delle Rime,* p. lxxvii^v.
39. Robert A. Georges and Alan Dundes, "Toward a Structural Definition of the Riddle," *Journal of American Folklore* 76 (1963): 113. For a thin overview of riddles, see Mark Bryant, *Riddles Ancient and Modern* (London: Hutchinson, 1983).
40. I have been able to locate no specific source for Franco's version of this riddle. Michele De Filippis in his study *The Literary Riddle in Italy to the End of the Sixteenth Century,* University of California Publications in Modern Philology, no. 34 (Berkeley and Los Angeles: Univ. of California Press, 1948), p. 4, omits any discussion of Franco "for obvious reasons." There are numerous riddles on the penis. See the "male organ" in the De Filippis index and the category of obscene riddles in *Anglo-Saxon Riddles of the Exeter Book,* trans. Paul F. Baum (Durham, N.C.: Duke University Press, 1963).

line of the sonnet might lead us to think that we are going to get either
a straight encomium or a paradoxical encomium (the latter is less a
possibility, certainly, in a collection of poems focused on Priapus). But
by the second line, Franco begins playing off a series of contradictive
elements that are a standard feature of many riddles. It does not have
feet, but it goes in and out; it is not armed, but it has great courage;
it does not have a cutting edge, but it can cause blood. What Franco
does is reverse what would be the expected pattern of the riddle where
the elements might be posed as questions: what goes in and out but
has no feet, what has great courage and is not armed, what causes
blood but has no cutting edge? Further, Franco gives the first part of
his riddle as a negative statement—it is this negation that should make
the function of the second part impossible. A comparison with
Georges' and Dundes's examples illustrates this process best. They state
that "the privational contradictive opposition results when the second
of a pair of descriptive elements is a denial of a logical or natural
attribute of the first."[41] They give as examples: something has an ear
and cannot hear (ear of corn); something has a nose and can't smell
(teapot); what has legs, but cannot walk (chair). In Franco's poem the
first element in the pair is given as a negative ("has no feet") and the
second part is given as a positive function ("goes in and out"). That
the function is positive whereas the attribute is negative is important,
for it makes the performance of the cock all the more remarkable; it is
a "great thing."

The second quatrain in the octave holds to this same pattern, and it
continues through the first three lines of the sestet. The poem concludes
with a causal contradictive. Here the second pair of descriptive elements
("comes out safe and sound") "explicitly denies the expected or natural
consequence of the action contained in the first descriptive element"
("entering in the body with infernal fury").[42] This contains the crucial
element of time, one thing being necessary prior to the other. Behind
Franco's use of the riddle lies his use of a central metaphor, something
Georges and Dundes note as first set forth by Aristotle.[43] The implied
comparison is obviously of a penis with man, and Franco imitates
Aretino at his best in carrying his conceit as far as he possibly can. In
the comparison it is man who is found wanting, for with so much less,
the penis can do so much more. While part of the effectiveness of the
comparison is carried through the sensory abilities of both penis and

41. Georges and Dundes, p. 115.
42. Ibid., p. 115.
43. Ibid., p. 116.

man, the metaphorical comparisons have even more force as we see the traditional sex-as-warfare theme played out, culminating in the heroic ability of the penis to escape infernal powers safe and sound.

A number of verses in Franco's *Priapea* are directed at the pope and the vices of the clergy; and these biting, often more obscene than humorous poems, along with some later scabrous anticlerical writings, were eventually to cost Franco his life.[44] One example of this type of poem should suffice. In it we see Franco do exactly what we would expect, accuse the clergy of buggery. Franco is always extreme, however; he has to single out the Pope for his gibes:

> Pappa, per la presente ti saluto,
>   Et ti mando di Ruche due cistelle,
>   Di quelle tenerelle tenerelle,
>   Di che piu volte gia ti se pasciuto.
> Ne senza gran proposito ho voluto
>   Mandarti di quest' herbe, come quelle,
>   Che son parenti de le pempinelle,
>   E fanno il cazzo tisico, e nerbuto.
> Che il douer vuole, e gia non e peccato,
>   Che tutti ci debbiamo ricordare
>   Del cazzo per hauerlo sempre a lato.
> Et che cosa Pontefici han da fare
>   Quando il collegio loro e feriato,
>   Se non mangiare, & bere, & buggierare?[45]

Pope, I greet you for the present, and I am sending you two sprigs of rocket, the super tender sort you have already fed on several times. Nor was it without good reason that I wanted to send you some of these greens, like those that are related to the vines and make the puny cock vigorous; because duty requires, and it is not a sin, for we should all remember to have a cock always at hand. And what else have the popes got to do when their college is not in session if not eat, drink, and bugger?

The major target throughout Franco's poems remains Aretino, however, and Franco's attack is carried off in the most obscene fashion imaginable. As I have mentioned, the obscenity in this attack belongs

44. For an account of Franco's problems with the Inquisition see Angelo Mercati, *I Costituti di Nicolo Franco (1568–1570) dinanzi L'Inquisizione di Roma* (Vatican City, 1955) and Simiani, *Franco*. The *Priapea* played only a minor role in Franco's ultimate demise. He had been jailed a short time for these verses, and the work was on the *Index*, but it was his later journal entitled *Avisi*, published in 1563 with continued attacks on Pope Paul IV, a target in other satires of Franco's, that led to his hanging in 1570. Also see Grendler, pp. 47–49.

45. Franco, *Delle Rime*, p. lxxvi[r].

in the context of the literary quarrel, for there was a tradition of insult, often obscene, between literary figures well established in the Renaissance long before Franco ever took up his pen against Aretino; further, Franco's attack on Aretino was only one of several to rage about the Scourge of Princes. The use of obscene insults in literary battles was a significant development in Renaissance writing, both in Italy and later in England. An important quarrel involving two literary figures earlier in the Renaissance engaged none other than Poggio Bracciolini. In his *Life of Poggio Bracciolini* William Shepherd has translated one of Poggio's letters attacking Filelfo Filelfi:

> Thou stinking he-goat! thou horned monster! thou malevolent detractor! thou father of lies and author of discord! May the divine vengeance destroy thee as an enemy of the virtuous, a parricide who endeavourest to ruin the wise and good by lies and slanders, and the most false and foul imputations. If thou must be contumelious, write thy satires against the suitors of thy wife—discharge the putridity of thy stomach upon those who adorn thy forehead with horns.[46]

While not exactly obscene, Poggio's attack hits Filelfo where the Italian male is most vulnerable, in his sexual pride, as Poggio offers the ultimate insult, the cuckold's horns. This kind of quarrel between two humanists might seem to be better categorized as "learned" erotica, given the authors and the audiences of such works, but while literary quarrels continued to be waged by the leading humanists in Italy, they were also quickly adopted by the popular writers, who added a great deal more obscenity in their vernacular works. Franco's attack on Aretino is a case in point.

The reasons for Franco's split with Aretino and subsequent attack are fairly well agreed upon. In 1538 a *Life of Aretino* supposedly by Francesco Berni (by then dead) appeared in print.[47] The book was an obscene exposé of Aretino's life and works. It was almost surely the work of Franco, hoping to make it on his own in the literary world.[48]

46. Shepherd, p. 252.
47. Berni did write a poem against Aretino in which he referred to Aretino's sisters as the pride of an Arezzo brothel. See Berni, *Rime Facete,* pp. 68–69; and Chubb, *Aretino,* p. 198.
48. See Chubb, *Aretino,* pp. 285–307; and Francesco Berni, *Vita di Pietro Aretino* (Milan: G. Daelli, 1864). Besides the 1864 edition, there is an expurgated edition done in 1888 in Turin. We find in this work such items as the reason for Aretino's name, "Dicesi che la madre la notte innanzi sognò partorir un otro di vino, il che forse è stato cagione ch'egli si sia chiamato di- vino" (p. 7; references are to the 1864 Milan edition) [They say that his mother the night before dreamt of giving birth to a container of wine, which may be the reason he is called di - vine (of the wine)]. We are told that in the

A rift was opened that was never to be closed; indeed Ambrogio degli
Eusebui, loyal to his master, went so far as to assault Franco with a
knife for his troubles. Franco's next attack upon Aretino came in his
verses. Some of these poems are addressed to famous friends of Aretino, asking them to withdraw their friendship; no fewer than eleven
are directed to Titian, for example. In most of the poems, however,
Franco attacks Aretino directly. His railings are obscene, schoolboy-
like insults. He makes fun of Aretino's diminishing cock; he calls him
a buggerer and cock-sucker; and he calls Aretino's sister a whore. An
example:

> Aretin, chi ti nomina ignorante
>   Ne mente per la gola, e se si pone
>   Cura a quel che tu sai, mai Cicerone
>   Cose non seppe che sien tali e tante.
> Tu prima sai ben 'esser furfante,
>   Tu sai dir ch'ogni Principe e beccone,
>   Tu sai che tua sorella e' vn puttanone,
>   Tu sai con tutti far il buon brigante.
> Tu sai a compiacenza ruffinare,
>   Tu sai fingendo vn santo esser vn ghiotto,
>   Tu sai senza vergogna buggerare.
> Tu sai mangiare vn cazzo e crudo e cotto,
>   Tu sai ne la mal'hora tanto fare,
>   Che pazzo e ben chi non ti chiamo dotto.[49]

Aretino, he who calls you ignorant certainly lies, because if one would think
what you know, he would realize that not even Cicero knew so many things
and so much. You know well that you are a rascal, you know how to say
that all Princes are cuckolds, you know that your sister is a big whore, you
know how to be a good rogue. You know how to procure anytime, you

---

dialogues Pippa is really Aretino's sister and Nanna his mother, that Pietro has cuckolded
the printer Francesco Marcolini, and we are given a description of Pietro in bed with
Perina Riccia (one of his loves) and Polo Bartolini (her husband): "Ivi Pietro, appoggiatala
al letto, la chiavò nella potta e nel culo; ma sopra tutto gli piacque il suo culo (ed in
ogni modo il culo è più dolce) perchè quelle chiappe ti tocchino il corpo, a tal che le
fanno andare in angoscia. Dormivano tutti tre in un letto; Polo chiavava Pietro, e Pietro
Perina; Pietro chiavava Polo, e Polo Perina, la quale, ingorda de' cazzi, apriva il culo e la
potta a ciascuno" (p. 28) [Here Pietro, putting her on the bed, fucks her in the cunt and
in the ass-hole; but above all he likes the ass-hole (and in any case the ass-hole is sweeter)
because those buttocks touch your body in such a way as to make you go into distress.
All three slept in one bed; Polo fucked Pietro, and Pietro Perina; Pietro fucked Polo, and
Polo Perina, who, filled with cocks, opened her ass-hole and her cunt to each]. Note
that Franco tries to make the work seem like Berni's by having him say that the anus is
the sweetest place for copulation.
49. Franco, *Delle Rime,* p. ix^v.

know how to pretend to be a saint instead of a greedy fellow, you know how to deceive without any shame. You know how to eat a raw or cooked cock, you know how to take advantage of a bad situation, therefore he who doesn't consider you wise, must be crazy.

On the one hand, this poem is like many in the classical *Priapeia* in that the acts Aretino is accused of committing are those threatened by Priapus on thieves in the garden. But of course, Franco is not threatening action but accusing a well-known writer of having committed those acts. This is obscenity with a vengeance, and it is certainly not inappropriate to say that this sonnet reminds one of the obscene insults of schoolboys. Before we saw Franco adapt the riddle to sonnet form; here he transforms the obscene insult, whose oral forms are certainly not far removed from the text, into literary invective. There is a sense in which this sonnet is a form of paradoxical encomium, for Franco does praise Aretino, but he praises him for the most base and vile acts. Folklorists who have studied verbal dueling rhymes and insults have noted general characteristics that have application here.[50] The analysis of Dundes et al. of Turkish boys' dueling rhymes is particularly enlightening. One of the principles of the game is to force one's opponent into a female, passive role.

> This may be done by defining the opponent or his mother or sister as a wanton sexual receptacle. If the male opponent is thus defined, it is usually by means of casting him as a submissive anus, an anus which must accept the brunt of the verbal duelist's attacking phallus. A more indirect technique is to disparage or threaten the opponent's mother or sister, which is a serious attack upon his male honor. Thus the victim either has to submit to phallic aggression himself or else watch helplessly as phallic aggression is carried out upon his female extensions, his mother or sister.[51]

Surely this is what Franco does here; he calls Aretino's sister a whore; he calls Aretino a buggerer, and worse, he accuses him of being the recipient of homosexual action—a sucker of all kinds of cocks.

Franco brings his sonneteering attack on Aretino even closer to an oral situation in the sonnet that follows:

50. See the articles by John Dollard, "The Dozens: Dialectic of Insult," and Roger Abrahams, "Playing the Dozens," reprinted in *Mother Wit from the Laughing Barrel,* ed. Alan Dundes (Englewood Cliffs, N.J.: Prentice-Hall, 1973) and Millicent R. Ayoub and Stephen A. Barnett, "Ritualized Verbal Insult in White High School Culture," *Journal of American Folklore* 78 (1965): 336–44; and especially see Alan Dundes et al., "The Strategy of Turkish Boys' Verbal Dueling Rhymes," in *Essays in Folkloristics* (Dehli: Folklore Institute, 1978).

51. Dundes, et al., "The Strategy," p. 73.

Aretin, che dirai di quel che io dico?
   Dirai forse ch'io dico la bugia
   Se t'appongo in infamia, che sia
   Il cazzo a la tua bocca tanto amico?
Se pur vuoi dir ch'io parli da nimico,
   Come non prendi la tua diceria?
   Parla su, fa che s'oda in ogni via
   Che tal mostro non sei sporco e' impudico.
Non ne vedi il dishonor che e troppo espresso?
   Che cosa t'impedisce il fauellare
   Onde risponder non ti fia permesso?
Ecco ch'e vero, ne me'l puoi negare,
   Hor lodato sia Dio che pur adesso
   Il cazzo hai in bocca che non puoi parlare.[52]

Aretino, what will you say about my statements? You will say, perhaps, that I am a liar, since I bring shame on you, because cock is such a friend to your mouth? If you want to say that I speak in this way being your enemy, why don't you begin your long discourse. Speak then, make it heard in every street that you are not such a dirty and immodest monster. Can't you see the dishonor that is so evident? What hinders you, is it the language which keeps you from speaking? See, it's true, you cannot deny it to me, for even now, blessed by God, you have the cock in your mouth so that you can't even speak.

Here Franco imagines his adversary as present; there is no false praise in this sonnet as he assails him. The humor of the sonnet depends on our being convinced of the dramatic situation, since it turns on Aretino's inability to answer. This is a contest with both combatants present; the reading audience replaces the crowd that attends in the oral tradition. Franco effects the perfect put-down. Not only does Aretino stand accused of being a cock-sucker, he loses the game of exchanging insults since his mouth is full. He is a loser as a human being given his perverse sexual habits, nothing but a receptacle; and perhaps even more cutting, he is a loser as a poet, he is verbally impotent as well. He gets no retort; he must accept, in Dundes's terms, "The brunt of the verbal duelist's attacking phallus." We have moved considerably beyond the grand insult of a Poggio, strong as it was in such a culture, to name-calling of the most obscene kind imaginable.

Niccolo Franco was not the only one of Aretino's secretaries to turn against him and attack him in print. Anton Francesco Doni, a man, as we have seen, willing to try anything to make his way in the world of letters, decided to try to gain one of Aretino's patrons as his own.

---

52. Franco, *Delle Rime,* p. xiᵛ.

Incurring the wrath of the Scourge, he retaliated with one of the best-concocted attacks on Aretino, the *Teremoto,* in 1556. The events leading up to Doni's attack are briefly these: Doni was befriended by Aretino when he came to Venice in 1547. Aretino helped him a great deal, but Doni began to want a literary reputation and power of his own, which in his case meant a powerful patron. He succeeded in gaining a gift of money from Guidiobaldo, Duke of Urbino; Aretino was outraged and wrote to the Duke attacking Doni. The battle was on, and Doni launched his counterattack in his *Teremoto* or *Earthquake.*[53]

The title page of the *Teremoto* trumpets, "Teremoto / Del Doni Fiorentino / Con la rouina d'un gran Colosso bestiale Antichristo della / nostra eta. Opera scritta a honor de Dio e della santa Chiesa /p difesa nō meno de Prelati: che de buō Christiani & salute."[54] At the outset of his work, Doni attacks Aretino as the Antichrist and further states, "Tu scriuendo male: uiuendo peggio: & con le Pippe e le nanna: & sporche cortigiane hai le tristitie publicate"[55] [You, writing badly, living worse, with your Pippa and Nanna and dirty courtesans have published your scoundrelly affairs]. Doni reiterates the worst that had been said about Aretino's life by Franco—that he has cuckolded the printer Marcolino, that he is no more of a whoremaster than a sodomite—all of this is old hat. Doni does introduce some new wrinkles that are fairly entertaining. He names all of the famous figures of the time who had favored Aretino and points out what unhappy ends they all have come to; Doni even has some fun with the letters of Aretino's name: ". . . quel P & quell' A e dicena Poltrone Asino Pezzo d' Asino: Pazzo As-

---

53. See Chubb, *Aretino,* pp. 439ff. Another interesting barometer of the Doni-Aretino relationship can be found in the various editions of Doni's *La Libraria. La Libraria* is a work in which Doni listed all of the important authors and their books and commented upon them. As he wrote on the title page of the 1558 Venice edition, this was a book "necessario, & utile, a tutti coloro che della cognitione della lingua hāno bisogno, & che uogliono di tutti gli autori, libri, & opere sapere scriuere, & ragionare" [necessary and useful for all who have need of knowledge of the language and who want to know how to write and talk about all the authors, books, and works]. In other words this was another Renaissance handbook for the man who wanted to be *au courant* in literature. In the 1550 edition of the *Libraria* all of Aretino's works are listed, along with three pages of the highest praise for Aretino (pp. 39ᵛ–40ᵛ). In the 1558 edition Doni says that he will exclude all of those authors who have been forbidden, suspect, or damned by the Church and the world (p. 13), although he does not omit such authors as Berni, Caro, and Molza, so he is not paying attention to any of the *Indexes.* Aretino has been completely eliminated from this version except for a listing under books no longer in print for his *Fondamento Christiano.*

54. Doni, *Teremoto* (n.p., 1556). There is a letter from the printer to Doni from Rome, which was probably the place of publication.

55. Ibid., sig. Aiᵛ.

inaccio: Porco Asinone . . ."[56] [that P and that A mean coward ass piece of ass, crazy bad ass, pig big ass]. All in all, Doni's attack comes off as something quite above Franco's *Life* in its ingenuity.

As one might expect, Aretino did not take all of this passively. His various counterattacks are best recorded in his letters: there are letters directly to Franco and Doni in which Aretino openly attacks them; there are letters to people in power asking them to withdraw their favor from these two men; and there are shifts made within the new editions of the letters designed to withdraw any favorable comments Aretino might have made at an earlier time. The last-mentioned category is of some interest for showing how a man of letters might work in such a matter. In the first edition of his letters (1538) Aretino included a letter written in 1537 to Benedetto Varchi in which he praised some sonnets of Franco's and said that Franco would be "another me."[57] In the third edition of the letters (1542), this letter is omitted entirely. A famous letter against pedants, originally addressed by Aretino to Franco in the first edition, is addressed to Lodovico Dolce in the third edition.[58]

Aretino's fullest exposé of the life and talents of Franco came in a letter not to any prince, but to Lodovico Dolce. Aretino begins by noting that Franco has not really hurt anyone by his attacks; he does not have the power to do that. "Il meschino simiglia un cane da ogniuno scacciato e a tutti odioso, il quale, adocchiato l'osso che non può mordere, comincia ad abbaiar sì forte che è forza che altri intenda che egli si muor di fame"[59] ["The rogue is like a cur that is kicked around by everybody and despised by everybody, and then when he sees a bone into which he cannot get his teeth, begins to growl so loudly that it is plain to all that he is starving to death"].[60] Aretino then launches into a characteristic building of epithets to be applied to Franco: "Io per me ho visto de i pazzi, de gli insolenti, de gli invidiosi, de i maligni, de gli iniqui, de i frappatori, de gli ostinati, de gli arroganti, de i villani e de gli ingrati; ma de le spezie di cui è la pazzia, la insolenzia, la invidia, la malignità, la iniquità, la vanitade, la ostinazione, l'arroganza, la villania e la ingratitudine sua, non mai"[61] ["For my part, I have seen madmen, insolent men, spiteful men, destructive men, obstinate men, arrogant men, boorish men and ungrateful men, but I have never seen anybody whose madness, insolence, spitefulness,

56. Ibid., sig. Diii^v.
57. Aretino, *Lettere*, p. 430. "Che doppo me sarà un altro me. . . ."
58. Ibid., pp. 192–94. See notes on pp. 1045–46.
59. Ibid., p. 593.
60. Chubb, *Letters*, p. 149.
61. Aretino, *Lettere*, p. 593.

wickedness, vanity, obstinacy, arrogance, boorishness and ingratitude were like his"].[62] This is a good catalogue; Aretino effectively piles one bad quality on top of another, but he never slips into the obscene here. Aretino seems to be taking some pains not to have to lower himself to obscene epithets in order to respond to Franco. He takes more pains to thank Dolce, in fact, for his assertion that Aretino's earlier kindnesses to Franco did not spring from any regard for the literary talents of the young man, "Ma ringrazio il vostro dire che la lode ch'io gli attribuisco, non meritandola punto, è suta bontà de la mia natura e non difetto del mio giudizio"[63] ["I am grateful to you for saying that the undeserved praise I heaped upon him came rather from the goodness of my heart than from my faulty judgement"].[64] Aretino recounts the full story from his point of view of the villainy performed by Franco, and only once does he fire an obscene name at him—sodomite.[65] Aretino is careful to include derogatory comments made about Franco by Titian and Marcolino, and he continues to find fitting animal comparisons: "Chi ha visto un serpe rotto ne la schiena, il quale benché non possa moversi non resta di vibrar la lingua, di alzar il capo e di sputa veleno, vede il ghioton da forche sdossato dal piè de la istessa invidia, latrare come un Cerbaro . . ."[66] ["Anyone who has seen a snake with his back broken who, although he cannot crawl away, still thrusts out his tongue, lifts his head up and spits poison, has seen this tidbit for the gallows trampled underfoot by his own envy and yet snarling like a Cerberus"].[67]

Aretino seems to have realized that there was no outdoing Franco in obscenity, and so he took the best defense against that obscenity; he showed how base Franco was, and he ends his letter castigating himself for wasting ink on such a low creature: "Ma io merito che le penne di Pasquino mi cavino gli occhi del nome, poiché spendo gli inchiostri in ragionare di sì vil verme"[68] ["But I deserve to have the pens of Pasquino pick out the eyes of my good name for wasting ink to talk about so low a worm"].[69] Irony of ironies, Aretino takes the path of the righteous for his defense! Aretino understood such games well; he saw what his best defense would be, and he followed that strategy. Obscenity

---

62. Chubb, *Letters,* p. 149.
63. Aretino, *Lettere,* p. 595.
64. Chubb, *Letters,* p. 151.
65. Aretino, *Lettere,* p. 595.
66. Ibid., p. 597.
67. Chubb, *Letters,* p. 154.
68. Aretino, *Lettere,* p. 597.
69. Chubb, *Letters,* p. 155.

did not serve his purpose here; besides, what worse things could he say of Franco than Franco had said of him? The abused, bountiful, pitying, self-righteous sponsor of a man turned beastly mad was Aretino's best and certainly most effective defense.

Along with the art of pornography, the art of literary warfare, obscenity included therein, was skillfully developed in the first great era of the printing press. It was an art the English were to learn from some fifty years later when the self-styled English Aretino, Thomas Nashe, swung into battle.

In looking over the range of written Italian Renaissance erotica discussed in these three chapters, one is struck by its variety, richness, and inventiveness. For the literary scholar there is much to admire, from the boldest of jokes to the most sophisticated of bawdy scholarly spoofs. The humanists are seen in a new perspective through the prism of erotica, and the popular writers can be examined profitably setting conventions, grappling with problems of fiction, adapting both classical and Renaissance forms to the service of erotica. The comic works of the humanists reflect a dimension of their world that repays serious attention; it is significant that the world is recognizably that of the humanists and that the humor depends upon a sophisticated knowledge of their serious scholarly practices as well as an appreciation for the bawdy. The fictive world of the popular writers is one far removed from our typical view of Renaissance Italy, epitomized by the courts of Urbino and Mantua or the cities of Rome, Florence, or Venice. The dialogues and sonnets of the Aretines' fictive world promote no self-knowledge and no elevation of the soul; their aim is to arouse or offend.

To have the works of both the learned and popular purveyors of erotica before us is to extend our vision of the literary scene in Renaissance Italy considerably. In the next chapter I undertake to extend the visual scene as well.

CHAPTER 4

The Loves of Men and Gods: Erotica in the Visual Arts

What wrong is there in beholding a man possess a woman?
It would seem to me that the thing which is given to us by
nature to preserve the race, should be worn around the neck
as a pendant, or pinned onto the cap like a broach, for it is
the spring which feeds all the rivers of the people, and the
ambrosia in which the world delights in its happiest days.
　　　　　　　　　　　　　　Pietro Aretino, Letters

To turn from literary texts to the visual arts is a large step, and although a literary scholar must approach a different discipline gingerly, approach he must, for the visual arts hold a major place in the broad canvas that constitutes erotica in the Renaissance. Because the connections between literary and visual materials are so strong, because so many of the problems in dealing with materials in the two disciplines are analogous, such an inquiry is both necessary and fruitful. To present the full range of erotica in the visual arts of the Italian Renaissance would be an impossible task within the confines of this study, however; what follows is necessarily selective and exemplary; it is a study in which I try to give some sense of the way our view of erotica has been obscured, distorted, and occasionally ignored altogether. I focus particularly on problems of audience and audience response, especially as they relate to the question of allegorical readings.

The most crucial of points must be stated directly; there was, under many guises, some put on by Renaissance artists themselves, some applied by later scholars, a good deal of erotica produced in the visual arts in Renaissance Italy. If neoplatonism provided the philosophical program for many paintings, if allegory provided the dominant methodology of interpretation, love still provided much of the subject matter, and often the love that is depicted can be classified in terms of erotica— the bawdy, the pornographic, the erotic, and the obscene.

I should begin by stating that it is my sense that art historians have

118

always been better at using literary materials than literary historians have been at using the visual arts, and they certainly have paid better attention to questions of production, societal influence, and so on. Nor have they totally ignored the broad range of erotica; however, when confronted with that broad range in painting and engraving in Renaissance Italy, from a number of series of prints done in the manner of Giulio Romano to female nudes on canvas and copulating figures on walls of ducal palaces, they have tended to emphasize questions of style or the allegorical nature of such prints and paintings; where such interpretations or questions do not apply (or cannot be made to apply) they have dismissed the works as insignificant. What follows attempts to provide a different perspective; first, by seeing erotic materials within the context of erotica rather than some other construct, and second, by examining methods of allegorical interpretation and, by extension, audience response.

I

Renaissance prints offer what is perhaps an easier starting point than Renaissance painting in dealing with visual erotica, since issues of audience, intention, and meaning are less problematical. Renaissance prints offer their own problems, of course, not the least of which is finding authentic productions. Nowhere is that problem more acute than the famous *posizioni* of Giulio Romano.

The complicated history of the *posizioni* and their relationship with Aretino's sonnets have already been discussed, but the engravings themselves are worthy of attention.[1] Although we no longer have any original "editions" of the *posizioni,* we can be fairly certain of what the drawings were like through evidence offered by the sixteenth-century woodcut version and Count Waldeck's copies executed in the 1830s. The drawings have an intrinsic interest for the student of erotica, and they are also the beginning of a number of Renaissance series of prints in the same mode, often entitled "The Loves of the Gods." Further, it seems to me that these prints of Giulio's have a strong relationship to some of his paintings done at the Palazzo del Tè at Mantua, and finally they become important in dealing with the concepts of High Renaissance style, Mannerism, and Antimannerism.[2]

1. See chapter 2, pp. 46–57.
2. The problems of classification and terminology are immense in this field, particularly for a student of literature. For the debate over the term Mannerism see Jacques Bousquet, *Mannerism* (Munich: Braziller, 1964); Walter Friedlaender, *Mannerism and Anti-Mannerism in Italian Painting* (New York: Schocken Books, 1967); E. H. Gombrich, *Norm*

It is something of a commonplace among art historians to place Giulio Romano in the forefront of the Mannerist movement in Renaissance art. As might be expected, there is considerable ambiguity attending the term Mannerism, an ambiguity that has obscured Romano's precise achievement. Linda Murray assures us that once we have carefully defined the limits ("a label only for certain works of a certain kind produced by certain artists between about 1520 and 1590, and only in certain parts of Italy"), Mannerism "can be quite easily recognized and defined."[3] Art historians talk of the anticlassical nature of the work of artists following the death of Raphael, of the subjective nature of the work, of a concern for style for its own sake, of "a concentration on the nude, often in bizarre and convoluted poses, and with exaggerated muscular development; with subject matter either deliberately obscure, or treated so that it becomes difficult to understand—the main incident pushed into the background or swamped in irrelevant figures serving as excuses for displays of virtuosity in figure painting; with extremes of perspective, distorted proportions or scale—figures jammed into too small a space so that one has the impression that any movement would burst the confines of the picture space; with vivid colour schemes, employing discordant contrasts, effects of 'shot' colour, and the use of colour, not for descriptive or naturalistic purposes, but as a powerful adjunct to the emotional impact of a picture."[4] Further, our attention is continually drawn to the sense of psychic disorder one notes in Mannerist works. Jacques Bousquet, for instance, states, "For the first time in the history of art importance was also given to the expression of the psychic world: evocations of melancholy and the world of dreams are common in Mannerist painting. There is also a strong current of eroticism in this art, frequently tinged by perversion."[5] But Peter Murray, John Shearman, E. H. Gombrich, and

---

and Form (London: Phaidon Press, 1966); Linda Murray, The Late Italian Renaissance and Mannerism (New York and Washington: Frederick Praeger, 1967); and John Shearman, Mannerism (Baltimore: Penguin Books, 1967). Literary scholars have also had more than their share of problems with the term. For a brilliant discussion about the problems and limitations of categorizing and labeling see Rosemond Tuve, "Baroque and Mannerist Milton?" in Essays by Rosemond Tuve, ed. Thomas P. Roche, Jr. (Princeton: Princeton Univ. Press, 1970), pp. 262–80.

3. Linda Murray, The Late Italian Renaissance, p. 30.
4. Ibid., pp. 30–31.
5. Bousquet, Mannerism, jacket. Bousquet takes a rather comprehensive look at Mannerism, and while he recognizes certain problems of definition, he does nothing to clear the issue. He blandly asserts, "No school of painting in the sixteenth century labelled itself 'Mannerist'; Mannerism, like Baroque, Rococo or Romanticism, is a term invented after the event and can be interpreted by anyone as he pleases, extending or limiting the

even Walter Friedlaender, who was himself instrumental in formulating the notion of a period of an anticlassical style following the High Renaissance, have given appropriate warnings against making too articulate a program and too neat a division between the artists following and those of the High Renaissance. Shearman reminds us that generalizations about Mannerism tend to reflect twentieth-century concerns,[6] and Friedlaender notes that "despite their antagonism, the anticlassic or manneristic style, and the High Renaissance have many and fundamental things in common."[7] All of this is a rather roundabout route to Giulio Romano's *posizioni,* but these are matters that cannot be avoided, since the only analysis of the Romano prints is rooted in the conception of Giulio Romano as a Mannerist.

Frederick Hartt is both wary and precise in discussing Giulio Romano's relationship to Mannerism. For Hartt, if Giulio is a Mannerist, he is one of a unique type whose Mannerism lies purely in his relationship to antiquity. Hartt makes much of Giulio's having grown up amidst the ruins of Rome: "Through the peculiar character of Giulio's relations to Roman antiquity one can understand strong elements in his style. . . . As in the case of no other artist the monuments of the Roman fora entered into Giulio's earliest experiences. Yet he did not, like the artists of the Quattrocento humanist movement dominated by Alberti, seek to revive, emulate, and continue Roman art. He seems rather to have identified himself in some way with the witnesses of a lost civilization, and to preserve in the content of his art the ambivalence of such an identification."[8] Hartt goes on to note an "uneasy quality" in Guilio's use of antiquity, and this is Guilio's Mannerism, a style stemming from "crisis."[9] It is from such a view of Guilio's relationship with antiquity that Hartt approaches the *posizioni,* "To the modern eyes the majority of them are funny," Hartt states; he points out that while the women are all youthful, the men vary in age; he comments upon the beds and other properties, and he concludes, "That such a series should exist at all and that it should be so avidly bought up, widely copied, and thoroughly destroyed is already a symptom. But

concept according to his whim" (p. 25). If this is true, then we have a hopelessly broad term, which would seem to be the case in Bousquet's book when he turns to literature and groups Spenser, Shakespeare, Webster, and Milton together as "all Mannerists to a greater or lesser extent" (p. 31).

6. Shearman, p. 135. Also see Peter Murray, "Italian Art from Masaccio to Mannerism," in *The Age of the Renaissance,* ed. Denys Hay (London: McGraw-Hill, 1967).

7. Friedlaender, p. 11.

8. Hartt, *Giulio Romano,* I, 6.

9. Hartt, I, 12.

the special emphasis on abnormal and spectacular attitudes, on acute physical strain, and on frustration is surely significant for the psychology of early Mannerism."[10] The humor with which Hartt views the *posizioni* at the outset of his analysis is at odds with the "special emphasis on abnormal and spectacular attitudes, on acute physical strain, and on frustration" he notes later. The "psychology of early Mannerism" that he is trying to convey is clearly not the easy humor with which he sees the modern viewer examining the works. Certainly there is the variety that Hartt notes in the various poses, and in some cases we are aware of the strain and muscular distortions involved (see figure 1). On the other hand, other figures, as is clear from an examination of the series, show distinct smiles of pleasure; at times we see some decidedly happy lovers. What we have in this series is a wide range of attitudes, both physical and psychological. And the emphasis above all else, in spite of the detail of beds, drapes, and vases, is on sexual intercourse—varieties of sexual intercourse. The prints, just as the sonnets of Aretino do, insist upon being viewed in terms of the act of sexual intercourse. If the detail of beds, drapes, statues, and vases is evocative of the Renaissance, it is also evocative of antiquity, as Hartt notes, and beyond that, the activity portrayed in the prints is supremely evocative of antiquity for the Renaissance mind. As we have already seen in chapter 1, to the Renaissance one of the things that typified the world of antiquity was sexual freedom.[11] Giulio's prints, in depicting classical couples copulating, are in one sense the ultimate in High Renaissance art if we mean by that term classical in form and spirit. This may be the ultimate step in the synthesis described by Seznec, for here we have a rehabilitation of classical activity in classical form.[12]

To view these prints in terms of Mannerism or High Renaissance style, or the "antique," may serve the purpose of those concerned with questions of defining artistic styles and periods, but such an analysis

---

10. Hartt, I, 282. Barolsky, p. 132, sees the *posizioni* as sexual comedy.

11. The idea of sexual freedom as characteristic of antiquity was carried by the Renaissance into its concept of the Golden Age. The addition of the sexual aspect to the Golden World was an addition of the Renaissance according to Harry Levin, *The Myth of the Golden Age in the Renaissance* (Bloomington and London: Indiana Univ. Press, 1969), pp. 24 and 36ff. Also see Otto Kurz, "'Gli Amori De' Carracci': Four Forgotten Paintings by Agostino Carracci," *Journal of the Warburg and Courtauld Institutes* 14 (1951): 227. Various Renaissance prints and paintings of the Golden Age show us that even in its most modest presentation it was seen as an era of sexual compatibility and freedom (see figures 22 and 34).

12. Jean Seznec, *The Survival of the Pagan Gods* (New York: Harper & Row, 1961), p. 213.

diverts us from the central point of seeing these prints in terms of erotica.

Giulio's prints, suppressed as they were in his own time, nonetheless inspired other artists to produce series of drawings depicting couples engaged in sexual intercourse. However, Perino del Vaga and Agostino Carracci felt the need to give such activity an Ovidian formulation by executing their respective series under the guise of the "loves of the gods." The Ovidian tradition is one that needs no rehearsing here, since it has already received so much scholarly attention. There is no question about a strong allegorical tradition adhering to Renaissance readings of Ovidian texts, especially the *Metamorphoses,* in both the literary and visual arts. Perino's depiction of the gods in what could be called his "positions" might have been a form of self-protection; he would have been able to claim the allegorical interpretation had he needed to. However, his prints stress not the allegorical but the very physical loves of the gods, and we see, as we did in Giulio's prints, a variety of attitudes, both physical and psychological.[13]

Occasionally in Perino's drawings we see the kind of physical contortion typical of Giulio's work, but we rarely get the same muscular strain (see figure 8). The contortion in this figure seems to emphasize the genitalia of Jove. While the title and verse of this print have clearly been misplaced, we have no difficulty in recognizing Jove in one of his many very human forms; in this case Jove is a shepherd, a form in which he coupled with Mnemosyne.[14] If we are to think of the nine muses resulting from the union depicted here, it is difficult to understand how. The emphasis is on genital action.

In figure 9 the bodies swing with ease into position, and the face of Jove shows none of the strain and fierceness we see in the preceding figure. Jove as a satyr (figure 10) is more intense (and tense), but curiously enough, in a number of cases while we may get a frontal view of the female, her legs spread apart and her face showing her quite aroused, more often than not the males are not depicted in a state of

13. From the prints I was able to see in the Gabinetto Nazionale delle Stampe in Rome, it was clear that two different printings of the works were used to fill out the set. All were sixteenth-century prints, however. Vasari, *Lives of the Most Eminent Painters, Sculptors & Architects,* trans. Gaston du C. de Vere (London: Macmillan, 1912–15) VI, 209, writes that Baviera commissioned Perino "to draw some of the stories of the Gods transforming themselves in order to achieve the consummation of their loves. These were engraved on copper by Jacopo Caraglio. . . ."

14. The title of this print is "Apollo di Hyacintho" and the verses relate to Apollo's love for the youth. A later print in the series (number 12), which depicts a youthful god with a young man, is entitled "Gioue in Pastore." Apparently the titles and accompanying verses got switched.

erection (see figure 11). Sometimes the males are depicted flaccid (see figure 12), and other times the male figure is presented as a dismembered statue in action (figure 13). This certainly suggests a kind of self-censorship, consonant with Perino's decision to present his "positions" as "loves of the gods." Yet there is little attempt to allegorize in these drawings. Whether explicit or not, the emphasis in these drawings is still on sexual activity itself, not on the "meanings" or "results" of such activity. And while the verses accompanying these drawings are a far cry from Aretino's sonnets, they too steer far away from any allegorical interpretations.

One should note that "seeing" is critical in these drawings. In three of the prints reproduced here (figures 8, 9, and 10) Cupid is present; in figure 8 he watches the action; in figure 9 his left hand is pushing into the very center of sexual intercourse. An allegorical reading would lead us to say that these drawings demonstrate the power of Eros, but we do not get much further than that. This is the power of a Cupid we will encounter in an English version of the "loves of the gods" in Spenser's *Faerie Queene* in the final chapter. The "seeing" of Cupid in figures 8 and 9, the angle of presentation in figure 10, and the viewing by both Mercury and Aglauros in figure 11 as Mercury prepares to take Aglauros' sister, Herse, give these prints strong overtones of voyeurism.[15] We are not merely looking at prints; they seem designed to remind us that we are voyeurs as well. Perino as an eroticist makes a strong appeal on this score, not Perino as an allegorist.

Agostino Carracci's drawings of the "loves of the gods" are remarkable in their insistence upon displaying as fully as possible the genitalia of both male and female figures.[16] Although these prints may be seen in the context of the return by Agostino Carracci to a "pre-manneristic" style should one again be asked to focus on questions of style, if one concentrates on questions of erotica, one must say that Agostino approaches his subject with a single-mindedness that is worthy of Sid Krassman and Boris Adrian, producer and director in Terry Southern's *Blue Movie,* as they attempt to shoot a "full vag-pen" scene in their greatest of all porno movies.[17] Of the twenty prints in the

15. In printing the title dropped an "a." "Mercurio parla a Glauros" should read "Mercurio parla ad Aglauros."

16. The dates of the prints were disputed. Bodmer puts the dates at 1584 and 1587. Maurizio Calvesi in a critical catalogue, *Le Incisioni Dei Carracci* (Rome: Communità Europea Dell'Arte e Della Cultura, 1965), p. 42, argues for 1588–89. Such was the fame of the Romano-Aretino prints that Agostino Carracci's prints became known in France as *L'Aretin D'Augustin Carrache.*

17. In the foreword to a recent translation of Giovanni Bellori's *The Lives of Annibale*

series, thirteen take great pains to show the penis either penetrating or about to penetrate; in four others full penetration has been achieved. The drapery, the vases, the couches, and the athletic, muscular bodies are reminiscent of Giulio's prints and worthy of attention, but the gods are only occasionally identifiable by various attributes included in the prints (see figure 14 of Hercules). Here as nowhere else the artist is intent upon showing us genitalia, and he often contorts his figures drastically to do so (figures 15 and 16). There is little attempt on the part of the artist to remind us that we are viewing the "loves of the gods." What we are viewing are couples engaged in sexual intercourse.

Figure 16 has been given the title "Julie and an athlete"; the latter is given his name with good reason. The focus of the artist throughout the series is remarkable; one looks either straight into the pudendum (figure 17) or nearly so (figures 18 and 19), and the faces are usually expressionless and unimportant in this celebration of genitalia. Sexual intercourse is of the greatest importance here, an importance emphasized by the inclusion of a satyr having intercourse with a nymph, a satyr watching Pandora, and most remarkably, a satyr and satyress copulating (figure 20).

Scholars are divided in their opinion of Agostino Carracci as a print-maker in general and the value of this series in particular. To Denis Mahon the great limitation of Agostino generally is that his heart, except on rare occasions, is never engaged: "I suoi disegni hanno un carattere freddo e cerebrale che raramente è riscaldato da una vena di sentimento."[18] One senses some of that detachment even in "The Loves of the Gods" when one looks at the faces, but rarely is our attention drawn there, and Maurizio Calvesi in his evaluation of the Carracci in general and these prints in particular sees a new use of myth, one in which classical myth is used anecdotally, not iconographically, so that while "a nymph in the country setting for Giorgione may be a double symbol of the creative mystery of nature, for the Carracci it is only an

---

and *Agostino Carracci,* trans. Catherine Enggass (University Park and London: Pennsylvania State Univ. Press, 1968), p. vii, Robert Enggass states: "Critics of their day and of our own agree that through their efforts the tide of Mannerism was at last stemmed and Italian painting returned to the main channel of classically inspired realism that had impelled its movement from the time of Giotto onward." Such an evaluation of the contribution of the Carraccis is a commonplace among art historians, but Denis Mahon warns against seeing Agostino as involved in a set theoretical program. See his "Eclecticism and the Carracci: Further Reflections on the Validity of a Label," *Journal of the Warburg and Courtauld Institutes* 16 (1953): 303–41.

18. Denis Mahon, *Mostra Dei Carracci. Catalogo Critico Dei Disegni,* trans. Maurizio Calvesi, 2nd ed. (Bologna, 1963), pp. 10–11.

appetizing woman."[19] Calvesi calls Agostino's prints an expression of naturalism; I would term them an embodiment of the Renaissance conception of classical sexual freedom, a freedom that artists like Romano and Carracci felt they could represent without self-conscious allegorical meanings. This, finally, is the great importance of these series of prints; they were well known, more than by word of mouth, and they show that Renaissance artists could in fact present classical subjects or forms performing classical deeds in a manner free from overt involvement in allegory. Clearly this was not the case with all prints that dealt with erotic subject matter. Some of the woodcuts in Francesco Colonna's *Hypnerotomachia* (famous for its 1499 edition) are frank enough in their depiction of the effects of Bacchus and the worship of Priapus, but these prints are presented in a work that is obviously highly allegorical and fanciful.[20] And while one does see animals copulating in some of Antonio Tempesta's prints, they are, after all, only animals, and we should expect this in prints of "May" and "The Golden Age" (see figures 21 and 22). We are dealing with exceptions in the cases of the Romano, del Vaga, and Carracci series, but their popularity, and the fact that the subject matter was repeated in such close succession, gives these works a significance of their own and has important implications for much Renaissance painting that was allegorical.[21]

II

One need only look at the paintings of Giulio Romano and Titian to find proof of the assertion that late Renaissance and Manneristic painting shows an increased interest in nudity, especially female nudity. But nudity had a long tradition in Renaissance painting; indeed nudity in one context or another was not unusual in Medieval art. It is the context that raises difficulties for the viewer and the historian, for questions of how to read allegory and, ultimately, audience response become critical. In many respects the problems are similar to those which arise in reading tales of lust that supposedly teach by negative example or which arise in reading any allegory for that matter.

The Medieval tendency to deal with fleshliness in the most religious

---

19. See Calvesi, *Le Incisioni Dei Carracci*, p. 8; the translation is mine.

20. For an informative discussion of Colonna's *Hypnerotomachia* see Edgar Wind, *Pagan Mysteries in the Renaissance* (Harmondsworth, Middlesex: Penguin Books, 1967), pp. 103ff. Wind also discusses the *Hypnerotomachia* in his *Bellini's Feast*, pp. 34–35.

21. Morse Peckham includes a discussion of these prints in *Art and Pornography*, pp. 289–94.

of contexts, and to see that representation in an allegorical manner, has been amply demonstrated.[22] A late Medieval representation of the Seven Deadly Sins in San Gimignano affords an excellent example of such a use of nudity. Painted by Taddeo di Bartolo (ca. 1396) in the Church of La Collegiata, the punishments in Hell of the Seven Deadly Sins are rendered with horrifyingly effective use of nudity. Human forms are distorted to show how we are corrupted as humans by our sins. Thus in the depiction of gluttony (figure 23) we see a body in the foreground that is so distorted as to make it look at first glance as if the man has his head on backwards. The punishment of lust (figure 24) is even more incredible—a serpent strikes at the woman's pudendum while a hideous female devil with tremendous sagging breasts pokes, perhaps with a torch, at the same area. There is nothing attractive about the nudity here, and certainly the viewer is not going to be enticed or excited by these fleshly forms. Such frescoes are like the attacks of theologians on lechery in which sexually loaded language is used, but it is a language that is loaded in a repulsive, debasing way, and we are in no danger of "misimagining" with the distorted forms in front of us.[23]

The case is rather different with Luca Signorelli's *Last Judgment* in the Duomo of Orvieto. Fleshliness is everywhere, and even those who are being carted off to Hell are given distinctly attractive human forms (figure 25). The human forms of the damned are no more attractive than those of the saved, but the point is that an emphasis on physical beauty of this luscious kind is not *necessarily* going to inspire thoughts of the afterlife.[24] It is true that we are to worry about what happens to

22. See Erwin Panofsky, *Studies in Iconology* (New York: Harper Torchbook, 1962), pp. 155ff; also D. W. Robertson, *A Preface to Chaucer* (Princeton: Princeton Univ. Press, 1962).

23. See, for example, Godfrey Goodman, *The Fall of Man* (London, 1616), pp. 322–23; Richard Cooke, *A White sheete, or a warning for Whoremongers* (London, 1629), pp. 18–19; Philip Stubbes, *The Anatomie of Abuses* (London, 1583), pp. 94^v, 98^r, 99^v, and 121^v.

24. In writing on Bosch's triptych *The Garden of Delights*, H. W. Janson deals with the same kind of problem. Janson sees Bosch depicting "man's life on earth as an unending repetition of the Original Sin of Adam and Eve, whereby we are all doomed to be the prisoners of our appetites." He continues:

So profound is Bosch's pessimism—if we read the meaning of the triptych correctly—that some scholars have refused to take it at face value; the center panel, they claim, is really an unusual vision of Paradise according to the beliefs of a secret heretical sect to which Bosch supposedly belonged. While their view has few adherents, it does point up the fundamental ambiguity of the *Garden*: there is indeed an innocence, even a haunting poetic beauty, in this panorama of sinful mankind. Consciously, Bosch was a stern moralist who intended his pictures to be visual sermons, every detail packed with didactic meaning. Unconsciously, however, he must have been so enraptured by the sensuous appeal of the world of the flesh that the images he coined with

those beautiful bodies (and souls), but one can easily be arrested by the physical forms here. The problem is analogous to the one examined by Professor Samuel Edgerton in his work on *pitturi infammati*. The audience (or the subject) could hardly find defaming paintings of human forms, even if depicted upside down, when those forms were executed as beautifully as Andrea del Sarto seems to have done.[25] Or to take another analogous situation, the audience of a sermon that attacks lechery in a provocative manner might have difficulty concentrating on the subject as a sin *to be avoided*.[26]

The problems of audience response become much more acute, however, when we turn from paintings in a religious context to those that are more secular. With Botticelli, with Giulio Romano, with Titian, with Annibale Carracci, we are most often exhorted not to dwell on the overt meaning of any painting but to note the cumulation of iconographical details that lead us ultimately to the allegorical significance of the painting. Now the work of Panofsky, Wind, and others is brilliant and often convincing, and in the discussion that follows I do not mean to imply that allegorical interpretations are not applicable; they surely are, but what I do think needs reexamining is our way of looking at allegory. As Barolsky has recently reminded us in his study of wit and humor in Italian Renaissance art, not all Renaissance secular paintings need be explained by neoplatonism.[27]

Study of the last decades devoted to reading Renaissance allegory, especially with reference to Spenser, is particularly enlightening here. Thomas P. Roche, Jr., in his excellent study of Books Three and Four

---

such prodigality tend to celebrate what they are meant to condemn. That, surely, is the reason why *The Garden of Delights* still evokes so strong a response today, even though we no longer understand every word of the sermon.

History of Art (New York: Prentice-Hall & Harry N. Abrams, 1964), p. 299.

25. Samuel Y. Edgerton, Jr., *Pictures and Punishment: Art and Criminal Prosecution during the Florentine Renaissance* (Ithaca and London: Cornell Univ. Press, 1985), p. 122.

26. For an example of this see Richard Cooke's sermon, *A White sheete, or a warning for Whoremongers*. The sermon is filled with sexually suggestive language through which Cooke castigates one of his parishioners who had been condemned for practicing fornication with his maidservant. As Jeremy Taylor advised in *Holy Living* (1650), one was better off not speaking to the issue of lust; "When a temptation of lust assaults thee, do not resist it by heaping up arguments against it, and disputing with it, considering its offers and dangers, but fly from it, that is, think not at all of it; lay aside all consideration concerning it, and turn away from it by severe and laudable thought of business." "If you hear it speak," Taylor continues, "though but to dispute with it, it ruins you; and the very arguments you go about to answer, leave a relish on the tongue." *The Rule and Exercises of Holy Living* (London: W. Pickering, 1852), p. 73.

27. Barolsky, pp. 166 and 209ff.

of *The Faerie Queene,* reminds us that allegory is totally dependent upon narrative and that at no point is it separate from that narrative:

Renaissance rhetoricians showed their awareness of the dependence of allegory on narrative by defining it as "continued metaphor," the use of which "serueth most aptly to ingraue the liuely images of things, and to present them vnder daepe shadowes to the contemplation of the mind, wherein wit and iudgement take pleasure, and the remembrance receiueth a long lasting impression. . . ." Here the emphasis is decidely on "the liuely images of things" that give rise to the allegorical meanings, that is, on the tenor of this continued metaphor which the vehicle (narrative) illuminates. Only through the "daepe shadowes" of particulars can the universals, which are the repository of allegorical meanings, be presented to the human mind. This is not to say that the universal allegorical meanings are stuffed into the particulars of the narrative. The allegory is contained by the narrative in the same way and to the degree that universals are contained by particulars. Particulars figure forth universals; the narrative figures forth the allegory. The narrative presents itself and under the guise of its deep shadows lures the mind toward a vision of those lively images it embodies, toward those universals that are the ground and form of *these* particulars.[28]

I am aware that such a statement does not explain allegory in Renaissance painting, but it goes a long way toward helping us even the balance somewhat by calling our attention to the importance of the narrative sense that "contains" the allegory.[29] Roche is careful to caution that "at no point is the allegory independent of the action as presented in the narrative. If the critic grants independence to the allegory, chaos is come again, for he is in fact denying the primacy of that golden world we enter when we read literature."[30] Or view paintings, we might add, for art historians have eagerly pointed to the complexity of Renaissance allegory, but the discussion always seems to center on the multi-layers of possible meanings *beyond* the narrative, never on the narrative itself.[31]

Edgar Wind's defense of an iconographical approach to Renaissance art is a sound and thorough one; it deserves citation here since it is so relevant to the matter at hand. Wind stresses our need to know more

28. Thomas P. Roche, Jr., *The Kindly Flame* (Princeton: Princeton Univ. Press, 1964), pp. 4–5.

29. Roche is careful to talk about the various senses of the narrative rather than levels of meaning that encourage clear breaks between narrative and allegory (ibid., p. 10).

30. Ibid., p. 4.

31. See Linda Murray, *The High Renaissance* (New York and Washington: Frederick A. Praeger, 1967), p. 46; also Rensselaer W. Lee, "*Ut Pictura Poesis*: The Humanistic Theory of Painting," *Art Bulletin* 22 (1940): 197–269.

about Renaissance arguments than the painter needed to know, since we are attempting to recover something lost. The reward of an iconographical approach "in the study of Renaissance mysteries, is that it may help to remove the veil of obscurity which not only distance in time (although in itself sufficient for that purpose) but a deliberate obliqueness in the use of metaphor has spread over some of the greatest Renaissance paintings. They were designed for initiates; hence they require initiation."[32] Wind then addresses himself to the problem of visual and intellectual satisfaction:

> Aesthetically speaking, there can be no doubt that the presence of unresolved residues of meaning is an obstacle to the enjoyment of art. However great the visual satisfaction produced by a painting, it cannot reach a perfect state so long as the spectator is plagued by a suspicion that there is more in the painting than meets the eye. In literature, the same sort of embarrassment may be caused by Spenser's, Chapman's, or even Shakespeare's verse in a reader who has been advised to surrender himself to the music of the poetry without worrying whether he understands every line or not. But it is doubtful how long that attitude, however justified as a preliminary approach, can be sustained without flattening the aesthetic enjoyment.[33]

No one would wish to have his aesthetic enjoyment flattened, but one might wonder exactly where the "perfect state" of visual satisfaction lies. I would argue that in our eagerness to explain the iconography, to become "initiated" into the privileged world of learning, we have responded too little to the visual impression and dealt too little with the problems of audience response to those impressions—concerns that are critical in dealing with art that is highly erotic.[34] It is certainly true that Renaissance artists did not paint simple *posizioni*. Giulio Romano and Titian, for example, place their erotic subjects within the context of allegory, but that fact should not blind us to the eroticism of their works.

We have already noted how scholars agree that Giulio Romano excelled in dealing with classical subjects in classical forms;[35] that ability

32. Wind, *Pagan Mysteries,* p. 15.
33. Ibid., pp. 15–6.
34. I am obviously in complete agreement that one must consider all of the various senses of a painting; indeed one can tire quickly of the narrative sense. This is why modern, photographic pornography is often so boring; there is nothing but the narrative, a narrative that is often barren. Nevertheless, we must make allowance for response to the literal sense; the narrative, after all, is quite different from the "music of the poetry."
35. Hartt, p. xvii, has stated with regard to Giulio's understanding of classical stories, "In any event he understood their spirit, and was able to project them vividly in his great narrative cycles. In content as in form, Giulio's attitude toward antiquity might

of Giulio's is everywhere in evidence in the Palazzo del Tè in Mantua. The context in which the "anciently modern and modernly ancient" frescoes were painted by Giulio is emphasized by both the subject matter and the form of the paintings, for the Palazzo del Tè was above all a place for festivity and relaxation.[36] Frederick Hartt's study of Giulio Romano is admirable in many ways, and he makes every effort to do justice to the full visual impact that the Palazzo del Tè and the Sala di Psiche in particular have on the viewer. Hartt gives an iconographical and finally allegorical explanation of the Sala di Psiche, and I must confess that I find his neoplatonic interpretation convincing—up to a point.[37] However, even as he acknowledges the erotic proclivities of the patron, Hartt minimizes that aspect in providing an overall interpretation of the room as a neoplatonic ascension. And Hartt gives very little attention to the audience here, especially the way in which a festive

---

be described as a folklore classicism, whimsical, comical, poetic, atavistic, magical, rather than scholarly." E. H. Gombrich strikes something of the same note in *Norm and Form,* pp. 126–27, "This brief list must suffice to explain in principle what may be described as assimilation as distinct from imitation. Assimilation demands a degree of generalization. The artist must learn how to create a figure that embodies his idea of the classical style. The ease with which Giulio did this was proverbial. Like the other great decorators of his time, like Polidoro or Perino, he could cover whole palaces with motifs that impressed his generation as evocations of the Antique, though few were literal quotations. Any one motif of the Palazzo del Tè, such as the conch with its six fields and four stucco medallions, not to speak of its frieze with a battle of Lapiths and Centaurs, for which the rapid drawing is preserved, exemplifies this inexhaustible stream of invention *all'antica,* to which Aretino referred in a typical letter: 'For invention and grace the world prefers you to anyone who has ever touched compass and brush. Even Apelles and Vitruvius would agree if they had only had experience of the buildings and paintings you have made and designed in this city, embellished and glorified as it is by the spirit of your conceptions—anciently modern and modernly ancient.'"

36. Linda Murray, *The Late Renaissance,* p. 34. Hartt argues that there are two distinct periods in the interior design. "The first, extending from 1527 [to 15]29, betrays in the uninterrupted speed of its execution the impatience of the young Federigo Gonzaga to occupy his pleasure palace, and in the consistency of its pagan eroticism the hedonistic nature of the prince. This campaign comprises the three small decorated chambers facing the city in the northwest apartment, and the entire northeast apartment centering around the Sala di Psiche" (I, 106–07). The second period (1530–35) shows Federigo's new preoccupation with power.

37. Hartt interprets the whole as a neoplatonic *ascensio* (I, 136–37). John Shearman in his review of Hartt's book points to some of the problems of fitting all into a neoplatonic plan: see *Burlington Magazine* 101 (1959): 456–60. And Gombrich in *Symbolic Images,* 2nd ed. (London: Phaidon Press, 1978), pp. 118, 227–78, points to Aretino's influence on Federigo at this time. Wind, writing on Alfonso d'Este, notes that "Alfonso had a predilection for mythological *erotica*; and in this he was followed by his nephew, Federigo Gonzaga, Isabella d'Este's son, who having shared the companionship and tastes of Aretino, ordered from Coreggio the famous *Io, Leda,* and *Danaë* (not to speak of the *Olympias* and *Pasiphae* painted for him by Giulio Romano" (*Bellini's Feast,* p. 45).

gathering of Italian Renaissance nobility might have reacted to such a room. Several details should serve to make the point. If the scene of Jupiter and Olympias is an example of carnal love (figure 26), it is alluring in its carnality; indeed this "orgiastic world" of the wall frescoes is made highly attractive. With the Jupiter and Olympias we are reminded of the *posizioni*; the painter is careful to show us Jupiter's erection, which could easily be hidden by Olympias' knee had Giulio wished to be more modest. The point is that Giulio did not want to be more modest; he wanted to show more, not less.

The preparations for the wedding feast, as Hartt points out, take place on this earth, and they are also filled with fleshliness—satyrs are in full erection, a swan appears almost to be engaged in fellatio with a man to the left side back (figure 27); even the marriage couple are lusciously fleshy. But given Hartt's interpretation, we should expect this; we are on an earthly level, one that he can describe as orgiastic. As we ascend to the lunettes and the ceiling, however, we enter the more spiritual spheres of neoplatonic love. The realm ruled by Desire and the three Graces presents an extraordinary view. It is extraordinary because of the perspective from which we see the Graces (figure 28) and because of the incredible fleshliness of these figures; faces are indistinguishable, but breasts and buttocks abound. One must wonder, I think, about how completely neoplatonic the thoughts of the viewer are made by such a presentation.[38] Granted the sense of the celestial is surely there, especially in the airy figures of the center fresco of the ceiling, but this is such a small portion of the whole of the room. So if we are to see this room allegorically as a celebration of neoplatonic love, then we may perhaps wonder how successful it was as an allegory. This is not to suggest that a neoplatonic interpretation of this room is invalid, but the immediate emphasis seems to be on the literal level and on the earthly sphere; throughout the frescoes the human form and fleshly love are celebrated. Allegory and narrative, if we accept Hartt's interpretation, may be at odds here, for the effect on the viewer is to overwhelm him with luscious human forms even in the heavenly realms. That the artist who created the first great series of Renaissance

38. I am particularly indebted to Professor John Benton for stimulating my thinking about audience response. In a paper entitled "Class, Audience, and Meaning," delivered at the conference on "The Medieval Artist and the Expectations of His Audience" at the Center for Medieval and Renaissance Studies of Ohio State University in 1971, Professor Benton raised what seem to me to be essential questions with regard to class analysis, shared values, and allegorical reading. Barolsky, pp. 133–38, has pointed to several comic elements in this room, including a *putto pisciatore*. For Barolsky's more extended commentary on "mictural comedy," see pp. 161ff.

posizioni should be able to present such a splendid display of fleshliness should not surprise us at all.[39]

The paintings of Titian, especially his many Venuses, provide us with a most complex and fascinating set of problems in dealing with the literal and the allegorical. With Titian, the problems have been recognized by such great scholars as Panofsky, Saxl, and Wind.

The *Venus Urbino* (figure 29) provides an excellent starting point for our discussion of Titian, since it has been viewed on the one hand as a painting of "an expensive and successful courtesan"[40] and on the other hand as an image of "harmonious, faithful love."[41] The latter interpretation is based on an iconographical study of the various elements in the painting besides the nude Venus—the lapdog, the roses, and the myrtle (all of which Reff argues are symbols of marital fidelity); yet it seems to me that here again we have such a celebration of sensuality and fleshliness in the figure of the nude herself that the viewer's response must be first and foremost to the nude Venus. Even Reff, who pushes an allegorical interpretation of this painting the furthest, realizes the difficulties at the outset of his article where he confesses, "Admittedly, the symbolic and the sensual in Titian's art, the disguised mythological allusion and the vividly rendered natural form, are often so thoroughly fused as to render a strict iconographic analysis difficult: we shall attempt, nevertheless, to investigate the specific meaning of the work and the context in which it was created."[42] It is Reff's insistence upon separating the sensual and the iconographic—especially to the point of excluding any important consideration of the nude herself—that confuses his analysis. Reff is so intent upon establishing the specific historical context for the painting (a wedding anniversary present for Eleanora Gonzaga, he argues) and upon finding the allegorical significance, that he loses sight of the sensuality of this painting. This sensuality is called dramatically into focus by comparing Titian's *Venus Urbino* with Giorgione's *Venus* (figure 30), a comparison undertaken most brilliantly by Fritz Saxl in his article on the relationship of Titian

39. In fact, Hartt must sense that placing an emphasis on the neoplatonic aspect of the room is at odds with his statement that this room fits the character of the young prince "in consistency of its pagan eroticism," which matched the "hedonistic character" of Federigo (see note 36). Presumably for the patron paying the bills the emphasis was on the fleshly.

40. Linda Murray, *The High Renaissance,* p. 137.

41. Theodore Reff, "The Meaning of Titian's Venus of Urbino," *Pantheon* 21 (1963): 362.

42. Ibid., p. 359.

with Aretino.[43] Whereas the Giorgione Venus is asleep, and the viewer of the painting must play the part of the onlooker, Titian's Venus is awake and "has thrown off all that reminds one of Venus."[44] Saxl continues:

> The classical sculptures which Titian introduced as decorations into his earlier pictures preserved their character of ancient marbles; but in the Uffizi picture classical sculptural beauty seems to be overpowered by what one would call real life. Giorgione painted the sacred sleeping goddess lying like a beautiful marble which has by chance been brought into a modern landscape. The goddess has preserved her intangible beauty. In Titian's work the attitude of the marble goddess is preserved, but it is a lovely modern young woman who assumes it in the surroundings of her everyday *levée*. It is impossible to imagine anything further removed from the ideals of Cardinal Bembo and all the pedants of the time, who preached that only by imitating Cicero and the classical authors can beauty be created. What Titian created in this Venus is rather an expression of what at that time was called real nature, that is, realism elevated by the antique ideal.[45]

Saxl focuses his attention where Titian undeniably places it—on the nude figure, and more specifically, I would argue that our attention is drawn to the pudendum by the gesture of the Venus *pudica* (figure 31), a gesture which Panofsky notes so often "emphasizes what it pretends to conceal."[46] If Titian's *Venus Urbino* is a study of "harmonious, faithful love," it is a strange one indeed, for Titian's colors, textures and above all his nude Venus appeal to the sensual.

Panofsky's study of Titian's group of paintings entitled *Venus and a Musician* is among the most intriguing of all his iconographic studies of Titian, for he states at the outset that this group of pictures deals "with a novel subject calculated to stimulate the carnal passions (by

43. Fritz Saxl, *A Heritage of Images* (Harmondsworth, Middlesex: Penguin Books, 1970), pp. 71–87. Also see Erwin Panofsky, *Problems in Titian: Mostly Iconographic* (New York: New York Univ. Press, 1969), pp. 9–13 and chapter 2.

44. Saxl, p. 77. Linda Murray in *The High Renaissance* makes a similar comparison. Of Giorgione's *Venus* she says, "Her peaceful sleep divorces her entirely from the spectator's world, and there is none of that self-consciousness later found in Titian's *Venus of Urbino*" (p. 124). Of Titian's Venus she writes, "This Venus is no goddess, caught unawares on a summer afternoon; this is an expensive and successful courtesan, her hair tumbling from her diadem over her creamy shoulders, her lovely face empty of all expression but that of self-confident self-admiration, displayed with the trappings of her art upon an all too suggestive bed, with her maids in the background laying aside her worldly store in rich chests while she lies contentedly, 'for where your treasure is, there will your heart be also'" (p. 137).

45. Saxl, pp. 77–78.

46. Panofsky, *Problems,* p. 149.

the juxtaposition of a nude woman with a fully dressed gentleman) as well as to intrigue the mind. . . ."[47] This is an important point, for the sensual response is given equal consideration with the intellectual, and indeed, as Panofsky's study of the painting shows, the literal and the allegorical are at one here. The issue, as Panofsky carefully establishes, is the relationship of the senses to beauty. In the Renaissance conception of the problem, only the senses of sight and hearing enabled the mind to perceive beauty. What we get in this group of paintings is a working out of the debate as to the relative merits of the senses of sight and hearing.[48] Panofsky traces a change in iconographic detail, showing how sight and hearing are eventually accorded equal weight in the *Venus with a Lute Player.* It is the earliest rendering of the topic that is of interest for this study, however. In the Berlin *Venus with the Organ Player* (figure 32) Panofsky sees the sense of sight as having triumphed completely over the sense of hearing; the organ player "has lost all contact with his instrument. Both hands are off the keyboard and his right leg is swung over the bench so that, apart from the other leg, his whole body is turned toward the reclining goddess at whom he looks with rapt attention."[49] Because the organist seems to look at all of Venus (his gaze is not directed solely at her pudendum, as it is in the two Prado paintings), I am hesitant to argue that we see only the erotic triumphant here—both literally and allegorically. But certainly sensual, physical beauty is strong in its appeal here, and the delight of this painting is that the literal and allegorical are so closely fused—the iconography, the triumph of the sense of sight over the sense of hearing, the inability of the organ player to keep his eyes off of Venus, all are at one with the literal presentation of physical beauty. The organ player responds as we respond, and the statement made by

47. Ibid., p. 121.
48. Ibid., pp. 119ff. This was an issue that greatly interested Renaissance artists. Elsewhere I have argued that Spenser treats this in Book IV of *The Faerie Queene* (see "The Union of Florimell and Marinell: The Triumph of Hearing," *Spenser Studies* 6 [1985]: 115–27).
49. Panofsky, *Problems,* p. 123. In the two Prado paintings of the same subject Panofsky notes that the "triumph of the sense of sight over the sense of hearing is less complete. Here the legs of the organist are still turned to the left. In order to look at the nude woman he must turn sharply at the hip and must lean over backward, thus enabling the beholder to see the keyboard (invisible in the Berlin picture) and to realize that one or—in the signed version—both of the player's hands are still on the keys. This means, I think, that the supremacy of visible beauty (incarnate in the nude) over the audible charms of music is no longer uncontested. Far from abandoning his instrument altogether, the player now attempts to enjoy the world of sight while not cutting himself off from the world of sound" (p. 123).

this painting about the appeal of female beauty to the male viewer reminds us that the carnal passions as well as the intellectual are stimulated by Renaissance painters.[50]

Annibale and Agostino Carracci are credited with restoring Renaissance art "to the main channel of classically inspired realism,"[51] and we might reasonably expect a high degree of eroticism in their paintings, especially those of Agostino, in spite of the decrees of the Council of Trent and the Counter-Reformation. Agostino Carracci did in fact do four paintings on the subject of love which are now in Vienna. Of special interest is *Love in the Golden Age* (figure 34) where the concept of the golden age as one of sexual freedom is clearly depicted. There is no doubt about the nature of the activity of the various couples; two couples in the background are engaged in sexual intercourse, but genitalia are not much in evidence. The painting may be related "in spirit as well as in style," as Otto Kurz suggests, to the "loves of the gods," but in spite of the turned, if swaying bodies, the serenity of the landscape gives this painting something of a quietness the "loves of the gods" lack.[52] Nonetheless, the fact that Agostino would paint such a

50. Barolsky, pp. 165–70, sees the two Prado paintings as satirical and says, "The spirit of these paintings does not relate simply to the serious Neoplatonizing texts of Ficino, Bembo, Leon Ebreo, and Castiglione, but to the playful treatment of Neoplatonism that one finds in the humorous, if vulgar writings of Aretino and his circle. After all, the aperture of Venus's body at which Titian's musicians are looking in the two Madrid paintings is clearly not the Neoplatonic 'window' to the soul" (p. 169).

Another interesting set of pictures by Titian, his Danaë, is discussed by Panofsky, and here he is able to show how the late Danaë (figure 33) accentuates both the erotic and the ominous elements.

> The presence of a little dog, the rumpled bedclothes, the omission of the loin cloth in favor of a *Venus pudica* gesture (which, as so often, emphasizes what it pretends to conceal) lend a more intimate character to the scene; moreover, the expression on the blushing face of the de-heroized—and, if one may say so, de-Michelangelized—*Danaë* is so enraptured yet so remote that she seems to "die" in the Elizabethan sense of the word.
>
> On the other hand, the atmosphere is one of dark foreboding. The golden shower, almost reddish, bursts forth from the dark clouds in a somber, thunderous sky (Jove seems to appear not as a "Jupiter Pluvius" but as "Jupiter Tonans," manifesting himself not in a gently descending stream of gold but in a terrific explosion); and the hideous old nurse, who has replaced the Lysippian Cupid of the earlier version, serves not only to set off the youth and beauty of Danaë but also to stress the miraculous nature of an event which in the old woman excites only greed but transforms her young mistress into a chosen vessel destined to give a savior to the world. (*Problems*, pp. 149–50)

51. See note 17 above.

52. Kurz, p. 231, dates this painting in the late 1580s or early 1590s. He writes, "They are imbued with the spirit of Venetian art. . . . The landscape backgrounds with

picture with couples clearly engaged in intercourse shows that the impulse for painting mythological or classical scenes had not been snuffed out by the decrees of the Council of Trent. The verses printed under an engraving of the painting explain its meaning:

> Come la palma indicio è di vittoria
> Cosi d'Amor conveniente è il frutto
> Quella dolcezza, de cui vien produtto,
> Il seme, onde Natura, e'l ciel si gloria.

As the palm is a sign of victory, so the fruit of congenial love is that sweetness from which is produced the seed whence Nature and heaven are glorified.

No great allegory here, merely a celebration of the sweetness of physical love.

The most famous works of the Carracci, however, are the frescoes, executed primarily by Annibale, in the Palazzo Farnese in Rome. Giovanni Bellori in *The Lives of Annibale and Agostino Carracci* pointed to the iconography of the frescoes as early as the seventeenth century, and, interestingly enough, he saw the *Triumph of Bacchus* as a negative exemplum of the "theme . . . [of] human love governed by Heaven."[53] We see love displaying its power over all in the Gallery, says Bellori, and the bacchanal of the vault "is the symbol of drunkenness, the source of impure desires."[54] All subsequent interpretations of the frescoes of the Gallery must confront Bellori in one way or another, and there has been little agreement among critics, from John Martin's assertion that what we have here is the triumph of divine love to Charles Dempsey's interpretation of the frescoes as satiric, depicting a mock-epic triumph, a triumph not of valor and virtue, but of drunkenness and lasciviousness.[55] Whether we see the Gallery as satirical or as a depiction of the triumph of divine love by positive or negative example, the fact remains that a sense of the erotic does not dominate here as it does in the Palazzo del Tè. The erotic element is surely muted in the *Triumph of Bacchus*

---

their small figures lightly brushed in are truly Venetian. It is only in the almost life-size figures of the foreground that we can discern a certain dryness which is not Venetian. A Venetian's brush would have immersed his figures in the atmosphere of the surrounding landscape, while in Agostino's pictures the sculptural character of the large isolated figures and groups is evident."

53. Bellori, p. 51.

54. Ibid., p. 51.

55. John Martin, *The Farnese Gallery* (Princeton: Princeton Univ. Press, 1965); Charles Dempsey, 'Et Nos Cedamus Amori': Observations on the Farnese Gallery," *Art Bulletin* 50 (1968): 363–74; see also Donald Posner's review of Martin's book in *Art Bulletin* 47 (1966): 109–14. Wind's comments on the Renaissance tendency to treat the pagan gods in a facetious style are also relevant (see *Bellini's Feast*, pp. 6–8).

(figure 35), and even in a scene like the *Rape of Galatea* (figure 36)[56] we do not get much sense of the sensual. Genitalia are mostly covered, and in ways that are less suggestive than more so. There are two exceptions. In the *Venus and Anchises* fresco on the wall, the slung-leg motif may at least imply sexual union,[57] and the way in which the material stands stiffly over Anchises' penis may suggest an erection (figure 37), although much of the drapery in the fresco has a sculptured, baroque look, and the placcid look on Venus' face along with the inscription on the step, GENUS VNDE LATINVM, certainly keep the erotic at a minimum here.[58]

The other exception is the fresco of Jupiter and Juno (figure 38). This is supposed to be a picture of conjugal love, of course, but the doting way in which Jupiter looks upon Juno, the way his hand grasps her leg, and the figure of Juno herself, give this painting a comic eroticism missing in many of the other frescoes. Juno is wearing the girdle of Venus, and her breasts draw our attention to them as they stand firm and pointed as do no others in the gallery. Even while we note the effect of Juno's erotic posture on Jupiter, it is true that Jupiter's doting look is almost, as Dempsey says, "imbecilic."[59] Indeed, Dempsey finds this painting to be the most comic in the Gallery, as we have depicted here one of Jupiter's "most humiliating moments."[60] Comedy there is, I think, but it is a comedy derived from seeing the effect of Juno's undoubted eroticism on Jupiter.

On the whole in the Gallery, however, we have none of the lush sensuousness that pervades Titian and little of the eroticism of Giulio Romano. Allegory in whatever interpretation is triumphant in the Farnese Gallery; we are compelled, I think, to move quickly from the literal sense to the allegorical senses of the frescoes; we are not likely to be enthralled by the very lushness of the literal presentation. It may be that the Carracci returned Renaissance painting to the main channel

56. The identification of this fresco has been disputed. Martin, pp. 105–09, argues for Glaucus and Scylla; Dempsey, in "Two 'Galateas' by Agostino Carracci Re-identified," *Zeitschrift für Kunstgeschichte* 29 (1966): 67–70, wants to title it "Thetis Carried to the Bridal Chamber of Peleus."

57. For an excellent analysis of this motif see Leo Steinberg's chapter, "The Metaphors of Love and Birth in Michelangelo's *Pietas,*" in *Studies in Erotic Art,* ed. Theodore Bowie and Cornelia V. Christenson (New York and London: Basic Books, 1970).

58. Dempsey, " 'Et Nos Cedamus,' " p. 368, sees this as a mocking contrast to the Roman myth.

59. Ibid., p. 369.

60. Ibid., p. 369. Barolsky, pp. 205–06, also sees the gallery as comic and has noted such details as a nude next to Jupiter and Juno "who eccentrically covers his head with drapery."

of classical realism, but the classical spirit of the erotic, as conceived and presented by earlier Renaissance painters, is muted or turned comic in the Farnese Gallery.

To pretend that most of the works discussed in this chapter do not belong in a study of erotica is to distort our view of the Italian Renaissance. Whatever other categories most of the prints and paintings discussed here might be put into—be they studies of style or Ovidianism in the Renaissance—however else we might "read" these works, if we do not acknowledge the fact that first they appeal to the erotic sensibility, we have missed much of the point.

Fig. 1   Waldeck drawing after Giulio Romano, *posizioni*. Reproduced by permission of the Kinsey Institute for Research in Sex, Gender, and Reproduction, Inc.

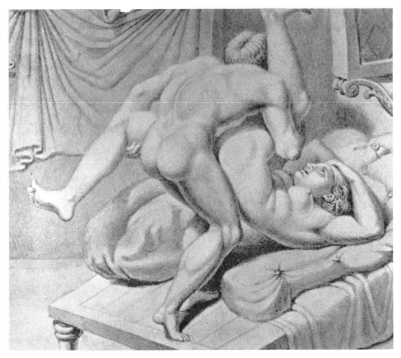

Fig. 2   Waldeck drawing after Giulio Romano, *posizioni*. Reproduced by permission of the Kinsey Institute for Research in Sex, Gender, and Reproduction, Inc.

Fig. 3   Jan Van der Noot, *A Theatre for Voluptuous Worldlings* (1569); (Wheeler).

Fig. 4   Jan Van der Noot, *A Theatre for Voluptuous Worldlings* (1569); (Wheeler).

Doe what we can, we must abide
the paine of being hornify'd.

The second part, To the same tune.

If they once bid vs goe,
we dare not twice say no,

Fig. 5 "Cuckold's Haven," in *The Roxburghe Ballads* (Wheeler).

A godly father sitting on a draught,
To do as neede, and nature hath us taught;
Mumbled (as was his maner) certen prayr's,
And unto him the Devil straight repayr's:
And boldly to revile him he begins,
Alledging that such prayr's are deadly sins;
And that it shewd, he was devoyd of grace,
To speake to God, from so unmeete a place.
The reverent man, though at the first dismaid;
Yet strong in faith, to Satan thus he said.
Thou damned spirit, wicked, false & lying,
Dispairing thine own good, & ours envying:
Ech take his due, and me thou canst not hurt,
To God my pray'r I meant, to thee the durt.
Pure prayr ascends to him that high doth sit,
Down fals the filth,[58] for fiends of hel more fit.

Fig. 6 "A godly father sitting on a draught" from Sir John Harington, *The Metamorphosis of Ajax* (Wheeler).

Fig. 7 "The Picture of Gabriell Haruey as hee is readie to let fly vpon *Ajax*," in Thomas Nashe, *Haue with You to Saffron-Waldon* (Wheeler).

Apollo di Hyacintho.

Nesun mincolpi, se del mio donzello
le guance io prezzo piu che gemme et oro
da poi che mi fu amor si crudo, et fello
per quella onde verdeggia il vago alloro

pero son fatto a quel desio ribello
et ardo sol per questo, et discoloro
et si mi piace ognhor la noua salma
chio le concedo dogni honor la palma

Fig. 8   Perino del Vaga, *Apollo di Hyacintho*. Reproduced by permission of the Istituto Nazionale per la Grafica, Rome (Gabinetto Fotografico Nazionale).

Gioue in fiamma.

Io, che co'l folgor ʒ'hauentar mi uanto   E'l tuo bel uiſo, donna, in me' puo tanto
La terra, e'l cielo, et ogni grande' alteʒʒa   C h'io corro in fiáma, et ho di cio uagheʒʒa
Vinto mi trouo da chi in doglia, e'n pianto   Hor che' farete' miſeri mortali
I ſuoi ſeguaci lungamente' aueʒʒa ,   S'io preſo cedo agli amoroſi ſtrali ?

Fig. 9   Perino del Vaga, *Gioue in Fiamma*. Reproduced by permission of the Istituto Nazionale per la Grafica, Rome (Gabinetto Fotografico Nazionale).

Fig. 10   Perino del Vaga, *Gioue in Satyro*. Reproduced by permission of the Istituto Nazionale per la Grafica, Rome (Gabinetto Fotografico Nazionale).

Mercurio parla a Glauros.

Poi che sei fatta per inuidia un Sasso
Ne uedi, u, l'empia uoglia ti trasporte,
E chiuder pensi, a chi non chiude il passo
Il crudo Rè dele tartaree porte;

In sasso trasformata qui ti lasso
Eterno esempio di si iniqua sorte,
Ma inuidia piu di me ti uince e sforza
Ch'ella quel dentro cangia, et io la scorza

Fig. 11 Perino del Vaga, *Mercurio parla a Glauros*. Reproduced by permission of the Istituto Nazionale per la Grafica, Rome (Gabinetto Fotografico Nazionale).

~: Parla Cupido :~

S'a me' son fatti i strali miei rubelli,   Qual herba trouarò, che mi diuelli
&r di mia propria mà me stesso i piago;   Dal cuor si cara, e si celeste imago;
Se tanto il uiso pomo, e gliocchi belli   Dunq̃ uoti porgete' a questa: io pgo
Di Psiche': che piu d'altro nó m'appago;   Amanti; ch'io son uinto; e ciò nó nego ·

Fig. 12   Perino del Vaga, *Parla Cupido*. Reproduced by permission of
the Istituto Nazionale per la Grafica, Rome (Gabinetto Fotografico
Nazionale).

17

. *Parla Vulcano a Ceres* .

Chi crederia, che i senſi, oue' souente'   Fuſſe altra fiamma mai tanto poſſente'
Fanueoſi penſier fanno dimoro,   C'haueſſe' loco fra le' fiamme' loro !
& occupati alla fornace' ardente'   & pur Ceres la tua trouato hà loco
Stan giorno e notte a far qualche lauoro,   Nel petto de Vulcano i mezo al foco

Fig. 13   Perino del Vaga, *Parla Vulcano a Ceres*. Reproduced by permission of the Istituto Nazionale per la Grafica, Rome (Gabinetto Fotografico Nazionale).

Fig. 14   Agostino Carracci, "Hercules and Deianira," in *L'Arretin d'Augustin Carrache*. Reproduced by permission of the Kinsey Institute for Research in Sex, Gender, and Reproduction, Inc.

Fig. 15 Agostino Carracci, "Antony and Cleopatra," in *L'Arretin d'Augustin Carrache*. Reproduced by permission of the Kinsey Institute for Research in Sex, Gender, and Reproduction, Inc.

Fig. 16 Agostino Carracci, "Julia and an Athlete," in *L'Arretin d'Augustin Carrache*. Reproduced by permission of the Kinsey Institute for Research in Sex, Gender, and Reproduction, Inc.

Fig. 17   Agostino Carracci, "Ovid and Corinna," in *L'Arretin d'Augustin Carrache*. Reproduced by permission of the Kinsey Institute for Research in Sex, Gender, and Reproduction, Inc.

Fig. 18   Agostino Carracci, "Jupiter and Juno," in *L'Arretin d'Augustin Carrache*. Reproduced by permission of the Kinsey Institute for Research in Sex, Gender, and Reproduction, Inc.

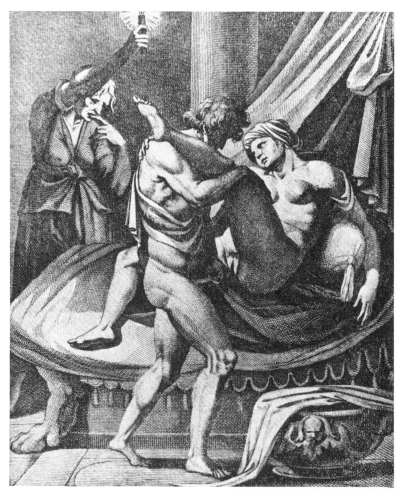

Fig. 19   Agostino Carracci, untitled, in *L'Arretin d'Augustin Carrache*. Reproduced by permission of the Kinsey Institute for Research in Sex, Gender, and Reproduction, Inc.

Fig. 20   Agostino Carracci, "Satyr and Satyress," in *L'Arretin d'Augustin Carrache*. Reproduced by permission of the Kinsey Institute for Research in Sex, Gender, and Reproduction, Inc.

Fig. 21 Antonio Tempesta, *Maggio*. Reproduced by permission of the Istituto Nazionale per la Grafica, Rome (Savio).

ÆTAS AVREA

Postquam regnis senex cæli faturnus haberet
Omne malum tenebris alta fatebat humus.

Et secura uener florebant gaudia mundo
Paxge coronatis uells regebat equis.

Non chipegus eustis erat fine numere trilligis
Obuia fecundas pandit amica sinus.

Fig. 22   Antonio Tempesta, *Aetas Aurea*. Reproduced by permission of the Istituto Nazionale per la Grafica, Rome (Savio).

Fig. 23   Taddeo di Bartolo, *Gluttony.* Basilica Collegiata di S. Maria Assunta, San Gimignano. Reproduced with the permission of the Basilica and the Soprintendenza Per i Beni Artistici E Storici per le Province di Siena e Grosseto (Fontanelli–Wheeler).

Fig. 24 Taddeo di Bartolo, *Lechery*. Basilica Collegiata di S. Maria Assunta, San Gimignano. Reproduced with the permission of the Basilica and the Soprintendenza Per i Beni Artistici E Storici per le Province di Siena e Grosseto (Fontanelli–Wheeler).

Fig. 25 Luca Signorelli, *Last Judgment* (detail). Duomo, Orvieto (Moretti–Wheeler).

Fig. 26 Giulio Romano, *Jupiter and Olympias*, in Room of Cupid and Psyche, Palazzo del Tè, Mantua. Reproduced by permission of the Palazzo Tè (Giovetti).

Fig. 27 Giulio Romano, *Wedding Feast of Cupid and Psyche*, in Room of Cupid and Psyche, Palazzo del Tè, Mantua. Reproduced by permission of the Palazzo Tè (Giovetti).

Fig. 28 Giulio Romano, detail of ceiling in Room of Cupid and Psyche, Palazzo del Tè, Mantua. Reproduced by permission of the Palazzo Tè (Giovetti).

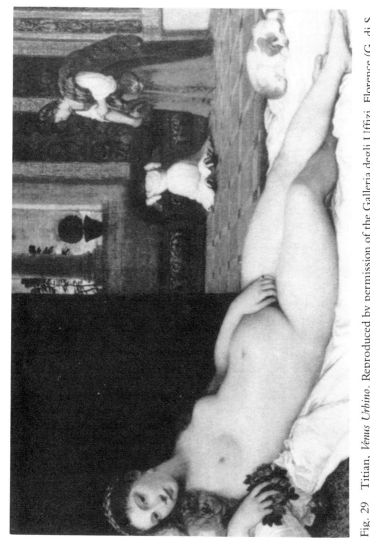

Fig. 29 Titian, *Venus Urbino*. Reproduced by permission of the Galleria degli Uffizi, Florence (G. di S. Becocci–Wheeler).

Fig. 30 Giorgione, *Venus*. Reproduced by permission of the Gemäldegalerie, Dresden.

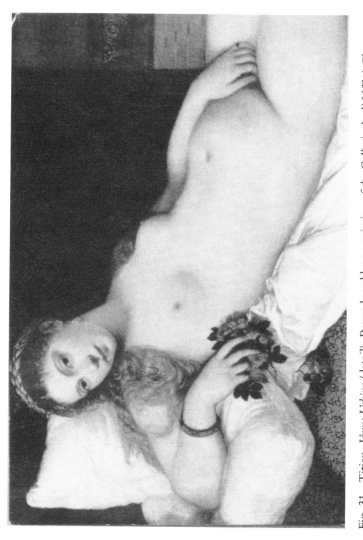

Fig. 31 Titian, *Venus Urbino* (detail). Reproduced by permission of the Galleria degli Uffizi, Florence (G. di S. Beccoci–Wheeler).

Fig. 32 Titian, *Venus with an Organ Player*. Reproduced courtesy of the Gemäldegalerie, Staatliche Museen, Berlin.

Fig. 33   Titian, *Danaë*. Reproduced by permission of the Museo del Prado.

Fig. 34   Agostino Carracci, *Love in the Golden Age*. Reproduced by permission of the Kunsthistorisches Museum, Vienna.

Fig. 35 Annibale Carracci, *The Triumph of Bacchus*. Palazzo Farnese, Rome. Reproduced by permission of the Istituto Nazionale per il Catalogo e la Documentazione, Rome.

Fig. 36 Annibale Carracci, *Galatea*. Palazzo Farnese, Rome. Reproduced by permission of the Istituto Nazionale per il Catalogo e la Documentazione, Rome.

Fig. 37 Annibale Carracci, *Venus and Anchises*. Palazzo Farnese, Rome. Reproduced by permission of the Istituto Nazionale per il Catalogo e la Documentazione, Rome.

Fig. 38 Annibale Carracci, *Jupiter and Juno*. Palazzo Farnese, Rome. Reproduced by permission of the Istituto Nazionale per il Catalogo e la Documentazione, Rome.

CHAPTER 5

A Study in Ambivalence: English Views of Italy

At yet ten Morte Arthures *do not the tenth part so much harme, as one of these bookes, made in* Italie, *and translated in England.*

Roger Ascham, The Scholemaster

Before I goe anie further, let me speake a word or two of this Aretine. *It was one of the wittiest knaues that euer God made.*

Thomas Nashe, The Vnfortunate Traveller

Ascham could attack Italian literature and morals, yet he felt one should read *The Courtier*; Spenser objected to Italianate abuses of courtly behavior, yet he drew on Ariosto and Tasso extensively in writing *The Faerie Queene*; Nashe condemned obscene literature, and yet he styled himself the English Aretino. On such paradoxes must one build a picture of England's attitude toward Italy; nowhere is that attitude better illustrated than in the realm of erotica.

The traditional historical thesis about England's relationship with Italy, set forth at the beginning of this century in Lewis Einstein's *The Italian Renaissance in England,* was that England's admiration and imitation of Italy early in the English Renaissance gave way to a period of revulsion.[1] This far too simplistic picture has been altered by later scholars,[2] and I think a more tenable position might be put in the following terms: England's attitude toward Italy throughout the Re-

1. Lewis Einstein, *The Italian Renaissance in England* (New York: Columbia Univ. Press, 1902).
2. John L. Lievsay, *The Elizabethan Image of Italy* (Folger Booklets on Tudor and Stuart Civilization, Ithaca, N.Y.: Cornell Univ. Press, 1964); R. C. Simonini, Jr., *Italian Scholarship in Renaissance England* (Chapel Hill: University of North Carolina Studies in Comparative Literature, no. 3, 1952); George B. Parks, "The Decline and Fall of the English Renaissance Admiration for Italy," *Huntington Library Quarterly* 31 (August 1968): 341–57.

naissance was ambivalent. On the one hand the English admired and imitated much in the way of Italian learning, general culture, and especially literature. On the other hand, the English abhorred and feared Italy as a land of Catholicism, lewd living, and lewd writing. Erotica allows us to see both sides of this ambivalence exceptionally well, for on the one hand it was made exemplary of all that was held to be evil in Italy, and on the other hand, to certain writers, it was an example of the fullest expression of literary freedom, and it provided models for imitation by English writers trying to make a living by the pen just as Aretino had. It is also important to remember that whatever the ambivalence in England's attitude toward Italy in the Renaissance, Italy's influence in England was extensive in many areas—scholarship, writing, music, portrait painting, language, commerce, courtiership, and printing, to name a few.[3] All of these areas have been the subject of specialized studies and need little elaboration here; nevertheless I think it would be wise to remind ourselves of some of the less publicized facts that are especially relevant to this study.[4]

While the *posizioni* of Giulio Romano were known by reputation in connection with the *sonetti lussuriosi* of Aretino, English knowledge of Italian erotica in the visual arts was for the most part limited to those who were able to view paintings on the continent or had access to copies of various kinds.[5] Written erotica was quite well known, however, and in the printing of certain Italian texts one finds some interesting connections between England and Italy.

John Wolfe was a prominent printer in England from 1579 to 1601; Sellers calls him "the most prolific and important printer in Italian

3. Parks, "Decline and Fall," p. 342.
4. To list some of the most prominent not already cited: Lievsay, *The Englishman's Italian Books, 1550–1700* (Philadelphia: Univ. of Pennsylvania Press, 1969); Lievsay, *Stefano Guazzo and the English Renaissance, 1575–1675* (Chapel Hill: Univ. of North Carolina Press, 1961); Parks, *The English Traveler to Italy* (Stanford: Stanford Univ. Press, n.d.); Giuliano Pellegrini, *Un fiorentino alla corte d'Inghilterra nel Cinquecento: Petruccio Ubaldini* (Turin: University of Pisa Studies in Modern Philology, n.s., vii, 1967); Mario Praz, *The Flaming Heart* (Garden City, N.Y.: Doubleday Anchor Books, 1958); Frances Yates, *John Florio* (1934; rpt. New York: Octagon Books, 1968); Lawrence Stone, *An Elizabethan: Sir Horatio Palavicino* (Oxford: Clarendon Press, 1956).
5. See chapter 3, n. 4. A traveler to Italy like Sir Philip Sidney certainly became familiar with Italian painters and painting. We know, for example, that Sidney sat for Veronese to have his portrait painted. See John Buxton, *Sir Philip Sidney and the English Renaissance* (London: Macmillan, 1954), pp. 69–71. Titian sent paintings to Philip II of Spain when he was in England in 1554. See Panofsky, *Problems,* p. 150. Everard Guilpin in his "Satyre Preludium," in *Skialetheia,* ed. D. Allen Carroll (Chapel Hill: Univ. of North Carolina Press, 1974), refers to "loues loues" as executed by Titian (ll. 55–56).

during Elizabeth's reign."[6] He is important because, as has been mentioned earlier, he published editions in Italian of works by Machiavelli and Aretino that had been banned in Italy. Wolfe gave his editions false or fictitious places of printing in Italy, probably to further his sales.[7] Sellers cites Giordano Bruno's statement made to the Venetian Inquisitor to the effect that, "All those books of mine which say in their imprint that they were printed in Venice, were printed in England, and it was the printer who would put on them that they were printed in Venice to sell them more easily."[8] Wolfe was a man with an eye for a good market, and he was shrewd enough to know that most readers would think that a book printed in Venice would be of superior quality. There is evidence that Wolfe worked at his trade in Florence in 1576, and soon after his return to England he started publishing Italian works.[9] Among these publications there were three books of Aretino's works, and the 1584 edition of *La Prima* and *Seconda Parte de Ragionamenti* was something of a success.[10] Thus there seems to have been a market for Italian erotica, and John Wolfe cornered most of the market. Someone admired Italian works that were not neoplatonic.

Even though we have long recognized the debts that Spenser and Sidney owe to Italian models, we have often failed to take into account the fact that English writers of bawdy, pornographic, and obscene literature admired and imitated Italian models as well. English jokes, paradoxes, literary quarrels, and obscene poems all were influenced by Italian works. If we look at the numerous English jest books, for example, we find that many of the jests are derived from Poggio's *Facetiae*.[11] Paradoxical encomia flourished in Renaissance England; Anthony Munday translated Lando's *Paradossi,* and in his *Metamorphosis of Ajax* Sir John Harington cites the precedents from which he is working,

6. Harry Sellers, "Italian Books Printed in England Before 1640," *The Library,* 4th ser., vol. 5, no. 2 (1924): 108.

7. Harry R. Hoppe, "John Wolfe, Printer and Publisher, 1579–1601," *The Library,* 4th ser., vol. 14, no. 3 (1933): 241–88.

8. Sellers, p. 111.

9. Hoppe, p. 243; and Sellers, p. 108n.

10. Sellers, p. 114. This edition of the *Ragionamenti* was unlicensed; the other works of Aretino, both licensed, were *Quattro Comedie* (1588) and *La Terza et Ultima Parte de Ragionamenti* (1589). The letters of Aretino were licensed to Wolfe in 1588 but were never published. Wolfe also published the works of Petruccio Ubaldini, the Florentine in London (Hoppe, p. 243; and Pellegrini, pp. 32–33) as well as the Harvey material in the Nashe-Harvey quarrel (Hoppe, p. 268). Hoppe feels that Harvey lived with Wolfe from September 1592 to April 1593.

11. See Mary Augusta Scott, *Elizabethan Translations from Italian* (Baltimore: Modern Language Association, 1895–99).

including Italians who have written in "honour of the Pox," in praise of "bawderie," and the *"Puttana Errante."*[12] In other literary modes Thomas Nashe styles himself the English Aretino, and we shall see him playing that role in his poetry and his literary warfare with Gabriel Harvey.[13] All of this English erotica will be examined in the following chapters; the point I wish to establish here is that Italian erotica was itself available in Renaissance England, and it did provide models for imitation by English writers. If an Englishman sat down to write erotica, he used Italian models, just as he did when he sat down to write an epic poem. And John Florio made sure that Italian erotica would be available to those who might not be sufficiently fluent in Italian through his Italian-English dictionary, *A Worlde of Wordes* (1598). Indeed, Florio's work through his successive editions in making Italian literature accessible to educated Englishmen is a remarkable barometer of English taste. Frances Yates, for example, has pointed out how Florio changed the tone and thrust of his *Second Frvtes* (1591) from the moralizing so prevalent in his *Firste Fruites* (1578) in order to give his work more popular appeal.[14] In the creation of his dictionary, Florio was equally attuned to English taste, and he took great pains to make contemporary Italian literature, especially learned erotica and pornography, available to his English readers as no lexicographer had done before him.[15] Florio had asserted that Italian literature was difficult to comprehend, for even in the Renaissance "Italian literature" meant primarily the works of Dante, Petrarch, and Boccaccio:

> And I haue seene the best, yea naturall Italians, not onely stagger, but euen sticke fast in the myre, and at last giue it ouer, or giue their verdict with An *ignoramus. Boccace* is prettie hard, yet vnderstood: Petrarche harder, but explaned: *Dante* hardest, but commented. Some doubt if all aright.[16]

But Florio also intended to make other Italian authors accessible, and he wondered:

> How then ayme we at *Peter Aretine,* that is so wittie, hath such varietie, and

---

12. Sir John Harington, *A New Discourse of a Stale Subject, called The Metamorphosis of Ajax,* ed. Elizabeth Story Donno (London: Routledge & Kegan Paul; New York: Columbia Univ. Press, 1962), pp. 63–64. All subsequent references to the *Metamorphosis* are to this edition.
13. Thomas Nashe, *Nashes Lenten Stuffe,* in *The Works of Thomas Nashe,* ed. R. B. McKerrow, rpt. ed. F. P. Wilson, 5 vols. (Oxford: Basil Blackwell, 1958), III, 152. All subsequent Nashe references are to this edition.
14. Yates, pp. 129, 136–37, 187.
15. See my article "Florio's Use of Contemporary Italian Literature in *A Worlde of Wordes,*" *Dictionaries* 1 (1979): 47–56.
16. Florio, *A Worlde,* sig. A4[r].

frames so manie new words? At *Francesco Doni,* who is so fantasticall, & so strange? At *Thomaso Garzoni* in his *Piazza vniuersale;* or at *Allessandro Cittolini* in his *Typocosmia,* who haue more proper and peculiar words concerning euerie seuerall trade, arte, or occupation for eureie particular toole, or implement belonging vnto them, then euer any man heeretofore either collected in any booke, or sawe collected in any one language? How shall we vnderstand *Hanniball Caro,* who is so full of wittie iestes, sharpe quips, nipping tantes, and scoffing phrases against that graue and learned man *Lodouico Casteluetri,* in his *Apologia de' Banchi*? Howe shall the English Gentleman come to the perfect vnderstanding of *Federico Grisone,* his *Arte del Caualcare,* who is so full of strange phrases, and vnusuall wordes, peculiar onely to horse-manship, and proper but to *Caualarizzi*? How shall we vnderstande so manie and so strange bookes, of so seuerall, and so fantasticall subjects as be written in the Italian toong?[17]

In order to make these writers accessible Florio tells us that he has read their works, along with those of Berni and other sixteenth-century Italian writers.[18] Florio is consequently careful to include in his dictionary the bawdy definitions for all of Berni's fruits and vegetables, and he is equally careful to define all of the appropriate vulgar words.

Whereas Italian erotica was to some Englishmen yet another aspect of Italy to be admired and imitated, to most Englishmen, especially those of staunchly Protestant persuasions, it was very much a part of the grand papist plot to undermine England and bring about her return to Roman Catholic control. Roger Ascham warns that traveling in Italy is certainly an evil practice, but he also recognizes the power of the printed word, and this is even more to be feared:

> These be the inchantementes of *Circes,* brought out of Italie, to marre mens maners in England: much, by example of ill life, but more by preceptes of fonde bookes, of late translated out of *Italian* into English, sold in euery shop in London, commended by honest titles the soner to corrupt honest maners: dedicated ouer boldlie to vertuous and honorable personages, the easielier to begile simple and innocēt wittes. It is pitie, that those, which haue authoritie and charge, to allow and dissalow bookes to be printed, be no more circumspect herein, than they are. Ten sermons at Paules Crosse do not so moche good for mouyng mē to trewe doctrine, as one of those bookes do harme, with inticing men to ill liuing. Yea, I say farder, those bookes tend not so moch to corrupt honest liuyng, as they do, to subuert trewe Religion. Mo Papists be made, by your mery bookes of *Italie,* than by your earnest bookes of *Louain.*[19]

17. Ibid., sig. A4ʳ.
18. Frantz, "Florio's Use."
19. Roger Ascham, *The Scholemaster,* in *The English Works of Roger Ascham,* ed. W. A. Wright (Cambridge: Cambridge Univ. Press, 1904), pp. 229–30.

Ascham's ultimate concern, as we see here, is with religion, and it is this that Italian books influence detrimentally, he contends. Ascham's assertion is that thoughts of lechery lead to religious corruption. His assumption is that a man whose appetite rules his reason is most susceptible to the worst kinds of intellectual errors in the realm of theology. It is lust then, Italy's national vice, which is to be feared most as it is presented in Italian books; lust will entice the Protestant Englishman from the path of the true religion. The printing of bawdy Italian books is, says Ascham, a part of an insidious plot of the Papists who, seeing that their openly disputatious books have had no effect, have persuaded the "sutle and secrete Papistes" in England to translate bawdy Italian books to allure young minds and pave the way for Roman Catholic theology.[20] Ascham recalls that when "Papistrie, as a standyng poole, couered and ouerflowed all England," the main business of books in English lay in "two speciall poyntes, in open mans slaughter, and bold bawdrye," and he cites the *Morte Arthure*.[21] And yet, he continues in a famous passage, "ten *Morte Arthures* do not the tenth part so much harme, as one of these bookes, made in *Italie*, and translated in England." These books are dangerous because "they open, not fond and common wayes to vice, but such subtle, cunnying, new, and diuerse shiftes, to carry young willes to vanitie, and yong wittes to mischief, to teach old bawdes new schole poyntes, as the simple head of an English man is not hable to inuent, nor neuer was hard of in England before, yea when Papistrie ouerflowed all." Such insidious books carry the "will to vanitie," and once "good manners" are marred, minds are easily corrupted. Even so, only Englishmen Italianated would be so corrupted, were these books not being "made in English" in increasing numbers.[22]

Ascham is not alone in his fear of Italian books.[23] Stephen Gosson in his famous attack on the theater sees the evils of the stage stemming from the Devil's use of Italian books. Gosson claims that the Devil deals in subtlety and treachery and that "First, hee sente ouer many wanton Italian bookes, which being trāslated into english, haue poysoned the olde maners of our Country with foreine delights, they haue so hardned the readers harts & seuerer writers are trode vnder foote, none are so pleasunte or plausible as they, that sound some kinde of

20. Ibid., p. 230.
21. Ibid., p. 231.
22. Ibid., pp. 231–32.
23. As has been mentioned, Ascham's view of Italy and Italian books was not entirely negative. He was proud of his Queen's ability to speak Italian, and he cites *The Courtier* as a book that ought to be read.

libertie in our eares."[24] Consequently, he argues that good books are
neglected and ". . . the increase of vanity is the decrease of vertue.
Therefore the Deuill not contented with the number he hath corrupted
with reading Italian baudery, because all canot reade preseteth us Comedies cut by the same paterne, which drag such a monstrous taile after
thē, as is able to sweep whole cities into his lap."[25]

The English abhorrence of Italian lechery went far beyond Italian
books, of course. To most Englishmen Italy was the land of lust depicted in lascivious tales; for them fiction was reality. Ascham claimed
that he saw more "libertie to sinne" in the nine days he was in Italy
("I thanke God, my abode there, was but ix. dayes") "than euer I hard
tell of in our noble Citie of London in ix yeare."[26] William Thomas in
his *History of Italy* grudgingly admits that although he can recite many
virtues of the Italian "even so on the other side if I were disposed to
speak of vice I might happen to find a number as ill as in any other
men. . . ."[27] Thomas goes on to explain, "For whereas temperance,
modesty, and other civil virtues excel in the number of the Italian nobility more than in the nobility of any other nation that I know, so
undoubtedly the fleshly appetite with unnatural heat and other things
in them that be vicious do pass all the terms of reason or honesty."[28]

The practice of sending young men to Italy is bewailed by William
Harrison. In his *Description of England* he finds that young men sent to
Italy bring home nothing but "mere atheisme, infidelitie, vicious con-
uersation, & ambitious and proud behauiour," and he cites examples
of those who have returned full of what Englishmen came to regard
as Machiavellianism.[29] While Harrison does not convey Ascham's mor-
alistic fervor or eloquence, he plainly shares his abhorrence of a man
without religious convictions (better even to be a Papist!).

Ascham, Thomas, and Harrison all claim to be presenting fact; they
are giving a true picture of Italy and the Englishmen who went there,
they assert. The negative reaction to Italy continued to coexist with the
positive one of admiration and imitation throughout most of the Renaissance, but the negative view came to dominate much of Elizabethan
fiction and drama.[30] If one wanted to write about lechery and bloody

---

24. Stephen Gosson, *Playes Confuted in fiue Actions* (London, 1582), sig. B6[v].
25. Ibid., sig. B6[r&v].
26. Ascham, p. 234.
27. William Thomas, *The History of Italy (1549),* ed. George B. Parks (Ithaca: Cornell Univ. Press, 1963), p. 13. See also p. 80.
28. Ibid., p. 13.
29. William Harrison, *Description of England,* ed. from the first two editions of *Hol-inshed's Chronicle* by F. J. Furnivall (London: N. Trubner, 1877–81), pp. 129–30.
30. See Parks, "Decline and Fall."

revenge, one set the scene in Italy. Tale after tale, play after play is testament to this. John Marston set forth the dangers of Italy most expertly in *The Malcontent*. Malevole says to Bilioso, who is about to leave his wife behind at the palace in Genoa while he goes to Florence:

> At the palace? Now discretion shield man! For God's
> love, let's ha' no more cuckolds. Hymen begins to put
> off his saffron robe. Keep thy wife i' the state of
> grace. Heart o' truth, I would sooner leave my lady
> singled in a bordello than in the Genoa palace.
> Sin there appearing in her sluttish shape,
> Would soon grow loathsome, even to blushes' sense;
> Surfeit would choke intemperate appetite,
> Make the soul scent the rotten breath of lust.
> When in an Italian lascivious palace,
> A lady guardianless,
> Left to the push of all allurement,
> The strongest incitements to immodesty,
> To have her bound, incensed with wanton sweets,
> Her veins filled high with heating delicates,
> Soft rest, sweet music, amorous masquerers,
> Lascivious banquets, sin itself gilt o'er,
> Strong fantasy tricking up strange delights,
> Presenting it dressed pleasingly to sense,
> Sense leading it unto the soul, confirmed
> With potent example, impudent custom,
> Enticed by that great bawd, Opportunity;
> Thus being prepared, clap to her easy ear
> Youth in good clothes, well-shaped, rich,
> Fair-spoken, promising-noble, ardent, blood-full,
> Witty, flattering—Ulysses absent,
> O Ithaca, can chastest Penelope hold out?[31]

What enticement to lust is not present in the "Italian lascivous palace." All of the traditional allurements are there—sloth, gluttony, music, plays, custom, and opportunity. For Marston, as for Webster, Tourneur, and so many others, Italy is supremely the land of lust and revenge.[32] Even Ben Jonson, whose policy was to set his plays in contemporary London, moves the scene to Venice when it supports his theme. It is

31. John Marston, *The Malcontent,* ed. Barnard Harris (New York: Hill & Wang, A Mermaid Dramabook, 1967), III.ii.23–49.

32. We must be careful in dealing with the "worlds" of the Jacobean dramas set in Italy, however, as has been pointed out in an illuminating article by Robert C. Jones, "Italian Settings and the 'World' of Elizabethan Tragedy," *Studies in English Literature* 10 (1970): 251–68.

only natural that *Volpone,* a play dealing with avarice and lust, should be set in Venice, since that city was most famous for precisely those vices. Frances Yates made the case many years ago for the assistance Jonson received from John Florio in realizing his setting;[33] beyond the setting, Jonson details his Italian backdrop with very particular references to Italian erotica: the Romano-Aretino *posizioni* (Ill. ii. p. 51 and III. vi. p. 56), Berni's encomia (IV. I. p. 67), and the lustful actions of the *commedia dell' arte* (II. i. p. 36).[34] Jonson's use of an Italian setting may be less sensational than that of other dramatists, but he, more than most of his contemporaries, packs his play with realistic details that have a thematic function.

Finally, even the self-styled English Aretino, Thomas Nashe, uses the traditionally negative view of Italy when it serves his purpose. Only in Italy, one imagines, could the terrible rapes, murders, and revenges that occur in *The Vnfortunate Traveller* take place. But Nashe provides us with a difficult case in this work, since he strikes out at all views, opinions, attitudes, and beliefs in this incredible tour de force. Precisely because Nashe employs both the positive and negative views of Italy in a most telling and complex fashion in *The Vnfortunate Traveller,* I shall examine that work in this chapter, and then deal with Nashe as the English Aretino in chapter 7.

In *The Vnfortunate Traveller* Nashe has his narrator, Jack Wilton, relate adventures which take him through a series of pranks in an English war camp on the continent, to episodes back home in England, and on to observations of a number of events back on the continent in Northern Europe.[35] Finally Nashe moves the scene to Italy, where the bulk of the narrative is set.

We may suppose we are getting a typical use of an Italian setting when Jack and his master, the Earl of Surrey, arrive in Venice and are

---

33. Yates, pp. 277–83.

34. Ben Jonson, *Volpone,* in *Ben Jonson: Three Plays,* ed. Brinsley Nicholson and C. H. Herford (New York: Hill & Wang, A Mermaid Dramabook, 1957). All references in citation are to this edition.

35. The narrative situation is confused. At the outset the narrator tells us that Wilton commends himself to us and has left some papers behind with his tale. At the end of the Induction we are asked to take our places and "heare *Iacke Wilton* tell his owne Tale" (*The Vnfortunate Traveller,* in *Works,* II, 208). In the narrative proper then we are to imagine Jack talking, and the situation is one of a tavern: "There did I (soft, let me drinke before I go anie further) raigne sole king of the cans and black iackes . . ." (p. 209). The tavern situation is mentioned again (p. 212), but later we read, "Gentle Readers (looke you be gentle now since I haue cald you so) . . ." (p. 217). We are called "Auditors" once more (p. 219); thereafter we are treated as readers. The narrative situation is clearly not consistent.

duped by the machinations of a wily pimp, Petro de Campo Frego, and his whore, Tabitha. This is precisely the kind of thing we would expect. Englishmen, even one who has hitherto proven as clever a prankster as Jack Wilton, simply are no match for the Machiavellian Italians, especially those who trade in the flesh. But just when we think we are settled in a conventional Italian setting with conventional anti-Italian attitudes, Nashe brings Aretino to the rescue of the imprisoned Englishmen.[36] Suddenly, something Italian that is admirable is presented to us. It is typical of Nashe to keep his readers off balance in just this way.[37] The issue is complicated further; in the events that transpire in the prison before Jack and the Earl of Surrey are saved by the good offices of Aretino, we see Nashe holding up for ridicule an Italian ideal (and literary form) usually perceived as worthy of admiration and imitation—Petrarchan love in sonnet form. What Nashe manages to do in *The Vnfortunate Traveller* is to play upon *both* the conventional negative and positive myths of Italy to further his comic ends. And since these views are embedded in the literature Nashe knew so well, exaggeration, ridicule, and parody are his stock-in-trade for achieving his comic ends. The events in the Venetian prison make this abundantly clear. On a basic level the events in Venice surely play upon our seeing Italy as the land where one becomes "a fine close leacher," but one fulfills what was traditionally a negative expectation of confrontation with Italian life by failing to live up to a positive Italian ideal, ideal Petrarchan love. Nashe arranges to leave us very little safe ground.

The prison scene in Venice is rendered in great detail. Outwitted by Tabitha the Temptress and her pimp, Petro de Campo Frego, Jack Wilton and his master, the Earl of Surrey, have been imprisoned. They are joined in captivity by Diamante, a young wife accused of horning her husband, one Castaldo. Bawdy innuendo and parody of love literature of several kinds are Nashe's major devices in rendering Wilton's seduction of Diamante.

Wilton begins his reminiscence of the situation with a physical description of Diamante. There is nothing in it to suggest the Petrarchan lady; rather, Wilton would call to mind the priapian musings of Chauntecleer for Pertolete:

36. See chapter 7, pp. 186–87, for Nashe's praise of Aretino.

37. Walter R. Davis, in *Idea and Act in Elizabethan Fiction* (Princeton: Princeton Univ. Press, 1969), points out that Nashe is a master at bringing romance down to the level of satire through destructive juxtapositions, and he believes that "Jack Wilton's experience of reality throughout Europe constantly gives the lie to ennobling formulations of the real, be they literary conventions, intellectual aspirations, or codes of life" (p. 215).

> A pretie rounde faced wench was it, with blacke eie browes, a high forehead, a little mouth, and a sharpe nose, as fat and plum euerie part of her as a plouer, a skin as slike and soft as the backe of a swan, it doth me good when I remember her. Like a bird she tript on the grounde, and bare out her belly as maiesticall as an Estrich. With a licorous rouling eie fixt piercing on the earth, and sometimes scornfully darted on the tone side, she figured forth a high discontented disdaine; much like a prince puffing and storming at the treason of some mightie subiect fled lately out of his power. (II.261)

Diamante is remembered not as a disdainful, distant blonde beauty; she is dark and soft, a creature to be "trod." Her eye is at once a "licorous rouling" one and a fixed and scornful one. We are not sure what to make of her character, although it seems fairly clear from Wilton's analogy with the puffing prince that her scorn is much posturing. Might she not be as virtuous as Wilton first asserted? Wilton pursues this point in an equivocal fashion:

> Her very countenaunce repiningly wrathfull, and yet cleere and vnwrinkled, would haue confirmed the cleernes of her conscience to the austerest iudge in the worlde. If in anie thing shee were culpable, it was in beeing too melancholy chast, and shewing her selfe as couetous of her beautie as hir husband was of his bags. Many are honest because they know not howe to bee dishonest; shee thought there was no pleasure in stolne bread, because there was no pleasure in an olde mans bed. (II.261)

Wilton gives us conflicting testimony. He begins by assuring us that Diamante is truly chaste, determined to preserve her beauty (and we assume her chastity); but the terms have begun to shift with the movement from chastity to beauty. The sentence beginning "Many are honest because they know not how to bee dishonest" might lead the reader to expect the next clause to state that this is *not* the case with Diamante, since Wilton has begun the description by asserting the "cleernes of her conscience." But he concludes the sentence by affirming that her virtue is based on lack of experience; Diamante simply has not yet been introduced to the pleasures of sexual intercourse. We are thus quite well prepared for the action that ensues.

Wilton takes us by stages to the seduction. He provides a set piece that is ostensibly a contemplation of the relationship of wit and beauty:

> It is almost impossible that any woman should be excellently wittie, and not make the vtmost pennie of her beautie. This age and this countrie of ours admits of some miraculous exceptions, but former times are my constant informers. Those that haue quicke motions of wit haue quicke motions in euerie thing: yron only needs many strokes, only yron wits are not wonne without a long siege of intreatie. God easily bends, the most ingenious

mindes are easiest mooued, *Ingenium nobis molle Thalia dedit,* sayth *Psapho* to *Phao.* Who hath no mercifull milde mistres, I will maintaine, hath no wittie but a clownish dull flegmatike puppie to his mistress. (II.261)

The point of Wilton's cogitations on wit and beauty is simply that any woman of wit will use her beauty, and a woman of quick wit, one of exceptional worth, akin to gold, will be most malleable. It is the "mercifull milde mistres" that interests Wilton, and he concludes his description of Diamante by saying that she "was a good louing soule that had mettall inough in her to make a good wit of, but being neuer remoued from vnder her mothers and her husbands wing, it was not molded and fashioned as it ought" (II.261–62). It is clear that Wilton feels honor-bound to become Diamante's instructor, her molder, her fashioner. "Immaculate honest" she may have been prior to being thrust into prison with Jack and the Earl of Surrey, but "what temptations she had then, when fire and flax were put together, conceit with your selues, but hold my master excusable" (II.262).

Surrey, Jack tells us, "was too vertuous to make her vicious"; Surrey does, however, occasionally mistake Diamante for his beloved Geraldine, and he is driven to paroxysms of passion that Wilton records with great amusement. His master sighs for the touch of her hand; he kisses the ground on which she walks; he "assaults" her with rhymes. Nashe's parody of Petrarch on wooing and Petrarchan verse provides the comic counterpoint to the lusty actions of Wilton. The sonnet Nashe creates as Surrey's plea to Diamante is a case in point:

> If I must die, O let me choose my death:
> Sucke out my soule with kisses, cruell maide,
> In thy breasts christall bals enbalme my breath,
> Dole it all out in sighs when I am laide.
> Thy lips on mine like cupping glasses claspe,
> Let our tongs meete and striue as they would sting,
> Crush out my winde with one strait girting graspe,
> Stabs on my heart keepe time whilest thou doest sing.
> Thy eyes lyke searing yrons burne out mine,
> In thy faire tresses stifle me outright,
> Like Circes change me to a loathsome swine,
> So I may liue for euer in thy sight.
>   Into heauens ioyes none can profoundly see,
>   Except that first they meditate on thee. (II.262–63)

Nashe captures the mortal excess of the Petrarchan lover. Surrey is in such an extreme state that he can envision only death and the physical pleasures that will bring it on; he will expire suffocated on her breasts; her lips will fasten on his like cupping glasses sucking forth his soul;

she should squeeze the very breath out of him; her "faire tresses" should strangle him. Life is conceivable in such a person's imagination only if he were a loathsome swine (what Ascham of course says Englishmen Italianated are) living in the presence of a Circe. Surrey would be a Grill could he enjoy his Acrasia, his Geraldine. The comedy works on several levels. The most obvious, of course, is that Surrey is so besotted with passion that he cannot distinguish the dusky Diamante from his golden Geraldine, whom he left in England. Then there is Surrey's inability to understand how completely he is caught in the purely physical part of love—he expresses no desire to be led to virtue, to have his soul lifted to the Good; he can see only what he described earlier as "the funerall flame" of his folly. Wilton recognizes the absurdity of all of this; all is folly to the man who would take the realistic tack, and Wilton provides the proper gloss on it all, noting, "sadly and verily, if my master sayde true, I shoulde if I were a wench make many men quickly immortall. What ist, what ist for a maide fayre and fresh to spend a little lipsalue on a hungrie louer? My master beate the bush and kepte a coyle and a pratling, but I caught the birde: simplicitie and plainnesse shall carrie it away in another world" (II.263).

Wilton appeals to Diamante's desire for revenge on her husband; why not, he reasons, make Castaldo a true cuckold? She acquieces; "How I dealt with her, gesse, gentle reader, *subaudi* that I was in prison, and she my silly Iaylor" (II.263). That we are to catch the sexual innuendos in this statement is made clear when Wilton informs us that, upon being set free through the good offices of Aretino, "Diamante . . . after my enlargement proued to be with child. . . ." (II.266). The "prison" in which Diamante held Jack has proven liberal indeed; the "enlargement" that Jack caused in Diamante repays him severalfold, for he gains not only Diamante but also all her husband's goods once he is freed. This is "love" Italian-style in Nashe's picture of Italy. What ends up dominating the presentation of "love" in this part of the narrative is not Italy the land of lechery so much as Italy the land of foolish Petrarchan love, a land where wit has its bawdy way. Bawdiness seems to deflate Petrarchan notions of love.

Elsewhere in *The Vnfortunate Traveller,* Nashe plays up the negative image of Italy by presenting it as the land of lust, rape, blasphemy, torture, murder, and revenge. And so Jack Wilton recounts the horrible torture and execution of Zadoch the Jew; he takes us through the incredible revenge wrought by Cutwolfe on the archvillain Esdras, something so devilish that Cutwolfe himself refers to it as "some notable newe Italionisme, whose murderous platforme might not onely extend on his bodie, but his soul also" (II.325). We also see the torture and execution of Cutwolfe after his revenge on Esdras, and we are given, in great detail, an extended account of the rape of Heraclide by Esdras, an assault performed on top of the supposedly dead body of her husband in plague-infested Rome.

The rape of Heraclide is a telling example of Nashe's willingness to try the outrageous. Only Nashe, one supposes, would attempt to present an extended rape scene as comedy. All of the elements operating in the scene contribute to this effect. The exaggerated villainy of Esdras, the ineffable purity of Heraclide, her lament of operatic proportions, the continual exaggeration of all the particulars (using the husband as a pillow), the puns, the narrator's attitude at the end of the account, all contribute, hard as it is to imagine, to the rape scene as comedy.

Jack Wilton, we recall, has made his way from Venice through Florence, thence to Rome. He has been living at the house of a "noble & chast Matrone," Heraclide. The plague is raging through the city; Esdras, a "notable Bandetto," and his henchman, Bartol, have been ravaging the diseased populace. They break into Heraclide's house and easily subdue the cowardly Wilton. Bartol finds Jack in bed with Diamante and, as Jack relates, the villain "ranne at me ful with his rapier, thinking I would resist him, but, as good luck was, I escapt him and betooke me to my pistoll in the window vncharged. He, fearing it had beene charged, threatned to runne her through if I once offered but to aime at him" (II.287). Nashe pulls the rug from under his narrator deftly indeed. We see that Wilton has no intention of offering resistance, and so his subsequent protestations as Bartol drags off Diamante are ludicrous indeed. "Foorth the chamber he dragde her," Wilton tells us, "holding his rapier at her heart, whilst I cride out, Saue her, kill me, and Ile ransome her with a thousand duckets: but lust preuailed, no prayers woulde be heard" (II.287). The wild illogicality of Wilton's cry—it is his life or his wife's money he is willing to sacrifice—certainly draws our attention to his cowardice. And the details with which Nashe continues this description also emphasize that quality. Wilton is essentially tricked (quite willingly, we gather) into believing that he is being guarded, so finally "nowe I was alone," he dares "all the deuiles in hell . . . to come and fight with mee one after another in defence of that detestable rape. I beat my head against the wals & cald them bauds, because they would see such a wrong committed, and not fall vppon him" (II.288). For *this* rape we are given no details beyond the craven actions of Jack Wilton. Nashe's persistence in treating Jack comically is crucial to our approaching the second rape, that of Heraclide, to which Nashe shifts abruptly in the next sentence with, "To returne to *Heraclide* below, whom the vgliest of all bloud suckers, *Esdras* of *Granado,* had vnder shrift" (II.288)). First, we are told, "he assayled her with rough meanes, and slue hir *Zanie* at hir foote, that stept before hir in rescue," but soon Esdras tries "honie speech" and gifts, while Heraclide resists in the most exaggerated terms. She attempts, finally, to threaten him, claiming she will breathe the plague upon him. Esdras casts the threat back upon her contemptuously:

> Now thinkest thou that I who so oft haue escaped such a number of hellish dangers, onely depending vppon the turning of a fewe prickes, can bee scare-bugd with the plague? what plague canst thou name worse than I haue had? whether diseases, imprisonment, pouertie, banishment, I haue past through them all. My owne mother gaue I a boxe of the eare too, and brake her necke downe a paire of staires, because she would not goe in to a Gentleman when I bad her: my sister I sold to an old Leno, to make his best of her: anie kinswoman that I haue, knew I she were not a whore, my selfe would make her one: thou art a whore, thou shalt be a whore, in spite of religion or precise ceremonies. (II.291)

To the vile Esdras, all women are commodities to be used for pleasure and profit; we hardly expect such a ferocious criminal to be stopped by the threat of the plague, and Esdras moves quickly from words to actions:

> Therewith he flew vpon her, and threatned her with his sword, but it was not that he meant to wound her with. He graspt her by the yuorie throat, and shooke her as a mastiffe would shake a yong beare, swearing and staring he would teare out her weasand if shee refused. Not content with that sauage constraint, he slipt his sacriligius hand from her lilly lawne skinned necke, and inscarft it in her long siluer lockes, which with strugling were vnrould. Backward he dragd her, euen as a man backwarde would plucke a tree downe by the twigs, and then, like a traitor that is drawen to execution on a hurdle, he traileth her vp and down the chamber by those tender vntwisted braids, and setting his barbarous foote on her bare snowy breast, bad her yeld or haue her winde stampte out. She cride, Stamp, stifle me in my haire, hang me vp by it on a beame, and so let me die, rather than I should goe to heauen with a beame in my eye. No, quoth he, nor stampt, nor stifled, nor hanged, nor to heauen shalt thou go, till I haue had my wil of thee; thy busie armes in these silken fetters Ile infold. Dismissing her haire from his fingers, and pinnioning her elbowes therwithall, she strugled, she wrested, but all was in vaine. So strugling and so resisting, her iewels did sweate, signifying there was poison cōming towards her. On the hard boords he threw her, and vsed his knee as an yron ramme to beat ope the two leaud gate of her chastitie. Her husbands dead bodie he made a pillow to his abhomination. Coniecture the rest, my words sticke fast in the myre and are cleane tyred; would I had neuer vndertooke this tragicall tale. Whatsoeuer

is borne, is borne to haue an end. Thus ends my tale: his whorish lust was glutted, his beastly desire satisfied; what in the house of anie worth was carriageable, he put vp, and went his way. (II.291–92)

But Wilton does not end his "eligiacall historie" here; he instructs his readers to show compassion for this woman who has buried fourteen of her children in five days and borne this alone, without the support of her husband, who is no more than a "comfortles corse, a carrionly blocke" (II.292). Even here the tale does not end. Heraclide rises, gives several long speeches, stabs herself, and falls dead upon her husband's body. The force of her fall jolts him out of his swoon; he rises to accuse the cowering Jack Wilton of having committed these heinous acts.

It is impossible to take this seriously; from the implied pun on "sword" in the first sentence, through the adjectives describing Heraclide that remind us of Petrarchan poetry ("lilly lawne skinned necke," "siluer lockes," "snowy breast"), to the similies of Esdras' dragging Heraclide like a tree and Heraclide rising like a corpse from a hearse and the *fourteen* dead children to the use of the "dead" husband as a pillow, all of these are calculated to work against any serious reaction to the passage. And beyond these elements, the most telling factor compelling a comic reading is the attitude of the narrator. He wishes he had never undertaken this "tragicall tale," and he feels it is necessary to remind his readers to show compassion in responding to this "eligiacall historie." Were the tale meant to bring such compassion as a response, we would hardly need to be reminded of it. What Nashe's reminders make us aware of, of course, is that such absurd "tragicall tales" and "eligiacall histories" are commonplace enough and deserve spoofing.[38]

The last point is a crucial one. Just as Nashe ridicules literary forms and conventions that present a positive view of things Italian, so too will he ridicule "tragicall tales" and "eligiacall histories" that portray

38. Critics have debated about this sequence in *The Vnfortunate Traveller.* Both G. R. Hibbard, in *Thomas Nashe* (Cambridge, Mass.: Harvard Univ. Press, 1963), pp. 167–70, and Davis, pp. 226–29, are uneasy with the story, but Hibbard finally decides that the Heraclide story is to be taken seriously, and he takes Agnes Latham to task for her interpretation of the episode as a *reductio ad adsurdum* of revenge. See Agnes Latham, "Satire on Literary Themes and Modes in Nashe's 'Unfortunate Traveller,'" *English Studies* n.s. 1 (1948): 85–100. Davis takes into account both views and directs our attention to the intense self-consciousness that each character has at some moment in the story. His conclusion is that in the Heraclide part of the story "when the style occasionally falls into tragic ranting, we can with some show of probability ascribe it, as Hibbard does, to overwriting pushed so far as to become unconscious burlesque of itself" (Davis, p. 227). I must admit that I am inclined to agree with Ms. Latham and give Nashe credit for knowing what he was doing in this part of the book.

a negative view of Italy. We see another example of this following the Heraclide episode when a banished English earl saves Jack from execution for his alleged rape and murder of Heraclide. The earl admonishes Jack in a speech that is a wonderful replication of anti-Italian diatribes. Readers of Thomas, Harrison, and Ascham would have had little difficulty in catching Nashe's echoes of their pronouncements on the dangers of visiting Italy and seeing the strong elements of parody in this section of the work. The earl begins by wondering "what is the occasion of thy straying so farre out of *England* to visit this strange Nation? If it bee languages, thou maist learne them at home; nought but lasciuiousnesse is to bee learned here" (II.297). Since the readers have already experienced Jack's adventures in Venice, especially his seduction of Diamante, they are well aware that Nashe is meeting expectations of Italy as the land of lechery and Machiavellian manipulation. Englishmen, "the plainest dealing soules that euer God put life in," are just not prepared for the wiles of foreigners (II.298). "*Italy,*" exclaims the earl:

> . . . the Paradice of the earth and the Epicures heauen, how doth it forme our yong master? It makes him to kis his hand like an ape, cringe his necke like a starueling, and play at hey passe repasse come aloft, when he salutes a man. From thence he brings the art of atheisme, the art of epicurising, the art of whoring, the art of poysoning, the art of Sodomitrie. The onely probable good thing they haue to keepe vs from vtterly condemning it is that it maketh a man an excellent Courtier, a curious carpet knight: which is, by interpretation, a fine close leacher, a glorious hipocrite. It is nowe a priuie note amongst the better sort of men, when they would set a singular marke or brand on a notorious villaine, to say, he hath beene in *Italy*. (II.301)

The Vnfortunate Traveller ends in a way calculated to parody rogue histories, with Jack Wilton learning the "lesson" that the banished earl would have had him learn by precept. The episode that educates Jack is Cutwolfe's revenge on Esdras. Cutwolfe is the brother of Bartolo, formerly the confederate of Esdras, rapist of Heraclide. Esdras killed his confederate Bartol, and now Cutwolfe has revenged his brother's murder. The story is told by Cutwolfe himself prior to his execution with Jack as a witness. The account is preceded by a "glose vpon the text" in which the narrator tells us Heraclide has been revenged (II.320). Cutwolfe had devised a "notable new Italionisme" in his revenge, for he made Esdras renounce his God and salvation, and when Esdras had done so, he shot him in the mouth so that he could not repent. Cutwolfe then claims:

> This is the falt that hath called me hether; no true Italian but will honor me

for it. Reuenge is the glorie of armes, & the highest performance of valure: reuenge is whatsoeuer we call law or iustice. The farther we wade in reuenge, the neerer come we to $\frac{e}{y}$ throne of the almightie. To his scepter it is properly ascribed; his scepter he lends vnto man, when he lets one man scourge an other. All true Italians imitate me in reuenging constantly and dying valiantly. Hangman, to thy taske, for I am readie for the vtmost of thy rigor. Herewith all the people (outragiously incensed) with one conioyned outcrie yelled mainely, Awaie with him, away with him. Executioner, torture him, teare him, or we will teare thee in pieces if thou spare him. (II.326–27)

From this story Jack Wilton learns "One murder begetteth another: was neuer yet bloud-shed barren from the beginning of the world to this daie. Mortifiedly abiected and danted was I with this truculent tragedie of *Cutwolfe* and *Esdras*. To such straight life did it thence forward incite me that ere I went out of *Bolognia* I married my curtizan, performed many almes deedes; and hasted so fast out of *Sodom* of *Italy* . . ." (II.327). Certainly we are not to take this seriously: Why, after all, this execution of a revenger of one who performed his "notable new Italionisme" on one of the most foul villains imaginable should educate Jack Wilton is a wonder. It is true that Cutwolfe has set himself up as a judge and executioner, but Esdras has not been presented as deserving any mercy. *The Vnfortunate Traveller* is in no way the education of Jack Wilton; indeed, for one who seems to start out as a clever prankster in his own right, he falls easily into the wiles of others. And though Wilton flees Italy, he ends up exactly where he began, in an English camp of war on the Continent. I take Nashe's ending to be a convenient way to bring the story to a close and a comic thrust at all the adventure stories that do end with the conversion of the rogue. Indeed, Nashe ends his work by calling attention to the kind of book he has written and his reasons for writing it: "All the conclusiue epilogue I will make is this; that if herein I haue pleased anie, it shall animat mee to more paines in this kind. Otherwise I will sweare vpon an English Chronicle neuer to bee outlandish Chronicler more while I liue. Farewell as many as wish me well" (II.328).

Nashe never was to be an "outlandish chronicler more," for he had misgauged literary taste, and *The Vnfortunate Traveller* was not a notable success in its time.[39] What Nashe did see clearly was that all opinions

---

39. Barolsky, p. 9, points to the tradition of "the cruel humor of the Renaissance picaresque." One might argue with his assertion that we are not amused by such cruel humor, or at least with the implication that modern readers are not attuned to "dark humor," when our own literature is filled with it. Walsh, pp. 241–42, sees Nashe's work as being in the manner of Petronius and Apuleius.

about Italy held by the English were open to ridicule, whether they were positive or negative. This is what he shows us in *The Vnfortunate Traveller.* Nashe understood something else: that if one were willing to try anything to "make it" as a professional man of letters, including the writing of erotica, there was an Italian on whom he could model himself—the Divine Aretino. Nashe as the self-styled English Aretino is the subject of chapter 7.

When we examine a wide range of English erotica, from jests and paradoxical encomia to epigrams and pornographic poems, we see that other English writers were also aware of models and traditions, both Italian and classical. English authors played off earlier models and counted on their readers' knowledge of this tradition of erotica. The English variety of that tradition is the subject of the ensuing chapter.

CHAPTER 6

Albion's Festum: Erotica in England

Now is Pernassus *turned to the stewes:*
And on Bay-stockes the wanton Myrtle growes.
Joseph Hall, Virgidemiarum

If one took the railings of the English moralists, theologians, and satirists at face value, one would have to assume that every person who set pen to paper in Renaissance England was producing erotica. It would be easy enough to dismiss these attacks as the outpourings of moral or religious extremists; it would be equally easy to expose them by subjecting them to analyses that would point to language in them so sexually suggestive as to open the attacks themselves to the charge of leaving a "relish upon the tongue" (to use Jeremy Taylor's phrase).[1] Rather than dismiss these works outright, however, I would like to expand my discussion of them begun in the introduction, for these writers are important in establishing English attitudes toward erotica in the Renaissance. Joseph Hall and Gabriel Harvey are especially relevant, for they put the stable of salacious writers before us, showing remarkable agreement about who those writers were. Further, they demonstrate that Renaissance writers, like their modern counterparts, had great difficulty in categorizing the erotica they saw around them.

In his collection of satires, *Virgidemiarum,* Hall states that the muses used to be vestal maids, but, he laments:

> Now is *Pernassus* turned to the stewes:
> And on Bay-stockes the wanton Myrtle growes.
> *Cythêron* hill's become a Brothel-bed,
> And *Pyrene* sweet, turnd to a poysoned head
> Of cole-blacke puddle: whose infectuous staine
> Corrupteth all the lowly fruitfull plaine.[2]

1. Taylor, *Holy Living,* p. 73.
2. Joseph Hall, *Virgidemiarum,* in *The Collected Poems of Joseph Hall,* ed. Arnold Davenport (Liverpool: Liverpool Univ. Press, 1949), I.ii.17–22. All Hall references are to this edition.

This is a general attack, one that sees the realm of poetry turned into a whorehouse but does not seem to specify any particular writers who are fouling the land and waters on Parnassus; Hall is merely describing the general state of literature in England.[3] In another satire Hall is more specific as he attacks licentious writers. He sees Cupid crowning a new "Laureat," one who

> Rymed in rules of Stewish ribaldry,
> Teaching experimentall Baudery?
> Whiles th' itching vulgar tickled with the song,
> Hanged on their vnreadie Poets tongue.

He wonders why

> . . . if some *Shordich* furie should incite
> Some lust-stung letcher, must he needs indite
> The beastly rites of hyred Venerie,
> The whole worlds vniversall baud to bee?
> Did neuer yet no damned *Libertine,*
> Nor elder *Heathen,* nor new *Florentine,*
> Tho they were famous for lewd libertie,
> Venture vpon so shameful villanie.
> Our *Epigrammatarians* olde and late,
> Were wont be blam'd for too licentiate.
> Chast men, they did but glance at *Lesbias* deed,
> And handsomely leaue off with cleanly speed.
> But Artes of Whoring: stories of the Stewes,
> Ye Muses can ye brooke, and may refuse?
> Nay let the Diuell, and Saint *Valentine,*
> Be gossips to those ribald rymes of thine. (I.ix.1–36)

Hall has a number of targets in this satire. The lewd reader, for one, is singled out. Hall realizes that there are those who read with an "itching" to be "tickled" by the song of the poet. Primarily, Hall attacks the writers who fulfill the expectations of such readers. He seems to feel that such fulfillment is more blameworthy in English writers than in Italian, for he condemns those who write of their escapades with the whores of Shoreditch as being worse than Aretino and his kind. As in manners there is none worse than an "Inglese

3. There are poetic and emblematic precedents for Hall's description, as Davenport has noticed (*Collected Poems of Hall,* p. 164). In Van der Noot's *Theatre for Voluptuous Worldlings* we are shown the muses and nymphs in an unsullied state tuning their voices in accord "Vnto the gentel sounding of the waters fall" (see figure 3). In a later emblem, however, we are shown the nymphs assailed by faunes who set them to flight and "with their feet vncleane the water fouled" (see figure 4).

Italianato," so in letters there is nothing worse than an Englishman
who goes beyond the Italians in such writing. This idea becomes a
major point in Harvey's attack on Nashe.[4] Hall also distinguishes between poets who merely "glance" at sexual matters and "leaue off" at
the proper moment, the epigrammatists, and writers like Nashe (referred to through *Pierce Penilesse* and *The Choise of Valentines*), who do
more than glance. The Renaissance, we see, also had its problems in
distinguishing among various degrees of erotica. Most satirists, moralists, and theologians regarded a large body of popular literature as
obscene, but others, like Hall, differentiated between works that were
bawdy and those that were obscene. John Marston draws the same
distinction in *The Metamorphosis of Pigmalions Image*, as he avoids telling
us directly what Pigmalion does with his statue when she comes to
life, admonishing his poetry in this manner, "Peace idle Poesie, / Be
not obsceane though wanton in thy rhimes."[5]

In one of his attacks on Nashe, Gabriel Harvey expands Hall's list
of purveyors of erotica, and he allows that ". . . better a Confuter of
Letters, than a counfounder of manners: and better the dogges-meate
of Agrippa, or Cattes-meate of Poggius, then the swines-meate of
Martial, or goates-meate of Arretine." Harvey wonders, "cannot an
Italian ribald, vomit-out the infectious poyson of the world, but an
Inglish horrel-lorrel must licke it vp for a restoratiue; and attempt to
putrify gentle mindes, with the vilest impostumes of lewde corruption?" He concludes, "One Ouid was too much for Roome; and one
Greene too-much for London: but one Nashe more intolerable then
both; not bicause his witt is anye thinge comparable, but bicause his
will is more outragious. . . ." Harvey hopes for a new age of Spartan
temperance, which "hath no wanton leasure for the Comedyes of Athens; nor anye bawdy howers for the songs of Priapus, or the rymes of
Nashe. Had he begun to Aretinize, when Elderton begun to ballot,
Gascoigne to sonnet, Turberuille to madrigal; Drant to versify, or Tar-
leton to extemporise; some part of his phantasticall bibble-bables, and
capricious panges, might haue bene tollerated in a greene, and wild
youth: but the winde is chaunged, & there is a busier pageant vpon the
stage."[6] Harvey expresses several typical attitudes toward lewd literature. We see that as Hall does, he places the accepted stable of lascivious
authors—Poggio, Martial, and Aretino—on a scale according to the

4. See pp. 198ff, for a discussion of the Nashe-Harvey quarrel.
5. See introduction, pp. 5–6.
6. Gabriel Harvey, *Pierce's Supererogation*, in *The Works of Gabriel Harvey,* ed. A. B.
Grosart (London: Huth Library, 1884–85), II, 91–96.

degree of their salaciousness. On this scale he too finds that there is nothing worse than the Englishman who licks up the Italian "vomit," who decides to Aretinize.[7] Harvey implicates Nashe above all others on this score.

From these two representative attacks, we can see that Englishmen did struggle to determine the difference between what was, in their terms, "wanton" and what was "obscene." And if, like modern critics and legalists, Renaissance men could hardly be precise in finding that fine line between the wanton and the obscene, they were in remarkable agreement as to which authors were most salacious. In the estimation of its own critics, then, Renaissance erotica consisted of collections of jokes and epigrams, and the lascivious works of writers like Nashe, imitating Aretino. What is equally important, their agreement reflects a strong sense of the classical tradition of erotica, embodying, at the very least by reputation, the "songs of Priapus," the "Comedyes of Athens," and the "swines-meate of Martial." And English erotica indicates an awareness as well of the Italian tradition: Poggio's jests, Aretino's "goates-meate," and the learned erotica of the humanists. Such a sense of a tradition is important, for it suggests that the reading public at least knew *about* a body of material we might term erotica. It means that if a writer mentioned Aretino, his audience thought "lascivious Italian material." It means that a learned writer composing for a learned audience might reasonably expect that audience to know not just Ovid and Catullus, but Martial and the tradition of the paradoxical encomium.

We might not agree with the view of the moralists, theologians, and satirists that a literature of lust was inundating England, but we should not fall into the trap of assuming that such literature did not exist at all. Yet if one accepted much of the twentieth-century scholarly writing about Elizabethan literature and taste, one would assume that, with several noted aberrations, the Elizabethans produced little that was not highly refined, witty (yet serious), uplifting, decorous, and ultimately didactic. At least, there was nothing *worthwhile* produced—according to the critics—that could not be described by the foregoing adjectives. Nowhere is such an attitude better set forth than in John Buxton's *Elizabethan Taste,* where he assures us that the love of the ceremonious "is consistent with the principle of decorum which governed their taste:

7. For a similar attack see Everard Guilpin, "Satyre Preludium," in *Skialetheia,* ed. D. Allen Carroll (Chapel Hill: Univ. of North Carolina Press, 1974). All subsequent Guilpin references are to this edition. Nashe himself attacks bawdy writing in *The Anatomie of Absurditie,* in *Works,* I, 29–30.

man, who was made in God's image, must never forget the dignity of his condition, must act the part cast for him; and where he found that he shared the destiny of other animals, in love, in hunger, in death, all the more must he distinguish the unique quality of his humanity. No Elizabethan had cause to observe, as had an eighteenth-century wit, that the art of love had been reduced to the simple phrase, 'Lie down'."[8] The problem with such a view is that it wants to ignore not only the direct "lie down" but also all the different ways Elizabethans had for saying "lie down," or "let a fart," or "eat shit." Such a view gives an extremely limited sense of Elizabethan taste, not to mention some very strange readings of Shakespeare and Donne.[9]

While we would certainly hesitate to regard as obscene (according to the way the term has been defined in this study) some of the works that the moralists, theologians, and satirists attacked, there is a great deal of literature that is bawdy, some that is palpably pornographic, some that is clearly erotic, and some that is truly obscene (again according to the definitions set forth earlier).

I

Collections of jests were printed as early as 1525 in England, and the collections continued well into the seventeenth century. Many jests are fairly innocuous in terms of their sexuality, and not a few are innocuous in terms of their humor, but there are a fair number that we would term dirty jokes; they have sex as the prime source of their humor, and more often than not in the Renaissance this meant that cuckoldry was involved. An example from *Mery Tales, Wittie Questions and Quicke Answers* (drawn from Poggio, whose boast that his jests flooded all of Europe was not an idle one) is tale number lxxiii:[10]

> A yonge man of Bruges, that was betroughed to a fayre mayden, came on a tyme, whan her mother was out of the way; and had to do with her. Whan her mother was come in, anone she perceyued by her doughters chere, what she had done; wherfore she was sore displeased, that she sewed a diuorse, and wolde in no wyse suffre that the yonge man shulde marye her daughter.
>
> Nat longe after, the same yonge man was maryed to an other mayden of the same parysshe: and as he and his wyfe satte talkynge on a tyme of the forsayde dammusell, to whome he was betrouthed, he fell in a nyce laughyng. Wherat laughe ye, quod his wyfe? It chaunced on a tyme (quod he), that she and I dydde such a thyng to gether, and she tolde hit to her mother.

8. Buxton, *Elizabethan Taste* (New York: St. Martin's Press, 1965), p. 21.
9. See ibid., pp. 295–99, 327–28.
10. Some of Poggio's *Facetiae* were included in Caxton's 1484 edition of Aesop.

> Therin (quod his wyfe) she playde the foole: a seruante of my fathers playde
> that game with me an hundred tymes, and yet I neuer tolde my mother.
> Whan he herde her saye so, he lefte his nyce laughynge.[11]

In the best jest fashion the husband is made a fool of. Not only has he
taken for a wife someone who is "damaged goods" (much like the
young woman to whom he was betrothed); his wife has "played the
game" with a servant! The wife, as so often happens in such jests, has
the last laugh.

The Sackful of News (ca. 1558) provides jokes that range from innocuous situational humor to the obscenely bawdy. As with Poggio, there
are discernible targets—foolish country bumpkins, stupid cuckolds, sly
priests, and especially foreigners. In these "detached jests" the targets
vary, however; sometimes as in the eleventh jest, our sympathies are
engaged on behalf of the outcasts of society, and sometimes the foreigner gets the bawdy riposte, as in the fifteenth.[12]

The third jest of this collection is merely a retelling of Boccaccio's
seventh story on the seventh day of the Decameron in which a wife and
her lover trick the foolish husband by sending him disguised as the
wife to the garden, where he is beaten by the servant for being a
faithless wife. More typical of English humor is the scatological twen-
tieth jest. For the English, as we shall see, the scatological was especially prominent. The jest is short and to the point:

> There was a man and his wife lying in bed together, and the good man laid
> his buttocks on his wife's knees, and so they lay sleeping; and the man
> dreamed that he was dead and, as he thought, was carried into heaven; and
> being there, he dreamed that he did shit through the moon into the world,
> but he did shit into his wife's lap. And when he awaked, he told his wife
> his dream; and as she would have turned on the other side, she felt she was
> all to-beshitten.
>
> "Cock's body," quoth she, "you have dreamed fair, for you have all to-
> beshitten my knees." And so they were both fain to rise and make them-
> selves clean.[13]

The humor is entirely situational here, and it is entirely scatological.
We may see little that is comic, but from Chaucer's Miller's Tale and

---

11. *Mery Tales, Wittie Questions and Quicke Answers,* in *Shakespeare Jest-Books,* ed. W.
Carew Hazlett (London, 1864; rpt. New York: Burt Franklin, 1964), LXXIII; XCVII
in 1581 Florence edition of Poggio. Also see Keith Thomas, "Place of Laughter," pp. 77–
81.

12. *Sackful of News,* in *Elizabethan Prose Fiction,* ed. Merritt Lawlis (New York: Odyssey Press, 1967), p. 27.

13. Ibid., p. 29.

Friar's Tale through Ben Jonson's *Alchemist* and beyond, the English show themselves particularly obsessed with the scatological, and they used it for a variety of effects from the bawdy and satiric to the obscene.[14] A more comic example of this humor from the *Sackful* is the twenty-first jest:

> There was a lady dwelt in the country which had a fool that did use to go with her to church; and on a time as his lady sat in the church, she let a great fart escape so that all the people heard it; and they looked on the fool that stood by her, thinking that it was he; which when the fool perceived, he said, "Truly, it was not I that let the fart; it was my lady." Whereat she was ashamed and went out of the church and chid the fool because he said that it was not himself.
>
> Then the fool ran into the church again and said aloud, "Masters, the fart which my lady let I will take it upon me, for she commanded me to say so." Whereat all the people laughed more than they did before, and the lady was much more ashamed.[15]

The joke has a nice doubling effect in the humor; the fool is indeed a fool, but the lady is of course more of the target. This jest also shows the Renaissance tendency to go beyond the joke, to give more than the punch line, to round the narrative off.

Jests were certainly abundant in English collections, and one could go on culling examples from them, but the epigram seems to have been an even more popular medium for English writers of bawdy humor. While more than one book has been devoted to the epigram in English, very little has been said about bawdy, satirical, and obscene epigrams, a neglect that is more than benign, since any reading in Renaissance collections of epigrams offers up a wide range of examples.[16] Practitioners of the art of the bawdy, the scurrilous, and the obscene in epigrammatic form range from notables like Sir John Harington, godson to Queen Elizabeth, to obscurities like Henry Parrot and Samuel Pick.

The fact that some notables, like Harington, did write epigrams, is surely the reason that they have drawn what little attention they have, for we are well aware that Elizabethans themselves held a hierarchical view of poetry with the epic at the top and all else far below. To Elizabethans the epigram was hardly very important literature, but this

---

14. This obsession remains current, as any viewer of Monty Python or Benny Hill knows. Philip Roth captures the literary tradition in the prologue of *The Great American Novel*.

15. *Sackful*, p. 29.

16. See H. H. Hudson, *The Epigram in the English Renaissance* (1947; rpt. New York: Octagon Books, 1966); and Harington, *The Letters and Epigrams of Sir John Harington*, ed. N. E. McClure (Philadelphia: Univ. of Pennsylvania Press, 1930).

does not mean that it was not very popular. And certainly the expectation was for the epigram to be bawdy at the very least. As Everard Guilpin says in one of his epigrams addressed to the Reader:

> Excuse me (Reader) though I now and than,
> In some light lines doe shew my selfe a man,
> Nor be so sowre, some wanton words to blame,
> They are the language of an Epigrame. (No. 47,p. 52)

Sir John Harington's commentary in his *Preface or rather, A Brief Apologie of Poetrie* attached to his famous translation of Ariosto's *Orlando Furioso* is very much to the point here. In answering a battery of objections raised against poetry, Harington addresses a last reproof, poetry's imputed "lightnes and wantonnes."[17] "This is indeed an Objection of some importaunce," Harington tells us, since "as Sir *Philip Sidney* confesseth, *Cupido* is crept even into the Heroicall Poems . . ." (p. 8). Harington notes that epic is the "least infected" with this disease, and as for other kinds "it may bee sayd where any scurrilitie and lewdnesse is founde there Poetry doth not abuse us but writers have abused Poetrie" (p. 8). This is a traditional defense, but Harington does not stop here; he goes on to characterize "scurrilitie and lewdnesse" in different kinds of poetry. He finds little of it in tragedy; in comedy, when rightly used, it is there "so as to make vice scorned and not embraced." The satiric is free from the charge since it is "wholly occupied in mannerly and courtly reproving of all vices." With the sonnet and epigram, Harington finds himself on more dangerous ground. He says, "though many times they savour of wantonness and love and toying and now and then breaking the rules of Poetry go into plaine scurrilitie, yet even the worst of them may be not ill applied and are, I must confesse, too delightfull, in so much as Martiall saith: *Laudant illa, sed ista legunt*" (p. 9). Provide all the justifications you want, Harington seems to be saying, the fact is that "wantonnesse" and "scurrilitie" in epigrams are fun. And Harington goes on to cite an additional verse from Martial that focuses on the enjoyment of the reader. *Erubuit posuitque meum Lucrecia librum, / Sed coram Bruto: Brute recede, legit.* Harington explains the verse, "*Lucrecia* (by which he signifies any chast matron) will blush and be ashamed to read a lascivious booke, but how? not except *Brutus* be by, that is if any grave man should see her read it, but if *Brutus* turne his backe, she will to it agayne and

---

17. Ariosto, *Ludovico Ariosto's "Orlando Furioso,"* trans. Sir John Harington, ed. Robert McNulty (Oxford: Oxford Univ. Press, 1972), p. 8. All subsequent references are to the Preface in this edition.

read it all" (p. 9). Harington is aware (as Martial was aware before him) that not all readers are willing to admit their appreciation for the bawdy as openly as he is, but he asserts that even the most chaste of readers enjoys such works.

The epigram was a favorite form from very early times in the English Renaissance; John Heywood began putting forth epigrams by the hundreds (600 by the 1562 edition, which forms the basis of John S. Farmer's edition of 1906). Heywood's epigrams are not remarkable in any way, being generally devoid of wit, bawdy or otherwise. Several do demonstrate the English obsession with bums and farts, however. In the first hundred of epigrams we read:

> 72. "Of Blowing"
> What wind can there blow that doth not some man please?
> A fart in the blowing doth the blower ease.[18]

And in the sixth hundred of epigrams we get:

> 90. "Of Things Unlike"
> Like will to like, men say; but not always so:
> Contrary to contrary ofttimes doth go.
> When folk be most open, their low parts most loose,
> Then go they to stools that be made most close.[19]

A close stool is, of course, a chamber pot (one that is mounted on a stool and covered), and Heywood's epigram turns on a nice paradox here.[20] It certainly would not be fair to classify Heywood as a bawdy epigrammatist, however, on the basis of two out of six hundred epigrams. A good number of Heywood's epigrams have to do with the conflicts between husbands and wives, and they make us conscious of the fact that epigrams often have targets, just as jokes do, and not surprisingly, the targets are the same ones we have seen in the joke literature—lustful women and cuckolds. Further, because epigrams are in a sense so much more literary than jokes, being built on a classical heritage, especially that of Martial, they frequently have as targets creatures loathsome to poets—rival poets and poet-haters.

Sir John Harington's epigrams, although not collected and published in his own lifetime, were well known through circulation in manu-

18. John Heywood, *The Proverbs, Epigrams, and Miscellanies of John Heywood,* ed. John S. Farmer (London: Early English Drama Society, 1906), p. 144.

19. Ibid., p. 293.

20. See Eric Partridge, *Shakespeare's Bawdy* (1948; paperback rpt. New York: E. P. Dutton, 1960), p. 88.

script; most of them were written between 1585 and 1603.[21] The learned and witty Harington, famous for his translation of Ariosto's *Orlando Furioso* (the translation of the whole poem was purported to have been a penance for his translation of the bawdy canto 28), wrote "that of all poems, the epigram is the plesawntest, & of all that writes Epigrams, Martiall is counted the wittyest."[22] The editor of Harington's epigrams, Norman McClure, counts Harington in the top rank of English epigrammatists, and I find no reason to quarrel with this. He is, as McClure points out, often indebted to Martial, but Harington always makes Martial's epigrams his own. For Harington the epigram was a congenial and flexible form. He could observe women in the "trade" or his own marital relations with equal facility. The court, the baths, the city, all provided grist for his mill. Here is Harington on a "commercial" woman:

> *Lesbia* doth laugh to heare sellers and buyers
> Cald by this name, Substantiall occupyers:
> *Lesbia,* the word was good while good folke vsed it,
> You mard it that with *Chawcers* iest abused it:
> But good or bad, how ere the word be made,
> *Lesbia* is loth perhaps to leaue the trade.[23]

This epigram turns on the double meaning of "occupy," which had as a bawdy meaning (as we recall from Florio) "to iape, to sard, to fucke, to swiue." According to Harington, "occupy" acquired this bawdy meaning from Chaucer.[24] Lesbia laughs to hear the word used in a commercial sense, but this is ironic since she herself deals in "occupying" commercially.[25]

To his wife Harington writes the following:

---

21. McClure in Harington, *Letters and Epigrams,* p. 52.

22. Harington, *Metamorphosis,* p. 97. Supposedly Harington had translated the tale of Iocondo in Canto 28 of *Orlando Furioso* and amused the ladies of the court by circulating his work. When the Queen discovered this, she set as his penance the translation of the entire poem. See McNulty in Ariosto, *Ludovico Ariosto,* p. xxv; and D. H. Craig, *Sir John Harington* (Boston: Twayne Publishers, 1985), p. 12.

23. Harington, *Letters and Epigrams,* p. 151. All citations of Harington's epigrams are from McClure's edition. Subsequent references are given in the text.

24. Thomas W. Ross, *Chaucer's Bawdy* (New York: E. P. Dutton, 1977), does not cite any bawdy meanings for occupy. McClure gives several Renaissance uses of the word in its bawdy sense and refers the reader to Spurgeon's *Five Hundred Years of Chaucer Criticism and Allusion,* which helps with the phrase "Chaucer's jest," but I have not been able to find a place where Chaucer uses occupy in any bawdy way.

25. See also epigram no. 305, Harington, *Letters and Epigrams,* p. 270.

My *Mall,* I mark that when you mean to proue me
To buy a Veluet gowne, or some rich border,
Thou calst me good sweet heart, thou swearst to loue me,
Thy locks, thy lips, thy looks, speak all in order,
Thou think'st, and right thou think'st, that these doe
  moue me,
That all these seuerally thy sute do forder:
  But shall I tell thee what most thy suit aduances?
  Thy faire smoothe words? no, no, thy faire smooth haunches. (No. 26,
  p. 159)

Harington's alliterative fourth line anticipates the turn he will give the epigram in the final line in this slice of his domestic life.

A number of Harington's epigrams have to do with matters excremental (nos. 132, 139, and 227), not surprising for the author of a discourse on privies, and Harington was not above an obscene jest at the expense of sycophantic courtiers. He gives us an extremely unpleasant picture of an aspiring courtier, precisely the kind we expect the epigrammatist to paint:

A Courtier, kinde in speech, curst in condition,
Finding his fault could be no longer hidden,
Went to his friend to cleere his hard suspition,
And fearing left [sic] he might be more than chidden,
Fell to a flattering and most base submission,
Vowing to kisse his foote, if he were bidden.
  My foote? (said he) nay, that were too submisse,
  But three foote higher you deserue to kisse. (No. 275, p. 261)

As we would expect, the cuckold is also a target of Harington's humor. We see this in a fine adaptation of one of Martial's epigrams:

What curld-pate youth is he that sitteth there
So neere thy wife, and whispers in her eare,
And takes her hand in his, and soft doth wring her,
Sliding her ring still vp and downe her finger?
Sir, tis a Proctor, seene in both the Lawes,
Retain'd by her, in some important cause;
Prompt and discreet both in his speech and action,
And doth her busines with great satisfaction.
And thinkest thou so? a horne-plague on thy head:
Art thou so like a foole, and wittoll led,
  To thinke he doth the business of thy wife?
  He doth thy business, I dare lay my life. (No. 335, p. 280)

A comparison with Martial's epigram is instructive:

Crispulus iste quis est, uxori semper adhaeret
  qui Mariane, tuae? crispulus iste quis est?
nescio quid dominae teneram qui garrit in aurem
  et sellam cubito dexteriore premit?
per cuius digitos currit levis anulus omnis,
  crura gerit nullo qui violata pilo?
nil mihi respondes? "Uxoris res agit" inquis
  "iste meae." sane certus et asper homo est,
procuratorem voltu qui preaferat ipso:
  acrior hoc Chius non erit Aufidius.
o quam dignus eras alapis, Mariane, Latini:
  te successurum credo ego Panniculo.
res uxoris agit? res ullas crispulus iste?
  res non uxoris, res agit iste taus.

Who is that spark who is always clinging to your wife's side, Marianus? Who is that curled spark, he who whispers some trifle into the lady's tender ear, and leans on her chair with his right elbow, round each of whose fingers runs a light ring, who carries legs unmarred by any hair? Do you make no reply? "That individual does my wife's jobs," you say. To be sure! he is a trusty and rugged fellow who flaunts factor in his very face: Chian Aufidius will not be sharper than he. Oh, Marianus, how you deserve the buffets of Latinus! You will be successor I fancy to Panniculus. He does your wife's jobs, does he? That curled spark do any? That fellow doesn't do your wife's jobs: he does yours.[26]

Both Harington's and Martial's epigrams depend on the same punch line, the turning from the "wife's business" to the husband's "business" with its sexual innuendos ("res uxoris agit? res agit iste tuas"). In both epigrams the young man is curly-headed, but beyond that detail Harington changes particulars to make an English work out of Martial's Roman. The rings that help paint the portrait of a Roman fop are transformed into a sexually suggestive action in Harington's poem as the young man slides the wife's ring up and down her finger. Part of the humor here stems from the fact that the husband does not see this action as sexually suggestive. The comic actors of Roman mime, Latinus and Panniculus, are dropped completely. Rather than adhere slavishly to his Roman model, as he might easily have done, Harington takes the punch line of the epigram and uses it as a way of expanding an English context. English terms for cuckoldry express specifically what kind of a fool the husband is—a "wittoll" deserving a "horne-plague"—and Harington expands the "business" metaphor to include

26. Martial, *Epigrams,* trans. Walter C. A. Ker (London: William Heinemann, 1930), II, 338–39.

the legal world. The youth is seen by the husband as a proctor (one who manages the affairs of others) practiced in both civil and canon law.[27] Harington anticipates the punch line of the epigram by suggesting that the proctor is prompt and discreet not only in word but also in deed, a deed that might be innocent enough were he not to add, "And doth her business with great satisfaction." "Satisfaction" had well-established sexual overtones by this time; here it certainly makes the sexuality of business unmistakable. Harington supports the sexual innuendoes of the epigram through these details, an effect Martial achieves through the "sharp" work of Chian Aufidius, a notorious libertine.[28] Harington's ending is less concise than Martial's, but he drives home the point of cuckoldry more dramatically by adding the opinion of the poet that all this is done, "I lay my life," for that opinion becomes sexually suggestive, taking us back, through the rhyme, to the only thing that is actually being "laid," the wife.

An example that shows the close relationship of lengthier epigrams to jests is Harington's on the "Lady that sought remedy at the Bathe." Here, however, Harington gives his verse local coloring as he plays on the physician as the doctor with the proper remedies of love. A man at the baths asks the maid of a comely lady why her mistress is there. The maid replies that an old physician had convinced her:

> These Bathes haue power to strengthen that debility,
> That doth in man or woman breed sterrilitie.

What is noteworthy in terms of the form here is the length of the epigram and its movement toward a punch line, so typical of a Poggian jest.

> Tush, said the man with plaine & short discourse,
> Your Mistris might haue tane a better course.
> Let her to Oxford, to the Vniuersitie,
> Where young Physicians are, and such diuersitie
> Of toward spirits that in all acts proceede,
> Much fitter than the Bathe is for the deede.
>   No, no, that will not serue, the Maide replide,
>   For she that Physike hath already tride. (No. 206, pp. 232–33)

The reputation of lusty university "clerks" ready to perform the "deed" is in fact a not-surprising commonplace from Chaucer's *Miller's Tale* and *Reeve's Tale* on.

---

27. See the *OED* for the citations of proctor under Law. VII.p.iv.1415.
28. Ker in Martial, *Epigrams,* I, 339n.

Harington was as adept at the shorter epigram as he was at the longer type noted above:

A vertuose Lady sitting in a muse,
As many tymes fayr vertuous Ladies vse,
Leaned her Ellbow on one knee full harde,
The other distaunt from it halfe a yarde.
Her knight, to tawnt her by a privy token,
Said, "Wife, awake, your Cabbinet stands open."
    She rose and blusht and smylld and soft doth saye,
    "Then lock it yf yow list: yow keepe the kaye." (No. 404, p. 312).

Bawdy innuendo begins with "yarde," a common term for penis. The "privy token" suggests private parts of course, and the ensuing reference to a cabinet makes it clear that this is what the poet intends; the wife's bawdy rejoinder is one that we understand even without knowledge of the particularly sexual meaning of locking with keys in Italian erotica.

In spite of the claims made by his most recent editor and the remarks of his contemporaries, the epigrams of Sir John Davies are among the least striking of Renaissance efforts in this vein. The reader plows through Davies's writings with a great deal more effort than is required for a reading of all twelve books of Martial's epigrams.[29] One epigram is particularly noteworthy, however:

When Francus comes to sollace with his whoore
He sends for rods and strips himselfe stark naked:
For his lust sleepes, and will not rise before,
By whipping of the wench it be awaked.
    I envie'him not, but wish I had the powre,
    To make my selfe his wench but one halfe houre.[30]

Kreuger is the soul of discretion in dealing with this poem; in fact, he avoids annotating it in any way. His failure to do so is symptomatic of why we have no comprehensive sense of Renaissance erotica. A scholar, editing and annotating in the 1970s the works of a significant Renaissance poet, chooses to ignore in his commentary a quite remarkable epigram, a genre that traditionally deals in the bawdy and the obscene. This particular epigram is remarkable because it is one of the few Renaissance poems to mention whipping, a practice that was to become *the* commonplace of Victorian pornography. The poem also demands

29. Davies, *The Poems of Sir John Davies,* ed. Robert Krueger (Oxford: Clarendon Press, 1975), pp. l, liii, and lx.
30. Ibid., p. 143.

some explication. Does the poet really wish he could be whipped for half an hour? I take it we are to interpret the "By whipping of the wench" to mean "By whipping *by* the wench"; she does the whipping, and the poet wishes he could replace her in performing that act.

As we have already seen, Everard Guilpin, the satirist, also wrote epigrams, ones in which he met the bawdy expectations of the genre. His sixth is a case in point:

> Since marriage, *Faber's* prouder then before,
> Yfayth his wife must take him a hole lower. (No. 6, p. 40)

As Carroll notes in his excellent edition of Guilpin's works, there is a "quibble on the sense 'sexually excited, swelling' " for "prouder." Carroll suggests that "take him a hole lower" should be read in light of the proverbial ' "take one a button-hole lower,' that is, to humiliate one," but I would submit that there is a sexual suggestion here as well, one that suggests that prior to marriage Faber might have had to depend on anal intercourse.[31] Guilpin reflects the English obsession with the scatological in:

> *Sextilius* sigh'd, for *Leuca* let a fart,
> Hath not the youth a meruailous kind hart? (No. 23, p. 45)

Carroll glosses kind hart as "a) loving disposition, b) *natural* mistress, 'heart' being a term of endearment."[32] What Guilpin captures is the English appreciation for all jokes having to do with the scatological; his sense of this works far better than Davies's epigram on the same subject.[33]

Guilpin also has a number of epigrams that derive their bawdy humor from puns on musical terms. No fewer than five of his seventy epigrams fall into this category. The best of these, one using the most common of Renaissance jokes, follows:

> The world finds fault with *Gellia*, for she loues
> A skip-iack fidler, I hold her excus'd,

31. Carroll in Guilpin, p. 104.
32. Ibid., p. 114.
33. Davies, *Poems,* pp. 134–35:

> Leuca in presence once a fart did let,
> Some laught a little, she forsooke the place:
> And mazde with shame, did eke her glove forget,
> Which she returnde to fetch with bashfull grace:
> And when she would have said, this is my glove,
> My fart (quoth she) which did more laughter move.

> For louing him, sith she her selfe so proues:
> What, she a fidler? tut she is abus'd?
> No in good faith; what fidle hath she vs'd?
>   The *Viole Digambo* is her best content,
>   For twixt her legs she holds her instrument. (No. 46, p. 51)

Carroll points to three other instances of this punch line in other Renaissance works, and certainly there are more. It is not surprising that a society so well schooled in music, in which poetry was closely allied with music, should have found it such a rich source for bawdy epigrams.

Henry Parrot's collection of epigrams, *Laquei ridiculosi: or Springes for Woodcocks,* is an excellent compendium of typical Renaissance bawdy epigrams. On the lust of women he has several selections. For example:

> *Kate,* for a need, deals in Astronomie,
>   And can of times and things prognosticate;
> For as they vse vpon their backs to lie,
> And censure of the weathers changing state;
>   So she (her body laid) can prophesie
>   Whether it shall proue colde, hot, moyst, or dry.[34]

In another he writes of the proverbial lust of the widow:

> A Souldier once a Widdow would haue woo'd,
>   But being poore and loath to be deni'd,
> Durst not impart how he affected stood,
> Which she as soone thus censur'd as espi'd:
>   *You may be valiant (sir) but seeme vnlusty,*
>   *That either haue no weapon, or tis rusty.* (I, 121)

The humor is reinforced here by the fact that it is a soldier, usually presented as the lustiest of men, who seems unable to meet the demands of the widow.

Parrot employs some of the most typical sexual imagery, that drawn from the world of horsemanship, in the following epigram:[35]

> Lesbia the fair, that would be woo'd of none,
>   Hath since beene won by many more than one:

---

34. Henry Parrot, *Laquei ridiculosi: or Springes for Woodcocks* (London, 1613), I, 12. All Parrot references are to this edition.

35. It is prominent in emblem books, and we find it used in poems like *Venus and Adonis.* Adonis' horse went after his love; Venus falls down with Adonis on her, and we are told: "Now is she in the very lists of love, / Her champion mounted for the hot encounter / All is imaginary she doth prove, / He will not manage her, although he mount her" (11.595–98). This and all subsequent Shakespeare references are to *The Riverside Shakespeare,* ed. G. Blakemore Evans (Boston: Houghton Mifflin, 1974).

And like a flower, whose colour soone doth fade,
With often riding, proues a hackney Iade. (II, 128)

A final example from Parrot, which again shows how close the epigram
is to the jest, is the fourteenth epigram of Book Two of the *Laquei*:

When *Cacus* was accused of Rape,
  For stealing secretly to his maids bed,
He hardly could the doome of law escape,
Had he not thus the matter coloured:
  That tooke his oath (nor did he sweare amisse)
He went not into her bed, (for t'was his.) (II, 14)

The narrative situation—the stealing to the maid's bed, the accusation
of rape, the trial proceedings—could be drawn out at length in a jest;
here all is condensed to six lines.

One finds many of Parrot's verses in a later collection entitled *Festum
Voluptatis, or the Banquet of Pleasure,* by Samuel Pick. Pick shows his
predilection for the sexual metaphor in the following epigram about
Amy:

Ay me (quoth *Amy*) who would ere have thought,
  So great a mischiefe should arise of naught,
Which had she knowne ere she began to swell,
Each yard of pleasure should have prov'd an ell.[36]

The major pun here is on "yard," one that we have seen several times
before, and Pick plays on the double meaning well here in carrying out
the associations of measuring terms.

Pick also includes Parrot's epigram on the preeminent source of
bawdy humor, the cuckold:

Old doting *Claudus* doth in haste desire,
  With beauteous young *Penelope* to wed,
Whose frozen appetite is set on fire,
Untill the match be thoroughly finished.
  Indeed as good dispatch as make delay,
That must be horned on his wedding day.[37]

One could go on presenting examples, but it seems sufficient here
to conclude this section by noting that the bawdy epigram deserves this
attention as a favorite form of erotica in the English Renaissance. It was

36. Samuel Pick, *Festum Voluptatis, or the Banquet of Pleasure* (London, 1639), pp. 31–
32. On Pick's borrowings, especially from Parrot, see H. E. Rollins, "Samuel Pick's
Borrowings," *Review of English Studies* 7 (1931): 204.
37. Pick, p. 42.

a form in which English poets felt at home, from the most gifted of them to the lowliest hack, and they put that form to a variety of uses. They adapted the frequently bawdy and obscene epigrams of Martial to English taste, and they often transferred the jest to verse form with notable success. It may be that epigrams rightfully are a lower rung on the ladder of literature, but clearly Renaissance poets and readers, even while recognizing the place of epigrams, enjoyed them, else they would not have produced them in such abundance. We are reminded, through them, that Elizabethan taste was not confined to the lofty and uplifting. Along with the dramatists, the epigrammatists give us a strong sense of the Renaissance enjoyment of ribald humor.

II

Even though the paradoxical encomium enjoyed a certain vogue in England, it never caught on as a vehicle for writing about sexual matters to quite the same degree that it did in Italy. Two notable exceptions are William Fennor's *Cornv-copiae, Pasquil's Night-cap, or Antidote to the Headache* and Sir John Harington's *Metamorphosis of Ajax*. We have already seen the prominence of cuckoldry as a source of ribald humor in the jest material. Indeed, it is safe to assert that the Renaissance obsession with cuckoldry as the staple of jest, insult, and comic plot at some point reduces every teacher of Renaissance literature to agreement with Marston's Malevole when he cries out, "For God's love, let's ha' no more cuckolds!"[38] The breadth and depth of the obsession can readily be demonstrated to readers unfamiliar with Renaissance literature by reference to Machiavelli's *Mandragola*, Gascoigne's *Adventures of Master F.J.*, Book III of *The Faerie Queene*, *As You Like It*, and *Othello* (for a tragic playing of the number). To pursue the topic further here, even through a reading of Fennor's neglected poem, would seem perverse in the extreme.[39] Harington's *Metamorphosis of Ajax* is another matter;

38. John Marston, *The Malcontent*, ed. M. L. Wine (Lincoln: University of Nebraska Press, 1964), III.ii.23–24.
39. There are several ballads on the subject of cuckoldry. The most notable are "The Cooper of Norfolke, or a Pretty Iest of a Brewer and the Coopers Wife: And how the Cooper served the Brewer in his kind"; "Household Talke: or Good Councill for a Married Man"; and "The Merry Cuckold." These can be found in *The Roxburghe Ballads*, ed. Charles Hindley (London: Reeves & Turner, 1873), I.135; II.60; and II.463–68. There is also a ballad called "Cuckolds Haven" that is accompanied by a woodcut (see figure 5). The case for Fennor as author of the *Cornv-copiae* cannot be made conclusively. Jean Robertson, in her 1952 edition of Nicholas Breton's poems (Liverpool: Liverpool Univ. Press, 1952), pp. cliii–clv, combined an earlier assertion by A. B. Grosart that *Pasquils Palinodia* and the *Cornv-copiae* had the same author, a fellow named William F., with the

for although it has enjoyed scholarly attention that attention has downplayed rather than highlighted its place as a piece of erotica. This is so, I believe, because Harington's work reflects that English fascination with the most unsavory of topics, scatology.

Harington's work, rarely obscene but often bawdy, deals with the glories of defecating and the proper construction of privies. The *Metamorphosis* is a work that partakes of several kinds, as scholars have noted, being partly satire, partly moral tract, and partly a work dealing with a useful invention.[40] But above all, Harington presents his work as a mock encomium, for he was aware of the indelicacy of his subject matter and understood the advantages that such a vehicle afforded him. From the outset of the *Metamorphosis* Harington defends his endeavor in part by placing himself in the tradition of the paradoxical encomium:

> Sure I am that many other country men, both Dutch, French & Italians, with great prayse of wit, though small of modestie, have written of worse matters. One writes in prais of follie. 2. an other in honour of the Pox. 3. a third defendes usurie. 4. a fourth commends Nero. 5. a fift extolls and instructs bawderie. 6. the sixt displayes and describes *Puttana Errante,* which I here will come forth shortly in English. 7. A seventh (whom I would guesse by his writing, to be groome of the stoole to some Prince of the bloud in Fraunce) writes a beastly treatise onely to examine what is the fittest thing to wype withall, alledging that white paper is too smooth, brown paper too rough, wollen cloth too stiffe, linnen cloth too hollow, satten too slipperie, taffeta too thin, velvet too thick, or perhaps too costly: but he concludes, that a goose necke to be drawne betweene the legs against the fethers, is the most delicate and cleanly thing that may be. (Pp. 63–64)

Counting on his readers' knowledge of this material, Harington does not go into great detail to provide the context he wants, mere mention of praising the pox or rendering *Puttana Errante* in English being sufficient to do this. Rabelais is cited in more detail since the subject matter is so much nearer his own.

In a letter set at the beginning of the work, Harington's cousin,

---

attribution in Pollard and Redgrave's *Short Title Catalogue* of the *Palinodia* to William Fennor and declared Fennor the author of the poem. However, the attribution of the *Palinodia* to Fennor is uncertain, for he had a habit of appropriating the works of others.

40. Donno, p. 18, is of the opinion that Harington's purpose in writing this treatise on privies was partially serious, for he did build an exceedingly fine privy for his manor house at Kelston. Donno states, "Emphasis on the utility of his invention remains a persistent, and more than mock-serious, element in the work." Craig, pp. 68–83, deals with the work under the following headings: "The Reformed Privy as an Invention," "The *Metamorphosis* as Satire," "The Reformed Privy as Metaphor," and "The Mock Encomium."

dubbed Philostilpnos, Lover of Cleanness, expresses his anxiety that Harington will be unable to abandon the high style of the epic:

> But all my feare is that your pen having bene
> inured to so high discourse,
> *Of Dames, of Knights, of armes, of loves delight.*
> will now disdaine to take so base a subject,
> *Of vaults, of sinkes, privies & draughts to write.* (P. 57)

Harington answers his cousin's reference to his loftier work of translating Ariosto by pointing to the utilitarian aspects of his work, and he expresses the hope that

> . . . if I should fortune to effect so good a reformation, in the pallace of Richmond, or Greenwich (to which Pallace, many of us owe service for the tenure of our land) I doubt not but some pleasant witted Courtier of either sex, would grace me so much at least; as to say, that I were worthy for my rare invention, to be made one of the Privie (and after a good long parenthesis come out with) chamber, or if they be learned and have read *Castalios Courtier* they will say, I am a proper scholer, and well seene in *latrina lingua*. (Pp. 61–62)

Harington's self-conscious use of bawdy implications is caught well in his "Privie (and after a good long parenthesis come out with) chamber," and his "*latrina lingua*." He goes on, however, to defend his writing on less utilitarian grounds by placing it squarely in the tradition of the paradoxical encomium.

Harington begins the discourse proper with a defense of seemingly obscene matters and words:

> I feare the homely title prefixed to this treatise (how warlicke a sound so ever it hath) may breed a worse offence, in some of the finer sort of readers; who may upon much more just occasion condemne it, as a noysome and unsavory discourse: because, without any error of equivocation, I meane indeed, to write of the same that the word signifies. But if it might please them a little better to consider, how the place we treate of (how homely soever) is visited by them selves, once at least in foure and twentie houres, if their digestion bee good, and their constitution sound; then I hope they will do me that favour, and them selves that right, not to reject a matter teaching their owne ease and cleanlinesse, for the homelinesse of the name; and consequently, they will excuse all broade phrases of speech, incident to such a matter, with the old English proverbe that ends thus; *For Lords and Ladies do the same*. I know that the wiser sort of men wil consider, and I wish that the ignorant sort would learne; how it is not the baseness, or homelinesse, either of words, or matters, that make them foule & obscenous, but their base minds, filthy conceits, or lewd intents that handle them. (Pp. 82–83)

Harington takes the traditional defense here; nothing is dirty in its own right; it is only thinking dirty that makes it so. Professor Donno is convincing in her argument that Harington in fact avoids scurrility wherever possible—direct scurrility, that is. She notes that

> Harington maintains a certain reticence in his treatment. This can definitely be ascertained by checking his sources with the modifications he introduced when citing them. For example, he is careful to translate the epigrams of Sir Thomas More by decorous paraphrase (pp. 99, 100); his memory of Heywood's epigrams on two occasions is 'no better' than he 'would have it' (p. 104); he forbears to quote a ribald epigram of Sir John Davies since 'without his consent it is no good manners to publish it' (p. 103); he leaves questionable passages, whether they derive from merry Martial or learned divines like Dr. Humphrey or Dr. Rainolds (p. 104), in their original Latin; in recounting an amusing if impolite anecdote about an Italian lady and her physician, he likewise leaves the key line in Italian. Thus Harington's method is to work by suggestion, equivocation, puns, and witty allusions. The reason is manifest: he is writing for a courtly circle of readers. As he had admitted in his letter to Lady Russell, the first two leaves (i.e., sheets) contained almost nothing but 'skurrill and toying matter,' but the rest he considered "pleasaunt and harmeles," and he had taken occasion earlier to read 'the moste part of it' aloud to her. Thus by means of circumlocution and indirection Harington intended to keep his work within the bounds of propriety, fit not only for courtiers of either sex but also for 'the magnificent majestie of a Mayden Monark.'[41]

There can be little quarrel with Donno's assertion that "suggestion, equivocation, puns, and witty allusions" are keynotes of Harington's method, although one might want to add that Harington gets more bawdy mileage out of his allusions and puns than most writers get out of more direct use of bawdy. Harington is nothing if not aware of the suggestive power of words. What is disturbing about Donno's analysis is her implied view of Harington's audience, for it can be reduced to the assumption that courtly audiences do not like scurrility. The implication would seem to be that writing for a courtly audience is more refined, more moral than, say, writing for a middle-class audience. This was surely not the case in Elizabethan England.[42] If the bawdy bits in courtly works and popular drama did not please what Ann Cook has

41. Donno, pp. 15–16.
42. I do not doubt that the court was the deciding factor at this time under Elizabeth, but the implication is that all courtly writing is going to be more refined or more moral than say, middle-class writing. This was certainly not the case when one considers the tenor of most middle-class works. See Louis B. Wright, *Middle Class Culture in Elizabethan England* (Chapel Hill: Univ. of North Carolina Press, 1935), especially chapters 4, 5, 8, and all of Part III. See also his chapter 4, pp. 230–33.

called the "privileged" of the age, why are they so pervasive?[43] Donno's statements here are akin to Buxton's arguments about Elizabethan taste. They are assertions buttressed by no proof that an Elizabethan audience, especially a learned and aristocratic one, is not likely to have appreciated the bawdy. Does leaving phrases in Latin really show a "reticence in his treatment," or is it merely a sign that Harington does not *need* to translate such phrases since they could be read easily enough by his audience? We would do well to remember that in the Preface to his translation of *Orlando Furioso* Harington sketches a picture of readers who enjoy bawdy rather than abhor it. In defending Ariosto from the charge of lasciviousness, Harington manages to mention most of the incidents in the *Orlando Furioso* in which Ariosto is most "lascivious" as "in that of the baudy Frier, in *Alcinas* and *Rogeros* copulation, in *Anselmus,* his *Giptian,* in *Richardetto* his metamorphosis, in mine hosts tale of *Astolfo,* and some few places beside. . . ." Harington asks his readers to pardon Ariosto "this one fault." "I doubt too many of you (gentle readers) wil be to exorable in this point," he continues, "yea me thinks I see some of your [*sic*] searching already for these places of the booke and you are halfe offended that I have not made some directions that you might finde out and read them immediatly" (p. 11). An author who can imagine readers like this is not going to pass by opportunities to titillate them, whether by direct or by indirect scurrility.

Harington proceeds in his work by showing how important his subject is for all mankind. His pose is that of the philosopher, the wise man of experience who knows that if we merely avoid the troubles of this life we have done well. "Surely," he avers, "if we would enter into a sober, and sad consideration of our estates, even of the happiest sort of us, as men of the world esteeme us; whether we be noble, or rich, or learned, or beautifull, or healthy, or all these (which seldome happeneth) joyned together: we shall observe, that the joyes we enjoy in this world, consist rather *in indolentia* (as they call it) which is an avoyding of grievances and inconveniences, then in possessing any passing great pleasures; so durable are the harmes, that our first parents fal hath layd on us, and so poore the helpes that we have in our selves" (p. 83). Harington is able to conclude this speculation by stating that "so short, & so momentarie the contentments that we fish for, in this Ocean of miseries, which either we misse, (fishing before the net, as

43. Ann Cook, *The Privileged Playgoers of Shakespeare's London, 1576–1642* (Princeton: Princeton Univ. Press, 1981).

the proverbe is) or if we catch them, they prove but like Eeles, sleigth & slipperie" (pp. 83–84).

Having established the general fallen condition of man, Harington continues on to examine "the chiefest of all our sensuall pleasures, . . . the sweet sinne of letcherie, though God knowes, it hath much sowre sawce to it; for which notwithstanding, many hazard both their fame, their fortune, their friends, yea their soules" (p. 84). We expect Harington to continue as the moral philosopher, perhaps even the preacher, as he contemplates the oft-breaking of the sixth commandment, but here our philosopher turns anecdotalist, presenting us a vignette in which his sinners are remarkably like the readers of his translation of the *Orlando Furioso.* When his sinners hear the sixth commandment read in church, "they leave the words of the Communion booke, and say, *Lord have mercie upon us, it grieves our hearts to keepe this Law.* And when the Commination is read on Ashwednesday, wherein is read, *Cursed be he that lyeth with his neighbours wife,* and let all the people say, *Amen;* all these people either say nothing, or as a neighbour of mine said, *he hem*" (p. 84). Harington's attention to audience response in the little drama he creates here demonstrates vividly the turning of the sacred to the profane—*Amen* to *he hem.*

Harington concludes this passage as a man of the world who knows that the pleasures of sex may be great, but that they are as fleeting as youth itself and filled with "sowre sawce." "I say this surpassing pleasure, that is so much in request, and counted such a principall solace, I have heard confessed before a most honourable person, by a man of middle age, strong constitution, and well practised in this occupation, to have bred no more delectation to him (after the first heate of his youth was past) then to go to a good easie close stoole, when he hath had a lust thereto (for that was his verie phrase.)" (p. 84). A "good easie close stoole" is a pleasure to be enjoyed again and again, and so he prefers "this house" he minds "to speake of, before those which they so much frequent" (p. 84).[44]

Having played philosopher, Harington takes on the role of scholar to give us the noble lineage of the prime elements of his subjects. The pagans, he informs us, had a god and goddess for these necessaries of life, Stercutius and Cloacina. His subject is not so ignoble as to have been ignored by the creators of emblem books either:

. . . But come we now to more particular & not so serious matter; have not

---

44. Keith Thomas, *Religion and The Decline of Magic* (New York: Charles Scribner's Sons, 1971), p. 6, makes the point that in Renaissance England "the well-to-do ate too much meat and were frequently constipated."

many men of right good conceit, served them selves with diverse pretie emblemes, of this excrementall matter, so that in Alciat, to shew that base fellowes oft-times swimme in the streame of good fortune, as well as the worthiest:

Nos quoque poma natamus.

Or as the old proverb, as wel as emblem, that doth admonish men not to contend with base and ignominious persons.

Hoc scio pro certo, quod si cum stercore certo
Vinco ceu vincor, semper ego maculor.

I know if I contend with dirtie foes,
I must be soild, whether I win or lose. (Pp. 95–96)[45]

From emblems Harington is able to move on to poetry, "And thus much for Emblemes. Now for poesie (though Emblemes also are a kind of poesie) . . ." (p. 97). "It is certaine," he writes, "that of all poems, the Epigram is the pleasawntest, & of all that writes Epigrams, Martiall is counted the wittyest" (p. 97). And Martial, as Harington shows through quotation, was not averse to writing about matters excremental. He anticipates the next objection: "But now it may be some man will say, that these wanton and ribald phrases, were pleasing to those times of licentiousness, and paganisme that knew not Christ. . . ." (pp. 98–99). This charge he meets by quoting some of Sir Thomas More's bawdy epigrams. Harington is thus able to conclude his first section justifying "the use of the homelyest wordes" (p. 81) with the following sally:

Thus you must needes confesse, it is more then manifest, that without reproofe of ribaldrie, or scurrilitie, writings both holy, and prophane, Emblemes, Epigrams, Histories, and ordinarie and familiar communication; admits the use of the words, with all their apurtenances; in citing examples whereof, I have bene the more copious, because of this captious time, so readie to backbite every mans worke, and I would forewarne men not to bite here, lest they bite an unsavorie morsell. But here me think it were good to make a pause, & (as it were at a long diner) to take away the first course; which commonly is of the coursest meate, as powdred biefe and mustard, or ratner (to compare it fitter) fresh biefe and garlicke; for that hath three properties, more suting to this discourse: viz. to make a man winke, drinke, and stinke. Now for your second course, I could wish I had some larks, & quailes, but you must have such as the market I come from will affoord, always remembred, that our retiring place, or place of *rende vous* (as is expedient when men have filled their bellies) must be Monsieur

45. See figure 6.

A Jax, for I must still keepe me to my tesh: wherfore as I say, here I will make the first stop, and if you mislike not the fare thus far, I will make the second course, make you some amends. (Pp. 110–11)

Harington's wit makes a good show here. "Backbiters" suggests eating, and Harington has the metaphor for his discourse that Fielding was to exploit so extensively in *Tom Jones*. In fact, Harington's narrator comes across in a manner that also strikes a familiar note for those who have journeyed through *Tom Jones*. The narrator is both chef and waiter; he is in total control, serving up that which has been prepared from the market place where he has shopped. Of course his metaphor is most appropriate, for eating is ever the road to Harington's principal subject.

In the second section of the *Metamorphosis* Harington sets out to prove "the matter not to be *contemptible*" (p. 111), and he does this by citing all of the great men who have "employed their wits, their care, and their cost, about these places . . ." (p. 111). Worthies both pagan and Christian are marshaled forth to prove his point, and along the way Harington shows us the kind of verbal fun that is typical of his writing. Translating some Latin, he sends for a dictionary to help him with the "straunge word" *confornicari*:

Looke it sirra there in the dictionarie. *Con, con.* Tush what dost thou looke in the French? thou wilt make a sweete peece of looking, to looke for *confornicar* in the French: looke in the Latin for *fornicor. F, fa, fe, fi, fo for, foramen, forfex, forica, forma, fornicator,* (now I think I am neare it) *fornix, fornicor, aris, are.* There, there, what says he of that? A vault or Arche, to vault or arch any thing with a compasse. (Pp. 135–36)

This is Harington at his best, poking fun at pedants and slipping bawdy insinuations in all along the way.[46] Professor Donno explains the passage well—up to a point. She notes that "in imitating the process of word hunting, Harington illustrates a kind of selective serendipity, picking out items that have a suggestive relevance to his text. In defiance of alphabetical order—as well as that of Elyot and Cooper—he inserts the passive *fornicor, fornicaris,* 'to commit fornication' before the active *fornicare* 'to make an arche or a vault,' thus permitting his observation that Elyot and Cooper place these two words 'too neare together.' A 'vaulting house' was one of the cant terms for a brothel."[47] Some of

---

46. Earlier in this passage Harington mentions the dictionary maker Thomas Thomas, who was one of the prefects at Eton when Harington was a student there. See *Metamorphosis*, p. 135; and Craig, p. 6.

47. Donno, p. 135.

Harington's other Latin words in this passage seem carefully chosen as well, and Donno's reticence in her commentary is symptomatic of her unwillingness to show Harington's bawdy for all that it is. *Foramen* means an opening or a hole, *forica* a privy, and we note as well Harington's adeptness in French with his *con, con*. Harington's method may be one of insinuation and punning, but the effect is to *increase* the rollicking bawdy of the passage. There is precious little "reticence" on the part of Harington here.

The final section of the book deals with "the forme, and how it *may be reformed*" (p. 159). Harington ends this section of the book with comments that are most enlightening in terms of recognition of certain types of readers. Defending himself against the charge of being "fantastical," especially with regard to the titling of his book, Harington writes:

> I must needes acknowledge it fantastical for me, whom I suppose you deeme (by many circumstances) not to be of the basest, either birth or breeding, to have chosen, or of another mans choise, to have taken so straunge a subject. But though I confesse thus much, yet I would not have you lay it to my charge, for if you so do, I shall straight retort all the blame, or the greatest part of it, upon your selfe: and namely, I would but aske you this question, & even truly between God and your conscience, do but answer it. If I had entituled the booke, *A Sermon shewing a soveraigne salve for the sores of the soule. Or, A wholsome haven of health to harbour the heart in. Or, A mervellous medicine for the maladies of the minde.* would you ever have asked after such a booke? would these grave and sober titles have wonne you to the view of three or foure tittles? much lesse three or foure score periodes. But when you heard, there was one had written of A Jax, straight you had a great mind to see what strange discourse it would prove, you made enquirie who wrote it, where it might be had, when it wold come forth. You prayed your friend to buy it, beg it, borow it, that you might see what good stuffe was in it. And why had you such a mind to it? I can tell you; you hoped for some meriments, some toyes, some scurrilitie, or so to speake plaine English, some knaverie. And if you did so, I hope now your expectation is not altogether frustrate. (P. 181)

Harington realizes that one kind of audience at least is the licentious reader, the reader Hall noted with an "itching" to be scratched; Harington himself had drawn a portrait of just such a reader in the preface to his translation of the *Orlando Furioso;* he knows that this work has had enough bawdy in it to scratch that itching. He captures very well the spirit of anticipation in the vignette he imagines of such a reader asking a friend to "buy it, beg it, borow it" to see "what good stuffe" is in it. Such readers have a relish for "meriments," "toyes," "scurrilitie," "knaverie." Harington goes on to point to the moral lessons ("pretie pils") the reader has gained as well, but what emerges from this passage most clearly is his sense of what will attract readers to a text.

Harington also recognizes another kind of reader, when he defends himself against the charge of "scurrilitie":

> The second fault you object, is scurrilitie, to which I answer, that I confesse the objection, but I denie the fault, and if I might know whether he were Papist or Protestant that maketh this objection, I wold soone answer them: namely thus; I would cite a principall writer of either side, and I would prove, that either of them hath used more obscenous, fowle, and scurrill phrases, (not in defence of their matter, but in defacing of their adversarie) in one leafe of their bookes, then is in all this. Yet they professe to write of the highest, the holiest, the waightiest matters that can be imagined, and I write of the basest, the barrennest, and most witlesse subject that may be described.
>
> *Quod decuit tantos cur mihi turpe putem?*
>
> I forbeare to shew examples of it, least I should be thought to disgrace men of holy and worthie memorie. (P. 182)

Harington was well aware of how base, how obscene, how sexually suggestive the language of theologians and moralists could be; his own work, he realizes, is not nearly so bad. Harington is certainly exaggerating here, but it is an exaggeration that had some basis in fact, as readers of controversial religious pamphlets knew.

In the same vein as his defense of "scurrilitie" is Harington's answer to the charge that his *Metamorphosis* is too satirical; and he concludes his work with the following couplet:

> To keepe your houses sweete, cleanse privie vaults,
> To keepe your soules as sweete, mend privie faults. (P. 186)

Harington's work is a first-rate paradoxical encomium and first-rate bawdy as well. His success in writing stems, I think, not only from his wit and verbal dexterity, but also from a knowledge of his readers with an "itching" to be tickled and a knowledge of other "salacious" writers. He knows the weaknesses of the moralists, theologians, and satirists as writers on matters sexual because he understands the potentiality for language to become suggestive once the subject of sex has been announced in any form.

There remains one major figure at the center of the canvas of English erotica, Thomas Nashe, the self-styled English Aretino. He is the subject of the next chapter.

CHAPTER 7

Thomas Nashe: The English Aretino

Of all stiles I most affect & striue to imitate Aretines
Thomas Nashe, Lenten Stuffe

Thomas Nashe must surely have been pleased to find himself acclaimed as a literary figure more notorious than Pietro Aretino. For a poor university man come to London to make it on the literary scene, notoriety, as long as one stayed out of jail and was able to keep one's work in print, was certainly preferable to anonymity. And to find oneself branded as the English Aretino was certainly a reflection of successful self-promotion.

Early in his publishing career Nashe had trumpeted the call, "giue me the man whose extemporall veine in any humour will excell our greatest Art-maisters deliberate thoughts; whose inuentions, quicker then his eye, will challenge the prowdest Rhetoritian to the contention of like perfection with like expedition" (III, 312). He meant the reading public to see one Thomas Nashe answering that call, and his own model in shaping his career, as he makes clear in any number of his works, was Pietro Aretino. Nashe tells us in the prefatory epistle to his *Lenten Stuffe* (1599) that "of all stiles I most affect & striue to imitate *Aretines,* not caring for this demure soft *mediocre genus,* that is like water and wine mixt togither; but giue me pure wine of itself, & that begets good bloud, and heates the brain thorowly: I had as lieue haue no sunne, as haue it shine faintly, no fire, as a smoothering fire of small coales, no cloathes, rather than weare linsey wolsey" (III.152). In this passage Nashe is clearly talking about imitating only Aretino's style, one that is full-bodied, powerful, and heady, but in an earlier praise of Aretino in *The Vnfortunate Traveller* (1594) Nashe displays considerable knowledge of Aretino's literary life. Nashe has his narrator, Jack Wilton, interrupt his story to offer extended praise of the Italian, one in which Wilton praises Aretino's wit, his satirical acuity, and his independence. Wilton informs us that "Foure vniuersities honoured *Aretine* wyth these rich titles, *Il flagello de principi, Il veritiero, Il deuino,* & *L'vnico Aretino*"

186

(II.265). He goes on to list most of Aretino's works and to defend his "lasciuious" writing and living: "If lasciuious he were, he may answere with *Ouid, Vita verecunda est, musa iocosa mea est*; My lyfe is chast though wanton be my verse. Tell mee, who is trauelled in histories, what good poet is, or euer was there, who hath hadde a lyttle spice of wantonnesse in his days?" (II.266).

As we have already seen, one must be wary of taking anything at face value that Nashe has his narrator say in *The Vnfortunate Traveller.* His "Induction to the Dapper Monsieur Pages of the Court" at the outset of the work should be warning enough, for there he writes, "A proper fellow Page of yours called *Iack Wilton* by me commends him vnto you, and hath bequeathed for wast paper here amongst you cer- taine pages of his misfortunes. In anie case, keepe them preciously as a *priuie* token of his good will towardes you" (II.207). But the praise of Aretino just cited seems unironic to me; it is set off from the rest of the work by the manner in which it is introduced and concluded ("Before I goe anie further, let me speake a word or two of this *Are- tine. . . .* My principall subiect pluckes me by the elbowe" [II.264– 66]), and the sentiments expressed in praise of Aretino are ones that Nashe held dear to himself. When Nashe is ironic, the reader usually does not have to search too long to find the cutting edge. I find none here in what I take to be extended praise and defense of the infamous Italian.[1]

Whether Nashe knew Aretino's works at first hand has never been conclusively demonstrated.[2] What is clear, however, is that Nashe

---

1. Nashe mentions Aretino a number of times in his writings. In *Pierce Penilesse* Nashe refers to Aretino as an exposer of evils (I, 242). In *Strange Newes* he mentions Aretino in connection with his comedies (I, 259), and as a writer who has brought in "a new kind of quicke fight" (I, 283 and I, 324).

2. See F. P. Wilson, ed., *The Works of Nashe,* V, 128–29; and McPherson, pp. 1551– 58. McPherson, however, states that his findings on Aretino support Parks's argument that the negative Italian myth is only a later development in England. As I think I have shown, England's response was ambivalent from an early date.

While Nashe's direct knowledge of Aretino remains open to debate, we do know that he was a friend of John Florio's. See Yates, pp. 194–212. The connections between the two show up in a way relevant to this study. In his definitions for *fottere* in *A Worlde of Wordes* Florio gives: "To iape, to sard, to fucke, to swiue, to occupy." As we know, this is one of the earliest printed uses of "fuck," a slang expression that rarely appears in Elizabethan literature. "Occupy" and "iape" were popular slang terms used throughout the Renaissance in literature. "Swiue" was of course well known and used in literature. "Sard" is the most curious term of all. It is such an obscure word that the *OED* felt safe in including it (with "jape" as the definition). According to the *OED* the word can be found in the Lindisfarne Gospels (950), the *Castle of Perseverence* (1425), Jehan Palsgrave's *Lesclaricissment de la langue francoyse* (1530), Lindesay's satires (1535), and Florio. There

understood what Aretino was famous for—sparkling wit, daring (and detailed) flagellation of sins, a proud independence, and lascivious writings. In Aretino's life and reputation, if not his writings, Nashe had a model of a man who had made it, a man who had become the Scourge of Princes, the Divine Aretino, all through the power of his pen. Nashe, from the outset of his career, showed the same daring willingness to try anything to succeed in the London literary world; and so, Aretino-like, he wrote moral tracts and pornography, drama and prose fiction; above all, he engaged in literary warfare, a field where his genius most readily manifests itself. As I argued in chapter 5, Nashe is a perfect reflection of England's paradoxical response to Italy in the Renaissance. He understood that if one wanted to write a tale of horror, rape, and revenge, one set it in Italy, reflecting the negative view of Italy. He also understood that if one wanted to write pornography, there were models to be imitated and traditions to be alluded to; Italy provided these as well. To the moralists and theologians, lascivious books were the epitome of all that was evil in Italy; to a writer trying to establish himself as a professional man of letters, Italian erotica was only one more of the products of Italy to be used as a model for his own creations. Indeed, the reputation of a writer who had been successful in such endeavors was sufficient precedent and authority for Nashe.

Seeing Nashe as a self-styled English Aretino is important in terms of understanding his achievement. Although Nashe ranged widely in his writing, trying many different genres, he produced relatively little in dramatic and poetic genres. That fact alone has limited the scholarly attention he has received. But even where Nashe's genius has been recognized, say as a literary combatant of extraordinary dexterity and possessor of one of the liveliest prose styles in English, the Aretinesque elements related to the world of erotica have been given scant attention or ignored altogether. Thus an author who chose to locate himself in the world of erotica has never been focused upon precisely in that realm. I shall do so in this chapter through an examination of *A Choise of Valentines* and several pamphlets from his battle with the Harveys.

Certainly Nashe followed directly in the footsteps of his esteemed Aretino when he composed his *Choise of Valentines*. As we have already seen, this work, even though it circulated only in manuscript form,

---

is one citation after Florio, Howell's *English Proverbs* (1659). Florio might have come across the term in Palsgrave's *Lesclaricissment,* where it is used as a definition for *fou.* But he might also have gotten the word from Nashe, for Nashe uses it in his *Praise of Red Herring,* a work, however, that postdates Florio's dictionary by one year. As far as I have been able to discover, Nashe and Florio are the only Renaissance writers to use "sard."

gained great notoriety for Nashe; his enemies constantly maligned him for producing such "filthy," such "bawdy," such "obscene" rhymes. The poem has not fared well at modern critical hands either. McKerrow includes a version of the poem in his *Works of Nashe,* but it is placed at the very end of all of the texts under a category of "Doubtful Works." Since the authorship of the *Choise* has never been a question, McKerrow must have found it "doubtful" on other grounds. It is, as Charles Nicholl says, a work "more often mentioned than described or examined," and the few treatments it has received have been curious indeed.[3]

Nicholl himself has the good sense to place the poem within the context of Marlowe's translations of Ovid's *Elegies,* though his own analysis is not extensive and his assessment is a rather brief and breezy: "As a piece of pornography (which by the yardsticks of the day it was) it is thoroughly wholesome: ribald rather than decadent, naughty rather than nasty. . . . Nashe's 'Dildo' is an erotic *vignette:* comic, titillating, full of cartoon-like visual touches."[4] Hibbard gives the poem short shrift indeed, and Keach virtually ignores it in his study *Elizabethan Erotic Narratives.* Keach labels the poem "the most obscene Elizabethan poem known to us."[5] The poem is not of much interest to Keach because his concern, as the subtitle of his book indicates, is with "Irony and Pathos in the Ovidian Poetry of Shakespeare, Marlowe, and Their Contemporaries." He is not concerned with Ovidian poetry as erotica. One can hardly fault Keach for putting the emphasis where he has; the Ovidian works of Shakespeare and Marlowe can no doubt be most profitably examined by focusing on irony and pathos rather than on eroticism. Jonathan Crewe in his study, *Unredeemed Rhetoric,* gives considerable attention to the poem, and he provides what is the most provocative analysis of it to date; but he also completely ignores the tradition of erotica, so intent is he on proving certain theses about Nashe's work.[6] Thus Crewe discusses the poem within the context of contemporary critical approaches and finds that "the poem stages a

3. Charles Nicholl, *A Cup of News: The Life of Thomas Nashe* (London: Routledge & Kegan Paul, 1984), p. 92.

4. Ibid., p. 92.

5. See Hibbard, p. 56–59; William Keach, *Elizabethan Erotic Narratives* (New Brunswick, N.J.: Rutgers Univ. Press, 1977), p. 158.

6. Jonathan Crewe, *Unredeemed Rhetoric* (Baltimore: Johns Hopkins Univ. Press, 1982), pp. 48–54. For Crewe the poem is in part about the loss of "an ideal poetic order" and "an ideal pastoral order" (p. 48). Crewe asserts that "recoveries may be attempted, either under the guise of moral satire or on some paradoxical mode of urban pastoral, the prospects of full recovery remain questionable" (p. 48).

radical dislocation and consequent loss of ontological security, not only for its speaker, but for love poetry as such."[7] What Crewe's and all the preceding comments reveal is that through an exclusionary practice of characterization, classification, and thesis-making, scholars have found convenient ways to avoid consideration of the most notorious piece of Elizabethan erotica as erotica.

Nashe's poem owes a general debt to Chaucer, with its setting on Valentine's Day reminiscent of that of the *Parliament of Fowls* and verbal touches that no doubt suggested Chaucerian expressions to his readers; but the primary debt is to Ovid's *Amores* III.vi, where the poet-lover laments his impotence.[8] It is typical of Nashe to go further than either his general or specific models, however, to reach Aretinesque heights in his rendering of a Valentine poem involving a dildo. Whether Nanna's use of a dildo in Aretino's *Dialogues* was known to Nashe (and thus a direct debt to the Italian master is involved) cannot be proven conclusively.

What Nashe does is adapt his Chaucerian echoes and Ovidian situation to contemporary London, and, typically, he carries them to an extreme. A comparison with the narrative situation in Ovid's poem is instructive. The poet-lover in the Ovidian poem writes in retrospect of a shameful situation. He could not get an erection during an encounter with a particularly luscious courtesan. "Yet like as if cold hemlock I had drunk, / It mocked me, hung down the head, and sunk" (ll. 13–14). The poet assures us that this situation is not normal for him, for only recently "boarded I the golden Chie twice, / And Libas, and the white cheeked Pitho thrice. / Corinna craved it in a summer's night, / And nine sweet bouts we had before daylight" (ll. 23–26). The poet-lover, upset over his inability to perform, finds that his sense of failure only adds to his feelings of inadequacy; indeed "shame to perform it quailed me, / And was the second cause why vigour failed me" (ll. 37–38). The poet-lover must confess that the woman in question on this occasion was everything a man might desire; she might have moved

---

7. Ibid., p. 51. In offering his provocative reading of the poem, Crewe concludes, "If 'The Choice of Valentines' and its impotent persons cannot redeem themselves—unless pornographically—they nevertheless establish the shift to the city as a moment of profound dislocation and loss" (p. 53). I obviously argue that his parenthetical "unless pornographically" is a telling quality for Nashe.

8. See Christopher Marlowe, *The Complete Poems and Translations,* ed. Stephen Orgel (Harmondsworth, Middlesex: Penguin Books, 1971), pp. 171–73. I have used Marlowe's translation, since Nashe knew Marlowe at Cambridge and it seems likely that he was familiar with Marlowe's translation of the *Amores*. See Nicholl, pp. 29–30. All subsequent citations to Ovid's poems are to this translation and edition.

"huge oaks" and "hard adamants"; her words might have caused deaf rocks to have loved, but all was in vain, "like one dead it lay, / Drooping more than a rose pulled yesterday" (ll.65–66). And here Ovid strikes a truly comic touch, for suddenly, in remembrance of all of this, the would-be poet-lover gets an erection: "Now, when he should not jet, he bolts upright, / And craves his task, and seeks to be at fight" (ll.67–68). He curses his offending appendage, telling it to "lie down in shame" for it has "cozened" him. Even the mistress's most ardent actions failed on that occasion:

> . . . the wench did not disdain a whit
> To take it in her hand and play with it,
> But when she saw it would by no means stand,
> But still drooped down, regarding not her hand,
> 'Why mock'st thou me,' she cried, 'or being ill,
> Who bade thee lie down here against thy will?
> Either th'art witched with blood of frogs new dead,
> Or jaded cam'st thou from some other's bed.' (ll.73–80)

The poet's penis, a traitor to him, is offensive to the mistress as well, a flaccid insult to her sexual attractiveness and wiles. The poem ends with *her* attempt to hide her humiliation, "And lest her maid should know of this disgrace, / To cover it, spilt water on the place" (ll.83–84).

Ovid's poem is far more comic than pornographic. While great pains are taken to ensure our acceptance of the young woman as sexually desirable, and while the overtly sexual nature of the encounter is certainly emphasized, including the attempts of the mistress to bring the poet to an erect state, the poem is finally calculated to expose the poet-lover to ridicule. The action is kept in the past; no sexual actions are described in extended detail; the mistress is concerned only with her reputation as a desirable sexual partner, not with satisfying her lust. The ultimate irony is that only in remembering the charms of the courtesan does the poet-lover seem to recover from his total impotency. It is a memory calculated to make us laugh at him, not calculated to give his readers an erection in reading it.

Nashe's *Choise of Valentines* is surely meant to be comic, but it is meant to be pornographic as well, and this can be plainly seen in the scenes of extended sexual activity, in the shifting of tenses to enhance the immediacy of that sexual activity (and thus involve the reader more fully), and in the depiction of the Valentine herself, a young nun of Venus driven by the need to satisfy her sexual appetite.

The poem begins by referring to that time of year "When yong-men

in their iollie roguerie / Rose earelie in the morne fore breake of daie /
To seeke them valentines so trimme and gaie" (ll.2–4). The speaker
describes several native customs of seeking mates and tells us he went
as a "poore pilgrim" to his lady's shrine "To see if she would be my
valentine" (ll.17–18). To his chagrin he discovered that

> Good Iustice Dudgein-haft, and crab-tree face
>   With bills and staues had scar'd hir from the place;
> And now she was compell'd for Sanctuarie
>   To flye unto an house of venerie.
> Thither went I, and bouldlie made enquire
>   If they had hackneis to lett-out to hire,
> And what they crau'd by order of their trade
>   To lett one ride a iournie on a iade. (ll.21–28)

This is hardly the Chaucerian world of Valentine's Day; the world
of natural love in a state of *otium* is transferred to the city, in a state of
negotium.[9] Nashe uses a traditional bawdy metaphor for sexual intercourse ("ride a iournie on a iade"), but this is clearly a world of commercial sex; this ride will be a hired one ("hackneis to lett-out to hire").
The commercial aspect of the pursuit of the valentine is detailed in the
speaker's dealings with the Madame of the brothel. The image of the
valentine on a pilgrimage is combined neatly in the Madame's demand:

> Com, laye me a Gods-pennie in my hand;
> For, in our Oratorie siccarlie,
>   None enters heere to doe his nicerie.
> But he must paye his offertorie first,
>   And then perhaps wee'le ease him of his thirst. (ll.36–40)

The would-be lover crosses the Madame's palm and is brought to a
room "Where venus bounzing vestalls skirmish oft" (l.48), and he is
shown several "prettie Trulls" whom he rejects; he must have "fresher
ware" (l.54). The sexual terminology is fairly traditional and metaphorical to this point, and we are constantly reminded that this pilgrimage is both sexual and commercial. The speaker tells the Madame
that he wants his special valentine, Mistress Francis.[10] She applauds his
choice but tells the pilgrim that if he wants to "swiue with hir" his
"purse-strings shall abye-it deare" (ll.61–62). The Madame means only

---

9. Crewe, pp. 48–49, sees the same shift.
10. Francis (with its variants Franceschina and Francissina) is a name commonly used
for a whore in the Renaissance. See Philip C. Kolin, "The Names of Whores and Their
Bawds and Panders in English Renaissance Drama," *Midwestern Journal of Language and
Folklore* 6 (1980): 41–50. A notable example is Marston's Franceschina in *The Dutch
Courtesan*.

that Francis will cost the poet a good deal of money, but purse was often used to suggest the male scrotum; as we shall see, the point of the poem is that it too will be taxed severely.[11]

Francis is brought in

> Sweeping she coms, as she would brush the ground,
>> Hir ratling silke's my sences doe confound.
> Oh, I am rauish't; voide the chamber streight,
>> For, I must neede's upon hir with my weight. (ll. 77–80)

There follows a description of Tomalin's (Francis's pet name for the speaker) approach to his valentine. It begins in a manner that indicates little beyond a full Elizabethan Ovidian treatment, except that Nashe plays a variation on the *topos* of the descending catalogue. Traditionally a beautiful woman was described from the head down to the toe.[12] Kiernan's contention is that any catalogue or description "greatly emphasizes an audience's sense of participation in the act of inspecting the beautiful body," and a reversal of the normal tradition "usually suggests a lasciviousness on the part of the viewer, and this, too, tends to embarrass the participating audience. In the best poems the type of description conforms with the type of viewer and, willy-nilly, the audience is incorporated into the poet's design."[13] One would quibble here only with the notion that the audience need be embarrassed. Nashe clearly wants the audience to be aroused sexually, so what follows is rendered in the present tense to increase the immediacy of the event. Tomalin begins his progress by lifting those silken skirts

> I com, I com; sweete lyning be thy leaue,
>> Softlie my fingers, up theis curtaine, heaue
> And make me happie stealing by degreese.
>> First bare hir leggs, then creepe vp to hir kneese.
> From thence ascend unto hir mannely thigh.
>> (A pox on lingring when I am so nighe)
> Smock climbe a-pace, that I maie see my ioyes,
>> Oh heauen, and paradize are all but toyes,
> Compar'd with this sight, I now behould,
>> Which well might keepe a man from being olde. (ll. 99–108)

The journey is swift indeed; Nashe does not waste too much time on

11. See Ross, pp. 172–73; and J. S. Farmer and W. E. Henley, *Slang and Its Analogues* (1890–1914; rpt. n.p.: Arno Press, 1970), p. 329.

12. Kevin Kiernan, "The Art of the Descending Catalogue, and a Fresh Look at Alisoun," *The Chaucer Review* 10 (1975): 1–16.

13. Ibid., p. 2.

loving details of the legs. A standard Elizabethan treatment of this discovery would not be overly explicit about what reveals itself when the smock is lifted completely; Nashe's poem is:

> A prettie rysing wombe without a weame,
>   That shone as bright as anie siluer streame;
> And bare out lyke the bending of an hill,
>   At whose decline a fountaine dwelleth still,
> That hath his mouth besett with uglie bryers
>   Resembling much a duskie nett of wyres. (ll.109–14)

The speaker is undone by all his viewing and anticipation:

> Hir arme's are spread, and I am all unarm'd
>   Lyke one with Ouids cursed hemlock charm'd,
> So are my limm's unwealdie for the fight,
>   That spend their strength in thought of hir delight.
> What shall I doe to shewe my self a man?
>   It will not be for ought that beawtie can.
> I kisse, I clap, I feele, I view at will,
>   Yett dead he lyes not thinking good or ill. (ll.123–30)

The reader of Ovid recognizes the situation, of course; indeed Nashe reminds his audience of Ovid's poem by referring to Tomalin's state as being like one affected with "Ouids cursed hemlock." But there is a difference. We realize that Tomalin's previous "I com, I com" carries a specific significance and that he is temporarily impotent because he has already ejaculated. Realizing this, Francis responds with a display of unadulterated lust in action, and that action is initially the same as that practiced by Ovid's mistress: "Vnhappie me, quoth shee, and wilt' not stand? / Com, lett me rubb and chafe it with my hand" (ll.131–32). While Francis's actions are the same as those of Ovid's mistress, her state is quite different; she is concerned not with maintaining her reputation but with satisfying her desire. This fact is emphasized in the lines that follow:

> Perhaps the sillie worme is labour'd sore,
>   And wearied that it can doe no more.
> If it be so (as I am greate a-dread)
>   I wish tenne thousand times, that I were dead.
> How ere it is; no meanes shall want in me,
>   That maie auaile to his recouerie.
> Which saide, she tooke and rould it on hir thigh,
>   And when she lookt' on't, she would weepe and sighe,
> And dandled it, and dance't it up and doune,
>   Not ceasing, till she rais'd it from his swoune.

> And then he flue on hir as he were wood,
>> And on hir breeche did thack, and foyne a-good;
> He rubd', and prickt, and pierst hir to the bones,
>> Digging as farre as eath he might for stones.
> Now high, now lowe, now stryking short and thick;
>> Now dyuing deepe he toucht hir to the quick.
> Now with a gird, he would his course rebate;
>> Streite would he take him to a statlie gate,
> Plaie while him list; and thrust he neare so hard,
>> Poore pacient Grisill lyeth at hir warde,
> And giue's, and take's as blyth and free as Maye,
> And ere-more meete's him in the midle waye. (ll. 131–54)

No other poem of the Elizabethan era is so explicit, and Nashe drags out his description of the sexual act through another seventy lines. Tomalin, unlike the poet-lover in Ovid's poem, has been able to act, and Nashe delights in describing that action for us. Such extended description is meant to arouse the reader. As I have argued earlier, one of the myths on which pornography is built is that of sexual potency, the readiness of the players to engage in sexual athletics at all times. Clearly, part of the humor in Nashe's poem lies in the depiction of the limited potency of Tomalin. Francis, however, is presented as the insatiable, sex-starved female of pornographic fantasy, and the shift to her and her drive for pleasure remains the focus for the rest of the poem.

The speaker tells us, after a lengthy description of the effect of viewing one and other, that they "perseuer, / But what so firme, that maie continue euer?" (ll. 177–78). Francis fears it all may end too fast:

> Oh not so fast, my rauisht Mistriss cryes,
>> Leaste my content, that on thy life relyes
> Be brought too-soone from his delightfull seate,
>> And me unwares of hoped bliss defeate.
> Togeather lett our equall motions stirr
>> Togeather let vs liue and dye my deere
> Together lett us marche unto content,
>> And be consumed with one blandishment. (ll. 179–86)

Tomalin strives to meet her ardor, describing the action now with metaphors that emphasize the keeping of a beat:

> As she prescrib'd, so kept we crotchet-time,
>> And euerie stroake in ordre lyke a chyme.
> Whilst she, that had preseru'd me by hir pittie,
>> Vnto our musike fram'd a groaning dittie. (ll. 187–90)

The pace picks up, and the speaker gives us both immediacy of action and conversation in the present tense:

> With Oh, and Oh, she itching moues her hipps,
>   And to and fro, full lightlie starts and skips.
> She ierks hir leggs, and sprauleth with hir heeles,
>   No tongue maie tell the solace that she feeles.
> I faint, I yeald; Oh death rock me a-sleepe;
>   Sleepe—sleepe desire, entombed in the deepe.
> Not so my deare; my dearest Saint replyde;
>   For, from us yett thy spirit maie not glide
> Vntill the sinnowie channels of our blood
>   Withould their source from this imprisoned flood;
> And then will we (that then we will com to soone)
>   Dissolued lye as-though our dayes were donne. (ll. 199–210)

The emphasis now shifts entirely to Francis and her frustration with Tomalin's inability to satisfy her. In her lament, she combines images of time, and by extension water, in ways that end up being most appropriate:

> Time ner'e looke's back, the riuers ner'e returne;
>   A second spring must help me or I burne.
> No, no the well is drye that should refresh me,
>   The glasse is runne of all my destinie. (ll. 223–26)

The passage of time brings forth the image of the river; it is another flood that Francis desires, but all is dry; the sands have all run out from her glass; the purse has been taxed indeed. There is a nice irony in the image of time's running out through the glass, for Francis is about to turn to her dildo, also an instrument of glass that she will fill with warm liquid to satisfy herself. Francis bids adieu to Tomalin's dwindling organ and turns to her dildo:

> Adiew faint-hearted instrument of lust,
>   That falselie has betrayed our equale trust.
> Hence-forth no more will I implore thine ayde,
>   Or thee, or men of cowardize upbrayde.
> My little dilldo shall suplye their kinde:
>   A knaue, that moues as light as leaues by winde;
> That bendeth not, nor fouldeth anie deale,
>   But stands as stiff, as he were made of steele,
> And plays at peacock twixt my leggs right blythe,
>   And doeth my tickling swage with manie a sighe;
> For by Saint Runnion he'le refresh me well,
>   And neuer make my tender bellie swell. (ll. 234–46)

McKerrow suggests in his notes that "Saint Runnion" is "presumably the 'ronyon,' i.e., mangy wretch, of *Merry Wives,* IV.ii.195, and *Macbeth,* I.iii.6," but it seems more likely that Nashe means to remind us of Chaucer here, for we recall that both the Host and the Pardoner swear by Saint Ronyan.[14] A meaning "runnion" came to have was the male organ, and that, of course, would be a most appropriate saint for Francis to swear by.[15] The dildo is described at great length, gets personified as a youth, and his actions are detailed (ll.269–86), but finally the speaker breaks off; he can go on no more. He tells us that she lies breathless and that he is "taken doune." Nashe concludes with a tag from Virgil's *Eclogues,* neatly changing *pueri* to *Priape* in his version, "Claudite iam riuos, Priape, sat prata biberunt." It seems gratuitous for Nashe to go on to tell us, as he does in an epilogue, that we are dealing here with "lasciuious witt." If there are parts that are witty in the modern sense of the word, there are many parts that are simply lascivious, nothing more nor less, and they exist to appeal to the salacious reader. The *Choise of Valentines* is one of the few unadulterated pornographic works of the English Renaissance. It purports no moral end; it does not say that it is trying to teach by negative example; it does not condemn lust. It appeals frankly to those who have an itching to be scratched. As pornography, it is not entirely successful. There are lengthy passages filled with metaphors and similes that are not salacious (ll.155–76, her viewing of his organ) or that do not further the work in any significant fashion (ll.290–epilogue, the poet's tedious attempt to end the poem and apologize for it). Nashe's presentation of his speaker, Tomalin, is comic, and this too detracts from the salacious effect of the poetry. But there are still the extended passages of lust in action, and always there is the sexual drive of Francis. While a modern sensibility might view Francis's actions as unsettling and propel one to a Derridean interpretation of the poem, a reader familiar with Renaissance erotica recognizes that Nashe is working in a tradition in which female masterbation with a dildo is one of the conventions confirming male fantasies about the sexual drive of females.[16] While the poet may fail to satisfy this drive, the male reader is nevertheless amused, confident in his own ability to meet the demands of a Francis. And while that confidence may be based on a mythic view of one's own powers, we must remember that erotic poetry like this is written for those

14. See McKerrow's comment in *Works of Nashe,* IV, 482; and Wilson's in the supplemental notes in ibid., V, 73.
15. See Ross, pp. 194–95; and the *OED.*
16. See Crewe, pp. 52–54.

indulging in just such fantasies. That is one reason Nashe treats Tomalin comically; he creates distance between the speaker and the reader
so that the reader can maintain his fantasies.

In the final analysis, while the poem is certainly not up to Aretino's
work, dress it out as Nashe will with Chaucerian and Ovidian ac-
coutrements, it nonetheless has its moments of both humor and salacious lubricity. In *Haue With You to Saffron-Walden* (1596), taxed with
the charge that he has been "prostituting" his pen "like a Curtizan,"
Nashe replies, ". . . well it may and it may not bee so, for neither will
I deny it nor will I grant it; onely thus farre Ile goe with you, that
twise or thrise a month, when *res est angusta domi,* the bottome of my
purse is turned downeward, & my conduit of incke will no longer flowe
for want of reparations, I am faine to let my Plow stand still in the
midst of a furrow, and follow some of these newfangled *Galiardos* and
Senior Fantasticos, to whose amorous *Villanellas* and *Quipassas* I prostitute my pen in hope of gaine" (III.30–31). Nashe's palpably sexual
imagery offers a telling counterpoint to his poem. When his financial
status is taxed like Tomalin's sexual status, the only solution open to
Nashe, he claims, is to "prostitute" his pen by putting it in the service
of amorous appetites. If Nashe did this, however, the evidence has not
come to light; his *Choise of Valentines* remains a unique work. In its
own time it was instantaneously notorious as the most lascivious poem
in English.

But if Nashe was not quite up to Aretino when it came to writing
pornography, he surely surpassed his master with his stunningly effective use of sexual insults and scatology in waging literary warfare with
Gabriel Harvey and his brothers.

The events in the Nashe-Harvey quarrel have been sufficiently well
chronicled elsewhere so as to need no extensive reworking here. What
does bear further investigation is the *way* in which Nashe so effectively
dissected Gabriel and his brother Richard.[17] The *general* qualities that
characterize Nashe's genius in his warfare with the Harveys were well
stated several years ago by David McPherson in his article on the Nashe-
Harvey quarrel. He writes, "Harvey, one might say, was like a Spanish
galleon—heavily armed but slow and awkward; Nashe, like an English
man-o-war—light, swift, maneuverable."[18] McPherson argues that
Nashe chose as his persona the Aretine railer but says that he adopted

17. See the accounts in *Works of Nashe,* V, 65–110; Nicholl; and Virginia Stern, *Gabriel Harvey: His Life Marginalia and Library* (Oxford: Oxford University Press, 1979), especially chapter 6.
18. McPherson, p. 1558.

a lighter tone such as is found in the "flytings." McPherson points out that "from the beginning of the quarrel Nashe had been able to hide any real anger he felt and to display an amusing self-congratulatory interest in his own abilities with language. After giving Richard Harvey a good going over, he stops, turns to his audience, and asks: 'haue I not an indifferent prittye vayne in Spurgalling an Asse? . . . but onely to shewe howe for a neede I could rayle, if I were throughly fyred.' "[19] While one would find little to quarrel with in this description, the fact is that some of the most telling *particulars* in Nashe's arsenal, especially his use of sexual insults and scatology, are almost entirely ignored by McPherson and others who have written on the Nashe-Harvey quarrel. It seems fairly astonishing that even where "erotica," comprehensively defined as it has been in this study, has been recognized since his own time as a keynote for understanding Nashe, we have steadfastly refused to look closely at that quality. Any careful reading of Nashe shows how perverse such silence by critics and editors alike is; for from the very beginning of the quarrel with Harvey, Nashe proved willing to stoop without compunction, and his attacks are filled with sly sexual insults and blunt scatological attacks. Of the two, as we shall see, the scatological predominates, consonant with the English predilection in such matters.

Let us begin with an analysis of Nashe's use of sexual insults. The circumstances of Gabriel Harvey's life played into Nashe's hands in such a way as to enable him to take events as various as the very real amorous difficulties of Harvey's younger sister, innocent remarks made by Gabriel about his reception in London in 1592, and the religious fervor of Richard Harvey, and use them in shaping offensive sexual insults in his literary battles with the Harveys. Certainly Nashe needed no circumstances to do this kind of thing. He says to Harvey at one point, "Take truths part, and I will proue truth to be no truth" (I.305); such a stance characterizes a part of Nashe's genius in such a game. He can (and will) argue anything with ease in a sprightly fashion. Is Harvey upset with Nashe's attacks on his lineage, Harvey's father having been a rope maker (allowing Nashe to make fun of Harvey through innovative name calling—Archibald Rupenrope, HempenHampen Slampamp)? Nashe would never be upset by such a charge; "Had I a Ropemaker to my father, & somebody had cast it in my teeth, I would foorthwith haue

---

19. Ibid., p. 1556. McPherson praises the lighter tone achieved by Nashe, but one must wonder if he has in fact delved into Aretino's literary quarrels; he points out that in contrast to Nashe's light tone, Aretino "seems to dwell upon sexual perversion" in his name-calling, and as an example he cites some epithets from *La Cortegiana*—hardly a product exemplary of Italian pamphlet-style warfare.

writ in praise of Ropemakers, & prou'd it by soūd sillogistry to be one of the 7. liberal sciences" (I.270). This ability to move facilely from position to position without regard for truth or fact is part of what suited Nashe so well for literary warfare, and this is what critics have fastened upon. However, circumstances of the Harvey family did provide Nashe with enough "facts," suggestions, and half-truths to fire his imagination in a masterful deployment of the sexual insult. And Nashe was never constrained by half-truths and suggestions; when all else failed he simply fabricated.

Nashe was able to get good mileage, for example, out of the difficulties of Gabriel Harvey's younger sister Mercy (or Marcie). A youthful Philip Howard, Earl of Surrey, living with his wife at Audley End about three miles from the Harvey home in Walden, saw the young Harvey girl in a farm field and was so attracted to her that he attempted to seduce her. Gabriel intervened deftly and discreetly and was able to prevent the seduction.[20] Harvey's success in maintaining virtue all around was hardly a hindrance to Nashe once he got wind of the affair. In *Haue With You to Saffron-Walden* Nashe at one point alludes to the tribulations of Mercy Harvey:

> I will not present into the Arches or Commissaries Court what *prinkum prankums* Gentlemen (his nere neighbors) haue whispred to me of his Sister, and how shee is as good a fellow as euer turnd belly to belly; for which she is not to be blam'd, but I rather pitie her and thinke she cannot doo withall, hauing no other dowrie to marie her. Good Lord, how one thing brings on another; had it not bin for his baudy sister, I should haue forgot to haue answerd for the *baudie rymes* he threapes vpon me. Are they *rimes*? and are they *baudie*? and are they *mine*? Well, it may be so that it is not so; or if it be, men in their youth (as in their sleep) manie times doo something that might haue been better done, & they do not wel remember. (III.129)

Under cover of forgiving, or at least offering an explanation for Mercy's actions (lack of a proper dowry), Nashe moves beyond accusation to conviction. Certainly it is far worse to have a "baudy sister" than to have written "baudie rymes" in one's youth.

In *Strange Newes* (1593), a response to Gabriel Harvey's *Foure Letters* (1592), Nashe takes on both Gabriel Harvey and his clerical brother, Richard, who had attacked Nashe in his treatise *The Lambe of God* (1590).[21] As Nashe prepares to wield his scalpel in anatomizing

---

20. Stern, pp. 35–38.
21. The work was entered at the Stationers' Register on 12 January 1593 (new dating system). For a discussion of the dates of composition see McKerrow, *Works of Nashe*, I, 245–51; and Nicholl, pp. 139–42.

Harvey's *Foure Letters,* he stops to consider Richard Harvey's work and decides, "Before I vnbowell the leane Carcase of thy book any further, Ile drinke one cup of lambswooll *to the Lambe of God and his enemies*" (I.272). His side skirmish with Richard Harvey begins by exposing Richard's "inckehornismes" and ridiculing his citation of various authorities: "All which hee reckons vp to make the world beleeue he hath read much, but alleadgeth nothing out of them: Nor, I thinke, on my conscience, euer read or knew what they meane, but as he hath stole them by the wholesale out of some Booksellers Catalogue, or table of Tractats" (I.272). Nashe follows with examples of Richard's "profounde Annotations," most having to do with matters sexual in the Bible, beginning with Jacob's being tricked into taking Leah as wife instead of Rachel and his use of "pilled rods" for prenatal influence (I.273). Nashe does not leave matters here; all has been a feint, preparing the way for a charge of sexual impropriety:

> It was not for nothing, brother Richard, that *Greene* told you you kist your Parishioners wiues with holy kisses, for you that wil talk *of opening the senses by carnal mixture* (the very act of lecherie) in a Theological Treatise, and in the Pulpit, I am afraide, in a priuater place you will practise as much as you speake. *Homines rarò nisi malè locuti malè faciunt. Olet hircum, olet hircum,* anie modest eare would abhorre to heare it.
>
> Farewell vncleane Vicar, and God make thee an honest man, for thou art too baudy for mee to deale withall. (I.273)

The pose of offended innocence works well for Nashe in his attack on Richard Harvey; he continues the game in the same work when he begins his confutation of Gabriel Harvey's *Foure Letters.* And again, Nashe brings charges of sexual impropriety to the fore.

In September of 1592 Gabriel Harvey had come to London on business with letters of introduction from a Walden native, one Christopher Bird, to a Dutchman in London, Emmanuell van Metern (or Demetrius). In Harvey's account, given in a letter to Christopher Bird, he says that upon his arrival in London ". . . in the absence of M. *Demetrius,* I deliuered your letter vnto his wife, whome I found very courteous" (I.162). Such a remark was all Nashe required to charge the innocent comment of Harvey with the powder of sexual innuendo:

> *Maister* Bird, *in the absence of M.* Demetrius. Perge porrò. *I found his wife curteous*; barlady sir, but that is suspitious.
>
> A woman is well holpen vp that does you any curtesie in the absence of her husband, when you cannot keep it to your selfe, but must blab it in print.
>
> If it were any other but Mistris *Demetrius* (whome I haue heard to be a

modest sober woman, and indued with many vertues) I would play vpon it a litle more. In regard that shee is so, I forbeare; and craue pardon in that I haue spoken so much.

Yet would I haue her vnderstand how well *the generall scholler* her guest, hath rewarded hir for his kind entertainment, by bringing her name in question in print. (I.276)

Only the "innocent" treatment by Nashe could now spur one to think that Mrs. Demetrius's name was "brought into question" by Harvey's account.

Nashe's use of the sexual insult never reaches the level of Franco's attacks on Aretino in its virulence, especially in charges of sexually deviant behavior; but when it came to the scatological, he pulled out all the stops. As the English seemed to take special pleasure in the scatological in their jokes, they likewise found it particularly suited for their literary quarrels. Nashe consistently portrayed the Harveys' works as dung, fit only for the privy. For the English this equation seems to have been a more powerful insult than charges of sodomy or cuckoldry. And in painting with his scatological brush, Nashe was anything but subtle. He daubed the Harveys on the walls of the jakes that his pages became. Sir John Harington, master of the privy, had seen the game clearly and understood it was one that Harvey could not win; in his epigram "*To Doctor* Haruey *of Cambridge*" he wrote:

> The prouerbe sayes, who fights with durty foes,
> Must needs be soyld, admit they winne or lose.
> Then think it doth a Doctors credit dash,
> To make himselfe Antagonist to *Nashe*. (No. 132, p. 199)

Nashe employed the scatological from the very first in his battle with the Harveys. In *Pierce Penilesse* (1592) he takes notice of Richard Harvey's *Lambe of God,* "I haue read ouer thy Sheepish discourse of the Lambe of GOD and his enemies, and entreated my patience to be good to thee wilst I reade: but for all that I could doe with my selfe, (as I am sure I may doe as much as another man) I could not refraine, but bequeath it to the Priuie, leafe by leafe as I read it, it was so vgly, dorbellicall, and lumpish" (I.198). It is not just that Richard Harvey's work is fit for the privy as a book; Nashe makes it quite clear that the work is fit for the privy because it is like excrement itself: noisome, lumpish, dull, and unseemly.[22]

22. The *OED* defines "dorbel" as "The English form of Dorbellus, i.e. Nicholas de Orbellis (died 1455), a professor of Scholastic Philosophy at Poitiers, and a vehement supporter of Duns Scotus. Hence, A scholastical pedant, a dull-witted person, dolt. . . . Anything that has an unseemly appearance." Both Harvey and Nashe use the term; Nashe employs it several times in a variety of works.

Nashe goes on to accuse Harvey of tasteless plagiarism, "thou hast skumd ouer the Schoolmen, and of the froth of theyr folly made a dish of diuinitie Brewesse, which the dogges will not eate" (I.198). As always, Nashe seems to find the perfect words to describe Richard Harvey's brewing. He has not skimmed over the pedants; he has "skumd" over them, a process that suggests skimming of a festering cesspool. Out of the scum atop a pool, Harvey has created something so foul even dogs will not eat it. If a printer, Nashe concludes, "haue any great dealings" with Harvey, "hee were best to get a priuiledge betimes, *Ad imprimendum solum,* forbidding all other to sell waste paper but himselfe, or else he will bee in a wofull taking" (I.198). Nashe's final gibe is virtually a step up in his scatological attack, for at least Harvey's works are equated here with waste paper rather than with excrement itself.

In *Strange Newes,* Nashe's reply to Gabriel Harvey's *Foure Letters,* Nashe warns "broome boyes, and corncutters (or whatsoueuer trade is more contemptible)" not to get in the way of Harvey's fury, "for else in the full tide of his standish [i.e., his inkwell], he will carrie your occupations handsmooth out of towne before him, besmeare them, drowne them: downe the riuer they goe *Priuily* to the Ile of Dogges with his Pamphlets" (I.280–81). Nashe's point is wonderfully ironic: the lowest tradesmen, those who sweep (or sell) brooms or those who cut the corns from people's feet, will not escape befouling from Harvey's inkstand; they will be covered, drowned, washed in excremental effluence down to the standing waste at the Ile of Dogges if Harvey lets fly at them. Of course it is Nashe who does the besmearing in accusing Harvey of doing so. Indeed, Nashe begins his response to Harvey with a scatological dig in the very title of this work, as Nicholl has noted. Nashe's full title is *Strange Newes of the intercepting of certaine Letters and a Conuoy of Verses, as they were going Priuilie to victuall the Low Countries;* in other words, Harvey's words were going to feed those lower regions of the privy. This notion is carried forward in the Epistle Dedicatorie: "*There is a* Doctor and his Fart *that haue kept a foule stinking stirre in Paules Churchyard*" (I.256). Harvey, Nashe would have us believe, is causing a stench at the center of London's book trade. While it is true, then, that Nashe exploits any weakness he sees in Harvey, be it personal or textual, his chief device for condemning the work of Harvey is the attack scatological. Creation in Harvey's case is depicted as an act of evacuation.

Nashe begins *Strange Newes* proper with a short example of the method he will employ, commentary on particular statements cited from Harvey's *Foure Letters.* Phrases from the *Foure Letters* he designates

L; those are followed by a comment designated C. At first, Harvey's work is presented as nothing worse than vomit:

L. *A Letter to M. Emanuel Demetrius, with a sonnet thereto annexed.*
C. That is, as it were a purgation vpon a vomit, buskins vpon pantophles.
(I.266)

Actually, Nashe claims, Harvey's work is worse than mere vomit; it is one purgation on top of another, since it is a letter and a sonnet, boots and slippers. In short order, however, Nashe descends to the excremental:

L. *A Letter to euerie fauorable and indifferent Reader.*
C. *Id est,* An exhortation to all Readers, that they shall reade nothing but his works.
L. *Another letter to the same, extorted after the rest.*
C. By interpretation, a Letter whereof his inuention had a hard stoole, and yet it was for his ease, though not for his honestie: and so forth, as the Text shall direct you at large. (I.266)

Part of Nashe's purpose in writing *Strange Newes* had been to defend his recently deceased friend, Robert Greene, a major target of Harvey's *Foure Letters.* This Nashe does in a section of *Strange Newes* that begins by attacking a sonnet that had been included in the first of the *Foure Letters.* That letter is not in fact one by Harvey; it was written by Christopher Bird to introduce Harvey to Emmanuell Demetrius in London. Along with this letter Harvey had printed additional comments and a sonnet, supposedly by Bird, that attacked Greene and defended the Harveys. The sonnet requires citation, since with it the scatological mud-slinging begins:

> *Greene* the Connycatcher, of this Dreame the Autor,
> For his dainty deuise, deserueth the hauter.
> A rakehell: A makeshift: A scribling foole:
> A famous bayard in Citty, and Schoole.
> Now sicke, as a Dog: and euer brainesick:
> Where such a rauing, and desperate Dick?
> Sir reuerence, A scuruy Master of Art,
> Aunsweared inough with a Doctors fart.
> He scornes other Aunsweare: and Enuy salutes
> With shortest vowels, and with longest mutes.
> For farther triall, himself he referres
> To proofe, and sound iudgement, that seldome erres.
> Now good Robin-good-fellow, and gentle Greene sleeues,
> Giue him leaue to be quiet, that none aggreeues. (I.161)

The sonnet is certainly at odds with the reasonable tone Harvey takes on in his Epistle Dedicatorie. It has been his intention, he says, "so to demeane my selfe in the whole, and so to temper my stile in euery part: that I might neither seme blinded with affection, nor enraged with passion: nor partiall to frend, nor preiudiciall to enemy: nor iniurious to the worst, nor offensive to any: but mildly & calmly shew, how discredite reboundeth upon the autors: as dust flyeth back into the wags Eyes, that will nedes be puffing it vp" (I.157). Had Harvey meant this, he should surely have omitted the sonnet, since it introduces the scatological motif and invites Nashe to reply in kind—an invitation Nashe hardly needed.

Nashe begins his riposte to the sonnet in some verses of his own:

> Put vp thy smiter, O gentle Peter,
> Author and halter make but ill meeter.
> I scorne to answer thy mishapen rime,
> Blocks haue cald schollers bayards ere this time. (I.275)

"I would trot a false gallop," Nashe says, "through the rest of his ragged Verses, but that if I should retort his rime dogrell aright, I must make my verses (as he doth his) run hobling like a Brewers Cart vpon the stones, and obserue no length in their feete; which were *absurdum per absurdius*, to infect my vaine with his imitation" (I.275). Nashe strikes the appropriately comic note with his image, carrying as it does an auditory association as well, of a brewer's cart on uneven stones. To respond in kind is to become infected, Nashe avers, and the whole of the verse against Greene has been so without sting that Nashe is able to characterize it in the following terms: "an olde mechanical meeter-munger would faine raile, if he had anie witte. If *Greene* were *dogge-sicke* and *braine-sicke,* sure he (poore secular Satirist) is dolt-sicke and brainlesse, that with the toothless gums of his Poetry so betuggeth a dead man" (I.275). It is hard to imagine that there could be a more effective description of a dull and feeble attack than to personify it as a toothless dotard gumming on a corpse.

Naturally, Nashe was not going to let the scatological remarks pass without a response in kind. Nashe cannot, finally, accept the sonnet as Bird's; it must, he concludes, be a fabrication, a weaving of Harvey himself:

> But I cannot be induced to beleue a graue man of his sort should be ere so *rauingly* bent: when all coms to all, *shortest vowels and longest mutes* will bewray it to bee a webbe of your owne loomes, M. *Gabriel*: you *mute* foorth many such phrases in the course of your booke, which I will point at as I passe by. (I.275)

The insult turns on the pun in "mute," for while we understand the meaning of "mute" as "silent" when used as an adjective, when used as a verb, it means "to void excrement." We may wonder if the pun is intended in the Harvey work; with Nashe it pointedly is.

Nashe concludes his commentary on this section by likening Harvey's style in the sonnet to that of the "olde Vice in the Morrals, as right vp and downe as may be," and he plays the scene for us:

> Let. *Greene, the Connycatcher, of this dreame the author,*
>   *For his daintie deuise deserueth the hauter.*
> Vice. Hey nan anon sir, soft let mee make water,
>   Whip it to go, Ile kisse my maisters daughter.
>   Tum diddy, tum da, falangtedo diddle;
>   Sol la me fa sol, conatus in fiddle.
>
> I am afraide your *Doctors fart* will fall out to be a fatall foyst to your breeches, if we followe you at the hard heeles as we haue begun.
>   Thou shalt not breathe a whit, trip and goe, turne ouer a new leafe. (I.275–76)

The editors of Nashe are marvelously silent on this passage as a whole, no doubt not wishing to have the material prove a "fatal foyst" to their leaves. While Nashe can be wildly abusive without resorting to scatology, he nonetheless continues to employ it through *Strange Newes*. And while part of what makes Nashe so successful in literary warfare is his unwillingness to be bound by any side or any truth, his dexterity, and his delight in the game, there is simply no way to ignore the fact that an integral part of his weaponry is his constant equating of his opponents' creative processes with voiding excrement and their works themselves with dung. As he says at a later point in *Strange Newes:*

> *Gabriell,* if there bee anie witte or industrie in thee, now I will dare it to the vttermost: write of what thou wilt, in what language thou wilt, and I will confute it and answere it. Take truths part, and I will proue truth to be no truth, marching out of thy dūg-voiding mouth. (I.305)

Near the end of the work, Nashe elevates the scatological to epic proportions, when, in addressing his Muse, he compares himself to Hercules cleansing the Augean stables: "Thus, O Heauenly Muse, I thanke thee, for thou hast giu'n mee the patience to trauel through the tedious wildernesse of this Gomorian Epistle. Not *Hercules,* when he cleansed the stables of *Aegeas,* vnder-tooke such a stinking vnsauorie exploit" (I.326). So elevated and restrained a use of scatology is hardly the norm for Nashe, however. His usual device is fierce, direct, scatological invective, a practice he was to continue in later attacks on Harvey.

Two examples from *Haue with you to Saffron-Walden* (1596) should suffice to conclude this argument. At one point Nashe piles on to Gabriel and Richard Harvey a series of abusive epithets that become increasingly repulsive. At first they are fools, "a paire of poore ideots, being not only two brothers, two block-heads, two blunderkins, hauing their braines stuft with nought but balder-dash." Next they become diseases, "they are verie botts & the glanders to the gentle Readers, the dead Palsie and Apoplexie of the Presse, the *Sarpego* and the *Sciatica* of the 7. Liberall Sciences."[23] The diseases culminate with effluent illnesses: they are the "surfetting vomit of Ladie Vanitie." "Ladie Vanitie" opens the way for a sexual insult: they became "the sworne baudes to one anothers vain-glorie." He concludes where a reader of Nashe has come to expect him to conclude: they are "the most comtemptible *Mounsier Aiaxes* of excrementall conceipts and stinking kennel-rakt vp inuention that this or anie Age euer afforded" (III.ll).

In perhaps the most unpleasant instance in this kind, Nashe plays a variation on his scatological theme, making Harvey neither the producer of excrement, nor the waste itself, but the recipient of Nashe's feces. He says, "How he hath handled Greene and Marloe since their deaths, those that read his Bookes may iudge: and where, like a iakes barreller and a *Gorbolone,* he girds me *with imitating of* Greene, let him vnderstand, I more scorne it than to haue so foule a iakes for my groaning stoole as hys mouth" (III.132).

If critics and editors have been reluctant to treat the salacious in Nashe, they have been even more chary of the scatological. This is easy enough to understand. With so much to admire in Nashe's attacks on Harvey that is witty, clever, outrageous, and inventive and *not* tainted by the excremental, why bother to touch so unsavory a subject? But to ignore this aspect of Nashe is to ignore one of the major devices employed in this notorious literary skirmish. To take note of and understand Nashe's use of the scatological is not to diminish his achievement. Rather, it pushes us to reexamine our sense of an Elizabethan context, for we see that such a context must include the bawdy, the salacious, and the scatological if we are to have the whole picture. When we look closely at a writer like Nashe we realize that our sense of "the Elizabethan context" has been sharply and unfairly confined, that we have let mistaken notions of "Elizabethan taste" close our eyes to a significant aspect of Elizabethan literature. Once that context has been extended, our reading of many writers of the English Renaissance is enriched indeed. The final chapter is intended to show just how this is so with examples from Marston, Donne, Shakespeare, and Spenser.

23. A bott is a parasitic larva or maggot. Glanders is a contagious disease in horses; its chief symptoms are glandular swelling and a mucous discharge from the nostrils. Sarpego or serpigo is a creeping or spreading skin disease.

CHAPTER 8

The Context of Erotica: Marston, Donne, Shakespeare, and Spenser

Come come Luxurio, *crowne my heade with Bayes,*
Which like a Paphian, wantonly displayes
The Salaminian titillations,
Which tickle vp our leud Priapians.
        John Marston, *"The Authour in prayse*
          of his precedent Poem"

In chapter 6 I purposely omitted any discussion of many writers and works that rightfully have a place in a study of Renaissance erotica. Indeed, it would be only a small exaggeration to say that almost all of the "fiction" of the English Renaissance (poetry, drama, and prose fiction) contains some element of erotica, be it the bawdy, the obscene, or the erotic. Sidney's *Astrophel and Stella,* Shakespeare's *Venus and Adonis* or his "Will" sonnets, Spenser's Bower of Bliss, the works of all the satirists—the mind boggles at what might be included. Some of these works would surely be classified as erotica—Shakespeare's "Will" sonnets, for example; most, however, would not be classified primarily as erotica, even though they partake of it. They use it, or some facet of it, and it is the use of erotica and its context that is the focus of this chapter. I have chosen to confine myself to four examples out of the many I could have picked. I could have discussed Gascoigne's use of bawdy in the *Adventures of Master F.J.;* I could have gone over the obscenity of the satirists at length; I could have examined once again Shakespeare's "Will" sonnets; I could have returned to the Bower of Bliss for an extended stay; I could have probed the bawdy in Renaissance drama; I could have written forever. The foregoing chapters provide the context in which to examine the way artists use certain aspects of erotica. If our reading of major authors is not radically altered by a knowledge of Renaissance erotica, it is at least deepened in a number of significant ways. As Colman has stated in his study of Shakespeare's bawdy, "It is the perennial weakness of all aspective criticism that it is too narrow, but if it serves to open up fresh possibilities of interpre-

208

tation and evaluation in other directions, its limited perspective may be justified."[1]

An understanding of the relationship between the readers of erotica and the works themselves is an element exploited comically by John Marston in his narrative poem, *The Metamorphosis of Pigmalions Image.* In his elegies we see John Donne employ sexual imagery to a variety of comic and obscene effects. In *The Merry Wives of Windsor* Shakespeare exploits the conventions of jest literature and creates a comic character bound to hear bawdy in even the most innocent of circumstances. In Book III of *The Faerie Queene* Spenser examines the ramifications of viewing the loves of the gods.

I

It was characteristic of Renaissance writers to produce works that could easily be identified as being in a specific genre, and it has been no less characteristic of modern critics to treat Renaissance works accordingly. While this approach has been unquestionably valuable, it has also occasionally produced misunderstanding and confusion. This is especially true where poets were writing in genres less well known to us, like pornography, or creating works not readily categorized. Nowhere are the misunderstanding and confusion brought on by a strictly generic approach more apparent than in the criticism of John Marston's *Metamorphosis of Pigmalions Image.* Defining precisely what *kind* of a poem Marston's work is has proven a tricky business indeed. And it has been that endeavor to find a *kind* for Marston's poem, at the expense of examination of the poet's strategy, that seems to me to have steered most critics wide of the mark in commenting upon this poem. Further, because strategy, and consequently one kind of audience, have been ignored, the less well-known genre central to an understanding of the poem, Renaissance pornography, has not been considered. Though considerations of genre are certainly important to an understanding of Marston's *Metamorphosis,* the reader must first understand the poet's strategy.

"I seriously protest / I slubber'd vp that Chaos indigest, / To fish for fooles," W.K., Marston's satiric persona, tells us in *The Scourge of Villanie.*[2] This is the first point, of course. From his dedication "To the Worlds Mightie Monarch, Good Opinion," which he signs W.K., we see that Marston wants us to understand that the "poet" of the

1. E. A. M. Colman, *The Dramatic Use of Bawdy in Shakespeare* (London: Longman Group, 1974), p. 170.
2. Marston, *The Scourge of Villanie,* in *The Poems of John Marston,* VI, ll. 69–71.

Metamorphosis is William Kinsayder, the "maculate," crude, foul, melancholy creature about to become a "barking satyrist."[3] While critics have made much of Marston's need (through W.K.) to offer explanations for his *Metamorphosis*, they have been singularly unwilling to grant him his defense.[4] A careful reading of Marston's various defenses, however, coupled with a knowledge of Renaissance pornography in addition to the more well-known Ovidian poetry of the Renaissance, helps, I think, in placing Marston's poem in its proper perspective.

In "The Authour in prayse of *precedent Poem*," Marston has W.K. offer his first defense for his *Metamorphosis* by calling out:

> Come come *Luxurio,* crowne my head with Bayes,
> Which like a Paphian, wantonly displayes
> The Salaminian titillations,
> Which tickle vp our leud Priapians. (ll .3–6)

W.K. goes on to ask, "Ends not my poem then surpassing ill?" (l. 33), and he hastens to answer the question himself:

> . . . fore others me deride
> And scoffe at mee, as if I had deni'd
> Or thought my Poem good, when that I see
> My lines are froth, my stanzaes saplesse be. (ll. 39–42)

Deride him they did, however; in the "Satyre Preludium" to his *Skialetheia,* Everard Guilpin wrote:

> A third, that falls more roundly to his worke,
> Meaning to moue her were she Iew or Turke:
> Writes perfect *Cat and fidle,* wantonly,
> Tickling her thoughts with masking bawdry;
> Which read to Captaine *Tucca,* he doth sweare,
> And scratch, and sweare, and scratch to heare
> His owne discourse discours'd: and *by the Lord*
> *It's passing good: oh good!* at euery word:
> When his Cock-sparrow thoughts to itch begin
> He with a shrug sweares't *a most sweet sinne.*[5]

---

3. Kernan, p. 96, suggests that "Kinsayder is apparently a pun on Marston (Marstone) since 'kinsing seems to have been an operation which castrated unruly dogs and docked their tails.'" See *The Poems of John Marston,* ed. Davenport, p. 265.

4. The critical positions are well laid out by Arnold Davenport in his edition of *The Poems of John Marston,* pp. 7–11. See also G. Cross, "Marston's 'Metamorphosis of Pigmalions Image': A Mock-Epyllion," *Etudes Anglaises* 13 (1960): 331–36; and P. Finkelpearl, "From Petrarch to Ovid: Metamorphoses in John Marston's *Metamorphosis of Pigmalions Image,*" *English Literary History* 32 (1965): 333–48.

5. Guilpin, "Satyre Preludium," ll. 25–34, in *Skialetheia.*

Modern scholars have been equally eager to attack Marston for his defenses; C. S. Lewis labels Marston "the most odious of literary characters, the man who publishes work he is not prepared to stand by and then pretends that he has been writing 'with his tongue in his cheek.' "[6] And Marston's most recent editor, while he does not think that the *Metamorphosis* is a parody of Ovidian poetry, cannot bring himself to label the poem as totally satirical either.[7] I find Hallett Smith's critical suggestion more fruitful, however; he sees the poem as satirical, and he finds that "the principal indication of the satirical purpose of the poem lies in the author's attitude toward the reader."[8] He argues:

> As he approaches the more salacious parts of the narrative he ridicules the reader's expectation which he has been carefully building up. He supposes that his reader is following him with a "wanton itching eare" (stanza 33), and he flatly tells the "gaping eares that swallow vp my lines" (stanza 38) to expect no more. This point of view toward the reader could hardly have been maintained if Marston had ever taken his own material seriously.[9]

Marston may have written the *Metamorphosis* as a parody of Ovidian poetry, but he seems to be more interested in playing a comic game with a particular kind of reader than he is in parodying a kind of poetry. And the particular kind of reader he plays his comic game with is the salacious reader, one who is probably better understood as a reader of Nashe's *Choise of Valentines* and Aretino's dialogues than as a reader of Marlowe's *Hero and Leander*. Seen in this context, Marston's defense through W.K. makes more sense. It is the "leud Priapians" who read

6. C. S. Lewis, *English Literature in the Sixteenth Century Excluding Drama* (Oxford: Clarendon Press, 1954), p. 472.

7. *The Poems of John Marston,* pp. 7–11.

8. Hallett Smith, *Elizabethan Poetry* (1952; rpt. Cambridge, Mass.: Harvard Univ. Press), p. 239.

9. Smith, pp. 239–40. John Scott Colley, in his article " 'Opinion' and the Reader in John Marston's *The Metamorphosis of Pigmalions Image,*" *English Literary Renaissance* 3 (1973): 221–31, also directs attention to the reader. Colley argues that in the *Metamorphosis* ". . . a major thrust of the poem is directed at a segment of its reading public, and accuses the reader of the same type of foolishness that had enveloped Pigmalion. . . . Pigmalion is deluded by a vain, empty imitation of a woman. The reader, in turn, is deluded by a vain, empty poetic imitation of the true experience of lovemaking" (p. 222). However, Cooley makes his point about the reader in order to pursue his analysis of Marston's examination of "opinion" in the poem, and his final evaluation is, "If Marston's satiric aims in the *Metamorphosis* are misunderstood, it is because he overdoes the 'teasing' and fails to provide his reader with clear signs of the ironies involved in the poem. The poet's burlesque is to heavy-handed and his satire too subtle. The poem is not an accomplished piece of work. It was perhaps more clever in design than execution" (p. 228).

for "titillations" in works we would describe as pornographic, not merely Ovidian, that he is after. W.K.'s later defense in satire vi of *The Scourge of Villanie* makes this position most plausible. He tells us that he "wrot / Those idle rimes to note the odious spot / And blemish that deformes the lineaments / Of moderne Poesies habilements" (*S.V.*, VI, 23–26). Poets have invoked a variety of inspirations in this degraded age:

> Here's one must invocate some lose-legg'd dame,
> Some brothell drab, to helpe him stanzaes frame,
>
> . . . . . .
>
> Another makes old *Homer, Spencer* cite
> Like my *Pigmalion,* where, with rare delight
> He cryes, O *Ouid.* This caus'd my idle quill,
> The worlds dull eares with such lewd stuffe to fill,
> And gull with bumbast lines, the witlesse sence
> Of these odde naggs; whose pates circumference
> Is fild with froth! O these same buzzing Gnats
> That sting my sleeping browes, these Nilus Rats,
> Halfe dung, that haue their life from putrid slime,
> These that doe praise my loose lasciuious rime:
> For these same shades I seriously protest
> I slubber'd vp that Chaos indigest,
> To fish for fooles, that stalke in goodly shape,
> *What though in veluet cloake, yet still an Ape.*
> *Capro* reads, sweares, scrubs, and sweares againe,
> Now by my soule an admirable straine,
> Strokes vp his haire, cryes passing passing good,
> Oh, there's a line incends his lustfull blood. (*S.V.,* 33–76)

As Davenport notes, Capro suggests the lustful he-goat, and it is just such a reader who finds the salacious parts of his poem to be "passing passing good" whom W.K. singles out as his target.[10] Further, he suggests something of the method he employs in the poem when he tells us that he decided to "fish for fooles." Marston did not set out to bludgeon lustful readers into senselessness; he set out his line with W.K. as his fisherman to have some sport. While much has been made of Marston's obsession with lust, and while it may be true that he "like many another censor of society, derived a vicarious gratification from detailed accounts of the vices he attacked," that problem need not concern us here.[11] The point is that for whatever reason, Marston under-

---

10. *The Poems of John Marston,* p. 325.
11. Douglas Bush, *Mythology and the Renaissance Tradition in English Poetry,* rev. ed. (New York: W. W. Norton, 1963), p. 183.

stood one kind of reader very well and knew how to angle for that reader skillfully through W.K.

Marston prepares for his warfare with the salacious reader before he begins the *Metamorphosis* proper. As Douglas Bush has noted, there is an "undercurrent of mockery and jocularity that runs from the prefatory verses 'To his Mistress' through the poem itself."[12] At the outset Marston has his narrator establish a technique of authorial intrusion designed to play upon a number of members in his audience. The narrator assumes his readers to be, at various times, his mistress, the general reader, lady readers, and, increasingly, the salacious reader.

In fact, W.K. begins that "undercurrent of mockery and jocularity" in his dedication "To the Worlds Mightie Monarch, Good Opinion" in a fine parody of dedicatory verses; he then moves on to a prefatory verse "To his Mistress" where he holds out hope for the lewd reader, as he directly addresses his Mistress, saying that his "wanton Muse lasciuiously doth sing / Of sportiue loue, of louely dallying" (ll. 1–2). He proceeds to establish a jesting tone as he asks his Mistress not to make him envy his Pigmalion—in short his poem is meant as a plea to his Mistress that she grant him the favors that Pigmalion gained. When she does this, the poet says, then he will "gladly write" her metamorphosis. The poem is thus meant on one level to be an argument for seduction. With such a purpose, the salacious reader can certainly be hopeful of some juicy passages to whet his appetite.

In the *Metamorphosis* proper, W.K. no longer addresses his Mistress directly, but he does aim a number of comments in her direction so that we are always aware of that purpose of the poem. In stanza 2 the narrator merely states that his Mistress may be the only one as beautiful as Pigmalion's statue, but in stanza 11 he expresses his envy of Pigmalion, who in "blameles" manner is able to look upon the place where "*Venus* hath her chiefest mantion" (st. 9). He wishes, "O that my Mistres were an Image too, / That I might blameles her perfections view" (st. 11). The narrator here clearly identifies with Pigmalion, who can best be described as the ultimate voyeur. Pigmalion is described as virtually overcome with *looking* at the image he has created. He is "enamored" through "admiring"; he is "allured" by her nakedness in stanza 4, and in stanza 5 he thinks he sees the blood "run through the vaine / And leape, and swell with all alluring meanes." He stands "as in an extasie." All of his senses are touched; his amorous thoughts feed on her cheeks (st. 6); her breath "doth perfume the ayre" (st. 7). His

12. Bush also sees the poem as satirical, however. See ibid., p. 182.

eye rests chiefly, however, on "Loues pauillion" (st. 9), and in stanzas 13, 16, and 17 Pigmalion fondles her. For example:

> And fondly doting, oft he kist her lip.
> Oft would he dally with her Iuory breasts.
> No wanton loue-trick would he ouer-slip,
> But full obseru'd all amorous beheasts.
>   Whereby he thought he might procure the loue
>   Of his dull Image, which no plaints coulde moue. (St. 13)

I take this emphasis upon the wanton nature of Pigmalion's desire with which the narrator identifies to be an important factor in the strategy of the poem, for it allows the salacious reader to suspect that, given the nature of W.K., he can expect some graphic descriptions in the appropriate places. Marston's comic strategy is one of raising the expectations and arousing the reader through identification with the lascivious natures of both W.K. and Pigmalion and then abruptly having W.K. remember his satiric purpose and turn on the reader at the critical moments.

As he approaches the climactic moments in the metamorphosis, W.K. avoids any authorial intrusion. We have no such comparisons with contemporary mores as appear in stanzas 10 and 14 where "citty-dames" and papists are described. The last intrusions occur in stanzas 19–20, where he appeals to the readers to find his poem a "mirror to posteritie," for here the lady readers will see a love that inspires a lover to more than kissing. Indeed, W.K. turns the logic of the poem so that it fits the seduction idea suggested at the outset in his comments to his Mistress:

> I oft haue smil'd to see the foolery
> Of some sweet Youths, who seriously protest
> That Loue respects not actuall Luxury,
> But only ioy's to dally, sport, and iest:
>   Loue is a child, contented with a toy,
>   A busk-point, or some fauour still's the boy.
>
> Marke my *Pigmalion,* whose affections ardor
> May be a mirror to posteritie.
> Yet viewing, touching, kissing, (common fauour,)
> Could neuer satiate his loues ardencie:
>   And therefore Ladies, thinke that they nere loue you,
>   Who doe not vnto more then kissing moue you. (St. 19–20)

From stanzas 21–27, W.K. describes the ardor of Pigmalion and his prayer for life for his statue. Without interruption, W.K. leads us to the critical moment, and then he intrudes once again—to tell us:

> Yet all's conceit. But shadow of that blisse
> Which now my Muse striues sweetly to display
> In this my wondrous metamorphosis. (St. 28)

The narrator implies that up to this point all has been but a "shadow"; the salacious reader can only proceed with renewed expectations of what is to come. But W.K. will not let the reader off without further authorial intrusion from here to the end of the poem. In stanza 29 he jocularly explains the reason for the metamorphosis—"Tut, women will relent / When as they finde such mouing blandishment"—and in stanza 32 the narrator once again wishes that he could do to *his* Mistress what Pigmalion has done to his statue:

> O wonder not to heare me thus relate,
> And say to flesh transformed was a stone.
> Had I my Loue in such a wished state
> As was afforded to *Pigmalion,*
>   Though flinty hard, of her you soone should see
>   As strange a transformation wrought by mee. (St. 32)

Again at a critical point the narrator strongly identifies with Pigmalion, thus raising the hopes of the lewd reader.

Finally, Marston can put off the salacious reader no longer. He says:

> And now me thinks some wanton itching eare
> With lustfull thoughts, and ill attention,
> List's to my Muse, expecting for to heare
> The amorous discription of that action
>   Which *Venus* seekes, and euer doth require,
>   When fitnes graunts a place to please desire. (St. 33)

W.K. (and Marston) clearly have been angling for the reader with a "wanton itching eare / With lustfull thoughts," and W.K. turns the task back on the priapian reader:

> Let him conceit but what himselfe would doe
> When that he had obtayned such a fauour,
> Of her to whom his thoughts were bound vnto,
> If she, in recompence of his loues labour,
>   Would daine to let one payre of sheets containe
>   The willing bodies of those louing twaine. (St. 34)

W.K. is clever in his combat with the reader; he says he will not report the events, he will not satisfy this "itching" reader, but he takes him far enough down the path so that the reader thinks he may not have to use his imagination after all, especially given the nature of the narrator:

> Could he, oh could he, when that each to eyther
> Did yeeld kind kissing, and more kind embracing,
> Could he when that they felt, and clip't together
> And might enjoy the life of dallying,
>   Could he abstaine mid'st such a wanton sporting
>   From doing that, which is not fit reporting? (St. 35)

It may not be "fit reporting," but the narrator does continue, and the priapian reader again proceeds hoping that the would-be priapian W.K. will fulfill his expectations.

> What would he doe when that her softest skin
> Saluted his with a delightfull kisse?
> When all things fit for loues sweet pleasuring
> Inuited him to reape a Louers blisse?
>   What he would doe, the selfe same action
>   Was not neglected by *Pigmalion*.
>
> For when he found that life had tooke his seate
> Within the breast of his kind beauteous loue,
> When that he found that warmth, and wished heate
> Which might a Saint and coldest spirit moue,
>   Then arms, eyes, hands, tong, lips, & wanton thigh,
>   Were willing agents in Loues luxurie. (St. 36–37)

Again W.K. has brought the salacious reader to the critical moment; for two stanzas he helps the reader imagine. He emphasizes the softness, the warmth, the action of the union. In the final lines of stanza 37 the limbs of the bodies seem to rush together. The narrator does then tell us what Pigmalion did in fact do—up to a point. And here W.K. pulls the rug from under his expectant priapian:

> Who knowes not what ensues? O pardon me
> Yee gaping eares that swallow vp my lines
> Expect no more. Peace idle Poesie,
> Be not obsceane though wanton in thy rhimes.
>   And chaster thoughts, pardon if I doe trip,
>   Or if some loose lines from my pen doe slip. (St. 38)

This stanza and the intentionally anticlimactic final stanza that follows should not come as a surprise to us, for Marston's strategy has been clear from the outset. It is clear, however, only when we give it the careful attention that Marston's poem demands. Moreover, it is a strategy that is fully meaningful only when we are aware of the tradition of the salacious reader and his literature. Against that background Marston's *Metamorphosis of Pigmalions Image* can be seen not as a poor rendition of an Ovidian poem, nor as an equally poor parody, but as a

poem that is comic from the outset and, through its careful manipulation of the narrator, wages skillful warfare with the "leud priapian"
readers of its day.[13]

II

A good deal of lip service has been paid to the sexual elements in the
poetry of John Donne.[14] Having given that service, however, scholars
have generally passed on to admire other qualities in Donne's poetry.
An attempt will be made here to redress the balance. While sexual
elements pervade much of Donne's poetry, both religious and secular,
from the satires to the holy sonnets, I wish to concentrate on his elegies
since they are, by virtue of their genre alone, predominantly concerned
with love—very often purely sexual love.

No scholar has written more cogently on Donne's elegies than J. B.
Leishman. His informative placement of Donne's elegies within the
tradition of Ovid's *Amores* and Berni's *capitoli* is in all places illuminating; his critical analyses of whole poems and individual lines are
always revealing and convincing.[15] His general statements about the

13. An excellent discussion of this poem is given in the unpublished M.A. thesis of
Esther Scheps, "Shade and Substance: The Problem of Morality in the Plays of John
Marston" (Ohio State University, 1975), pp. 6–7. In part, Ms. Scheps argues:

> Once the reader has accepted the basic situation, he realizes that Pigmalion is in love
> with a statue, a shadow, an image, a figment of his own imagination. And the sculptor
> succumbs to lust for what he has created. But the narrator has also shared an intimacy
> with the reader in his satiric commentary and, although both the reader and the
> narrator recognize Pigmalion's lust for an image, neither recognizes his own lust,
> albeit voyeuristic, until the narrator at stanza XXXIII indicates that he is aware of the
> reader's curiosity which decorum prevents him from satisfying. And so, ultimately,
> the satire is directed against the reader.

14. J. B. Leishman, *The Monarch of Wit* (New York: Harper & Row, 1966) does a
good job of attempting to treat Jack Donne and John Donne as one fabric. Rosemond
Tuve, in *Elizabethan and Metaphysical Imagery* (Chicago: University of Chicago Press,
1963), p. 380n, reminds us:

> The reaction against Victorian piety has reduced the sermon-reading of critics; this
> would matter little if it had not succeeded in splitting certain Metaphysicals into two
> men. Though scholarship has partly readjusted the balance, Humpty-Dumpty cannot
> be put together again without the glue of a sympathetic as well as studious reading,
> by many and not by a few, of the *complete* works of seventeenth-century poets. A
> session with the elegies for Donne is enough to show how much easier it was for the
> seventeenth century, than for us, to allow a poet and a divine to be one man.

15. Leishman, pp. 78–79, in discussing the elegies mentions Berni's *capitoli*, but it
seems to me that he does not go far enough. Leishman quotes De Sanctis, who does
point to the obscene nature of many of these, but Leishman cites *capitoli* in praise of
peaches, eels, etc., with no indication that part of the humor here lies in the bawdy
nature of the thing praised.

essential nature of these poems—that it is wit above all else that characterizes them—seem sound enough.[16] Indeed, it seems almost churlish
to criticize Leishman at all, for I must say at the outset of this discussion
that I am in deep agreement with Leishman's readings of Donne's
elegies, and I have learned a great deal by reading Leishman. But Leishman's treatment of Donne's elegies always stops just short of analyzing
precisely those elements in the elegies that make them so outrageous,
so witty, so shocking, so memorable—the bawdy and the obscene. It
is not that Leishman does not know that these qualities are there; it is
that he will not or chooses not to discuss just these qualities in any
detail. Any careful reading of the elegies will show that these qualities
cannot be ignored if the full impact of these poems is to be felt.

In his elegy "The Comparison," the speaker compares his mistress
with another man's mistress, and an outrageous note is struck at the
outset:

> As the sweet sweat of Roses in a Still,
> As that which from chaf'd muskats pores doth trill,
> As the Almighty Balme of th' early East,
> Such are the sweat drops of my Mistris breast,
> And on her necke her skin such lustre sets,
> They seeme no sweate drops, but pearle carcanetts.
> Ranke sweaty froth thy Mistresse's brow defiles,
> Like spermatique issue' of ripe menstruous boiles,
> Or like the skumme, which, by needs lawlesse law
> Enforc'd, Sanserra's starved men did draw
> From parboild shooes, and bootes, and all the rest
> Which were with any soveraigne fatnes blest,
> And like vile lying stones in saffrond tinne,
> Or warts, or wheales, they hang upon her skinne.
> (ll. 1–14)[17]

16. Leishman sees the "colloquial vigour of the language" as the most pervasive of
characteristics; he goes on to say, "For Donne, in these elegies, whether he is being
mainly dramatic, argumentative, impudent, paradoxical, dialectical, or ingenious, is always being witty. . . . The element of play, or of display, predominates: the reader's
attention is directed, not so much upon the subject, as upon what Donne is able to make
of it—upon what seemed to many of his contemporaries his miraculous ingenuity and
cleverness" (ibid., pp. 89–90). See pp. 54–109.

17. John Donne, "The Comparison," in *The Complete Poetry of John Donne,* ed.
John T. Shawcross (Garden City, N.Y.: Doubleday, 1967). All Donne references are to
this edition.

Donne[18] is making fun of conventional Petrarchan comparisons, to be sure; even the description of his own mistress as an ideal is undercut by the mere idea of contemplating the sweat drops on her breasts, but the outrageousness comes with his description of the other man's mistress and her rank sweat, which is like, as Shawcross renders the line, "germ filled pus which issues from the ripe boils (of venereal disease) around a woman's genitals."[19] One such comparison is not enough for Donne here; the sweat is also like the scum that resulted from boiling shoes, a necessity brought on by the siege at Sancere. While military metaphors are commonplace in love poetry, they are not of this kind. The *idea* of such comparisons is what is so outlandish; that is, that Donne has attempted to find the most repulsive images possible for the other mistress, and the language that drives home the point is the kind of sexual language one expects to find in a rough Elizabethan satire, not in an Elizabethan love elegy.[20] Donne goes on to compare the breasts of the two mistresses:

> Like Proserpines white beauty-keeping chest,
> Or Joves best fortunes urne, is her fair breast,
> Thine's like worme eaten trunkes, cloth'd in seals skin,
> Or grave, that's dust without, and stinke within. (ll. 23–26)

And Donne does not shy away from comparing their genital regions:

> Then like the Chymicks masculine equall fire,
> Which in the Lymbecks warme wombe doth inspire
> Into th'earths worthlesse durt a soule of gold,
> Such cherishing heat her best lov'd part doth hold.
> Thine's like the dread mouth of a fired gunne,
> Or like hot liquid metalls newly runne
> Into clay moulds, or like to that AEtna
> Where round about the grasse is burnt away.

18. I refer to the speaker as Donne, but I must concur with Leishman that we must resist the temptation to read these poems autobiographically. See Leishman, p. 58; also Joan Bennett, *Four Metaphysical Poets,* 2nd ed. (New York: Vintage Books, 1953), pp. 17–18.

19. *The Complete Poetry of Donne,* p. 47.

20. Donne in fact uses repulsive, excremental language in his second satire, where he rails against poets who plagiarize:

> But hee is worst, who (beggarly) doth chaw
> Others wits fruits, and in his ravenous maw
> Rankly digested, doth those things out-spue,
> As his owne things; and they' are his owne, 'tis true,
> For if one eate my meate, though it be knowne
> The meate was mine, th' excrement is his owne. (ll. 25–30)

> Are not your kisses then as filthy,' and more,
> As a worme sucking an invenom'd sore?
> Doth not thy fearefull hand in feeling quake,
> As one which gath'ring flowers, still feares a snake?
> Is not your last act harsh, and violent,
> As when a Plough a stony ground doth rent? (ll. 35–47)

Donne has succeeded in conjuring up all kinds of unpleasant sensations related to the "act" of sexual intercourse with the other man's mistress; we are repulsed by the comparisons of the other man's mistress's genitals to the "mouth of a fired gun" or a bald Mount Aetna, and we are repulsed by a comparison of sexual intercourse to plowing a stony ground. Donne's is a virtuoso performance; and what gives us the sense of impudence and insolence carried off with wit, the qualities so important for Leishman, is the startling sexuality of his imagery.

It is true that in some of the elegies it is only the situation that is sexual, for example "The Perfume," and the fun of the poem lies in the comedy of the situation (the speaker is betrayed to the "Hydroptique father" of the loved one by his own perfume) and not necessarily in sexual language, but other poems clearly depend upon such language for their impact.

Elegy 13 is an exercise very much in the Ovidian tradition; the poet-lover complains that he has taught his mistress all the tricks she knows about adultery, and now he fears that she is practicing her learning with others. The poem begins with an ambiguous, "Natures lay Ideot, I taught thee to love, / And in that sophistrie, Oh, thou dost prove / Too subtile" (ll. 1–2). Ostensibly, the mistress is addressed as "Natures lay Ideot," that is, a creature ignorant, without learning, and, as we understand the pun on "lay," a person ignorant in the business of sexual intercourse. Since by the second line of the poem the lover already laments that the mistress "proves" too subtile in that sophistry (deceptive reasoning), the "lay Ideot" may well be the lover as well.

Initially, he reminds his mistress, she did not understand

> The mystique language of the eye nor hand:
> Nor couldst thou judge the difference of the aire
> Of sighes, and say, this lies, this sounds despaire:
> Nor by the' eyes water call a maladie
> Desperately hot, or changing feaverously. (ll. 4–8)

She did not understand all of those wiles that Ovid so clearly delineated for his mistress in the *Amores,* giving her instructions on how to deceive her husband. He amplifies on this in the succeeding lines:

> I had not taught thee then, the Alphabet
> Of flowers, how they devisefully being set
> And bound up, might with speechlesse secrecie
> Deliver arrands mutely,' and mutually. (ll. 9–12)

The emphasis here is on the "art" of love, the trickery, the "secrecie," needed to carry out the affair. The speaker then "remembers when," as Leishman renders it, all the response the lady knew to give suitors was "I, 'if my friends agree" (l. 14). He tells her that she is not "by so many duties" her husband's

> That from the' worlds Common having sever'd thee,
> Inlaid thee, neither to be seene, nor see,
> As mine: who have with amorous delicacies
> Refin'd thee' into a blis-full paradise. (ll. 20–24)

The mistress is his creation; she is his land, his Common that he has "inlaid" for his own; she is not just his land, she is his fruit; he has refined her with "amorous delicacies" and made that land into a paradise. Her "graces and good words" are his "creatures" (l. 25); "I planted knowledge and lifes tree in thee," he asserts (l. 26). There can be no squeamishness about the phallic connotation of this image; the lover has taught her "knowledge" through sexual intercourse; he has "planted" on this land. Having asserted this, the lover concludes with a series of questions that describe his dilemma—others seem to be benefiting from his teaching:

> I planted knowledge and lifes tree in thee,
> Which Oh, shall strangers taste? Must I alas
> Frame and enamell Plate, and drinke in glasse?
> Chafe waxe for others seales? breake a colts force
> And leave him then, beeing made a ready horse? (ll. 26–30)

A paraphrase of these lines might go as follows: shall strangers taste the fruits of my labors? Must I fashion and enamel (covering with enamel for adornment) metal ware and then drink from mere glass? Must I heat wax for others to use in applying their seals? Must I tame a colt and then leave him ready for others to ride? Ostensibly, Donne's images have little connection; he draws on agriculture and its products, the working of expensive metal, the use of wax for seals, and the training of horses. They are all connected by the idea, conceit if you will, of creating something at great expense or effort and having someone else reap the benefits of that creation. But the full power of the wit involved, the impudence of the stance taken by the lover, and the assumptions about the true nature and end of love, are felt only when we acknowledge the sexual nature of these images.[21] The mistress is something he has created, probed, planted, tasted, made glorious, handled, warmed, and trained. The horse is a traditional symbol of lust, as we have seen, and he fears that he has made her one "ready" for riding by others.[22] This elegy works precisely because these images are so sexually suggestive; the wit, the tone, the pose, would not work without them.

Other elegies are filled with equally suggestive language, including the most widely anthologized of Donne's elegies, "Going to Bed," but as that poem has been treated extensively elsewhere, I pass it over in favor of "Loves Progress," a poem Leishman places in his witty category and praises for the "ingenious comparisons Donne uses in order to describe the lover's progress in terms of a voyage."[23] Leishman sees the impudence of the poem as Ovidian; the particular comparisons used by Donne are what make the poem work for him. No one would quarrel with Leishman's assessment of the power of Donne's comparisons, but what gives the poem its power is Donne's use of impudent logic and the variation he plays on the "descending catalogue" *topos*. We noted earlier Nashe's use of this *topos* in his *Choise of Valentines,* and scholars have pointed to the similarities between Donne's poem and Nashe's, but the differences are even more instructive.[24] Donne's poem rings variations on the descending catalogue *topos* in ingenious and inventive ways that culminate with an obscene jest. Helen Gardner has said that this "outrageous poem is a paradox, arguing that since the beauty of a woman is not what a lover desires in her, the foot should be studied rather than the face."[25] Such a reading ignores "the centrique part," the object of "Loves Progress." The speaker gives us not a simple description of a woman that moves by progression, rather, he is concerned with how one "travels," both poetically and physically, to "the centrique part."

The image of travel that underlies the poem is depicted as a sea voyage. This voyage is invoked in the first three lines of the poem:

21. Leishman, p. 56.

22. On horses as symbols of lust, see chapter 6, note 35.

23. Leishman, p. 76. For an excellent discussion of the elegy, "Going to Bed," see Clay Hunt, *Donne's Poetry: Essays in Literary Analysis* (New Haven: Yale Univ. Press, 1954), pp. 16–31.

24. *John Donne: The Elegies and the Songs and Sonnets,* ed. Helen Gardner (Oxford: Clarendon Press, 1965), p. 133.

25. Ibid., p. 133.

> Who ever loves, if he do not propose
> The right true end of love, he's one that goes
> To sea for nothing but to make him sick. (ll. 1–3)

Shawcross, who is everywhere attuned to the bawdiness of this poem, suggests that by "true end of love" the speaker means sexual intercourse, and he further suggests that a graphic pun on "end" is intended given the final jest of the poem. There is nothing farfetched in this reading of the poem; it is entirely consonant with the outrageous logic, violation of poetic conventions, and overall character of the elegies. At first reading, of course, the "right true end of love" is ambiguous enough. The next three lines, however, suggest the sexual nature of love as the speaker begins to define it:

> Love is a bear-whelp born, if we o're lick
> Our love, and force it new strange shapes to take,
> We erre, and of a lump a monster make. (ll. 4–6)

Literally, the speaker argues that love is like a young bear when born; it takes its proper form from being licked into shape; if we make it assume strange and unusual forms, we make a mistake and turn a formless thing into a monster.[26] Lovers ought to make a "lump" (one physical mass) not a monster, created, one supposes, by some "unnatural inverted sexual position."[27] To the twisted mind of an Iago the "beast with two backs" is monstrous; to the speaker of this elegy, departure from that "lump" is monstrous. The speaker continues with this idea of the monstrous by asking, "Were not a Calf a monster that were grown / Face'd like a man, though better then his own?" (ll. 7–8). The speaker deftly moves his description back to a question of the form and end of things. A man's face is better than a calf's, but it would not be fitting on a calf. Both the logical thrust of the poem and the descriptive progress are prepared for in the next two lines: "Perfection is in unitie: preferr / One woman first, and then one thing in her" (ll. 9–10). We get here the strong sense of the speaker as the experienced man of the world, dispensing advice to those who may be less experienced. This is part of what gives Helen Gardner the notion that the elegies "give an overwhelming impression of masculinity." It is not just that the " 'masculine persuasive force' of the language and the reckless, overbearing argumentativeness match an arrogance that in some of the poems amounts to a brutal contempt for the partner of his pleasures . . ."; the impression of masculinity is brought into focus

26. See Shakespeare's *3 Henry VI*, III.ii.161.
27. *The Complete Poetry of Donne*, p. 65.

by the very strong sense of man talking to man, telling him how to really go about the business (or sport) of getting a woman.[28] The reader (an imagined auditor) surely expects from Donne an explanation at this point of the "one thing in her," but it is here that Donne's perverse logic, love of inventive comparisons, and careful exploitation of expectations dominate the poem. The idea of preferring one thing, the *essential* thing of an object, receives the speaker's attention for the next several lines:

> I, when I value gold, may think upon
> The ductilness, the application,
> The wholsomness, the ingenuitie,
> From rust, from soil, from fire ever free:
> But if I love it, 'tis because 'tis made
> By our new nature (Use) the soul of trade. (ll. 11–16)

From contemplating the essential quality of woman, the speaker considers by analogy the essential quality of gold. That the speaker should think in terms of gold in such a situation is not altogether exceptional. Both gold and women are presumably things of great worth; that the speaker thinks of women as valued objects is important, for ultimately the poem will turn on the connections between sexual intercourse and money. As the speaker "values" his gold, considers the qualities that make it what it is, he tells us he might think of its "ductilness," its malleableness; its "application," its use, but also that which can be put onto another; its "wholsomness," its healthiness, but also its completeness; its "ingenuitie," its freedom. It is free from rust, soil, and fire; all of these are the qualities of gold that the speaker might value (weigh with judgment).[29] "But if I love it," the speaker continues " 'tis because 'tis made / By our new nature (Use) the soul of trade." The distinction here is between what we judiciously value in something and what we love in something, for we love the essential thing—in gold that essential thing is that quality which man has invested it with, ultimate worth in world of trade. Gold is given a new nature through use by man. The speaker has established some interesting possibilities in his analogy of women and gold. The speaker now shifts to consideration of women:

> All these in women we might think upon
> (If women had them) and yet love but one.
> Can men more injure women then to say
> They love them for that, by which they're not they? (ll. 17–20)

28. Gardner, in *John Donne,* p. xxiv.
29. Shawcross, in *The Complete Poetry of Donne,* p. 65, glosses soil as "both 'stain' since gold is untarnishable and 'earth' since they can easily be separated."

I take the "these" to refer to the qualities suggested in considering gold. One might think of these qualities in women if they had them and yet love only one of those qualities. The implication, of course, is that women do not have these qualities; they have other ones, but the speaker slyly suggests through the lines that follow that in fact women and gold *do* share many of the same qualities. At this juncture, however, he is intent upon establishing his logical point, that we must love things for their one essential quality. He proceeds to consider different, traditional qualities that have been held to be the essential quality of women. The speaker rejects virtue, beauty, and wealth. This is consistent with his pose throughout; he is hot-blooded, and he leaves "virtuous" loving to "barren" angels, especially because one cannot find a woman "wise and good" (1.22). His emphasis here is on "make love" not merely "love"; it is an action, and that action becomes ever more prominent in the poem. Any man who "strayes" from the essential thing in woman to those that are mere qualities she happens to have, that man is more adulterous than if he "took" such a woman's maid. Donne condemns the wrong-headed lover in sexual terms; he is an adulterer, one who acts incorrectly, as bad as a lover who forces himself sexually on a lady's maid. The speaker's condemning wrong-headed lovers for sexual intercourse (when that is precisely the case he is going to make as the true end of love) is one of the nice reversals in the poem, and it has the effect of heightening further the reader's attention to sexual innuendo.

If love is not in virtue or beauty or wealth, it must be somewhere, and the speaker leads us there by connecting love, through Cupid, back to gold:

> . . . Search every sphear
> And firmament, our *Cupid* is not there:
> He's an infernal god and under ground,
> With *Pluto* dwells, where gold and fire abound;
> Men to such Gods, their sacrificing Coles
> Did not in Altars lay, but pits and holes:
> Although we see Celestial bodies move
> Above the earth, the earth we Till and love:
> So we her ayres contemplate, words and heart,
> And virtues; but we love the Centrique part. (ll. 27–36)

Cupid does not live in heaven; his abode is underground where gold and fire abound. The suggestion is that money and heat have a great deal to do with Cupid, and men sacrifice not on altars, but in pits and holes (those vile receptacles the theologians of the age railed against).

Men cultivate and love the earth, the body, not "ayres," "words," "hearts," and "virtues." Men like the speaker love the "centrique part."

As surely as Chaucer's Miller directs our attention to Alisoun's middle parts, so the speaker directs those who love properly to *the* essential quality of women, that quality alone which is worth having women for. But it has taken thirty-six lines to get there, and the fun has only begun. Any analysis of the poem to this point cannot help but notice those characteristics of Donne's poetry that readers have been pointing to for years—a dramatic quality, outrageous logic, and inventive metaphors—all of which show off the poet's wit (a wit, one might add, that is less and less fashionable since it shows itself off in such a "masculine" or sexist fashion). What follows in the poem draws on Donne's use of conventions, especially the *topos* of the descending catalogue; it is a catalogue that continues to employ the idea of a journey, a journey to the place that has finally been identified. The speaker tells us, "But in attaining this desired place / How much they erre; that set out at the face!" (ll. 39–40) Since they "erre" who set out from the face, we might expect the speaker to pass over just such an exercise, but here our expectations are thwarted; the journey, a descending catalogue, has begun, and the speaker sets forth to have his fun with the convention.

The journey down from the face is rendered as a voyage, and it is one that is beset with difficulties from the outset. The hair is a "Forest . . . of Ambushes," the brow "becalms us when 'tis smooth and plain," and when it is "wrinckled" it is worse, it "shipwracks us again" (ll. 41–44). The shift in person from line 40, "How much *they* erre" that set out from the face to the first person plural indicates that the speaker has entered into the journey himself—presumably he has erred too, and this is what he is showing us.

From the brow, the speaker descends to the nose, and Donne's penchant for geographic imagery dominates the rest of the voyage.[30] There are several strategic and surprising ports of call. The nose cleaves both the eyes and cheeks (a "rosie hemisphere / On either side") and "directs us where / Upon the Islands fortunate we fall" (ll. 50–51). These fortunate islands are not the "faint *Canaries,* but *Ambrosiall*"; that is, they are not the Canary Islands, where ancient cosmographers placed the division of eastern and western hemispheres, where a sweet wine is made, but the drink of the gods; these islands are her "swelling lips." Donne has not exactly punned here; he works by association; in the

---

30. A reading of the elegies does nothing but confirm the commonplace that Donne is the most powerful and interesting of Renaissance writers in his use of geographic imagery.

Canary Islands there is produced a light sweet wine; on the islands of this woman, her swelling lips, there is produced the drink of the gods. When we come to those lips, he says, "We anchor there, and think our selves at home, / For they seem all" (ll. 54–55). The speaker makes it clear that this is an illusion, that men only "think" they are at home here; the lips merely seem all, but he tells us what "seems" at the lips, "there Syrens songs, and there / Wise Delphick Oracles do fill the ear" (ll. 55–56). And inside those lips, "There in a Creek where chosen pearls do swell / The Rhemora her cleaving tongue doth dwell" (ll. 57–58). Gardner glosses these lines by explaining that the "remora, or sucking fish, was believed to be able to stop any ship to which it attached itself, as a woman's tongue will delay her lover's progress to the desired port."[31] Since songs and wise sayings seem to be the activities of the tongue, there is no need to insist upon a sexual reading here; surely the primary reading is the one suggested by Gardner, but we must also remember that the "true end of love" can be perverted; it can be forced to take "new strange shapes" if we "o're lick" it. The speaker pushes on, the voyage continues and moves swiftly, not even the breasts cause further delay:

> . . . and the streight *Hellespont* between
> The *Sestos* and *Abydos* of her breasts,
> (Not of two Lovers, but two loves the neasts)
> Succeeds a boundless sea, but yet thine eye
> Some Island moles may scatter'd there descry. (ll. 59–64)

The speaker has shifted person again, now he is describing the voyage for a "you"; he has separated himself out, done away with the "we," perhaps because of the danger that lies ahead. the voyage moves apace toward "*India*"—that which is rich and sumptuous. Sailing that way he tells the person, you

> . . . Shall at her fair Atlantick Naval stay;
> Though thence the Current be thy Pilot made,
> Yet ere thou be where thou wouldst be embay'd,
> Thou shalt upon another Forest set,
> Where many Shipwrack, and no further get. (ll. 66–70)

In fact the shifting of person is confusing, and one has the sense that Donne is careless through this part of the poem. He certainly is intent upon separating himself from anyone who would attempt such a voyage, for, as he changes metaphors, he announces that once you arrive

31. *John Donne*, p. 135.

at this "Forest" where many shipwreck, "When thou art there, consider what this chace / Mispent by thy beginning at the face" (ll. 71–72). The forest suggests the metaphor of chase; what is especially interesting is the speaker's return to a term from the monetary realm—all that effort is "mispent." The speaker has spent thirty-five lines defining the "essential quality" of woman and another thirty-seven lines describing the wrong way of arriving at that "quality." The reader is now fully prepared for an erotic trip like Nashe's when the speaker announces, "Rather set out below; practice my Art" (l. 73). After all, if the speaker can be so successfully suggestive in describing the wrong way to voyage, what sites will there not be to behold on the proper voyage! How Donne deludes such an expectant reader, for he discourses for thirteen lines upon that organ almost never catalogued, the foot![32] The speaker's reasoning is ingenious, the foot has "Some Symetry . . . with that part / Which thou dost seek" (ll. 74–75); it is least subject to disguise and change; it is the emblem of firmness, and it comes to bed first. And just as the kiss began at the face, it has since been transplanted to the hand and for emperors to the knee and for popes to the foot; "If Kings think that the nearer way, and do / Rise from the foot, Lovers may do so too" (ll. 85–86). The emphasis through these lines is not on a voyage, not on a catalogue of ascendance; it is on witty argumentation, ever a keynote in Donne.

With his starting place ever so elaborately defined, the speaker finally begins his ascent. But even here, it is not an ascent graphic in its detail reminiscent of Alisoun's stockings or the Valentine's "Mannely thigh" and "prettie rysing wombe"; it is virtually a void:

> For as free Spheres move faster far then can
> Birds, whom the air resists, so may that man
> Which goes this empty and AEtherial way,
> Then if at beauties elements he stay. (ll. 87–90)

The poem moves toward a conclusion with the objective finally achieved and described: "Rich Nature hath in women wisely made / Two purses, and their mouths aversely laid" (ll. 91–92). Here the monetary and sexual images are drawn together most vividly. Donne's anatomical description is not unique with him; although the "purse" is more often used as a metaphor for the male's scrotum in the Renaissance, it is also used for the female pudendum, and as we saw with Chaucer's Alisoun, her "purse" hanging from her belt carried such a suggestion.[33] In Donne's usage here "Rich Nature" has been generous;

---

32. Kiernan, p. 2.
33. *John Donne*, p. 135. See also chapter 7, note 11.

she has given woman two purses in her centrique part and laid their openings "aversely"—that is, in opposite direction to one another. Shawcross also suggests that aversely means "in an unfavorable position"; more to the point might be the sense that the mouths sit with aversion or dislike for one another.[34]

The poem ends with an obscene jest about these two purses:

> They then, which to the lower tribute owe,
> That way which that Exchequer looks, must go:
> He which doth not, his error is as great,
> As who by Clyster gave the Stomack meat. (ll. 93–96)

These lines might be paraphrased as follows: they who owe tribute to the lower purse (the one first arrived at by starting from below) must go the direction that such a receiver of payment looks; he who does not (owe tribute to that purse, that Exchequer, the female pudendum, but rather serves the anus) his error is as great as he who gives food to the stomach by an enema (rather than drawing food off). One has to be careful once one arrives at the "true end of love."

This is a bravura performance. For all the confusion caused by the shifting of person in this poem (and I think it is that), this poem is exemplary of Donne's elegies. The outrageous argument, the display of wit, the learned quality (Donne's poems are never an easy read), the combination of the strains of the *Amores* of Ovid and the Italian paradox—they are all there. And we understand Donne's use of all of these things when we see his poem within the full context of Renaissance erotica. In his elegies Donne shows himself capable of the pornographic, the erotic, the bawdy, and, as we have seen in "Loves Progress," even the obscene. It is instructive to move beyond acknowledgment to analysis. We might not find Donne's obscene jest at the end of "Loves Progress" very pleasant; nevertheless, his manipulation of the catalogue convention, his outrageous logic, his puns, his metaphors, his bawdy, surely earn our admiration.

III

Imagine a course in Renaissance drama devoid of erotica in one form or another, and you eliminate most of the great (and a good many of the mediocre) plays of the era. Renaissance dramatists exploited sex and sexual innuendo to its utmost; a study on lust alone would run volumes, as would one on sexual innuendo. Sexual action and sexual innuendo

---

34. *The Complete Poetry of Donne*, p. 67.

are inseparable in Renaissance drama, since there could have been little realistic heterosexual action on the stage with an audience always aware that boys were playing the parts of women.[35] A knowledge of plots of sexual intrigue found in a variety of sources, from novelle to jests, and a knowledge of the language of sexuality are essential for a full understanding of Renaissance drama, as both are used masterfully by a number of Renaissance dramatists to develop character, theme, and setting as well as plot. For example, the language of sexuality and the lust of certain characters become the means by which Malevole gains his revenge in *The Malcontent*; both elements turn out to be unmasking devices for Volpone in his attempted seduction of Celia, and our understanding of *Volpone*'s world is greatly informed by our knowledge of Italian erotica. The love of Romeo and Juliet is put into focus not only by the early posturings of Romeo as a Petrarchan lover but also by the bawdy humor of the Nurse and Mercutio; even in *King Lear* the subject of lust plays an important role; one could go on and on, for sex is everywhere in Renaissance drama in both major and minor ways. In Shakespeare's *The Merry Wives of Windsor* we can see both the jest literature and sexually suggestive language used in an exemplary manner.

It is true that there is no pornographic action in *The Merry Wives of Windsor;* there is bawdy language in good plenty, but it is not used to shock or arouse. On the surface, then, it would seem an unpromising play for study even under the category of "the context of erotica." But the actions of the play, the plots, are everywhere informed by a knowledge of ribald stories, especially in the form of jests or merry tales; and the English language, "hacked" and made "fritters" of, is bawdy run rampant to great comic effect.

The commonplace with regard to the sources for *The Merry Wives* is that there is no one *known* source for the plot of Falstaff and the wives, but there are many analogues.[36] Editors have singled out stories from Ser Giovanni, Straparola, and Tarlton. Surely the merry tales and jests of the kind examined in chapters 1 and 6 of this book are what inform Shakespeare's plots, particularly the variations Shakespeare plays on them. Obviously, Shakespeare counted on his audience's familiarity with the jest material; his title was undoubtedly meant to

35. For an illuminating discussion of this problem see Gordon Lell, " 'Ganymede' on the Elizabethan Stage: Homosexual Implications of the Use of Boy-Actors," *Aegis* (1973): 5–15.

36. Editors have cited Ser Giovanni's *Il Percorone,* Day I story 2; Straparola's *Le tredici piacevoli notti,* "The Story of Nerisio of Portugal"; and Tarlton's *Newes out of Purgatorie,* "The Tale of Two Lovers of Pisa."

remind playgoers of the many collections of "merry tales" that continued to be printed throughout the English Renaissance. We recall that the conventional sexual jest story is one of cuckoldry in which a lusty wife usually manages to trick a foolish husband as she has an affair with a virile young lover. What Shakespeare does in the Falstaff-wives line of his play is to invert the conventional plot in several ways. In *The Merry Wives of Windsor* both the lover (an aging, money-grubbing lecher) *and* the jealous husband are duped and shamed by wives who are *chaste*.

It is confusing to talk about main plot and subplots in this play. The action might be described as follows. The play opens with Justice Shallow and his cousin Slender complaining to the Welsh parson, Sir Hugh Evans, about wrongdoings perpetrated on them by Sir John Falstaff. As has been noted many times, Shakespeare quickly drops this line of the plot and puts before the audience the question of the marriage of Anne Page. Shallow pushes his reluctant cousin to pursue this young maiden. The wooing of Anne Page thus provides the play with one major plot line, the conventional story of romantic comedy. In quick succession we understand that in addition to Slender, Anne Page has as suitors Dr. Caius, the French physician, and Fenton, the rake. This plot is complicated not only by the conventional parental intervention (Page on behalf of Slender, Mrs. Page on behalf of Dr. Caius), but also by the use of go-betweens. Slender engages Sir Hugh Evans on his behalf (who in turn solicits the help of Mistress Quickly), and both Dr. Caius and Fenton engage Mistress Quickly. This use of go-betweens in turn leads to conflict between Sir Hugh and Dr. Caius, a conflict fanned on to comic effect by the Host of the Garter Inn. The bringing together of these would-be combatants by the Host and the exposure of their foolishness leads ultimately to the cozenage of the Host by Sir Hugh and Dr. Caius.[37] So much for the bare bones of the romantic comedy plot.

The jest plot of Sir John and the merry wives also springs from the opening scene, where we see Sir John having troubles not only with Shallow but with his own followers as well. Falstaff discharges Nym and Pistol in the opening scenes and launches his campaign to seduce the wives with his page, Robin, as go-between. The wives in turn counterplot, using Mistress Quickly as their messenger. Mistress Quickly is thus involved as a go-between in both plots, and other characters interact as well. Early in the play Nym and Pistol, discarded by Falstaff, reveal the fat knight's plan to the jealous Mr. Ford. From

37. See note 47 below.

this follows Ford's plot to revenge himself on Falstaff by disguising himself as Brook and using the Host as an entree to the knight. The Host thus operates in both plots. Within the Falstaff-wives plot there are two major jests before act V—the basket jest and the old woman jest. By the beginning of act V, the two major plot lines have come together with one additional factor: Fenton has engaged the Host to aid him in his plot to secure Anne Page. The minor conflicts between the Host and Sir Hugh and Dr. Caius have been played out, the wives and Ford are working together, and only the final unmasking of Falstaff and marrying of Anne Page are left to be accomplished.

Such an accounting of the plots of *The Merry Wives* does not do justice to the sprightliness of the action, but it is necessary, I think, in making the central point about the plot or plots of the play—they are joined *thematically* throughout by being precisely that, plots or schemes of the kind found in jest books. Even in a play with so notable a character as Falstaff, all, even characterization, seems subordinated to plot.[38] This is not to say that the characters are not well drawn, but it does emphasize the primacy of the plot and plotting. References to "jest," "cosenage," "revenge," "plot," "trick," "invention," "device," "knaveries," "deceit," "foppery," "comedy," "scene," and "sport" abound in the play.[39] Our attention is constantly drawn to the "jest," the "comedy," the "sport" of the action, and of course the "sport" that all would play involves sexual intercourse—for the Anne Page plot within marriage, for the Falstaff plot in adultery. This is also a play in which Shakespeare creates a good deal of the humor from verbal sport, especially in his use of bawdy, which, given the nature of the plot, is never gratuitous but is always reminding us of the "sporting" game here. It is not insignificant that most of this very earthy play is in prose. To say all of this about the plots and language is not to deny the emphasis given *The Merry Wives* in earlier studies, studies that have approached the work as Shakespeare's Garter play or Shakespeare's only fully domestic comedy; rather, it is to emphasize what the plots and language of the play itself emphasize.[40]

38. Commenting on the play as farce in his introduction to the Pelican edition, Fredson Bowers notes that in such plays "The plot itself—usually of the intrigue variety—is the normal center of interest, and characters are necessarily subordinate. . . . the plot concerns itself with being a plot—with the rapidity, absurdity, and ingenuity of its twists and turns—and scarcely at all with holding a mirror up to life" (*The Complete Pelican Shakespeare,* ed. Alfred Harbage [Baltimore: Penguin Books, 1969], p. 336).

39. Words meaning "trick" appear at least fifty-eight times in the play.

40. One may call this a Garter play in terms of the occasion of composition, setting, and topicality of allusions, but the notion of the Order of the Garter has little to do with

Let us focus first on the plots of the play. In her introduction to the Riverside edition of the play Anne Barton makes the salient point that Shakespeare's *Merry Wives* is a "play which extends and, in a sense, violates the calculatedly limited form the merry tale."[41] She is not precisely clear on *how* the form is violated. She correctly points out that the wives are merry but chaste (as they are not in the analogous Italian stories), but she goes on to say that in Shakespeare's play, "It is the would be lover . . . who is cleverly deceived, not the husband."[42] The fact is that Shakespeare has it both ways; both the husband (the typical jealous type) and the lover (here transformed into a fat, old, money-seeking lecher) are deceived, and the wives remain chaste.

Shakespeare uses two major jest traditions, I think, in developing the plots of *The Merry Wives*—the Italian sexual jest and the English cony-catching jest exemplified by Greene's cony-catching pamphlets. Playgoers familiar with jest books, merry tales, and stories of cozenage would have seen from the outset that there was more than mere complication of the plots going on in terms of the thematic significance of such actions.[43] Even in the first plot, Shallow's argument with Falstaff, which goes nowhere in the play, the trouble has come from the cozenage of Slender by Bardolph, Nym, and Pistol, characters Slender calls "cony-catching rascals" (I.i.124). In Falstaff's plot to gain the merry wives the two jest traditions are joined. Falstaff tells his cronies, "I must cony-catch, I must shift" (I.iii.33–34), and the way in which he will cony-catch leads him into the machinations of a comic Italian sexual jest.

Falstaff's language as he describes his project is instructive. He tells his cronies "what he is about," and a series of puns follow:

> *Pist.* Two yards, and more.
> *Fal.* No quips now, Pistol! Indeed I am in the waist two yards about; but I am now about no waste; I am about thrift. Briefly—I do mean to

---

the central actions of the play. Even William Green, who argues most strongly for the play's being Shakespeare's Garter play in his book *Shakespeare's Merry Wives of Windsor* (Princeton: Princeton Univ. Press, 1962), admits at one point that "not one of the Court-Garter passages is essential to the action of the *Merry Wives*" (p. 96).

41. Anne Barton in her introduction to Riverside edition, p. 288.

42. Ibid.

43. Some very early punning by Falstaff is important in reminding us that many of the jest books built their jokes on precisely the kinds of misunderstandings Shakespeare presents in Act I scene i. At the outset we see that Slender has little mastery of English and Parson Evans even less, so that when Sir Hugh warns Sir John in his accented Latin and English, "*Pauca verba;* Sir John, good worts," Sir John replies, "Good worts? Good cabbage" (I.i.120–21). As readers familiar with *The Sackful of News* know, the whole of jest 16 is built around a foreigner's misunderstanding of the word "coleworts."

make love to Ford's wife. I spy entertainment in her. She discourses, she carves, she gives the leer of invitation. I can construe the action of her familiar style, and the hardest voice of her behavior (to be English'd rightly) is, "I am Sir John Falstaff's."

Pist. He hath studied her well, and translated her will, out of honesty into English. (I.iii.40–50)

Shakespeare seems to have been fascinated with the possibilities of punning on the language of grammar in the play, and this scene gives an early indication of what proves to be a rich mine for him. Falstaff wishes he were in a "waist" (we are reminded of "The expense of spirit in a waste of shame") with his yard, but he is not. He spies "entertainment" like a grammarian, for she discourses, and he construes her style and voice. Falstaff continues by employing some of the typically suggestive geographic imagery of Renaissance love poetry as he describes what he has taken to be Mrs. Page's affection for him:

O, she did so course o'er my exteriors with such a greedy intention, that the appetite of her eye did seem to scorch me up like a burning-glass! Here's another letter to her. She bears the purse too; she is a region in Guiana, all gold and bounty. I will be cheaters to them both, and they shall be exchequers to me. They shall be my East and West Indies, and I will trade to them both. Go, bear thou this letter to Mistress Page; and thou this to Mistress Ford. We will thrive, lads, we will thrive. (I.iii.65–74)

Traditional love imagery, yes, but we notice more in this speech. "Purse" may well have sexual connotations here, but the primary meaning for Falstaff is the financial one, and we note throughout this speech that Falstaff is at least as interested in money as in sex. It is financial cozenage above all that he wishes to practice, and this is surely a departure from the norm of Italian jests; it is in fact the typical concern of English cony-catching jests.[44]

What follows on the stage is not lewd behavior on the part of Falstaff; he never even gets as close as Volpone to stealing any secret fruits. What follows is intrigue upon intrigue, messengers, disguises, ruses— all the manipulation of foolish men by clever women. We know from the very moment that we see Mistresses Ford and Page together that Falstaff will not victimize them. They are not squeamish; their own

---

44. Colman, p. 78, notes that Falstaff "has a surprisingly small share of the bawdy lines in the earlier scenes. This may be because his plans to subvert the two wives are at this stage less lustful than financially interested: he spies *entertainment* (which means employment as well as sexual amusement), and he proposes to *trade* (sexually, but also for profit)."

conscious verbal dexterity as they compare their letters from Falstaff shows us this:

> *Mrs. Page.* Letter for letter; but that the name of Page and Ford differs! To thy great comfort in this mystery of ill opinions, here's the twin-brother of thy letter; but let thine inherit first, for I protest mine never shall. I warrant he hath a thousand of these letters, writ with blank space for different names (sure, more!); and these are the second edition. He will print them, out of doubt; for he cares not what he puts into the press, when he would put us two. I had rather be a giantess, and lie under Mount Pelion. Well—I will find you twenty lascivious turtles ere one chaste man.
> *Mrs. Ford.* Why, this is the very same: the very hand; the very words. What doth he think of us?
> *Mrs. Page.* Nay, I know not; it makes me almost ready to wrangle with mine own honesty. I'll entertain myself like one that I am not acquainted withal; for sure unless he know some strain in me that I know not myself, he would never have boarded me in this fury.
> *Mrs. Ford.* "Boarding," call you it? I'll be sure to keep him above deck.
> *Mrs. Page.* So will I; if he come under my hatches, I'll never to sea again. . . . (II.i.70–93)[45]

Falstaff of course is not the only victim; Ford, the jealous husband, must also learn a lesson. Both would-be lover and husband are to be victims of *chaste* wives; that is the marked departure from norms we have seen from Poggio on.

Ford furthers his own victimization by conceiving his plot of going to Falstaff as Brook, a would-be lover of Mrs. Ford's. Brook's approach to Falstaff highlights the issue of financial cozenage. Falstaff, we recall, noted that the wives would be "exchequers" to him, but until they become so, he has been spending, paying Mistress Quickly to help him (II.ii.131), but he has hopes: "Wilt thou, after the expense of so much money, be now a gainer?" (II.ii.140–41). Brook offers first sack and then money, "Such Brooks are most welcome," to Sir John. Whether the primary motivation for Falstaff is avarice or lust is not important; both are surely there, and the entrance of Ford as Brook into the plot reminds us that this is basically a cuckoldry story of the kind found in Poggio or Ser Giovanni or Tarlton. And Shakespeare keeps the business of cuckoldry before us by his use of the plot, the language, and visual presentations. By having Brook press Falstaff about Ford in their initial meeting, Shakespeare contrives to let the jealous fool fry in Falstaff's verbal fire. Does Falstaff know Ford?

45. Colman, p. 85, argues, "The bourgeois wives, although 'merry' enough for an occasional vulgar quip, are essentially too prim to be outspoken on sexual matters."

> Hang him, poor cuckoldy knave, I know him not. Yet I wrong him to call him poor. They say the jealous wittolly knave hath masses of money, for the which his wife seems to me well-favor'd. I will use her as the key of the cuckoldly rogue's coffer, and there's my harvest-home. (II.ii.270–75)

This speech would seem to reemphasize the financial motivation in Falstaff, and it does do that, but there is more. Falstaff sees Ford as a "cuckoldly knave," "a jealous wittolly knave," and he does hope to "use" Mrs. Ford; thus the image of the key and coffer is one of interesting transformation here. Falstaff parts from Brook speaking thus of Ford, "Hang him, mechanical salt-butter rogue! I will stare him out of his wits; I will awe him with my cudgel; it shall hang like a meteor o'er the cuckold's horns. Master Brook, thou shalt know I will predominate over the peasant, and thou shalt lie with his wife" (II.ii.278–83). Ford is left to contemplate "Terms! names!":

> Amaimon sounds well; Lucifer, well; Barbason, well; yet they are devils' additions, the names of fiends; but Cuckold! Wittol!—Cuckold! the devil himself hath not such a name. Page is an ass, a secure ass; he will trust his wife, he will not be jealous. I will rather trust a Fleming with my butter, Parson Hugh the Welshman with my cheese, an Irishman with my aqua-vitae bottle, or a thief to walk my ambling gelding, than my wife with herself. Then she plots, then she ruminates, then she devises; and what they think in their hearts they may effect, they will break their hearts but they will effect. God be prais'd for my jealousy! Eleven o'clock the hour. I will prevent this, detect my wife, be reveng'd on Falstaff, and laugh at Page. I will about it; better three hours too soon than a minute too late. Fie, fie, fie! cuckold, cuckold, cuckold! (II.ii.297–314)

We see here the power of the term "cuckold." Shakespeare is careful to maintain a comic tone throughout this speech; we never sympathize with Ford, but we are conscious of the horror the epithet holds for Ford. What Shakespeare makes comic here, he is able to turn frighteningly horrible in his later tragedies and tragicomedies with characters like Othello and Leontes.[46]

Through the meeting of Brook and Falstaff, the plot is prepared for the knight's first visit to Mrs. Ford. Ford has invited his friends to accompany him home, "You shall have sport; I will show you a monster" (III.ii.81), but the women have already made their plans to use the "buck" or wash basket. The entrance of Mrs. Page with news of the arrival of Ford cuts short Falstaff's first attempts at seduction, and he is quickly stuffed into the buck basket with the foulest of linen, taken past Ford and dumped into the Thames. Ford enters the scene with:

---

46. See *Othello*, III.iii.258–77 and IV.i.60–73; and *The Winter's Tale*, I.ii.179–207.

Ford. Pray you come near. If I suspect without cause, why then make sport at me, then let me be your jest, I deserve it. How now? Whither bear you this?
Serv. To the landress, forsooth.
Mrs. Ford. Why, what have you to do whither they bear it? You were best meddle with buck-washing.
Ford. Buck! I would I could wash myself of the buck! Buck, buck, buck! ay, buck! I warrant you, buck, and of the season too, it shall appear. Gentlemen, I have dream'd to-night; I'll tell you my dream. Here, here, here be my keys. Ascend my chambers, search, seek, find out. I'll warrant we'll unkennel the fox. . . . (III.iii.149–64)

As Parson Evans notes, "This is fery fantastical humors and jealousies," and Ford is the obvious object of the jest here; he wishes he were rid of his horns, and of course we know that he is not one of the forked order. But Falstaff must not be forgotten; Mrs. Ford later says, "I know not which pleases me better, that my husband is deceiv'd, or Sir John" (III.iii.178–79), and the wives decide to "lay a plot" to try Ford's jealousy and "have more tricks with Falstaff" (III.iii.190–91).

Falstaff's reaction to his ducking in the Thames is recorded first in conversation with Mistress Quickly, sent once again as a go-between by the wives. Mistress Quickly announces that she has come from Mrs. Ford, and Falstaff exclaims, "Mistress Ford? I have had ford enough. I was thrown into the ford; I have my belly full of ford" (III.v.35–37). Mistress Quickly responds with a wonderfully appropriate malapropism: "Alas the day! good heart, that was not her fault. She does so take on with her men; they mistook their erection" (III.v.38–40). Falstaff plays upon the nonbawdy sense of "erection" in his rejoinder. "So did I mine, to build upon a foolish woman's promise" (III.v.41–42), but we understand this in a sexual sense as well, knowing that Falstaff has indeed mistaken his "erection." Falstaff blames the failure of his mission to Brook on the jealousy of "the peaking cornuto," Ford. He has escaped, he explains, through a clever "invention" of the ladies, but he promises Brook he will carry on his plan, for he is on his way to Mrs. Ford's again, having received word that the jealous Ford has gone birding. Ford repairs to his house once more, hoping to catch his wife and Falstaff *in flagrante,* and this time he is tricked as Falstaff passes out of his house disguised as the old lady of Brainford. In this disguise Falstaff is roundly beaten as "an old cozening quean." The wives decide, finally, to reveal all to their husbands, for they have not yet done with Falstaff:

Mrs. Ford. I'll warrant they'll have him publicly sham'd and methinks there would be no period to the jest, should he not be publicly sham'd.

> *Mrs. Page.* Come, to the forge with it, then shape it. I would not have things cool. (IV.ii.220–24)

Thus does the cuckoldry plot move toward its great final scene, where it is joined by the wooing plot of Anne Page. The wives plan to have Falstaff meet them in Windsor forest at the oak disguised as Herne the Hunter with his "great ragg'd horns." Page asks that the "plot go forward. Let our wives / Yet once again (to make us public sport) Appoint a meeting with this old fat fellow . . ." (IV.iv.12–14). The "device" (l. 42), the "plot" (l. 46), is set, and Sir Hugh delightedly comments, "Let us about it. It is admirable pleasures and fery honest knaveries" (IV.iv.80–81). This has been one of Shakespeare's ironic reversals throughout, that the virtuous characters are the ones duping the plotting sinners; these have indeed been "honest knaveries," and this ironic reversal is brought home visually in the final scene in the forest.

Shakespeare links the cuckoldry and wooing plots through the very notion of plotting. With the scheme to humiliate Falstaff set, Page plans to have Slender steal his daughter away in the confusion. Mistress Page also plans to take advantage of the situation by having Dr. Caius carry off Anne. But Fenton is not to be caught off guard. He tells the Host that "Fat Falstaff / Hath a great scene; the image of the jest . . . (IV.vi.16–17). He knows of Page's plan to take advantage "While other jests are something rank on foot" (IV.vi.22) and Mrs. Page's plot "While other sports are tasking of their minds" (IV.vi.30), but he himself has what the Host calls a "device." Before this scene can be played out, however, indeed, before Fenton hatches his plot, Shakespeare introduces the scene where the Host learns he has been cozened. Whether we see the scene as unrelated to the Host's trickery practiced on Dr. Caius and the Parson or as part of an undeveloped revenge plot is not so important as the plot itself.[47] The scene opens with an apparently

47. This scene has troubled all commentators on the play. Green dismisses the idea that this is the culmination of an undeveloped plot by Dr. Caius and Parson Evans to get even with the Host, and he explains it as topically related to events surrounding the Duke of Wurtemberg's election to the Order of the Garter and some notorious horse-stealing affairs of the time. I myself think that it *is* part of an undeveloped plot by Dr. Caius and Parson Evans because they *both* appear to "warn" the Host, one right after the other, and they *both* assure the Host that they do this for "good will":

> *Evans.* Have a care of your entertainments. There is a friend of mine come to town, tells me there is three cozen-germans that has cozen'd all the hosts of Readins, of Maidenhead, of Colebrook, of horses and money. I tell you for good will, look you. You are wise and full of gibes and vlouting-stocks, and 'tis not convenient you should

curious exchange between Simple, Slender's servant, and Falstaff, where Simple asks Falstaff if the old lady of Brainford knows "whether one Nym, sir, that beguil'd him of a chain, had the chain or no" (IV.v.32–33). Falstaff replies that the old lady said "that the very same man that beguil'd Master Slender of his chain cozen'd him of it" (IV.v.36–38). Is Shakespeare at the eleventh hour resurrecting the Falstaff-Shallow plot? I think not. His concern here is to remind us of the thematic importance of plotting, for in rushes Bardolph shouting "cosenage! mere cozenage" (IV.v.63), and the Host Story follows. The scene draws to a conclusion with Falstaff's noting:

> I would all the world might be cozen'd, for I have been cozen'd and beaten too. If it should come to the ear of the court, how I have been transform'd, and how my transformation hath been wash'd and cudgell'd, they would melt me out of my fat drop by drop, and liquor fishermen's boots with me. I warrant they would whip me with their fine wits till I were as crestfall'n as a dried pear. I never prosper'd since I forswore myself at primero. Well, if my wind were but long enough to say my prayers, I would repent. (IV.v.93–103)

The greatest transformation is yet to come, of course, as the "sport" devised by the citizens moves to a conclusion.

The final scene of the play begins with Falstaff's excursus on transformations brought on by lust, and here for once we see him motivated more by lust than greed:

> The Windsor bell hath strook twelve; the minute draws on. Now the hot-bloodied gods assist me! Remember, Jove, thou wast a bull for thy Europa, love set on thy horns. O powerful love, that in some respects makes a beast a man; in some other, a man a beast. You were also, Jupiter, a swan for the love of Leda. O omnipotent love, how near the god drew to the complexion of a goose! A fault done first in the form of a beast (O Jove, a beastly fault!) and then another fault in the semblance of a fowl—think on't, Jove, a foul fault! When gods have hot backs, what shall poor men do? For me, I am here a Windsor stag, and the fattest, I think, i'th' forest. Send me a cool

---

be cozen'd. Fare you well.
> *Caius.* Vere is mine host de Jarteer?
> *Host.* Here, Master Doctor, in perplexity and doubtful dilemma.
> *Caius.* I cannot tell vat is dat, but it is tell-a-me dat you make grand preparation for a duke de Jamany. By my trot, dere is no duke that the court is know to come. I tell you for good will; adieu. (IV.v.75–89)

That both men should come out of "good will" within ten lines makes it look suspiciously like an agreed-upon phrase, bound to hit the Host where he feels most proud, in his "good will." Nothing evil need be thought of the Doctor and the Parson, for nothing in *fact* need to have happened except for them to have employed Bardolph.

rut-time, Jove, or who can blame me to piss my tallow? Who comes here?
My doe? (V.v.1–15)

Mrs. Ford enters, and Falstaff thinks he will finally play out his adulterous act:

> My doe with the black scut? Let the sky rain potatoes; let it thunder to the
> tune of "Green-sleeves," hail kissing-comfits, and snow eringoes; let there
> come a tempest of provocation, I will shelter me here. (V.v.18–21)

As Anne Barton comments, "scut" is a slang term "for the female
pudenda," "sweet potatoes" were thought to stimulate sexuality,
"Green-sleeves" was a popular love song, kissing-comfits were "per-
fumed candies, used by women to sweeten their breath," eringoes were
thought an aphrodisiac, and "provocation" here means "sexual incite-
ment."[48] Falstaff is ready for sexual action, and the entrance of Mrs.
Ford only incites him further:

> Divide me like a brib'd-buck, each a haunch. I will keep my sides to myself,
> my shoulders for the fellow of this walk—and my horns I bequeath your
> husbands. Am I a woodman, ha? Speak I like Herne the hunter? Why, now
> is Cupid a child of conscience, he makes restitution. As I am a true spirit,
> welcome! (V.v.24–29)

But the horns, which Falstaff would graft upon the husbands' heads,
are his indeed as a sign of one who has been fooled. He learns that he
is the object of the jest as the "faeries" assault him.[49] When the jest is
revealed, Mrs. Ford says, "Sir John, we have had ill luck; we could
never meet. I will never take you for my love again, but I will always
count you my deer." Falstaff replies, "I do begin to perceive that I am
made an ass"; to which Ford adds, "Ay, and an ox too" (V.v.116–20),
so that transformations, which began verbally with Falstaff's invoca-
tion to the gods, then were brought visually into play on the stage, are
reinforced verbally once again as the scene draws to a close. The play
ends with the revelation of the "cosenage" of Slender and Dr. Caius,
and Fenton notes that since all has been for the good "this deceit loses
the name of craft" (V.v.226). Ford remarks that "In love, the heavens
themselves do guide the state; / Money buys lands, and wives are sold
by fate" (V.v.232–33). Mrs. Page wishes Fenton well and bids "us every
one go home / And laugh this sport o'er by a country fire" (V.v 241–
42). All has been turned to "admirable pleasures and fery honest knaveries"; the would-be horner wears the horns, although even he is in-

---

48. *Riverside Shakespeare,* p. 319n.
49. Colman, pp. 79–80, sees the scene in terms of ritual.

cluded in the festive circle at the end in Shakespeare's reworking of the typical cuckold jest.

If reversal of the cuckold jest explains much of *The Merry Wives of Windsor*, it does not explain a scene like IV.i, where young William Page is run through his schoolboy's paces by his teacher, Parson Evans. The scene is one filled with sexual innuendo provided by the Welsh accent of the Parson and the bawdy inferences of Mistress Quickly. The scene is not gratuitous bawdy provided for the groundlings, as has been suggested (when commented on at all; most editors leave much of the scene conspicuously uncommented); rather, it is a scene that plays upon the already developed comic characteristics of the Parson and Mistress Quickly and upon the "sport" that this play is about. Parson Evans provides comedy throughout the play as one who "makes fritters of English," but Mistress Quickly provides humor as one who both inadvertently speaks bawdy and willfully hears bawdy where none is intended. As Anne Barton has noted, "Mistress Quickly is scandalized by what seem to her to be the bawdy syllables uttered by a small boy rehearsing his Latin declension, but herself habitually blunders into unconscious obscenities about which Freud might have had a good deal to say."[50]

In Act I scene iv, Mistress Quickly is caught by her master, Dr. Caius, with Simple at the Doctor's house. Simple is soliciting her aid in Slender's pursuit (through Parson Evans) of Anne Page. Quickly assures the Doctor that the young man "is an honest man" and that he need fear nothing. Dr. Caius decides that he will handle this situation initially by writing a letter to Sir Hugh, and a relieved Mistress Quickly (unaware that Dr. Caius is penning a "shallenge") speaks to Simple in an aside:

> *Quick.* I am glad he is so quiet. If he had been throughly mov'd, you should have heard him so loud and so melancholy. But notwithstanding, man, I'll do you your master what good I can; and the very yea and the no is, the French doctor, my master (I may call him my master, look you, for I keep his house; and I wash, wring, brew, bake, scour, dress meat and drink, make the beds, and do all myself)—
> *Sim.* 'Tis a great charge to come under one body's hand.
> *Quick.* Are you avis'd o' that? You shall find it a great charge; and to be up early and down late; . . . (I.iv.89–102)

How much of the bawdy play is intended here on the part of Mistress Quickly is not entirely clear. Shortly after, her penchant for malaprop-

50. *Riverside Shakespeare*, p. 288.

isms leads her into a bawdy blunder when she says to Fenton, now come to enlist her aid:

> *Quick.* . . . Have not your worship a wart above your eye?
> *Fent.* Yes, marry, have I, what of that?
> *Quick.* Well, thereby hangs a tale. Good faith, it is such another Nan;
> but (I detest) an honest maid as ever I broke bread. (I.iv.146–51)

Mistress Quickly thinks she is a mistress of language, one attuned to nuances, for when she comes to Falstaff in Act II he greets her:

> *Fal.* Good morrow, goodwife.
> *Quick.* Not so, and't please your worship.
> *Fal.* Good maid then.
> *Quick.* I'll be sworn
> As my mother was the first hour I was born. (II.ii.34–38)[51]

Falstaff's response is that he believes the swearer, for he senses she is no maid. Mistress Quickly's erring tongue leads her into other comic blunders; she tells Falstaff that Mrs. Page is "as fartuous a civil modest wife . . . as any is in Windsor," and that Mrs. Page wants Falstaff to send his little page to her for "Her husband has a marvellous infection to the little page . . ." (II.ii.97 and 114–15).[52] Mistress Quickly worries about the use of the page as go-between, however. She urges Falstaff to use care so that "the boy never need to understand any thing; for 'tis not good that children should know any wickedness. Old folks, you know, have discretion, as they say, and know the world" (II.ii.127–30).

It is as the protector of children from licentiousness that Mistress Quickly reads into the innocent drilling of William Page by Parson Evans in Act IV scene i a host of dirty meanings. Through the Parson's Welsh renderings and Mistress Quickly's bawdy inferences, Shake-

51. We are reminded here of the exchange between Mistress Quickly as hostess of the Boar's Head Tavern and Falstaff in *1 Henry IV*:

> *Host.* I am no thing to thank God on, I would thou shouldst know it. I am an honest man's wife, and setting thy knighthood aside, thou art a knave to call me so.
> *Fal.* Setting thy womanhood aside, thou art a beast to say otherwise.
> *Host.* Say, what beast, thou knave, thou?
> *Fal.* What beast? why, an otter.
> *Prince.* An otter, Sir John, why an otter?
> *Fal.* Why? she's neither fish nor flesh, a man knows not where to have her.
> *Host.* Thou art an unjust man in saying so. Thou or any man knows where to have me, thou knave, thou! (III.iii.118–30)

52. In Act III scene iii ll. 236–37, Dr. Caius, because of his accent, is made to say, "If there be one or two, I shall make-a turd."

speare presents a scene entirely in keeping with the business of the play. We have seen elsewhere his propensity for punning on grammar, printing, and books themselves. In this scene he reminds us of Harington's presentation of dictionary searching as he gives us a rollicking bawdy scene. Mistress Quickly, the child-protector with the mind ready to see bawdy anywhere, is the key to the scene, for it is she who invests the contextually innocent terms with "dirty" meanings. Shakespeare shows us that he understands precisely how a "dirty" mind works, for it can invest anything with a bawdy meaning. Evans's fractured pronunciation is partly to blame, of course, and critics, especially Colman, have stressed Parson Evans's unconscious use of sexual innuendo, but it is Mistress Quickly, with her willful mishearings, who provides most of the humor.

Mistress Quickly begins mishearing innocently enough. When William Page says there are two numbers in nouns, Mistress Quickly thrusts in with "Truly, I thought there had been one number more, because they say, 'Od's nouns'" (IV.i.23–24). Thereafter, it is bawdy she hears. At William's rendering of "fair" as "*pulcher*" she interrupts. "Poulcats? There are fairer things than poulcats sure" (IV.i.28–29). She understands "poulcats" as a cant term for whores. Mistress Quickly does not comment on a rare pun by Shakespeare on "fuck." Evans asks William, "What is the focative case, William?," and William replies, "O-*vocativo*, O." (IV.i.50–52). In Colman's opinion "there is the jingle *focative / fuck*, arising through Evan's Welshified pronunciation. And . . . there is the coital suggestion, in such a context, of *case* (as meaning vagina) and of the repeated O sound, which can be thought of as either a pudendal symbol or the echo of an orgasmic cry."[53] Mistress Quickly does supply the bawdy when Parson Evans tells William that "focative is *caret*." This elicits from Mistress Quickly the idea that "that's a good root" (IV.i.53–54). And when William gives the "genitive case plural," "*Genitivo, horum, harum, horum*," Mistress Quickly cannot contain herself: "Vengeance of Jinny's case! Fie on her! never name her, child, if she be a whore" (IV.i.56–63). Mistress Quickly invests "case" with its bawdy meaning of vagina, as she hears "horum" as whore and "genitive" as Jinny. She tells the parson:

> You do ill to teach the child such words. He teaches him to "hic" and to "hac," which they'll do fast enough of themselves, and to call "horum,"— fie upon you! (IV.i.65–68)[54]

53. Colman, p. 82.

54. Colman, p. 82, points out that the "puns *genitive case/Jenny's case* and *horum/whore* are straightforward enough. Less obvious to the modern ear is what may also be a pun

As the scene draws toward a conclusion, Evans asks William to decline pronouns, something William has forgotten how to do. This elicits some final unintentional bawdy from the Parson, who tells William, "It is *qui, quae, quod:* if you forget your *qui's,* your *quae's,* and your *quod's,* you must be preeches" (IV.i.77–79). Colman is dubious about allowing a pun on "qui's" (keys / penises); "quod's" (cods / testicles) he feels is likely. Given what we have in this scene an argument for the pun, as made by Helge Kökeritz, does not seem at all far-fetched.[55]

Colman has commented on this scene as a whole that "Although we are nowadays too many removes from Lily's Latin Grammar to enjoy Sir Hugh Evans and Mistress Quickly to the full, it is easy to imagine that some word-conscious theatergoers of 1597 or 1598 would have found them funny. If, also, we bear in mind that the audience at any court performance—during a Feast of the Garter, for example—would have had a great deal more than 'small Latine', it becomes easy to envisage Shakespeare indulging himself and them by returning, at least for one short scene, to bawdy for simple laughter's sake."[56] It may be that we as casual theatergoers are too many removes from the propensities of the past to appreciate this scene fully, but those knowledgeable in the kinds of literature examined in this study can of course appreciate the humor fully. This scene may be bawdy "for simple laughter's sake," but it is not at all out of place in a play that is informed by bawdy literature throughout.[57] And it is a brilliant example of Shake-

---

Harum/hare—assuming, that is, that in Shakespeare's own day the Latin word would have been given the pronunciation ['hearan]. From classical times, and very extensively in medieval art, both the hare and the rabbit have enjoyed associations with lust and fecundity, and if a director of *The Merry Wives* were to ask his Mistress Quickly to register indignation over William's *Harum* he could quote in support Mercutio's "old hare hoar' jingle. . . ."

55. Helge Kökeritz, *Shakespeare's Pronunciation* (New Haven: Yale Univ. Press, 1953), p. 119.

56. Colman, p. 83.

57. Since Colman is interested in tracing Shakespeare's development in his use of bawdy, he sees the play as a whole in the following terms (p. 84):

In broad outline, then, the use of bawdy in *The Merry Wives* of Windsor comes to look like this: Falstaff speaks commercially at the start, erotically near the end, thus providing some immediate pretext for his ill-treatment, but also, paradoxically, increasing the kind of authority with which the play endows him; the Host speaks with corpological mockery of the French physician, who in turn helps Sir Hugh Evans and Mistress Quickly to mangle and confuse the language of everyday middle-class life. Ford, lonely in his supposed cuckoldom, mutters and shouts jealously, obsessed by the thing he fears. The bourgeois wives, although 'merry' enough for an occasional vulgar quip, are essentially too prim to be outspoken on sexual matters. Slender, for all his awkwardness, only once blunders into impropriety—'three veneys for a dish

speare's ability to create a mind bound to see bawdiness everywhere, as he does with Mistress Quickly.

The reader of Shakespeare's *Merry Wives* finds his understanding of the play enriched throughout by a knowledge of Renaissance erotica, for such a reader understands the variations Shakespeare plays on the typical jest plot, appreciates the rich punning throughout, and admires the comic use Shakespeare makes of a mind bound to see bawdiness even in the most innocent of places. Even if *The Merry Wives* is not one of Shakespeare's great plays, it is one that we can still enjoy immensely, and it is one in which the enjoyment grows within the context of erotica.

IV

Perhaps no poet of the English Renaissance recognized more clearly the power in the sense of sight to arouse erotic impulses than Edmund Spenser. *The Faerie Queene* brims with episodes, major and minor, where characters and readers alike are enticed, tempted, and tested by the allure of physical female beauty. Such instances are not confined to Petrarchan catalogues of angelic hair, death-dealing eyes, rosy cheeks, coral lips, ivory necks, and alabaster skin. For example, in Guyon's encounter with the maidens at Acrasia's fountain in the Bower of Bliss in Book II (long ago dubbed Cissie and Flossie by C. S. Lewis) both Guyon and the reader are enticed and tempted by the naked maidens as they frolic in the water. No "dainty parts" are hidden from view here. The scene in which Calepine watches the Saluage Nation prepare Serena for Sacrifice in Book VI is another episode in which the poet explores the issue of voyeurism and the power of female nudity.[58] The

---

of stewed prunes'; whereas his contrasting rival, the courtly young Fenton, never sullies his elegant verse with anything indecent.

In 1602 the First Quarto promised on its title-page "A Most pleasaunt and excellent conceited Comedie". If some loose ends in the plot and an air of hurry in the writing somewhat limit the excellence of its 'conceit', this is still a viable farce that has stood the searching test of the stage. Where the study of Shakespeare's developing use of bawdy is concerned, we should note that the indecencies here are more varied in tone and effect than in any other play so far. *The Merry Wives* can be regarded as a signpost to the increasingly specialised types of bawdy that are to operate in the plays Shakespeare writes after the turn of the century.

58. For the comments of C. S. Lewis see *The Allegory of Love* (Oxford, 1936; rpt. New York: Oxford Univ. Press, 1958), p. 331. Also see Arlene N. Okerlund, "Spenser's Wanton Maidens: Reader Psychology and the Bower of Bliss, *Publications of the Modern Language Association* 88 (1973): 62–68. On Serena and the Saluage Nation see A. C. Hamilton, *The Structure of Allegory in The Faerie Queene* (Oxford: Clarendon Press, 1961), pp. 196–99; Paul Alpers, *The Poetry of The Faerie Queene* (Princeton: Princeton Univ.

power of female beauty is perhaps most centrally examined in the Florimell-Marinell story in the middle books of the poem, where Spenser involves himself in the neoplatonic debate as to which sense, sight or hearing, is best suited to the apprehension of beauty, a debate we have seen treated in the paintings of Titian.[59]

All of the episodes mentioned above might be profitably reexamined within the context of erotica. Of even more interest within this context, however, because it is written by one who understands the power of images and the meaning of myths, is Spenser's treatment of the loves of the gods as they appear in two sets of tapestries in Book III of *The Faerie Queene,* the story of Venus and Adonis depicted in Malecasta's Castle Joyous in the first canto of Book III and the tapestries in the House of Busyrane in canto xi of Book III. If a Perino del Vaga found the loves of the gods a convenient cover for presenting sexually explicit material, Spenser, learned reader and master shaper of myth, understood that whatever allegorical interpretations one might find in the loves of the gods, the actions of the narratives presented a fundamental truth—the gods, when driven by what was essentially lust in the pursuit of mortal loves, were examplars of bestiality and destructiveness. That Spenser should present the amorous escapades of the gods within his poem as narratives depicted in tapestries brings a further complexity and richness to his treatment, concerned as he is with audience response, for here both reader and a viewer within the poem serve as audience.

C. S. Lewis pointed out that Spenser "is fond of describing pictures or tapestries" and that "he usually put such artefacts in places which he thinks are evil." Lewis goes on to note that it "would be rash to infer from this that the poet disliked pictures: his practice is probably a calculated device and not a mere slavish obedience to temperament."[60] What Lewis so adeptly demonstrates is that Spenser often "uses art to suggest the artificial in its bad sense—the sham or imitation" and such art is contrasted with the natural.[61] One of the examples Lewis uses to

---

Press, 1967), pp. 321–24; Humphrey Tonkin, *Spenser's Courteous Pastoral* (Oxford: Oxford Univ. Press, 1972), pp. 100–106; and James Nohrnberg, *The Analogy of The Faerie Queene* (1976; rpt. Princeton: Princeton Univ. Press, 1980), pp. 662–63, 710–16. One should note that Spenser's intention in the Serena episode is made clear in a number of ways, not the least of which is the variation he plays on the *topos* of the descending catalogue. The description of Serena omits her face entirely and begins with her ivory neck and alabaster breast.

59. See chapter 4, pp. 134–36; and my article "The Union."

60. Lewis, *Allegory,* p. 326.

61. Ibid., pp. 327–28.

illustrate his point is Spenser's use of the Venus and Adonis story. The "pictured Venus and Adonis" on the tapestries at the Castle Joyous in canto i of Book III is a "bad Venus," a Venus not of " 'lust in action' but of lust suspended—lust turning into what would now be called *skeptophilia.*"[62] In contrast, the Venus and Adonis in the Garden of Adonis in the center of Book III, canto vi, are not artificial but real and good, "actual fruition."[63] These two instances serve admirably to illustrate Spenser's adept use of myth, shaping it in one instance to further an understanding of generation and in the other to serve as an exemplum of lust, especially the central role the eyes play in fueling illicit fires.

The tapestry depicting the story of Venus and Adonis is only one of many elements in the Castle Joyous designed to provide an atmosphere in which the residents swim deeply in "sensuall desires."[64] For example, the Italianate nature of the Castle and its knights is an important part of this setting, but the emphasis on sight in the narrative told by the tapestry is a keynote for the actions of Malecasta and prepares us for the wounding of Britomart by Gardante at the end of the episode.[65]

When Red Cross Knight and Britomart are first brought into the great hall of the Castle Joyous their eyes are assaulted by a richness the poet claims he cannot display:

> The royall riches and exceeding cost,
> Of euery pillour and of euery post;
> Which all of purest bullion framed were,
> And with great pearles and pretious stones embost,
> That the bright glister of their beames cleare
> Did sparckle forth great light, and glorious did appeare. (III.i.32)

The "image of superfluous riotize" is everywhere, and the knights wonder at the "sumptuous guize" (III.i.33). The walls of the castle "apparelled / With costly clothes of *Arras* and of *Toure*" (III.i.34) present, in narrative detail, the traditional story of Venus and Adonis. As has already been noted, the tapestries do *not* depict lust in action; rather,

---

62. Ibid., pp. 331–32.
63. Ibid., p. 331.
64. Edmund Spenser, *The Faerie Queene,* ed. T. P. Roche, Jr. (Harmondsworth, Middlesex: Penguin Books, 1978), III.i.39. All subsequent references are to this edition.
65. This episode has been treated extensively. See especially Roche, *Kindly Flame,* pp. 70–71. On the Italian knights see Alastair Fowler, "Six Knights at Castle Joyous," *Studies in Philology* 56 (1959): 583–99. This episode serves as a nice example of the paradoxical relationship of England and Italy in the Renaissance. In the book in which he imitates and utilizes Ariosto most extensively, Spenser includes episodes that are most critical of Italianate behavior.

they depict Venus' obsession with Adonis, her attempts to win his love, her feasting upon him with her eyes:

> And whilst he slept, she ouer him would spred
> Her mantle, colour'd like the starry skyes,
> And her soft arme lay vnderneath his hed,
> And with ambrosiall kisses bathe his eyes;
> And whilest he bath'd, with her two crafty spyes,
> She secretly would search each daintie lim. (III.i.36)

I believe that Spenser chooses to emphasize viewing in the amorous actions described here because that is what serves his allegorical purpose at this point in the narrative of Britomart. As we will learn in the subsequent cantos, Britomart's initiation into love began with seeing an image of Arthegall in a mirror, so she has some understanding of this sense in a positive process of love. But the Knight of Chastity does not as yet understand the power of seeing as part of a negative process in "love." She is very much unschooled in the "art" of love, as her nocturnal encounter with Malecasta is to bear out. Britomart does not understand the import of the tapestries, and she does not read the telltale sign that Malecasta is "badly chaste": "Her wanton eyes, ill signes of womanhed, / Did roll too lightly, and too often glaunce, / Without regard of grace, or comely amenaunce" (III.i.41). Indeed, through the evening Malecasta will "roue at her with crafty glaunce" and throw "secret darts," but to no avail (III.i.50–51). Britomart, unlike Hellenore in Malbecco's castle, does understand such "lewd lore" (III.ix.28). The Venus of the tapestries is a lustful, predatory Venus, a fitting reflection of Malecasta to any sufficiently "initiated" to understand that fact. The love of this goddess is surely fitting at this stage of Britomart's development; depictions of Aretine "positions" would hardly be an appropriate test for Britomart (or the reader) at this juncture. The tapestries at the House of Busyrane at the end of Book III are quite another matter.

Britomart's encounter with Busyrane at the end of Book III, in which the Knight of Chastity frees Amoret from the vile enchanter, has received a great deal of critical attention ever since Roche's extended commentary on the episode in his book, *The Kindly Flame*. The House of Busyrane has been visited and revisited, interpreted and reinterpreted, considered and reconsidered.[66] Nonetheless it remains one of

66. See Roche, *Kindly Flame,* pp. 72–88; Nohrnberg, pp. 471–90; Helen Gardner, "Some Reflections on the House of Busyrane," *Review of English Studies* 34 (1983): 403–13; Roche, "Britomart at Busyrane's Again, or, Brideshead Revisited," *Spenser at Kalamazoo, 1983,* pp. 121–41; Alastair Fowler, *Triumphal Forms* (Cambridge: Cambridge Univ. Press, 1970), pp. 47–58.

the most elusive and complex episodes in the poem. This is so in part because Busyrane himself has never been explicated to everyone's satisfaction, and because the wound that Britomart receives continues to be a matter of controversy. There has not, however, been much controversy over the scenes depicted in the tapestries of the first room in the House of Busyrane—they depict the loves of the gods in intricate detail, all to the end of displaying cruel Cupid's "powre and great effort" (III.xi.46). These tapestries are themselves described in great detail, and in Roche's judgment the

> . . . description of these tapestries is one of Spenser's greatest poetic achievements. His mastery of the stanza never once falters. This passage has been quoted out of context so often that its function in may be overlooked. Its main purpose, however, is its depiction of the gods' debasing themselves in pursuit of love. Jove appears in all his animal metamorphoses, ravishing his mortal loves. The pull of the verse is overwhelming, showing the ease and attraction of sin, but we should not ignore the fact that it is a picture of love as bestiality. The description of Apollo's love illustrates another aspect of debasement. Apollo, the god of light, destroys his mortal loves—Daphne, Hyacinth, and Coronis; they are all transformed into flowers. And so it is with Neptune and Saturn and Mars and Venus and even Cupid himself. The love of a god and a mortal brings debasement for the god and possible destruction for the mortal.[67]

Any reader who has paused over these verses would hardly take issue with Roche's judgment about Spenser's command of his verse here. But I do not think that we are pulled by the verse to see the ease and attraction of sin. *That* is the test of Cissie and Flossie in Acrasia's pool. Spenser does not use the loves of the gods to test us with sexually explicit scenes; rather, these are Busyrane's tapestries, designed to depict the debasing and fearful power of lust. These are not depictions analogous to the drawings of a Giulio Romano, an Agostino Carracci, or a Perino del Vaga. Spenser would have us see the loves of the gods as unambiguous here. The first two stanzas introducing the tapestries signal the poet's intention. First we are told

For round about, the wals yclothed were
  With goodly arras of great maiesty,
  Wouen with gold and silke so close and nere,
  That the rich metall lurked priuily,
  As faining to be hid from enuious eye;
  Yet here, and there, and euery where vnwares
  It shewd it selfe, and shone vnwillingly;

67. Roche, *Kindly Flame,* pp. 84–85.

> Like a discolourd Snake, whose hidden snares
> Through the greene gras his long bright burnisht backe declares. (III.xi.28)

The "lurking" of the gold, pretending "to be hid from enuious eye" alerts us to a deceitful quality in the tapestry in terms of its richness, and the comparison with a snake is ominous indeed.

The second stanza describing the tapestries does tell us that in these works "Many faire pourtraicts, and many a faire feate, / And all of loue, and all of lusty-hed" are shown, but we are told what these are:

> And eke all *Cupids* warres they did repeate,
> And cruell battels, which he whilome fought
> Gainst all the Gods, to make his empire great;
> Besides the huge massacres, which he wrought
> On mighty kings and kesars, into thraldome brought. (III.xi.29)

In what follows, Spenser, reworking a passage from Ovid's *Metamorphoses* (VI.103–28) that tells the story of the weaving contest between Minerva and Arachne, describes twelve metamorphoses of Jove, four of Apollo, five of Neptune, one each of Saturn and Bacchus. The poet concludes with Mars' reduction to "wommanish teares" and shrieking for love of Venus and "many other Nymphes." In virtually every instance what is made explicit is the power of lust to debase, besot, and destroy. What is *not* made explicit is the sexual activity itself. As anyone who has read Spenser carefully knows, such an omission does not stem from any reluctance on Spenser's part to celebrate human sexual love. One example should suffice to illustrate this point. We are told of Jove that

> Twise was he seene in soaring Eagles shape,
>   And with wide wings to beat the buxome ayre,
>   Once, when he with *Asterie* did scape,
>   Againe, when as the *Troiane* boy so faire
> He snatcht from *Ida* hill, and with him bare:
>   Wondrous delight it was, there to behould,
>   How the rude Shepheards after him did stare,
>   Trembling through feare, least down he fallen should
> And often to him calling, to take surer hould.
>
> In *Satyres* shape *Antiopa* he snatcht:
>   And like a fire, when he *Aegin'* assayd:
>   A shepheard, when *Mnemsoyne* he catcht:
>   And like a Serpent to the *Thracian* mayd. (III.xi.34–35)

The one possible exception to this generalization about the tapestries is Spenser's depiction of Jove's rape of Leda:

> Then was he turnd into a snowy Swan,
>> To win faire *Leda* to his louely trade:
>> O wondrous skill, and sweet wit of the man,
>> That her in daffadillies sleeping made,
>> From scorching heat her daintie limbes to shade:
>> Whiles the proud Bird ruffing his fethers wyde,
>> And brushing his faire brest, did her inuade;
>> She slept, yet twixt her eyelids closely spyde,
> How towards her he rusht, and smiled at his pryde. (III.xi.32)[68]

Leda obviously does not object to her introduction to Jove's "trade"; indeed our attention is drawn to the fact that she sees what is happening and smiles at Jove's heated condition.[69] But we also do not forget that Jove has transformed himself from his majesty to a swan and that from this act will come "the broken wall, the burning roof and tower / And Agamemnon dead."[70]

All of the escapades of Jove serve the usurping claims of Cupid:

> Whiles thus on earth great *Ioue* these pageaunts playd,
> The winged boy did thrust into his throne,
> And scoffing, thus vnto his mother sayd,
> Lo now the heauens obey to me alone,
> And take me for their *Ioue,* whiles *Ioue* to earth is gone. (III.xi.35)

After some seventeen and half stanzas describing the loves of the gods, the poet can go no further in describing Cupid's triumph (in which he has included both himself and Venus):

> But to declare the mournfull Tragedyes,
> And spoiles, wherewith he all the ground did strow,
> More eath to number, with how many eyes
> High heauen beholds sad louers nightly theeueryes.
>
> Kings Queenes, Lords Ladies, Knights & Damzels gent
> Were heap'd together with the vulgar sort,
> And mingled with the raskall rablement,
> Without respect of person or of port,
> To shew Dan *Cupids* powre and great effort. (III.xi.45–46)

68. The Rape of Danaë in stanza 31 is rendered in less negative terms than some of the others, but there is no mention of the compliance or pleasure that is present in the Rape of Leda.

69. "Pride" was a term commonly used to describe animals in heat.

70. There are different versions of the myth; in some the result of Jove's union with Leda is said to be Helen; in others Castor and Pollux are mentioned as the offspring. The reduction of lovers to the bestial is given an interesting twist in Sidney's *Astrophel and Stella*. See Daniel Traister, "Sidney's Purposeful Humor: *Astrophel and Stella* 59 and 83," *English Literary History* 49 (1982): 751–64.

There is no order in a world where all are subject to the power of Cupid.

In this episode, Britomart understands what she sees, and so do we. In these stanzas we are not enticed or tempted, nor is Britomart. These loves of the gods are negative exempla and presented as such. Britomart's education is sufficiently advanced so that she sees lust for what it is and moves beyond the room of tapestries to the room of golden overlay and beyond that to her encounter with Busyrane. The embodiment of chastity, fruitful and faithful married love for Spenser, knows the difference between lust and the fruitful sexual intercourse of a loving husband and wife. If the loves of the gods of antiquity became for some Italian Renaissance artists a means by which they could explore human sexual activity, Spenser needed no such cover.

Spenser's treatment of the loves of the gods provides a fitting conclusion for this chapter, reminding us as it does of the Renaissance sense of a tradition of erotica, England's complex relationship with Italy, the relationship of the literary and visual arts, and problems of audience response. All of the writers treated in this chapter work with a context of erotica firmly in mind and count upon their readers' familiarity with that context as well. With the recovery of that context, we can see the works treated in this chapter in a richer, more varied light.

Conclusion

The range of materials covered in this study is wide in terms of time, place, context, and taste; general conclusions and speculations are best made with a good deal of scepticism. Indeed one conclusion which might be readily made is that this range itself has been yet another factor that has inhibited scholarly investigation of erotica. On one major point, however, I would hope that there could be little argument: that there is a significant body of Renaissance artistic material which is most appropriately called "erotica." It is a body that we have been reluctant to see, whereas Renaissance writers and painters and readers and viewers saw it, understood it, and worked within its contexts and traditions.

Beyond this primary point, there are questions, judgments, and puzzles of infinite variety. Were I to generalize, for example, about the quality of Renaissance erotica vis-à-vis the erotica of other eras, I would begin by saying that it is certainly as varied as that of any era. We find it in sprightly dialogues, sonnets, and prose fiction; we see it in paintings, prints, epigrams, epics, shorter narrative poems, paradoxical encomia, and plays. Some of it is superbly done; some of it is poorly done. This is readily apparent in contrasting the works of Aretino with those of his less talented disciples, or comparing a good Donne poem with a poor one. In my opinion Aretino's dialogues, Nashe's attacks on Harvey, Giulio Romano's prints, are masterpieces of their kind.

Of the kinds of erotica discussed in this study, it is notable that Italy produces a good deal more of what I have classified as pornography than does England. One wonders why this is so. Social, economic, religious, political, and intellectual conditions are all factors, of course. To an educated man in England a wide range of such literature was already available in Italian. Perhaps there was no need felt to produce a national pornography, as there was to produce a national epic; pornography appeals to the sexual, not the civic, nature of human beings, after all. The same kind of question might be asked about the visual arts in general and erotica in the visual arts in particular. Why does England produce so little compared with Italy? In part the answers to such questions are so deeply imbedded in a web of cultural and political

253

factors that it is impossible to tease them out. Can we explain with any sense of certainty why, for example, the English are so much more taken with the scatological in their jokes and insults than the Italians? Or why the English so favor the epigram as a form particularly fit for their bawdy? There is no end to such questions and speculations.

There is a final point to be made. I have argued, to return to the metaphor of my introduction, that there is a canvas in the Renaissance palazzo of artistic production that is rightly called "erotica." When we see this painting for what it is, the context and appreciation for our sense of all the paintings that constitute the "Renaissance" are forever altered, for we cannot pretend that it does not exist. The time may come when we will once again want to expurgate, alter, cover, extirpate, or hide away these materials, but if we do so, we shall impoverish ourselves and our view of the cultural creations of other people in other times. One hopes that this will never happen, especially because the canvas "Renaissance erotica" has not been completely revealed. In the opening of the final chapter I mentioned a number of topics that I might have covered; certainly they have a place on that canvas. And no doubt there is much still to be discovered in manuscript form or underneath frescoes of the seventeenth, eighteenth, and nineteenth centuries. Indeed there is still much to be discussed that is before us in print. We need only to look and then acknowledge what we see.

One might stop, if not conclude, by stating that there has been an explosion of erotica and writing about erotica in our time, and we are beginning to learn what questions to ask about it, even if we have not and will not ever explain this phenomenon in a satisfactory manner. Perhaps more significant study of erotica of the past in all of its manifestations will now be undertaken; this study ends with knowledge that it is only a beginning.

Bibliography

Primary Works

Alciati, Andrea. *Andreae Alciati Emblematum flumen abundans.* Lyons ed. by Bonhomme, 1551. Facsimile reprint. Edited by Henry Green. Manchester Pub. for the Holbein Society by A. Brothers, 1871.

———. *Andreae Alciati Emblematum fontes quatuor.* Augsberg ed., 1531: Paris ed., 1534; Venice ed., 1546. Facsimile reprints. Edited by Henry Green. Manchester Pub. for the Holbein Society by A. Brothers, 1870.

The Anathomie of Sinne. London, 1603.

Aretino, Pietro. *Aretino's Dialogues.* Translated by Raymond Rosenthal. New York: Stein & Day, 1971.

———. *Dubbi amorosi.* Paris: Grangé, 1757.

———. *Dubbi amorosi, altri dubbi, et sonetti lussuriosi.* "Fottropoli" [Paris?]: Grangé [?], n.d.

———. *La Prima (e seconda parte del Ragionamento).* "Bengodi" [London], 1584.

———. *The Ragionamenti.* 6 vols. Paris: Isidore Liseux, 1880.

———. *Sei Giornate.* Edited by Giovanni Aquilecchia. Bari: Gius. Laterza & Figli, 1969.

———. *Tutte le opere di Pietro Aretino.* Vol. 1. *Lettere, Il Primo e il Secondo Libro.* Edited by F. Flora. Milan: Arnoldo Mondadori, 1960.

———. *The Works of Pietro Aretino.* 2 vols. Translated by Samuel Putnam. New York: Covici-Friede, 1933.

Ariosto, Lodovico. *Commedie e satire.* Annotated by Giovanni Tortoli. Florence: Barbera, Bianchi, 1856.

———. *Ludovico Ariosto's "Orlando Furioso."* Translated by Sir John Harington. Edited by Robert McNulty. Oxford: Oxford Univ. Press, 1972.

L'Arretin d'Augustin Carrache. N.p., 1798.

Ascham, Roger. *The Scholemaster.* In *The English Works of Ascham.* Edited by W. A. Wright. Cambridge: Cambridge Univ. Press, 1904.

Athenian Sport: or, Two Thousand Paradoxes Merrily Argued. London, 1707.

B., R. *A Happy Husband.* London, 1618.

Beccadelli, Antonio. *L'oeuvre priapique des anciens et des modernes.* Paris: Bibliothèque des Curieux, 1907.

Berni, Francesco. *Opere Burlesche del Berni, Casa, Varchi, Mauro.* Venice, 1603.

———. *Opere di Francesco Berni.* 2 vols. Milan: G. Daelli, 1864.

———. *Rime Facete.* Edited by Ettore Bruni. Milan: Rizzoli, 1959.

————. *Vita di Pietro Aretino.* Milan: G. Daelli, 1864.

Bolton, R. *The Carnall Professor.* London, 1634.

Breton, N. *Poems.* Edited by Jean Robertson. Liverpool: Liverpool Univ. Press, 1952.

Bry, Joah. Theodorum de. *Proscenium vitae humanae, siue Emblematum Secularium.* Frankfurt, 1627.

Bryce, Thomas. *Against filthy writing.* N.p., 1562.

Burton, Robert. *The Anatomy of Melancholy.* Edited by A. R. Shilleto. 3 vols. London: Bell & Sons, 1893.

Campani, Niccolo. *Lamento.* Venice, 1523.

Caro, Annibale. *Commento di Ser Agresto da Ficarvolo, sopra la prima Ficata del Padre Siceo.* In *La Prima Parte de Ragionamenti di M. Pietro Aretino.* "Bengodi" [London], 1584.

————. *Rime.* Venice: Aldi Filii, 1569.

Cartari, Vincenzo. *Le Imagini de i Dei De gli Antichi.* Venice, 1571.

————. *Le Imagini de gli Dei Delli Antichi.* 2nd ed. Padua, 1626.

Castiglione, B. *The Book of the Courtier.* Translated by Charles S. Singleton. Garden City, N.Y.: Doubleday, Anchor Books, 1959.

————. *Il Cortegiano.* Translated by Thomas Hoby. In *Literature of Italy.* New York: National Alumni, 1907.

Cavallino, Antonio. *La Tariffa delle Puttane Di Venegia.* Paris: Isidore Liseux, 1883.

Certaine sermons appoynted by the Queenes Maiestie, to be declared and read, by all Parsons, Vicars, and Curates, euery Sunday and Holy day in their Churches: and ouerseene, for the better vnderstanding of the symple people. N.p., 1576.

Chubb, Thomas, trans. *The Letters of Pietro Aretino.* Hamden, CT: Shoe String Press, Archon Books, 1967.

Colonna, Francesco. *Hypnerotomachia Poliphili.* 2 vols. Edited by Giovanni Pozzi and Lucia Ciapponi. Padua: Antenore, 1980.

Conti, Natale. *Mythologiae.* Venice, 1568.

Cooke, Richard. *A White sheete, or a warning for Whoremongers.* Sermon. London, 1629.

Cornazano, Antonio. *Proverbs in Jests.* Literally translated into English with the Italian text. Paris: Isidore Liseux, 1888.

Cranley, T. *Amanda: or The Reformed Whore.* London, 1635.

Davies, Sir John. *Nosce Teipsum.* In *Silver Poets of the Sixteenth Century.* Edited by Gerald Bullett. London: Everyman Ed., 1962.

————. *The Poems of Sir John Davies.* Edited by Robert Krueger. Oxford: Clarendon Press, 1975.

The Deceyte of Women. London, 1569.

Dolce, Lodovico. *Dialogo della Pittura, Intitolato l'Aretino.* In *Tratti D'Arte Del Cinquecento.* Vol. 1. Edited by Paola Barocchi. Bari, 1960.

Domenichi, Lodovico. *Facetie.* Venice, 1568.

Doni, Antonio Francesco. *La Chiave.* In *Scelta di Curiosita Letterarie Inedite o Rare Dal Secolo 13 al 19.* Vol. 1. Bologna, 1862–present.

————. *La Libraria.* Venice, 1550. 3rd ed. Venice, 1558.

————. *I Marmi*. Venice, 1552–53.

————. *Pistolotti Amorosi*. Venice, 1552. 2 vols. Venice, 1554.

————. *Teremoto*. N.p., 1556.

————. *La Vita dello Infame Aretino*. Edited by Costantino Arlia. Citta di Castello, 1901.

Donne, John. *The Complete Poetry of John Donne*. Edited by John T. Shawcross. Garden City, N.Y.: Doubleday, Anchor Books, 1967.

————. *John Donne: The Elegies and the Songs and Sonnets*. Edited by Helen Gardner. Oxford: Clarendon Press, 1965.

Esame Critico sulla Vita di Pietro Aretino. Edited by Giuseppe Battelli. Turin, 1888.

Fennor, W. *Cornu-copiae*. London, 1612.

————. *Pasquils Palinodia and His Progress to the Taverne*. London, 1619.

Florio, John. *Queen Anna's New World of Words*. London, 1611.

————. *A Worlde of Wordes*. London, 1598.

Fracastoro, Girolamo. *The Sinister Shepherd: A Translation of Girolamo Fracastoro's Syphilides sive de morbo gallico libri tres*. Translated by William Van Wyck. Los Angeles: Primavera Press, 1934.

Franco, Niccolo. *Delle rime di M. Nicolo Franco contro Pietro Aretino, et de la Priapea del medesimo*. London, 1887.

————. *Dialogi Piacevoli*. Venice, 1554.

————. *Le Pistole Vulgari*. Venice, 1539.

————. *La Puttana Errante*. Bound in the back of Meursii, Johannes the Younger, *Elegantiae Latini Sermonis*. Venice, n.d.

————. *Sonetti lussuriosi e satirici con la priapea*. Alvisopoli, 1850.

Gallonio, Antonio. *Martyrvm Crvciatibus*. Rome, 1594.

Garzoni, T. *L'Hospidale De' Pazzi Incvrabili*. Venice, 1601.

————. *The Hospitall of Incvrable Fooles*. London, 1600.

————. *Opere*. Venice, 1605.

Goodcole, H. *Heavens Speedie Hue and Cry sent after Lust and Murthur*. London, 1635.

Goodman, G. *The Fall of Man*. London, 1616.

Gosson, S. *Playes Confuted in Fiue Actions*. London, n.d.

————. *The School of Abuse*. Reprint. London: Shakespeare Society, 1841.

Gosynhill, Edward. *The Scholehouse of Women*. N.p., 1561.

Gottifredi, Bartolomeo. *Specchio d'Amore*. In *Trattati d' amore del Cinquecento*. Edited by Giuseppi Zonta. 1912. Reprint. Bari: Gius. Laterza & Figli, 1967.

Greene, Robert. *The Life and Complete Works in Prose of Robert Greene*. Edited by A. B. Grosart. 15 vols. London and Aylesbury: Huth Library, 1881–86.

Guilpin, Everard. *Skialetheia*. Edited by D. Allen Carroll. Chapel Hill: Univ. of North Carolina Press, 1974.

Hall, Joseph. *The Collected Poems of Joseph Hall*. Edited by A. Davenport. Liverpool: Liverpool Univ. Press, 1949.

Harington, Sir John. *The Letters and Epigrams of Sir John Harington*. Edited by Norman E. McClure. Philadelphia: Univ. of Pennsylvania Press, 1930.

————. *A New Discourse of a Stale Subject, called the Metamorphosis of Ajax*.

Edited by Elizabeth Story Donno. London: Routledge & Kegan Paul; New York: Columbia Univ. Press, 1962.

Harrison, G. B. *The Elizabethan Journals.* Edited and abridged by G. B. Harrison. 2 vols. Garden City, N.Y.: Doubleday, Anchor Books, 1965.

Harrison, W. *Description of England.* Edited by F. J. Furnivall from the first two editions of *Holinshed's Chronicle:* 1577, 1587. London: N. Trubner, 1877–81.

Harvey, Gabriel. *Gabriel Harvey's Marginalia.* Edited by G. C. Moore Smith. Stratford-Upon-Avon: Shakespeare Head Press, 1913.

———. *The Works of Gabriel Harvey.* Edited by A. B. Grosart. 3 vols. London: Huth Library, 1884–85.

Hazlitt, W. C. ed. *Shakespeare Jest-Books.* 3 vols. 1864. Reprint. New York: Burt Franklin, 1964.

Heywood, John. *The Proverbs, Epigrams, and Miscellanies of John Heywood.* Edited by John S. Farmer. London: Early English Drama Society, 1906.

Hynd, J. *Eliosto Libidinoso.* London, 1606.

Jonson, Ben. *Volpone.* In *Ben Jonson: Three Plays.* Edited by Brinsley Nicholson and C. H. Herford. New York: Hill & Wang, A Mermaid Dramabook, 1957.

L., H. *Gratiae Ludentes. Iests From the Universitie.* London, 1628.

Lando, O. *Conmentario delle pui notabile et mostruose cose d'Italia.* Venice, 1548.

———. *Paradossi.* Venice, 1544.

———. *Quattro Libri de dubbi.* Venice, 1552.

———. *Sette Libri de Cathaloghi A Varie Cose, Appartenenti, Non Solo Antiche, Ma Anche Moderne: Opera Vtile Molto Alla Historia, et Da Cui Prender. Si Po Materia de Fauellare D'Ogni Proposito Che ci Occorra.* Venice, 1552–53.

———. *I Varii Componimenti.* Venice, 1552.

Ling, N. *Politeuphuia.* 3rd ed. London, 1598.

Lucian. *Selected Satires of Lucian.* Edited and translated by Lionel Casson. Chicago: Aldine Publishing Co., 1962.

Marlowe, Christopher. *The Complete Poems and Translations.* Edited by Stephan Orgel. Harmondsworth, Middlesex: Penguin Books, 1971.

Marston, John. *The Malcontent.* Edited by Barnard Harris. New York: Hill & Wang. A Mermaid Dramabook, 1967.

———. *The Malcontent.* Edited by M. L. Wine. Lincoln: Univ. of Nebraska Press, 1964.

———. *The Poems of John Marston.* Edited by A. Davenport. Liverpool: Liverpool Univ. Press, 1961.

Martial. *Epigrams.* Translated by Walter C. A. Ker. 2 vols. London: William Heinemann, 1930.

Molza, F. M. *La Figueide.* In *Caro.* N.p., 1886.

———. *Quattro Novelle.* Lucca, 1869.

Nashe, T. *The Works of Thomas Nashe.* Edited by R. B. McKerrow. Reprint edited by F. P. Wilson. 5 vols. Oxford: Basil Blackwell, 1958.

Parrot, H. *Laquei ridiculosi: or Springes for Woodcocks.* London, 1613.

Perkins, W. *The Works of William Perkins.* London, 1596–97.

Piccolomini, A. *Dialogo dove si Roggiona della Bella Creanza Delle Donne*. Venice, 1539.

Pick, S. *Festum Voluptatis, or the Banquet of Pleasure*. London, 1639.

Priapeia. N.p.: Erotika Biblion Society, 1888.

Poggio Bracciolini, G. F. *The Facetiae*. Translated by B. J. Hurwood. New York: Award Books, 1968.

Randall, J. *The Description of Fleshly Lusts*. London, 1622.

Rankins, William. *The English Ape, the Italian Imitation, The Foote-Steppes of Fraunce*. N.p., 1588.

———. *A Mirrour of Monsters*. London, 1587.

Ripa, Cesare. *Iconologia*. Rome, 1603.

Rowlands, S. *The Complete Works of Samuel Rowlands*. 3 vols. Glasgow: R. Anderson, 1880.

The Roxburghe Ballads. Edited by Charles Hindley. 2 vols. London: Reeves & Turner, 1873.

Sackful of News. In *Elizabethan Prose Fiction*. Edited by Merritt Lawlis. New York: Odyssey Press, 1967.

Salter, T. *The Mirrhor of Modestie*. London, 1579.

Shakespeare, W. *The Complete Pelican Shakespeare*. Edited by Alfred Harbage. Baltimore: Penguin Books, 1969.

———. *The Riverside Shakespeare*. Edited by G. Blakemore Evans. Boston: Houghton Mifflin, 1974.

Speght, R. *A Movzell for Melastomvs*. London, 1617.

Spenser, Edmund. *The Faerie Queene*. Edited by T. P. Roche, Jr. Harmondsworth, Middlesex: Penguin Books, 1978.

Stubbes, P. *The Anatomie of Abuses*. London, 1583.

Swetnam, J. *The Araignment of Lewde, Idle, Froward, and Vnconstant Women*. London, 1615.

Taylor, Jeremy. *The Rule and Exercises of Holy Living*. 1650. London: W. Pickering, 1852.

Thomas, Thomas. *Dictionarium Linguae Latinae et Anglicanae*. 1587. Reprint. Menston, Yorkshire: Scolar Press, 1972.

Thomas, William. *The History of Italy*. 1549. Reprint. Edited by George B. Parks. Ithaca, N.Y.: Cornell Univ. Press, 1963.

Timme, T. *A Discouerie of Ten English Lepers*. London, 1592.

Tofte, R. *The Bachelor's Banquet*. London(?), 1603.

Van der Noot, Jan. *A Theatre for Voluptuous Worldings*. 1569. Reprint. New York: Scholars' Facsimiles & Reprints, n.d.

Veniero, Lorenzo. *Tariffa delle puttane de Venegia*. Paris: Bibliothèque des Curieux, n.d.

———. *La Zaffetta*. Catania: Libreria Tirelli, 1929.

———. *La Zaffetta*. Paris, 1861.

Vignale, Antonio. *La Cazzaria*. Paris: Isidore Liseux, 1882.

———. *La Cazzaria*. 1530. Cosmopoli, 1863.

Wither, G. *Abuses Stript and Whipt*. London, 1613.

———. *A Collection of Emblems*. London, 1635.

Wright, T. *The Passions of the Mind in Generall*. London, 1604.

Secondary Works

Abrahams, Roger. "Playing the Dozens." In *Mother Wit from the Laughing Barrel*. Edited by Alan Dundes. Englewood Cliffs, N.J.: Prentice-Hall, 1973.

Allen, Morse. *The Satire of John Marston*. Columbus: n.p., 1920.

Alpers, Paul. *The Poetry of The Faerie Queene*. Princeton: Princeton Univ. Press, 1967.

Altick, Richard D. "Out of the Closet." *London Review of Books*, 20 August–2 September 1981, p. 12.

Anglo-Saxon Riddles of the Exeter Book. Translated by Paul F. Baum. Durham, N.C.: Duke Univ. Press, 1963.

Arber, Edward, ed. *A Transcript of the Registers of the Company of Stationers of London*. 1554–1640. London, 1876.

Arco, Mario dell'. *Pasquino E Le Pasquinate*. Milan: Aldo Martello, n.d.

Axelrad, A. J. *Un Malcontent Élizabéthain: John Marston*. Paris: Didier, 1955.

Ayoub, Millicent R., and Stephen A. Barnett. "Ritualized Verbal Insult in White High School Culture." *Journal of American Folklore* 78 (1965): 336–44.

Bachelard, Gaston. *The Poetics of Space*. Translated by Maria Jolas. New York: Orion Press, 1964.

Barocchi, Paola. *Il Rosso Fiorentino*. Rome: Qismondi Publ., 1950.

Barolsky, Paul. *Infinite Jest: Wit and Humor in Italian Renaissance Art*. Columbia: Univ. of Missouri Press, 1978.

Bartsch, Adam. *Le Peintre Graveur.* 21 vols. Leipzig: J. A. Barth, 1854–76.

Baumgartner, Leona, and Fulton, John. *A Bibliography of the Poem Syphilis sive Morbus Gallicus by Girolamo Fracastoro of Verona*. New Haven: Yale Univ. Press, 1935.

Bellori, Giovanni Pietro. *The Lives of Annibale and Agostino Carracci*. Translated by Catherine Enggass. University Park: Pennsylvania State Univ. Press, 1968.

Bennett, Joan. *Four Metaphysical Poets*. 2nd ed. New York: Vintage Books, 1953.

Bicknell, E. J. *A Theological Introduction to the Thirty-Nine Articles*. 3rd ed. rev. London: Longmans, 1961.

Bolgar, R. R. *The Classical Heritage*. Harper Torchbook Edition. New York: Harper & Row, 1964.

Bond, R. W. *Early Plays from the Italian*. Oxford: Clarendon Press, 1911.

Bonneau, Alcide. *Curiosa*. Paris: Isidore Liseux, 1887.

Bonora, Ettore. "Il Classicismo dal Bembo al Guarini." In *Storia della Letteratura Italiana*. Edited by Emilio Cecchi and Natalino Sapegno. Vol. 4. Milan: Garzanti, 1965–69.

Bousquet, Jacques. *Mannerism: The Painting and Style of the Late Renaissance*. Munich: Braziller, 1964.

Brown, A. "Citizen Comedy and Domestic Drama." *Jacobean Theater. Stratford-Upon-Avon Studies*. 1(1960): 62–83.

Brusendorff, O., and P. Hennigsen. *Love's Picture Book*. 4 vols. Copenhagen: Veta Publishers, 1960.

Bryant, Mark. *Riddles Ancient and Modern*. London: Hutchinson, 1983.

Bush, Douglas. *English Literature in the Earlier Seventeenth Century*. Rev. ed. Oxford: Clarendon Press, 1962.

———. *Mythology and the Renaissance Tradition in English Poetry*. Rev. ed. New York: W. W. Norton, 1963.

Buxton, John. *Elizabethan Taste*. New York: St. Martin's Press, 1965.

———. *Sir Philip Sidney and the English Renaissance*. London: Macmillan, 1954.

Caputi, A. *John Marston, Satirist*. Ithaca: Cornell Univ. Press, 1961.

Chastel, André. *The Golden Age of the Renaissance*. Translated by Jonathan Griffin. London: Thames & Hudson, 1965.

Charney, M. "Shakespeare's Antony: A Study of Image Themes." *Studies in Philology* 54 (1957): 149–61.

Chubb, Thomas Caldecot. *Aretino Scourge of Princes*. New York: Reynal & Hitchcock, 1940.

Clemen, W. *The Development of Shakespeare's Imagery*. New York: Hill & Wang, A Mermaid Dramabook, 1962.

Clements, Robert J. "Anatomy of the Novella." In Norton Critical ed. of Boccaccio's *Decameron*. Translated and edited by Mark Musa and Peter Bondanella. New York: W. W. Norton, 1977.

Cleugh, James. *The Divine Aretino*. New York: Stein & Day, 1966.

Colie, Rosalie. *Paradoxia Epidemica*. Princeton: Princeton Univ. Press, 1966.

Colman, E. A. M. *The Dramatic Use of Bawdy in Shakespeare*. London: Longman Group, 1974.

Colley, John Scott. "'Opinion' and the Reader in John Marston's *The Metamorphosis of Pigmalions Image*." *English Literary Renaissance* 3 (1973): 221–31.

A Concise Encyclopaedia of the Italian Renaissance. Edited by J. R. Hale. New York and Toronto: Oxford Univ. Press, 1981.

Cook, Ann. *The Privileged Playgoers of Shakespeare's London, 1576–1642*. Princeton: Princeton Univ. Press, 1981.

Craig, D. H. *Sir John Harington*. Boston: Twayne Publishers, 1985.

Crane, T. F. *Italian Social Customs of the XVI Century and Their Influence on Literature in Europe*. New Haven: Yale Univ. Press, 1920.

Crewe, Jonathan V. *Unredeemed Rhetoric: Thomas Nashe and the Scandal of Authorship*. Baltimore: Johns Hopkins Univ. Press, 1982.

Cross, G. "Marston's 'Metamorphosis of Pigmalions Image': A Mock-Epyllion." *Etudes Anglaises* 13 (1960): 331–36.

Curry, Walter Clyde. *Chaucer and the Mediaeval Sciences*. Rev. ed. New York: Barnes & Noble, 1960.

Curtius, Ernst Robert. *European Literature and the Latin Middle Ages*. Translated by Willard Trask. Harper Torchbook. New York: Harper & Row, 1963.

Davis, Walter. *Idea and Act in Elizabethan Fiction*. Princeton: Princeton Univ. Press, 1969.

De Filippis, Michele. *The Literary Riddle in Italy to the End of the Seventeenth Century*. University of California Publications in Modern Philology, no. 34. Berkeley and Los Angeles: Univ. of California Press, 1948.

Dempsey, Charles. "'Et Nos Cedamus Amori': Observations on the Farnese Gallery." *Art Bulletin* 50 (1968): 363–74.

———. "Two 'Galateas' by Agostino Carracci Re-Identified." *Zeitschrift für Kunstgeschichte* 29 (1966): 67–70.

Dollard, John. "The Dozens: Dialectic of Insult." In *Mother Wit from the Laughing Barrel.* Edited by Alan Dundes. Englewood Cliffs, N.J.: Prentice-Hall, 1973.

Dundes, Alan, ed. *Mother Wit from the Laughing Barrel.* Englewood Cliffs, N.J.: Prentice-Hall, 1973.

Dundes, Alan, et al. "The Strategy of Turkish Boys' Verbal Dueling Rhymes." In *Essays in Folkloristics.* Dehli: Folklore Institute, 1978.

Dunlap, Jan. *Palaces and Progresses of Elizabeth I.* New York: Taplinger Publishing Co., 1970.

Edgerton, Samuel Y., Jr. *Pictures and Punishment: Art and Criminal Prosecution during the Florentine Renaissance.* Ithaca and London: Cornell Univ. Press, 1985.

Einstein, L. *The Italian Renaissance in England.* New York: Columbia Univ. Press, 1902.

Farmer, J. S., and W. E. Henley. *Slang and Its Analogues.* 1890–1914. Reprint. N.p.: Arno Press, 1970.

Ferguson, W. K. *The Renaissance in Historical Thought.* Cambridge, Mass.: Houghton Mifflin, 1948.

Finkelpearl, P. "From Petrarch to Ovid: Metamorphoses in John Marston's *Metamorphosis of Pigmalions Image.*" *English Literary History* 32 (1965): 333–48.

Forberg, Friedrich Karl. *Manual of Classical Erotology.* New York: Grove Press, 1966.

Fowler, Alastair. "Six Knights at Castle Joyous." *Studies in Philology* 56 (1959): 583–99.

———. *Triumphal Forms.* Cambridge: Cambridge Univ. Press, 1970.

Foxon, David. *Libertine Literature in England 1660–1745.* New Hyde Park, N.Y.: University Books, 1965.

Frantz, David. "Florio's Use of Contemporary Italian Literature in *A Worlde of Wordes.*" *Dictionaries* 1 (1979): 47–56.

———. "The Union of Florimell and Marinell: The Triumph of Hearing." *Spenser Studies* 6 (1985): 115–27.

Freeman, R. *English Emblem Books.* London: Chatto & Windus, 1948.

Friedlaender, Walter. *Mannerism and Anti-Mannerism in Italian Painting.* New York: Schocken Books, 1967.

Fusco, Domenico. *L'Aretino Sconosciuto ed Apocrifo.* Turin: Libraria Editrice Berruto, 1953.

Gardner, Helen. "Some Reflections on the House of Busyrane." *Review of English Studies* 34 (1983): 403–13.

Garin, Eugenio. "La Letteratura degli Umanisti." In *Storia della Letteratura Italiana.* Edited by Emilio Cecchi and Natalino Sapegno. Vol. 3. Milan: Garzanti, 1965–69.

Georges, Robert A., and Alan Dundes. "Toward a Structural Definition of the Riddle." *Journal of American Folklore* 76 (1963): 111–18.

Giamatti, A. B. *The Earthly Paradise in the Renaissance Epic.* Princeton: Princeton Univ. Press, 1966.

Gilman, Richard. "There's a Wave of Pornography / Obscenity / Sexual Expression." *The New York Times Magazine,* 8 September (1968), pp. 36–37, 69–82.

Gombrich, E. H. *Norm and Form: Studies in the Art of the Renaissance.* London: Phaidon Press, 1966.

————. *Symbolic Images.* 2nd ed. London: Phaidon Press, 1978.

Gordon, Phyllis, trans. *Two Renaissance Book Hunters: The Letters of Poggius Bracciolini to Nicolaus de Niccolis.* New York and London: Columbia Univ. Press, 1974.

Gould, C. *National Gallery Catalogues; The Sixteenth-Century Italian Schools.* London, 1962.

Granville-Barker, H. *Prefaces to Shakespeare.* 2 vols. Princeton: Princeton Univ. Press, 1947.

Green, William. *Shakespeare's Merry Wives of Windsor.* Princeton: Princeton Univ. Press, 1962.

Grendler, Paul F. *Critics of the Italian World, 1530–1560: Anton Francesco Doni, Nicolo Franco and Ortensio Lando.* Madison: Univ. of Wisconsin Press, 1969.

Grierson, H. J. C. *Cross Currents in English Literature of the Seventeenth Century.* Baltimore: Penguin Books, 1966.

Haight, Elizabeth H. *Apuleius and His Influence.* New York: Longman, Green & Co., 1927.

Hamilton, A. C. *The Structure of Allegory in The Faerie Queene.* Oxford: Clarendon Press, 1961.

Hartt, Frederick. *Giulio Romano.* 2 vols. New Haven: Yale Univ. Press, 1958.

Hauser, Arnold. *The Social History of Art.* Vols. 1, 2. New York: Vintage Books, n.d.

Hay, Denys. *The Italian Renaissance in Its Historical Background.* Cambridge: Cambridge Univ. Press, 1962.

Hay, Denys, ed. *The Age of the Renaissance.* London: McGraw-Hill, 1967.

Hayden, H. *The Counter-Renaissance.* Evergreen Edition. New York: Grove Press, 1960.

Hibbard, G. R. *Thomas Nashe: A Critical Introduction.* Cambridge, Mass.: Harvard Univ. Press, 1962.

Holt, Elizabeth G. *A Documentary History of Art.* 2 vols. Garden City, N.Y. Doubleday, Anchor Books, 1958.

Hoppe, Harry R. "John Wolfe, Printer and Publisher, 1579–1601." *The Library.* 4th ser., vol. 14, no. 3 (1933): 241–88.

Hudson, H. H. *The Epigram in the English Renaissance.* 1947. Reprint. New York: Octagon Books, 1966.

Hunt, Clay. *Donne's Poetry: Essays in Literary Analysis.* New Haven: Yale Univ. Press, 1954.

Hunter, G. K. "English Folly and Italian Vice: The Moral Landscape of John Marston." *Jacobean Theater. Stratford-Upon-Avon Studies* 1 (1960): 85–112.

Hutton, Edward. *Pietro Aretino The Scourge of Princes.* London: Constable, 1922.

Hyde, Montgomery H. *A History of Pornography.* New York: Farrar, Straus & Giroux, 1964.

Le Incisioni Dei Carracci. A critical catalogue of the works by Maurizio Calvesi and Vittorio Casale with an Introduction by Maurizio Calvesi. Rome: Comunità Europea Dell'Arte e Della Cultura, 1965.

Janson, H. W. *History of Art.* New York: Prentice-Hall and Harry N. Abrams, 1964.

Jones, Robert C. "Italian Settings and the 'World' of Elizabethan Tragedy." *Studies in English Literature* 10 (1970): 251–68.

Judges, A. V. *The Elizabethan Underworld.* New York: E. P. Dutton, 1930.

Keach, William. *Elizabethan Erotic Narratives.* New Brunswick, N.J.: Rutgers Univ. Press, 1977.

Kearney, Patrick J. *The Private Case.* London: Jay Landesman Ltd., 1981.

Kernan, Alvin. *The Cankered Muse: Satire of the English Renaissance.* New Haven: Yale Univ. Press, 1959.

Kiernan, Kevin. "The Art of the Descending Catalogue, and a Fresh Look at Alisoun." *The Chaucer Review* 10 (1975): 1–16.

Kökeritz, Helge. *Shakespeare's Pronunciation.* New Haven: Yale Univ. Press, 1953.

Kolin, Philip C. "The Names of Whores and Their Bawds and Panders in English Renaissance Drama." *Midwestern Journal of Language and Folklore* 6 (1980): 41–50.

Kurz, Otto. " 'Gli Amori de' Carracci': Four Forgotten Paintings by Agostino Carracci." *Journal of The Warburg and Courtauld Institutes* 14 (1951): 221–33.

Kusenburg, Kurt. *Le Rosso.* Paris: Albin Michel Publ., 1931.

Latham, Agnes. "Satire on Literary Themes and Modes in Nashe's 'Vnfortunate Traveller.' " *English Studies* n.s. 1 (1948): 85–100.

Lawrence, D. H. *Selected Literary Criticism.* Edited by Anthony Beal. New York: Viking Press, 1966.

Lee, Rensselaer W. "*Ut Pictura Poesis:* The Humanistic Theory of Painting." *Art Bulletin* 22 (1940): 197–269.

Legman, G. *The Horn Book: Studies in Erotic Folklore and Bibliography.* New Hyde Park, N.Y.: University Books, 1964.

———. *Rationale of the Dirty Joke.* New York: Grove Press, 1968.

Leishman, J. B. *The Monarch of Wit.* Harper Torchbook ed. New York: Harper & Row, 1966.

Lell, Gorden. " 'Ganymede' on the Elizabethan Stage: Homosexual Implications of the Use of Boy-Actors." *Aegis* (1973): 5–15.

Lever, J. W. *The Elizabethan Love Sonnet.* University Paperbacks. London: Methuen & Co., 1966.

Levin, Harry. *The Myth of the Golden Age in the Renaissance.* Bloomington and London: Indiana Univ. Press, 1969.

Lewis, C. S. *The Allegory of Love.* 1936. Reprint. Galaxy Book ed. New York: Oxford Univ. Press, 1958.

——. *English Literature in the Sixteenth Century Excluding Drama.* Oxford: Clarendon Press, 1954.

Lievsay, John Leon. *The Elizabethan Image of Italy.* Folger Booklets on Tudor and Stuart Civilization. Ithaca, N.Y.: Cornell Univ. Press, 1964.

——. *The Englishman's Italian Books, 1550–1700.* Philadelphia: Univ. of Pennsylvania Press, 1969.

——. *Stefano Guazzo and the English Renaissance. 1575–1675.* Chapel Hill: Univ. of North Carolina Press, 1961.

Lopez, Robert S. *The Three Ages of the Italian Renaissance.* Charlottesville: Univ. Press of Virginia, 1970.

Loth, David. *The Erotic in Literature: A Historical Survey.* New York: Julian Messner, 1961.

Lowry, Martin. *The World of Aldus Manutius.* N.p.: Cornell Univ. Press, 1979.

Luzio, Alessandro. *Pietro Aretino Nei Primi Suoi Anni A Venezia.* Turin: Ermanno Loescher, 1888.

McPherson, David C. "Aretino and the Harvey-Nashe Quarrel." *Publications of the Modern Language Association* 84 (1969): 1551–58.

Mahon, Denis. "Eclecticism and the Carracci: Further Reflections on the Validity of a Label." *Journal of the Warburg and Courtauld Institutes* 16 (1953): 303–41.

——. *Studies in Seicento Art and Theory. Studies of the Warburg Institute* 16 (1947).

——, ed. *Mostra Dei Carracci. Catalogo Critico Dei Disegni.* Translated by Maurizio Calvesi. 2nd ed. Bologna, 1963.

Marcadé, Jean. *Roma Amor.* Geneva: Nagel Publishers, 1965.

Marcus, Steven. *The Other Victorians.* 1966. Reprint. New York: Bantam Books, 1967.

Martin, John R. *The Farnese Gallery.* Princeton: Princeton Univ. Press, 1965.

Martines, Lauro. *The Social World of the Florentine Humanists, 1390–1460.* Princeton: Princeton Univ. Press, 1963.

Mason, E. C. "Satire on Women and Sex in Elizabethan Tragedy." *English Studies* 31 (1950): 1–10.

Maylender, Michele. *Storia Delle Accademie d'Italia.* 5 vols. Bologna: Licino Cappelli, 1926–30.

Mercati, Angelo. *I Costituti di Nicolo Franco (1568–1570) dinanzi l'Inquisizione di Roma.* Vatican City, 1955.

Miller, H. K. "The Paradoxical Encomium with Special Reference to Its Vogue in England 1600–1820." *Modern Philology* 53 (1956): 145–78.

Murray, Linda. *The High Renaissance.* New York: Frederick A. Praeger, 1967.

——. *The Late Renaissance and Mannerism.* New York and Washington: Frederick A. Praeger, 1967.

Murray, Peter. "Italian Art from Masaccio to Mannerism. In *The Age of the Renaissance.* Edited by Denys Hay. London: McGraw-Hill, 1967.

Nicholl, Charles. *A Cup of News: The Life of Thomas Nashe.* London: Routledge & Kegan Paul, 1984.

Nohrnberg, James. *The Analogy of The Faerie Queene.* 1967. Reprint First Limited Paperback ed. Princeton: Princeton Univ. Press, 1980.

Okerlund, Arlene N. "Spenser's Wanton Maidens: Reader Psychology and the Bower of Bliss." *Publications of the Modern Language Association* 88 (1973): 62–68.

Panofsky, Erwin. *Meaning in the Visual Arts.* Garden City, N.Y.: Doubleday, Anchor Books, 1955.

———. *Problems in Titian: Mostly Iconographic.* New York: New York Univ. Press, 1969.

———. *Studies in Iconology.* Harper Torchbook. New York: Harper & Row, 1962.

Panofsky, Erwin, and Dora Panofsky. *Pandora's Box.* London: Routledge & Kegan Paul, 1956.

Parks, George B. "The Decline and Fall of the English Renaissance Admiration of Italy. *Huntington Library Quarterly* 31 (August 1968): 341–57.

———. *The English Traveler to Italy.* Vol. 1: *The Middle Ages to 1525.* Stanford, Calif.: Stanford Univ. Press, n.d.

Partridge, Eric. *Shakespeare's Bawdy.* New York: E. P. Dutton, 1960.

Peckham, Morse. *Art and Pornography: An Experiment in Explanation.* New York and London: Basic Books, 1969.

Pellegrini, Giuliano. *Un fiorentino alla corte d'Inghilterra nel Cinquecento: Petruccio Ubaldini.* Turin: University of Pisa Studies in Modern Philology, n.s., vii, 1967.

Prager, Leonard. "The Clown in *Othello.*" *Shakespeare Quarterly* 11 (1960): 94–96.

Praz, M. *The Flaming Heart.* Garden City, N.Y.: Doubleday, Anchor Books, 1958.

———. *Studies in Seventeenth Century Imagery.* 2 vols. London: Warburg Institute, 1939–47.

Putnam, George Haven. *Books and Their Makers During the Middle Ages.* 2 vols. 1896–97. Reprint. New York: Hilary House Publishers, 1962.

———. *The Censorship of the Church of Rome.* 2 vols. 1906. Reprint. New York: Benjamin Blom, 1967.

Reff, Theodore. "The Meaning of Titian's Venus of Urbino." *Pantheon* 21 (1963): 359–66.

Register of Erotic Books. Compiled by Alfred Rose. 1936. Reprint. 2 vols. New York: Jack Brussel, 1965.

Renda, Umberto, and Piero Operti. *Dizionario Storico della Letteratura Italiana.* New edition on original text by Vittorio Turri. 4th ed. Turin: G. B. Paravia & Co., 1959.

Richardson, John. "The Catch in the Late Picasso." *The New York Review of Books,* 19 July 1984, pp. 21–28.

Robertson, D. W., Jr. *A Preface to Chaucer.* Princeton: Princeton Univ. Press, 1962.

Robinson, Christopher. *Lucian and His Influence in Europe.* Chapel Hill: Univ. of North Carolina Press, 1979.

Robinson, Victor, ed. *Encyclopedia Sexualis.* New York: Dingwall-Rock, 1936.

Roche, T. P., Jr. "Britomart at Busyrane's Again, or, Brideshead Revisited." *Spenser at Kalamazoo, 1983,* pp. 121–41.

———. *The Kindly Flame.* Princeton: Princeton Univ. Press, 1964.

Roeder, Ralph. *The Man of the Renaissance.* 1933. Reprint. Cleveland: World, 1958.

Rollins, H. E. "Samuel Pick's Borrowings." *Review of English Studies* 7 (1931): 204.

Roskill, Mark W. *Dolce's "Aretino" and Venetian Art Theory of the Cinquecento.* New York: New York Univ. Press, 1968.

Ross, Lawrence J. "Shakespeare's 'Dull Clown' and Symbolic Music." *Shakespeare Quarterly* 17 (1966): 107–28.

Ross, Thomas W. *Chaucer's Bawdy.* New York: E. P. Dutton, 1977.

Rouchès, Gabriel. *La Peinture Bolonaise A La Fin Du XVIᵉ Siecle. Les Carrache.* Paris: Librairie Felix Alcan, 1913.

Rowland, Ingrid D. "Render unto Caesar the Things Which Are Caesar's: Humanism and the Arts in the Patronage of Agostino Chigi." *Renaissance Quarterly* 39 (1986): 673–730.

Sackton, A. "The Paradoxical Encomium in Elizabethan Drama." *Univ. of Texas Studies in English* 28 (1949): 83–104.

Samuels, Richard. "Benedetto Varchi, the *Accademia degli Infiammati,* and the Origins of the Italian Academic Movement." *Renaissance Quarterly* 29 (1976): 599–634.

Sander, Max. *Copertine Italiane Illustrate Del Rinascimento.* Milan: Hoepli, 1936.

Sandys, John Edwin. *A History of Classical Scholarship.* 2 vols. Cambridge: Cambridge Univ. Press, 1908.

Sanesi, Ireneo. *Il Cinquecentista Ortensio Lando.* Pistoia: Fratelli Bracali, 1893.

Saxl, Fritz. *A Heritage of Images.* Harmondsworth, Middlesex: Penguin Books, 1970.

Scheps, Esther. "Shade and Substance: The Problem of Morality in the Plays of John Marston." Master's thesis. Ohio State University, 1975.

Scott, M. A. *Elizabethan Translations from Italian.* Baltimore: Modern Language Association, 1895–99.

Seller, Harry. "Italian Books Printed in England Before 1640." *The Library.* 4th ser. vol. 5, no. 2 (1924): 105–28.

Sells, Arthur L. *The Italian Influence in English Poetry from Chaucer to Southwell.* Bloomington: Indiana Univ. Press, 1955.

Seznec, Jean. *The Survival of the Pagan Gods.* Harper Torchbook. New York: Harper & Row, 1961.

Shearman, John. *Mannerism.* Baltimore: Penguin Books, 1967.

———. Review of *Giulio Romano,* by Frederick Hartt. *Burlington Magazine* 101 (1959): 456–60.

Shepherd, W. *The Life of Poggio Bracciolini.* Liverpool: J. M'Creery, 1837.

Shugg, Wallace. "Prostitution in Shakespeare's London." *Shakespeare Studies* 10 (1977): 291–313.

Simiani, Carlo. *Nicolo Franco: La Vita e Le Opere.* Turin and Rome: L. Roux, 1894.

Simonini, R. C., Jr. *Italian Scholarship in Renaissance England.* Chapel Hill: Univ. of North Carolina Studies in Comparative Literature, no. 3, 1952.

Smarr, Janet, trans. *Italian Renaissance Tales.* Rochester, Mich.: Solaris Press, 1983.

Smith, H. *Elizabethan Poetry.* Cambridge, Mass.: Harvard Univ. Press, 1966.

Sontag, Susan. *Styles of Radical Will.* New York: Farrar, Straus & Giroux, Noonday Press, 1976.

Speroni, Charles. *Wit and Wisdom of the Italian Renaissance.* Berkeley and Los Angeles: Univ. of California Press, 1964.

Steinberg, Leo. "The Metaphors of Love and Birth in Michelangelo's *Pietas.*" In *Studies in Erotic Art.* Edited by Theodore Bowie and Cornelia V. Christenson. New York and London: Basic Books, 1970.

Steiner, George. "Night Words: High Pornography and Human Privacy." In *Perspectives on Pornography.* Edited by Douglas A. Hughes. New York: Macmillan and St. Martin's Press, 1970.

Stern, Virginia F. *Gabriel Harvey: His Life, Marginalia and Library.* Oxford: Clarendon Press, 1979.

Stone, Lawrence. *An Elizabethan: Sir Horatio Palavicino.* Oxford: Clarendon Press, 1956.

Storia della Letteratura Italiana. Edited by Emilio Cecchi and Natalino Sapegno. Vol. 4: "Il Cinquecento." Milan: Garzanti, 1965–69.

Struever, Nancy S. *The Language of History in the Renaissance.* Princeton: Princeton Univ. Press, 1970.

Sypher, Wylie. *Four Stages of Renaissance Style.* Garden City, N.Y.: N.p., 1955.

Tatum, James. *Apuleius and the Golden Ass.* Ithaca and London: Cornell Univ. Press, 1979.

Taylor, Archer. *English Riddles from Oral Tradition.* Berkeley and Los Angeles: Univ. of California Press, 1951.

———. *The Literary Riddle before 1600.* Berkeley and Los Angeles: Univ. of California Press, 1948.

Thomas, Keith. "The Place of Laughter in Tudor and Stuart England." *Times Literary Supplement* 3906 (21 Jan. 1977): 77–81.

———. *Religion and the Decline of Magic.* New York: Charles Scribner's Sons, 1971.

Thomason, Richmond F. *The Priapea and Ovid: A Study of the Language of the Poems.* Nashville, Tenn.: George Peabody College for Teachers, 1931.

Thompson, Roger. *Unfit for Modest Ears.* London: Macmillan, 1979.

Tillyard, E. M. W. *The Elizabethan World Picture.* 1943. Reprint. London: Penguin Books, 1963.

Tonkin, Humphrey. *Spenser's Courteous Pastoral.* Oxford: Oxford Univ. Press, 1972.

Toscanini, Walter. Unpublished letter to the Institute for Sex Research, 12 January 1962.

Traister, Daniel. "Sidney's Purposeful Humor: *Astrophel and Stella* 59 and 83." *English Literary History* 49 (1982): 751–64.

Tuve, Rosemond. *Allegorical Imagery.* Princeton: Princeton Univ. Press, 1966.

———. "Baroque and Mannerist Milton?" In *Essays by Rosemond Tuve.* Edited by Thomas P. Roche, Jr. Princeton: Princeton Univ. Press, 1970.

———. *Elizabethan and Metaphysical Imagery.* Chicago: Univ. of Chicago Press, Phoenix Books, 1961.

Van Marle, Raimond. *Iconographie de l'Art Profane au Moyen-Age et à la Renaissance.* 2 vols. The Hague: Martinus Nijhoff, 1932.

Vasari, Giorgio. *Lives of the Most Eminent Painters, Sculptors and Architects.* Translated by Gaston du C. de Vere. 10 vols. London: Macmillan and the Medici Society, 1912–15.

Vita, Alessandro Del. *Galanteria e lussuria nel Rinascimento.* Arezzo: Edizioni Rinascimento, 1952.

———. *Lusso, Donne, Amore nel Rinascimento.* Arezzo: Edizioni Rinascimento, 1960.

Walsh, P. G. *The Roman Novel.* Cambridge: Cambridge Univ. Press, 1970.

Watt, Ian. *The Rise of the Novel.* 1957. Reprint. Berkeley and Los Angeles: Univ. of California Press, 1959.

Watts, R. A. "The Comic Scenes in *Othello,*" *Shakespeare Quarterly* 19 (1968): 349–54.

Wedeck, Harry E. *Dictionary of Erotic Literature.* New York: Philosophical Library, 1962.

Weiss, Roberto. *The Renaissance Discovery of Classical Antiquity.* Oxford: Basil Blackwell, 1969.

Wethey, Harold E. *The Paintings of Titian.* London: Phaidon Press, 1969.

Willey, B. *The English Moralists.* Garden City, N.Y.: Doubleday, Anchor Books, 1967.

Wind, Edgar. *Bellini's Feast of the Gods: A Study in Venetian Humanism.* Cambridge, Mass.: Harvard Univ. Press, 1948.

———. *Pagan Mysteries in the Renaissance.* Harmondsworth, Middlesex: Penguin Books, 1967.

Wittkower, R. *The Drawings of the Carracci in the Collection of Her Majesty The Queen at Windsor Castle.* London: Phaidon Press, 1952.

Wright, Louis B. *Middle-Class Culture in Elizabethan England.* Chapel Hill: Univ. of North Carolina Press, 1935.

Yates, Frances A. *John Florio: The Life of an Italian in Shakespeare's England.* N.d. Reprint. New York: Octagon Books, 1968.

Young, Wayland. *Eros Denied: Sex in Western Society.* New York: Grove Press, 1964.

Zall, P. M. "John Marston, Moralist." *English Literary History* 20 (1953): 186–93.

Index